Education

and

Emigration

Educational Policy, Planning and Theory
Series Editor: Don Adams, *University of Pittsburgh*

Education
and
Emigration

Study Abroad and the
Migration of Human Resources

Robert G. Myers

The University of Chicago

DAVID McKAY COMPANY, INC. / NEW YORK

EDUCATION AND EMIGRATION

To My Mother and Father

CONTENTS

APPENDIXES

TABLES

ILLUSTRATIONS

ACKNOWLEDGEMENTS

Sitting down to write a set of acknowledgements, one quickly realizes that at best the result is a series of unsatisfactory under-statements, the real import of which can be felt only by the writer. Accordingly:

The research presented in this book was supported by the Carnegie Corporation of New York.

I am extremely fortunate to have benefited from the valuable suggestions, constructive criticism and friendly encouragement of C. Arnold Anderson and Mary Jean Bowman at all stages of the research and writing. To the latter, I am particularly indebted for her close cooperation while I was writing chapters 5, 6, and 8.

In the final stages of shaping the manuscript, the comments of the series editor, Don Adams, proved very helpful.

The Institute of International Education generously allowed me to exploit the data so laboriously collected from foreign students in the United States. The intricate programming involved in analyzing the IIE data was artfully handled by Ronald Skirmont.

Daniel Parrish and Igou Allbray successfully executed their difficult charge of locating and interviewing Peruvian students in United States colleges and universities. The students, almost without exception, were willing and enthusiastic participants; I owe Part IV of the book to their cooperative involvement.

Responsibility for interpretations as well as errors or omissions or both must, of course, be mine.

ACKNOWLEDGEMENTS

Finally (and in the most unsatisfactory understatement of all), my greatest debt is to my wife, Sally, for her sacrifices and for her help throughout the research.

RGM

Education
and
Emigration

INTRODUCTION

Brain drain, with its pejorative ring, captured the attention of policy-makers in the United States and elsewhere during the decade of the 1960s. International and national organizations rushed to pass resolutions, to set up conferences, and sometimes even to undertake research.[1] All manner of evil was initially attributed to the flow of high-level manpower from "poor" to "rich" nations in what has been termed "reverse foreign aid." Emigrating talent was not only tagged as a major contributor to lagging economic development, but was also associated in more emotional expositions of the "problem," with poor health standards, hunger, and the faltering quest for peace.[2]

When the United States changed its immigration law in 1965 from one of discrimination based mainly on national origins to one of discrimination based, among other criteria, on skill, concern about brain drain was heightened. Indeed, immigration statistics almost immediately reflected an increased number of talented persons "entering" the United States. Its conscience pricked, the United States Congress held hearings to examine the "New Immigration."[3] As is often the case, the policy-makers listened principally to arguments they wanted to hear—in this instance that developing nations were incurring significant losses (much greater than before the 1965 legislation) through brain drain. Not only was the drain hurting developing nations, but it was offsetting the foreign assistance efforts of the United States, so the argument went. Accordingly recommendations for moderating immigration of talent to the United States were made. Several bills were intro-

1

duced before an amendment to the 1965 Immigration Act was finally passed in April 1970.

By the time legislative action was taken in 1970, however, the emotional swell had subsided as more pressing international problems confronted policy-makers throughout the world. And Congress apparently felt it could afford to pass an amendment that would respond to pressures at home as well as to pressures from abroad. Consequently, while incorporating provisions to moderate the flow of high-level immigration, it also opened the door a bit wider.[4] I would not be surprised to find that the net result is an increase in the number of high-level migrants.

The migration of talent is continuing into the 1970s. How to interpret that migration is still being argued. Some nations persist in their preoccupation with talent "losses"; others wonder (usually unofficially), what they would do to absorb the talent if emigration ceased. Passage of the 1970 amendment and changing economic conditions within the United States will, I think, eventually lead to a reexamination of high-level migration flows to the United States and to another modification of the immigration law. Meanwhile, decisions are being made in many other areas of policy affecting migration.

There is a continuing need for careful, dispassionate description and analysis of "elite" migration and of the effects of various policies upon it. And there is also a need to sort out the burgeoning literature and to pull together the disparate, sometimes contradictory, research results that have already emerged from studies dealing with international migration of high-level manpower. This would provide a more solid, informed basis for the next official round of policy decisions. I hope this book will contribute to the effort.

Thus far, I have only touched upon one-half of the title—upon emigration. Where does education fit in? Educational attainment is, of course, one means (not necessarily the best) of differentiating "brainy" migrants from others. But in this book education will have more than just classificatory significance.

Brain drain statistics often pick up both migration for education and migration of the educated. We will be concerned primarily with the relationship between the two types of migration. The former (education abroad), it is alleged repeatedly, leads all too often to the latter (emigration through non-return of students). Getting behind the relationship is crucial not only for evaluating and explaining brain drain, but also for evaluating programs of international educational exchange. There is a widespread nationalistic feeling that the primary benefits of international educational exchange, whether political, cultural, or economic, are contingent on the return home of those who have studied abroad. Let us look, then, somewhat more closely at international educational exchange and at non-return.

EMIGRATION THROUGH EDUCATION ABROAD

What underlies increased national and international concern about the foreign student as an immigrant rather than an exchangee? [5] There is no doubt that the number of non-returning students has risen. In part this is simply a result of growing student enrollment with proportionally greater numbers of non-returnees. At the end of the 1960s approximately half a million students were enrolled in institutions of higher education outside the borders of their home country, as compared, for instance, with an estimated 50,000 in 1925; [6] in the United States alone there were about 120,000 foreign students in 1969.[7] But there is also a strong supposition (supported, in America, by statistical evidence [8]) that greater *percentages* of today's foreign student population are remaining abroad than did in previous years. The increases should not be surprising, migration of all types having been facilitated by improved transportation and communication and by spreading universalism of knowledge. And migration regu-

lations, while limiting the flow of the unskilled and the uneducated, are not particularly inhibiting for the educated or for those
who wish to acquire an education abroad. However, the increasing number of students remaining abroad is not, in itself, a cause
for expressing concern.

Discontent and the pressures for action to moderate student
non-return are closely related to the context within which international educational interchange occurs. In the 1960s, the context
changed. There appeared what might be labeled an international
preoccupation with economic development. In that "first development decade," international agencies, advanced nations, and developing nations alike emphasized economic growth rates and the
reduction of "gaps" between rich and poor nations. Accompanying
this accent on economic development was a recognition of the
importance of "human resources" in the development process, and
of education as the major component in developing human resources. As education became an "investment" item, educational
planning for human resource development became stylish—the
latest in a line of seemingly simple solutions to the problems of
promoting economic growth—and created the context for increased concern about migrating manpower.

With the emphasis on economic growth and on planning for
development came a more careful system of accounting. In those
national systems where high-level human resources become in-
creasingly scarce commodities as one moves from secondary to
university to post-graduate degree levels, statistics on who has
been trained in what fields and where are more frequently available—though they are not necessarily accurate. The numbers
game both reflects and induces new awareness of the importance
of education in economic development. And it provides a basis
(albeit sometimes misleading) for discussing effects of emigration
through foreign student non-return that was previously missing.

In such an environment it is not surprising to find that the early
post-World War II theme of international educational exchange—
international understanding—has slowly been subordinated to a

presumably more pragmatic view. Economic benefits have been substituted for cultural benefits and the role of study abroad in producing the classic cosmopolitan, cultured individual has been subordinated to its role in providing "needed" skills that can be used by nations at home in the development process. The following statement by the Organization for Economic Cooperation and Development (OECD) is typical of the current international attitude:

It is necessary that study abroad should be used as an integral part of the strategy of the advanced countries in extending help to the newly developing countries for the growth of their human resources.[9]

When we couple the economic emphasis with the suggestion that training nationals abroad is probably less costly for many developing nations than mounting programs at home, increased interest in minimizing non-return is understandable. By training manpower abroad, it is possible to export part (most?) of the educational expense, and countries can use scarce capital for other investments that are less capital-intensive than higher education.[10] On the other hand, emigration by those educated abroad could offset the potential advantages. There is the rub.

In the first development decade, then, there was an increase in the expectation of economic gains from education as well as a heightened sensitivity to potential economic losses that can occur when educated nationals emigrate, that is, to student-related "brain drain." The expectation continues into the second development decade. In addition there was, and is, a new awareness of who has been educated and who has migrated.

Preoccupation with economic development has probably done more to bring about a reexamination of gains and losses associated with study abroad and non-return than any other single idea or set of ideas. Accordingly, the framework for this book comes from the economics of education and of migration, although it would have been possible to adopt any one of several other equally valid approaches.

The evaluation of economic gains and losses associated with study abroad and/or non-return poses some problems. There is substantial disagreement among economists, educators and politicians about how to properly measure the economic values and consequently the economic effects of foreign student non-return. With respect to the United States, for instance, many would agree that the student brain drain constitutes ". . . a critical problem which seriously impedes the prospects for economic and social improvement in many underdeveloped countries." [11] Others would support the contention that ". . . training offered in the United States to foreign students is a clear net gain of large dimensions to both the students and the foreign countries." [12]

That foreign concern about brain drain through non-return is viewed sympathetically in the United States is suggested by a summary report of a House of Representatives Subcommittee, "Scientific Brain Drain from Developing Countries." The report includes a section titled "A Particularly Serious Aspect of the Immigration is the High Proportion Accounted For by Student Non-return" which states: [13]

Of the 7,913 scientists, engineers, and physicians immigrating to the United States from the developing countries in 1967, 3,772, or 48 per cent, were people who had originally entered the United States as students, with the declared intention of obtaining education or training and then returning home. Instead, these students *changed their minds* [italics mine—RGM] and immigrated.

". . . during the course of study, *many* [italics mine—RGM] students . . . become alienated from national needs and career opportunities in their own countries and pulled toward the needs and opportunities of the United States." [14]

As we will see, however, conclusions inspired by concern may, at best, be premature. For instance, referring to the quotes above, 1967 is not a particularly good year from which to draw conclusions about foreign student non-return; the 48 per cent figure means little by itself; and we have no real evidence that students did in fact change their minds or become alienated from national needs during their period of study. We cannot conclude from such statistics that the United States is acting as a seducer of foreign manpower, as is implied—it is possible that individuals were to some extent alienated *before* they came to study.

In the brain-drain setting, then, international educational exchange, once a "Beacon of Hope," [15] is being regarded with a much more skeptical eye. For instance, the House Committee cited above recommended that: [16]

The United States make clear to those developing countries that are concerned about their student emigration to the United States that we have no objection to their reducing the number of students sent for study to this country. . . .

The statement says little but implies a great deal. It implies not only that there was an objection before, but that now a reduction in the number of students sent to the United States would clearly benefit less developed nations in their drive for development. I would like to keep open, for the moment, the opposite possibility —that reducing the number of students could hurt, not help, developing nations.

As the halo of educational exchange slips and as the formerly sporadic and relatively restrained expressions of national regret at student failure to return home give way to more frequent and widespread concern, it is particularly important to approach that part of brain drain occurring through non-return in as rational a manner as possible. For discussion to be rational and constructive, it is necessary to take the topic out of its charged political context, to make clear the basic facts and figures about foreign student non-return, to point to areas of our ignorance, to determine the key factors promoting or retarding student migration, and to develop a variety of methods for assessing the effects of non-return. Such is one aim of this book, which, while focusing on non-return, is addressed to both the broader problem of evaluating programs of international educational exchange and the larger questions surrounding international migration of talent.

THE PLAN OF THIS BOOK

Part I provides a background for the rest of the volume in three ways. First, a migration paradigm is presented which can be used to put brain drain and foreign student non-return in perspective. The paradigm establishes alternative work-study sequences linked to migration. Second, a review of the literature dealing with high-level migration is undertaken. After examining more general work on the subject for insights into student migration, results of specific research are brought together. In the course of coordinating information about the volume, characteristics and motives of high-level migrants and foreign student non-returnees, it seems possible to make some crude generalizations and to clarify some current misconceptions about the nature of non-return. Third, an analytical note to Part I treats problems of definition and measurement that complicate interpretation and comparisons of available "facts."

In Part II, a previously unpublished analysis of the Institute of International Education's Survey of Foreign Students not only serves as a source of new facts and figures, but also as an example of the difficulties involved in using available statistics on foreign students in the United States. It is evident that even when statistics are broken down by country and field of study, simple interpretations of the causes of non-return are imprudent and that cross-national patterns are extremely complex.

Identifying migrant numbers and correlates and analyzing non-return cross-nationally in Parts I and II lead to the more important task of "valuing" migrants in Part III. In so doing, a third dimension is added to the migration paradigm of chapter 1. Several methods for valuing gains and losses are discussed and economic decision models for evaluating alternative study-work possibilities are presented. The economic models are applicable to either individual or social decisions when parameters are adjusted.

A case study of Peruvian students in the United States is presented in Part IV. In chapter 7, correlates of non-return are sought. In chapter 8, one of the economic decision models developed earlier is applied to the decision to remain in the United States or return to Peru. Even as decisions are analyzed from an economic viewpoint, the importance of non-monetary factors becomes clearer.

Finally, in Part V, several policy alternatives are examined; caveats are offered, and specific suggestions are made for moderating losses through non-return while taking full advantage of the potential gains associated with study abroad.

Arising as it has from the brain-drain debate, our discussion of education and emigration will focus on the migration of high-level talent and will be discussed primarily in the international sphere. The policy discussion will concentrate on policy concerning the return or non-return of foreign students.

There are, however, more general questions concerning education and emigration, viewed from an economic perspective, that need to be asked. Chapters 1, 5, and 6 are of this more general nature. And there are policy questions flowing from the more general discussion of education and emigration which apply internally as well as internationally. For instance, looking within the United States and at states or regions rather than at countries, we can ask:

To what extent does one state or region subsidize education that will be utilized elsewhere as graduates emigrate? Does this mean a loss to the states that did the training?

What are the costs and benefits associated with allowing (or promoting) study at state universities by out-of-state students? Do out-of-staters stay to work or do they return home? If they stay, does their presence offset the amount invested in their education?

Is there a general tendency toward under-investment in education because local or state political units realize many individuals will migrate? Is the national welfare decreased or increased as a result of high-level migration? Do individual states or regions give up their human capital resources without adequate compensation from those who receive the resources?

If a state wishes to retain its educated manpower, what strategies are most effective?

This book does not deal directly with such policy issues, but it does provide a framework within which these and similar questions might be approached.

I hope that this book will help policy-makers and researchers ask appropriate questions. It is probably more a source book for policy-makers than a policy statement. It is not a listing of simple policy solutions. Indeed, I hope the book will help to drive home the complexity of high-level migration and the need for similarly complex and tailored policies for moderating (or increasing) migration flows. I hope policy-makers will look for brain gains as well as brain drains associated with both temporary and permanent migration of talent. I trust that the value of looking at brain drain in a broader perspective—in comparison with non-migrants and incorporating re-migration—will be evident, and that the tendency to assign a *causal* role to study abroad in promoting brain drain, and to brain drain in retarding development, will be modified after reading this book.

NOTES

[1] See the research summary in chapter 2.

[2] Walter F. Mondale, "The Cost of the Brain Drain," *The Atlantic Monthly*, ccxx, No. 6 (December 1967), pp. 67–69.

[3] U.S. Senate Subcommittee on Immigration and Naturalization of the Committee on the Judiciary, *Hearings, International Migration of Talent and Skills,* 90th Congress, 1st Session, March 6 and 10, 1967; U.S. House Subcommittee of the Committee on Government Operations, *Hearings on the Brain Drain of Scientists, Engineers, and Physicians from the Developing Countries into the United States,* 90th Congress, 2nd Session, January 23, 1968; and U.S. House Committee on Government Operations, *Scientific Brain Drain from the Developing Countries,* H. R. 1215, 90th Congress, 2nd Session, March 28, 1968, Report 23.

[4] See discussion in the "Footnote to Part I," and in chapter 9. In the 90th Congress, 2nd Session, the following bills were introduced but not carried through to passage: H. R. 16509, H. R. 16863, and H. R. 17290. The 1970 amendment is Public Law, 91–225, 91st Congress, 1st Session, April 7, 1970.

[5] Gregory Henderson, "Foreign Students, Exchange or Immigration?" *International Development Review*, VI, No. 4 (December 1964), pp. 19–21. *The Foreign Student: Exchangee or Immigrant?* A statement prepared by The Committee on Educational Interchange Policy, Institute of International Education, New York, May 1958.

[6] The estimate of 500,000 is well above the UNESCO estimate of 375,000 for the school year, 1966, but it does not seem unrealistic for 1969–70. See UNESCO, *Statistical Yearbook, 1968* (Paris: UNESCO, 1969), p. 280.

While the number of students abroad has *increased*, it should be noted that the world ratio of foreign students to total students at the third level has *not changed* substantially in recent years and, in fact, seems to be decreasing. For the estimate of 50,000 students abroad in 1925, see Henry H. King, "Outline History of Student Migrations," *The Foreign Student in America*, ed. W. Reginald Wheeler, Henry H. King, and Alexander B. Davidson (New York: Association Press, 1925), p. 38.

[7] Institute of International Education (IIE), *Open Doors* (New York: Institute of International Education, 1970).

[8] See, for instance, Alan E. Bayer, "The Effect of International Interchange of High-Level Manpower on the United States," *Social Forces*, XL, No. 4 (June 1968), p. 469. Also, analysis of International Institute of Education statistics produces a non-return rate of 23 per cent for 1968–69 versus a 16 per cent rate for 1964–65. See chapter 3, footnote 19. On the other hand, non-return among post-doctoral foreigners seems to be decreasing. See National Academy of Science, *The Invisible University: Post-Doctoral Education in the United States* (Washington: The National Academy of Sciences, 1969), p. 221.

[9] Organization for Economic Cooperation and Development (OECD), *Policy Conference on Economic Growth and Investment in Education, V: International Flows of Students* (Paris: OECD, Directorate of Scientific Affairs, 1962), p. 5.

[10] This point is made by Gopal Dorai, *Economics of the International Flow of Students—A Cost-Benefit Analysis* (unpublished Ph.D. dissertation, Department of Economics, Wayne State University, 1968), pp. 65–67.

[11] John C. Shearer, "The Foreign Student 'Brain Drain,'" a statement prepared for hearing on January 23, 1968 of U.S. House of Representatives Research and Technical Programs Subcommittee, p. 1 (mimeographed).

[12] Charles V. Kidd. "Statement of Dr. Charles V. Kidd, Executive Secretary for Science and Technology, Office of Science and Technology, Before the Senate Immigration and Naturalization Subcommittee," *Hearings*, March 6, 1967, p. 105.

[13] U.S. House Committee on Government Operations, Report 23, Scientific Brain Drain from the Developing Countries, H. R. 1215, 90th Congress, 2nd Session, March 28, 1968, p. 7.

[14] *Ibid.*, p. 9.

[15] "There is no other international activity of our Government that enjoys so much spontaneous public approval, elicits such extensive citizen participa-

tion, and yields such impressive evidences of success. In a time when most international activities seem almost unbearably complex, hazardous and obscure in outcome, the success of educational exchange is a beacon of hope." *A Beacon of Hope—the Exchange of Persons Program,* a report from the United States Advisory Commission on International Educational and Cultural Affairs, Washington, D.C., April 1963, p. 6.

[16] U.S. House Report 23, p. 9.

PART I

Migration of Talent: An Overview

1

EMIGRATION, EDUCATION, AND EMPLOYMENT:

A Migration Paradigm

One of the main impressions which results from digging into the voluminous and diffuse literature about migration is that there are few, if any, generalizations that apply to all forms of migration and to all types of migrants. Indeed, migration researchers often deny the existence of "laws." [1] Nevertheless the search for explanation, if not laws, continues as social scientists of many persuasions attempt to capture a complex phenomenon in some manageable, meaningful way.[2] Typically, the study of migration has been approached through classification and typology; the latter being the highest form of abstraction.[3] Utility of a particular typology and/or classification is determined primarily by the particular analytical concerns of each researcher.

In this book, the type of migration singled out for attention is that which is often called "voluntary international migration," and emphasis is on that class of international migrants labeled high-level or "elite" migrants—including foreign students. It is difficult, however, to distinguish clearly between free (voluntary) and forced migration. And even though a workable definition might be established, statistics do not allow a tidy division into voluntary and involuntary migrants. In practice, then, "voluntary" is a

15

relative term and is useful only for sorting out the extreme cases in which individuals have been expelled from an area by physical force.[4] Although in many respects the distinction between international and internal migration is also questionable (variations within a country can be as great as variations between countries), international migration normally involves greater distances and sharper cultural disparities than internal migration. Furthermore, the existence of national immigration policies alone makes the international-internal distinction a necessary one.

WHY HIGH-LEVEL MIGRANTS?

There are pragmatic reasons for dealing with high-level (elite, skilled, talented) rather than low-level (mass, unskilled, untalented) migrants, quite apart from the obvious differences introduced by definition in terms of educational attainment or occupational level. As noted in the introduction, current concern with human resource building for economic development focuses attention on high levels of manpower and lends importance to the fact that high-level migration, as a proportion of total migration, seems to be increasing (even more rapidly than the proportion of high-level occupations in the labor force). A clear conception of high-level migration, then, is critical for those who are formulating immigration laws with economic development in mind. Furthermore, existing immigration laws often discriminate in favor of high-level migrants, thereby creating conditions peculiar to that group and necessitating separate study of it.

Existing theoretical literature seems to support several generalizations about the manner in which high-level migrants differ from other migrants. Consider the following: 1) In general, the propensity to migrate seems to increase as educational attainment increases. 2) Similarly, individuals tend to be more mobile the more prestigious their occupation. 3) The deterrent effect of distance on migration decreases as the educational level rises, and more-educated migrants will therefore make up a larger proportion of long than of short migration totals. 4) Although high-level migrants are more mobile in earlier than in later years (thus conforming to what is probably the most universal migration generalization), they are also mobile over longer periods of their life than other migrants.

These generalizations are based primarily on internal migration research, most of which was completed in the United States,[5] and which may or may not hold for international migration. There will undoubtedly be exceptions for particular inter-country flows, but *a priori* the generalizations seem logical for most international as well as most internal migration. In view of the immigration legislation of many nations favoring international flows of professional manpower, statements 1 and 2 seem even more plausible for international than for internal migration. When the percentage of scientists and engineers among migrants to the United States was compared with the percentage of scientists and engineers in the total population of several countries, it was found that on the average scientists and engineers were ten times more apt to migrate than persons in other occupations.[6] The educated professional presumably masters languages more easily, is more cosmopolitan, is more apt to be in fields where there are greater job opportunities, and where communication on the job is facilitated by the universalism of science. This makes plausible, as stated in generalization 3, that distance has less of a deterrent effect on high-level international migrants. Generalization 4, concerning age-connected variations between high- and low-level migration, is more open to question, but there seems to be no compelling reason for modifying it at this time.

In short, there is sufficient evidence to show that high-level migrants merit separate analysis. While specifying differences and similarities *among* migrants classified by educational and/or occupational levels, and detailing how the migration process is distinctive for each type would be a challenging task, our main concern here will be to make comparisons *within* the category of the high-level migrant.

HIGH-LEVEL STUDENT MIGRATION

But our topic will be even more sharply defined by taking as the main subject of this book foreign student migrants who do not return to their home country. These migrants are included in most discussions of brain drain, sometimes as a separate category, at other times under a more general heading.

Although he is often treated with other high-level migrants in general statistics and in discussions, the student migrant is different. He is usually younger and less experienced in an occupational role than other high-level migrants. His decision to migrate for study is probably less related to ultimate occupational objectives than the decision of an older, more mature professional person; and his decision to migrate following study, although linked to work goals, is made with less hindsight than that of the previously employed. His niche in the economic structure at home or "abroad" is not carved out and presumably his migration does not disturb a functioning economic system in the same way the migration of an established professional might. He is human capital in formation; he has more of his economically productive life ahead of him than most other high-level migrants (even though most non-student migration of professional manpower takes place before the age of thirty-five). It is not at all obvious, then, that the same generalizations applying to other high-level migrants will also apply to students.[7]

Student migrants have already made at least one migration decision, to study abroad. But they must face a second decision—to remigrate following study or to remain abroad, becoming a "permanent" rather than a "temporary" migrant.[8] If a student remains abroad, he enters the brain drain statistics, but until the decision is made, he represents a potential gain to his area of origin. Our discussion, then, should incorporate remigration.

MIGRATION AND REMIGRATION

Most migration research focuses on a single, "original" decision to migrate and on a one-way permanent move, even though the option to return and the decision to return or remain may be equally important. The original decision to migrate and the subsequent decision to remain abroad or to return may be associated with distinctive types of migrants; if these are analyzed as a simple group (i.e., if we look only at net migration) without taking into account potential differences, the result may be misleading from a number of perspectives, particularly that of determining gains and losses through migration. Remigrants differ from original migrants [9] but researchers continue to treat in- and out-migration streams with only token disaggregation and without adjusting for qualitative differences. The numerical importance of remigration has been recognized for some time,[10] but it has become the subject of systematic research only recently.[11]

The decision to remain abroad or to remigrate is probably more visible in the case of students than it is for most other types of migrants. Students usually go (or are sent) abroad for an initial period that is quite clearly specified. They are expected to return home to work following their period of study. If a student chooses to remain abroad, it is assumed that his decision is separate in time from his original decision. In fact, the two decisions may have been made concurrently. Study abroad may even have provided the means for carrying out a prior decision to emigrate.

On the other hand, migration and remigration by students are almost invisible in the international migration statistics. Most are based on intended residence abroad for one year or more, thus putting all students who plan more than one year of study abroad among permanent migrants rather than listing them as temporary migrants who will then remigrate.

There is basically not much difference between a remigrating student and non-student if we consider that both acquire additional knowledge and experience abroad. Therefore, although their contribution to the home country was at least partially "lost" during their stay abroad, the returning migrants will be more valuable and productive because of their newly acquired skills. This must be kept in mind when judging gains and losses connected with migration.

We are now ready to set up a migration paradigm based on our discussion of work, study, and remigration.

A MIGRATION PARADIGM

Consideration of the two migration decisions that have been described above—the first involving locus of study and the second involving locus of employment—leads to a simple but useful paradigm, facilitating comparison between non-returning foreign students and other high-level migrants or non-migrants. When locus of study (at home or abroad) is cross-tabulated with locus of work (at home or abroad) following study, the resultant paradigm arranges high-level migrants (or migrant decisions) into four categories, one of which covers all non-returning foreign students (or which represents the decision both to study and to stay abroad). See Figure 1.

The paradigm is not given here as a migration model; it is presented simply to organize consideration of questions related to study abroad and non-return, placing them in the larger context in which they should be viewed. It may be used to classify individuals already in the work force according to locus of their present employment and their past education or to classify students according to locus of their present education and expected future employment. Using such classifications, numerical gains and losses associated with migration for study and migration following study can be compared and/or aggregated.[12] From a slightly different perspective, the paradigm may be visualized as a set of study-work alternatives open to an individual or a society.[13] Each alternative has associated with it certain advantages or disadvantages (or benefits and costs) which can presumably be identified and compared to arrive at the "best" alternative (among those considered). This latter decision-making view will be developed further in Parts III and IV.

	WORK AT HOME	WORK ABROAD
STUDY AT HOME	I NON-MIGRANTS	II EMIGRANTS
STUDY ABROAD	III RETURNEES	IV NON-RETURNEES

FIGURE 1—A Migration Paradigm

I + II = Total studying at home
III + IV = Total studying abroad
I + III = Total entering home work force
II + IV = Total emigrating (brain drain)

Using the migration paradigm assures clear separation of two distinct components of the brain drain. Unfortunately, the migration of experienced professional manpower (the "trained brain drain") and the migration of students (the "untrained brain drain") are often indiscriminately lumped together in brain-drain analyses. To compare these brain-drain components for a particular country is to compare categories II and IV of the paradigm.

Other frequently overlooked comparisons are evident from a quick glance at the paradigm: Non-returnees can be compared with Returnees (III and IV); Non-migrants can be compared with Returnees, who are also in the home labor force but who were trained abroad (I and III); the total number of individuals trained at home can be compared with the total number trained abroad (I + II with III + IV); and the total home labor force can be compared with the total emigrant population (I + III and III + IV). The central place of foreign student non-return in two larger sets of overlapping questions is apparent from the paradigm. On the one hand are questions relating to the brain drain (approached mainly through comparisons of II and IV); on the other are questions concerning the place of study abroad in human resource development (involving comparisons between III and IV).

In this simple presentation, category III includes only returning students. By redefining locus of study to include on the job experience abroad, we could include remigrating non-students in category III and we could include as non-returnees (in category IV) migrants who receive training outside formal educational institutions. Generally, however, our discussion will focus on students, narrowly defined as those attending institutions of higher education.

Using the paradigm, let us now examine several hypothetical numerical examples, illustrating differences worth exploring. (See Figure 2.) Assume that each of three countries, A, B, and C, has a total of only 100 nationals with high-level training so that in referring to Figure 2, the entries in each education-employment category will represent both numbers and percentages of the total population.

LOCUS OF EMPLOYMENT

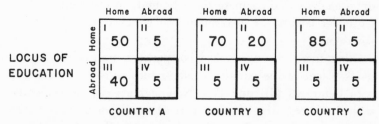

FIGURE 2—Hypothetical Distribution of Education—Employment Alternatives in a Context of Migration

Focusing on non-return (category IV) in Figure 2, it is evident that although the over-all percentage is the same in all three cases (5 per cent of all available manpower studied abroad and stayed abroad to work), the context is very different for each case. For instance, the rate of non-return *among foreign students* (IV divided by III plus IV) is 50 per cent for countries B and C, but only 11 per cent for country A. Although the rate of non-return among foreign students is the same for countries B and C, the relative importance of foreign student non-return in the total brain drain (IV divided by II plus IV) from the respective countries appears to be different—for country C, it constitutes 50 per cent of all emigration, trained and untrained, but for country B, it accounts for only 20 per cent of all emigration. Without going into more detailed comparisons or fabricating additional examples, the value of considering non-return in broader perspective is evident. This will be a recurrent theme throughout the book. It needs to be stressed even though it may seem obvious, in order to counter the tendency toward dependence on simple, unqualified numbers or even ratios to describe brain drains or non-return. The "summary statistic" is convenient, but often misleading.

As it stands, the paradigm is an obvious over-simplification and it pertains to only one country or region. However, it can be focused and/or elaborated and extended. Within each of the four large groups, sub-groups can and should be distinguished. If, for instance, the paradigm were applied to the analysis to high-level manpower in a particular country, sub-groups of engineers, scientists, doctors, etc., could be separated out within each cell. Or the paradigm could be applied only to engineers.

For fuller consideration of the brain-drain question, more than one country must be included and Figure 1 must be expanded. Implicit in the original paradigm is an unidentified area from which the Returnees (or remigrants) in Group III return. It can be made explicit quite easily by juxtaposing a similar paradigm for a second country (or for the rest of the world). In Figure 3, areas of loss or gain between country A and the world are presented from the viewpoint of country A; presumed gains and losses to A are represented by a "+" or a "−" respectively. The magnitude of the gains or losses would, of course, depend on the method used to calculate them. In Figure 3, the unwarranted assumption is made that only the number of migrants is relevant. Following that assumption, the brain *drain* from country A to the rest of the world (AII + AIV) is to be balanced against the brain *gain* to country A from the world (WII + WIV). In addition, those who study abroad and return to A (AIII) should be considered, at least in part, as a brain gain (to the extent that educational expenses are covered by sources outside country A) and must be set against the partial brain drain of those from abroad who were educated in country A at A's expense and who return to their respective home countries (WIII).

LOCUS OF EMPLOYMENT

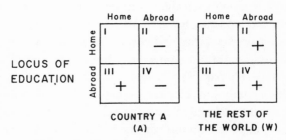

FIGURE 3—Two-Country Migration Paradigm

The two-country elaboration has been used by Bayer to calculate *numerical* gains and losses to the United States vis à vis the rest of the world.[14] Bayer's cautious analysis illustrates at once the potential of the paradigm and the limitations of current statistical information. He notes that the combination of the "untrained" and the "trained" brain *gain* to the United States ". . . yields . . . a substantial boost to the pool of high-level manpower in the United States which is not balanced by comparable outflows of United States citizens to other countries."[15] However, Bayer places the gain in perspective by indicating that the net gains of high-level manpower through immigration to the United States are relatively small, representing less than 5 per cent of the output of American institutions of higher learning.[16] He also points out that once numbers have been determined for the various migration streams, economic and possible other benefits should be assessed. Jumping ahead somewhat in our argument we can see that once we move beyond mere counting, the "gain" to the United States may not be the same as the "loss" to countries of origin.

With the extension to valuing migrants, we need a qualitative dimension of the migration paradigm. Indeed, simple counts of migrating students or other high-level talent as a means of determining "losses and gains" take into account neither the migrants' potential nor their opportunities to apply it to productive activity. The migrant's potential before and after he studies (or works) abroad depends, among other things, upon his age, ability, quality and level of previous schooling, experience, and motivation. The chance to utilize the potential in a "productive" manner depends on a student's "connections," on supply-and-demand conditions within the particular setting considered, and on the availability of necessary complementary resources. Thus a man's potential value or contribution in a given setting depends both on his own abilities and on the chances he will have to make use of them.

Because there are differences among migrating students with respect to capabilities and chances to utilize them, it would be possible for the contribution of one able, motivated, well-trained non-returning student (had he returned home) to have equaled that of a dozen less-talented students who did return (or vice versa). It is also possible that even though a nation has a general "shortage" of manpower (however defined), the particular individuals who are training and staying abroad could actually have contributed very little to the home country, either because complementary resources are not available there or because its social or political constraints would have prevented them from realizing their potential in home-country jobs.[17]

Adding a qualitative dimension to the paradigm would not be so important if no systematic differences existed among students in the various categories. However, these differences do exist between students who return, do not return, or are trained at home. And students differ from country to country in their characteristics and conditions of study. When comparing across nations, when comparing returnees and non-returnees, and when determining aggregate gains and losses associated with migration, it is therefore not enough to consider only the number of migrating individuals.

That the difference between counting migrants and attaching a particular social value to them is not trivial can be illustrated by a treatment of Canadian emigrants in which only one differentiating factor, educational attainment, is considered, and in which value is in terms of the cost of education:

It is worth noting that whereas professional, technical, and managerial groups comprise only 30.7 per cent of the absolute numbers of emigrants, valued in terms of costs of education, they equal 61.3 per cent of the total outlays on education of emigrants—double their previous weight.[18]

We might expect to find similar differences by sorting students into non-degree students below the level of a B.A. versus Ph.D. holders.

Granted that some method of valuing migrants is desirable, the problem becomes one of finding a conceptually sound methodology (or methodologies) that can be made operational. In Part III, this will be a major concern.

Adding a third dimension that can temporarily be labeled "value" to the migration paradigm of Figure 1 gives the revised version shown in Figure 4. Blocks replace the cells of the earlier diagram. The face of each block depicts, as did the former cells, the number of individuals in each category and the depth of each block is determined by the average "value" of an individual in that category.

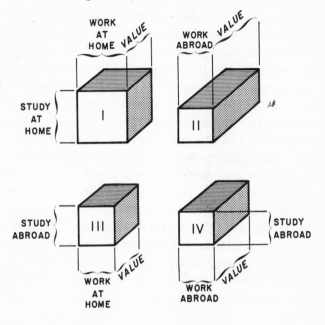

I = NON-MIGRANTS III = RETURNEES

II = EMIGRANTS IV = NON-RETURNEES

FIGURE 4—Migration Paradigm in Three Dimensions

Assuming knowledge of the numbers in each cell and an agreed-upon method of valuing students, one could compute the net effect of study at home (I minus II) and compare it with that of study abroad (III minus IV). This is essentially the approach taken in chapter 6 where decision models are presented based on the "value" of individuals in terms of human capital.

If the four categories of the revised paradigm are viewed as alternatives in an individual decision framework, we should be able to predict which of the alternatives will be chosen by comparing the manner in which each individual values himself in each of the situations described. In effect, the paradigm provides a starting point for developing hypotheses about the migration behavior of students (or of migrants in general). Furthermore, if the "value" placed on individuals within each of the categories is the value to society rather than the private value, then the models provide a basis for policy decisions about which of the education-employment alternatives the society should encourage. Such policy decisions would presumably be more firmly grounded than those made by simply counting migrants. And the comparative perspective overcomes problems that might arise from decisions made simply on the basis of valuing any one alternative.

Although our emphasis will be on using economic criteria to value migrants, non-economic measures may also be used effectively. For instance, in a study of doctorate recipients, Bayer adopted the "quality" of the institution attended as a proxy for the value of the migrating doctorate recipients.[19] Research focused on flows of persons who had received their doctoral degrees in selected science disciplines in the period 1957–60 and who reported their place of employment to the 1964 National Register of Scientific and Technical Personnel four to eight years after completion of the degree. Bayer used the migration paradigm to classify his population, adopting locus of high school study to designate the "home" region and locus of Ph.D. degree to indicate region of study. After receiving the doctoral degree, approximately one of two recipients left the area in which he received his degree.[20] Of those who originally migrated for study, 30 per cent were non-returnees who remained in the region of advanced study for employment, 29 per cent were returnees who remigrated to the region of their high school study, and 41 per cent were non-returnees, migrating to a third region.[21]

When the migrating student types were related to the quality of institutions attended, the most mobile group (non-returnees who moved to a third region for employment following their Ph.D.) was found to have attended the best institutions and the least mobile group (non-migrants) had attended the poorest institutions. Intermediate in quality of institution attended and in degree of mobility were the returnees, the non-returnees remaining to work in the area of their advanced study, and the "defectors" as Bayer calls those trained at home who then emigrate.

The quality of educational institutions is related to the locus of the institutions; some regions have higher quality schools, on the average, than others. As indicated above, quality is also related to migration propensities, both the propensity to migrate for education and to migrate following that education. Therefore, some regions attract and/or hold disproportionately, quality products of quality institutions. When adjustments for the quality of migrants, as defined by quality of institution attended, were made by Bayer, at least one region of the United States shifted from "loss" to "gain" status and others modified their position as relative gainers or losers through migration.[22] The need to attach qualitative weights to the migration streams was clearly upheld.[23]

SUMMARY

High-level migrants (defined by level of education or by occupation) differ from other migrants; they tend to move more frequently, for longer distances and over greater periods of their lives. However, there is substantial variation even among high-level migrants that must be incorporated when analyzing motives or assessing losses and gains through emigration. Not the least of the variations that should be considered is variation in the "quality" of the migrants and in their potential value to areas of origin and destination. In this book areas of origin and destination are defined by national borders and our primary concern is with international migration of high-level talent.

Students abroad are a special type of high-level international migrant, particularly those who remain abroad, thus becoming part of the brain drain (the so-called "untrained" part). An analysis of migration for education and of the change from temporary to permanent migrant status—as a decision is made to remain abroad—brings out relevant questions that are sometimes obscured if only migration for employment ("trained" brain drain) is considered. Attention is drawn to the decision to remain or return home as well as to the original decision to emigrate.

In chapter 1, a paradigm has been presented that can be used to classify migrants according to locus of education (home or abroad) and locus of employment (home or abroad). By thus defining education-employment sequences the paradigm should facilitate analysis of migration decisions and the assessment of aggregate gains and losses associated with emigration within a larger context of international high-level migration flows. The paradigm incorporates and emphasizes remigration, particularly the remigration of individuals educated outside their home area. A qualitative as well as quantitative dimension to migration has been included, setting the stage for assessing gains and losses using more than simple counts of migrating individuals, but still within a larger comparative framework.

In chapters 5 and 6, the paradigm will serve as the basis for elaborating economic models. First, however, some general observations on international flows of high-level manpower and on emigration through foreign student non-return will be made, followed by an analysis of non-return among foreign students in the United States.

NOTES

[1] This is probably a reaction against the early attempt by Ravenstein to establish what he called "laws." E. G. Ravenstein, "The Laws of Migration," *Journal of the Royal Statistical Society*, XLII, Part II (June 1885), pp. 167–235. For statements denying the existence of migration laws, see for instance: William Peterson, "Migration: Social Aspects," *International Encyclopedia of the Social Sciences* (New York: The Macmillan Company and the Free Press, 1968), pp. 286–92, or Donald J. Bogue, "Internal Migration," in *The Study of Population*, ed. Philip M. Hauser and Otis Dudley Duncan (Chicago: University of Chicago Press, 1959), p. 499.

[2] It is possible to extract from the migration literature literally hundreds of migration models designed to predict the volume and direction of migration flows, including student flows, to sort out significant factors in the decision calculus of migrating individuals or to compare migrants with non-

migrants. The models vary considerably in their emphasis on real and perceived characteristics of areas of origin (social, economic, political, etc. conditions); on intervening obstacles to migration (such as distance, legal barriers, intervening opportunities, and communication channels); and on the characteristics of the migrants (such as age, education, occupation, etc.). For present background purposes, migration models, qua models, are of less interest than the recurrent relationships which have emerged from the application of the various models to a wide range of migration situations. No attempt will be made here to summarize the migration literature. For two of the more complete bibliographies, see Gunnar Olsson, *Distance and Human Interaction* (Philadelphia: Regional Science Institute, 1965); and, J. J. Mangalam (with the assistance of Cornelia Morgan), *Human Migration, A Guide to Migration Literature in English, 1955–1962* (Lexington: University of Kentucky Press, 1968).

[3] Peterson, p. 289.

[4] Is an individual who is refused employment because he happens to be from the "wrong" background or from a minority any less "forced" to migrate than an individual who happens to be of the "wrong" political persuasion? Rarely is the latter individual actually physically forced to leave his home country, yet he will often be termed a political refugee and, as such, may be included with those migrants labeled involuntary or forced migrants. On the other hand, an individual from a minority background presumably makes a "free" choice and is grouped with the voluntary migrants.

Foreign student statistics in the U.S. include students who are refugees from Cuba, China, and elsewhere. They are included in most tabulations and introduce a bias. How to deal with that bias is another question.

[5] Support for these generalizations may be found, among other places, in such references as Bogue, pp. 499–502; Peter M. Blau and Otis Dudley Duncan, *The American Occupational Structure* (New York: John Wiley and Sons, Inc., 1967); Aba Schwartz, *Migration and Life Span Earnings in the U.S.* (unpublished Ph.D. dissertation, Department of Economics, University of Chicago, August 1968); Henry Shyrock, Jr., and Charles Nam, "Educational Selectivity of Interregional Migration," *Social Forces*, XLIII, No. 3 (March 1965), pp. 299–310; Albert M. Marckwardt, *Differentials of Recent Internal Migration in the United States* (unpublished Ph.D. dissertation, University of Michigan, 1968). But even these seemingly straightforward generalizations have their exceptions. For instance, R. Marvin McInnis has found the deterrent effect of distance increases with educational and occupational level. See "Age, Education and Occupation Differentials in Interregional Migration: Some Evidence for Canada," Discussion Paper No. 20 (Queen's University, Kingston, Ontario, 1970). Mimeographed.

[6] Herbert G. Grubel and Anthony Scott, "The Emigration of Scientists and Engineers to the United States, 1949–61," *The Journal of Political Economy*, LXXIV, No. 4 (August 1966), pp. 368–78.

[7] The student migrant has not received adequate treatment in spite of the fact that students constitute a not insignificant proportion of all migrating individuals in the United States, particularly within the 20–24 age groups. See Ann Miller, "Migration Differentials in Labor Force Participation: United States, 1960," *Demography*, III, No. 1 (1966), p. 60.

For the most complete analysis of student migration to date, see T. Groat,

"Internal Migration of a Population Subgroup, College Students, 1887–1958," *American Journal of Sociology*, LXIX (1964), pp. 383–94. See also Abbott Ferris, "Predicting Graduate Student Migration," *Social Forces*, XLIII (March 1965), pp. 310–19; and Charles S. Grossman *et al.*, *Migration of College and University Students in the United States* (Seattle: University of Washington Press, 1968).

[8] Note that both temporary migration (as in the case of the student who returns home) and permanent migration (as in the case of the immigrant or the student non-returnee) are within purview.

[9] Evidence from internal migration studies in the U.S. suggests remigration occurs by individuals who are less educated on the average than those who remain but who are nevertheless more educated than non-migrants. Marquardt, p. 71. It would be possible, therefore, for remigrants to have been "failures" in their new environment, yet to contribute at a higher level in the old than non-migrants (or even at a higher level of contribution than if they had remained at home). For an interesting example see Alan Sorkin, "Some Aspects of American Indian Migration," *Social Forces*, XLVIII, No. 2 (December 1969), pp. 243–50.

[10] The volume of return migration is affected by the size of the unit chosen for analysis. Generally, the smaller the unit, the less chance of encountering return migration. At the inter-county level, Marquardt (*op. cit.*, p. 71), found that return migration accounted for only 5% of all migration. At a regional level, the figures are higher (see chapter 5 of this book). On an international basis we might expect higher return rates. For instance Simon Kuznets and Ernest Rubin estimated that departures from the U.S. between 1878 and 1897 equaled about one-fourth of arrivals. Between 1899 and 1910 the rate rose to about one-half. Large percentages of those departing were remigrants. See *Immigration and the Foreign Born*, National Bureau of Economic Research Occasional Paper 46 (New York, National Bureau of Economic Research, 1954), p. 22.

[11] As in the Kuznets and Rubin study, most research incorporating remigration has been primarily concerned with migration of unskilled manpower rather than high-level manpower. See, for instance, Jose Hernandez Alvarez, *Return Migration to Puerto Rico* (Berkeley: University of California, Institute of International Studies, 1967); Organization for European Cooperation and Development (OECD), *Emigrant Workers Returning to Their Home Country* (Paris: OECD, 1967); R. T. Appleyard, "Determinants of Return Migration—A Socio-Economic Study of United Kingdom Migrants Who Returned from Australia," *Economic Record*, XXXVIII, No. 83 (1962), pp. 352–68. One example of the importance of remigration among high-level migrants comes from the work Goran Friborg, who notes that remigration from the U.S. to Sweden has been very high. See *Minerva*, VII, No. 4 (1969), p. 761.

[12] Alan Bayer, "Interregional Migration and the Education of American Scientists," *Sociology of Education*, XLI, No. 1 (Winter 1968), p. 92.

[13] Mary Jean Bowman and Robert G. Myers, "Schooling, Experience, and Gains and Losses Through Migration," *Journal of the American Statistical Association*, LXII, No. 319 (September 1967), pp. 875–98.

[14] Bayer, *Social Forces*, XLVI, No. 4, pp. 465–77.

[15] *Ibid.*, p. 475.

[16] *Ibid.*

[17] It is reasonably well established, for instance, that there is a brain drain from East African nations in the very fields where there are bottleneck shortages. The drain, however, is primarily of Asians who are victims of the politically important "Africanization" programs. See A. Baron Holmes, "Migration of Talent: A Case Study of East Africa," (mimeographed, n.d.) The study was part of the larger brain drain study being done by Education and World Affairs.

[18] Bruce W. Wilkinson, "Some Economic Aspects of Education in Canada" (unpublished Ph.D. dissertation, Massachusetts Institute of Technology, 1964), p. 114.

[19] Bayer, *Sociology of Education*, XLI, No. 1, pp. 90–102. "Quality" was determined by rating institutions according to Alan Cartter's graduate school ratings. See Alan Cartter, *An Assessment of Quality in Graduate Education* (Washington, D.C.: American Council on Education, 1966).

[20] Bayer, *Sociology of Education*, XLI, No. 1, p. 96.

[21] Calculated from Bayer, *ibid.*, p. 90, Table 3 (Mean Quality of Doctorate Education, by Migration Pattern and Major Field Area).

[22] *Ibid.*, pp. 99, 102.

[23] Locus can be broadly defined as a national or regional construct or it can be narrowed to particular institutions.

2

HIGH-LEVEL INTERNATIONAL MIGRATION:

Some General Observations

How many and who are the high-level international migrants? Why do they migrate? How does the propensity to migrate differ among them? From the migration paradigm developed in chapter 1, we switch to a description of high-level migration and migrants. In so doing, no "new" information will be presented. Rather, an attempt will be made to highlight and coordinate some of the existing literature.

The descriptive task is not a simple one. International migration statistics are scarce and those that do exist must be interpreted with extreme caution. And the mushrooming literature[1] is so diverse in both quality and viewpoint that integration is almost impossible. Even to keep abreast of the literature is almost a full-time task; most of the studies and articles which focus on high-level migration and the brain drain have appeared after 1960. Since then, however, there has been an extraordinary outpouring of material by special committees of international organizations, professional associations, policy-oriented institutes, United States Government groups, and academicians of various persuasions. With time, analyses have grown ever more elaborate. Fortunately they are becoming more rigorous and objective as well; accompanying the increased tempo of writing and research has been a change in style from the earlier demographic or manpower-oriented descriptions and speculative overviews to in-depth analyses revealing the more complex nature of correlates, motives, and effects.[2]

The reader must not expect a clear, focused, picture of high-level migration to emerge. If there is an overriding theme in this chapter, it is one of diversity. Indeed, after surveying the literature, one of the main conclusions to be drawn is that disaggregated analysis of high-level migration is essential. Because there are pronounced variations, groupings by country, occupation, educational attainment, and the like should be included in analyses. The paradigm of chapter 1, for instance, is best applied to sub-categories. And because there is such diversity, generalizations derived from "cases" must be treated skeptically.

The Magnitude and Direction of High-Level Migration

At a global level, we must leave unanswered the question, "How many high-level migrants are there?" There is no world-wide tabulation of high-level international migration that incorporates flows among all countries. Such neglect is not surprising, for general immigration and emigration statistics are still notoriously deficient at the national level. Even when national collection procedures are carefully monitored and are consistent, and even when definitions are relatively clear, available national figures are often of limited utility because critical disaggregation is impossible. Furthermore, remigration and multiple moves seldom surface in statistics even though they can be quantitatively and qualitatively important when considering gains and losses or when studying motives. Efforts are being made to sort out these migration flows, but as yet the larger picture remains blurred. When it sharpens to include counterflows and multiple moves, more can be said about gross flows as well as about the relative influences of conditions at origin and destination on migration patterns and about the effect of international migration on national as well as on world welfare.[3]

In the meantime, however, several observations can be offered about high-level international migration that are not particularly dependent on the pinpoint accuracy of statistics. First, there is little doubt that the percentage of all high-level talent in the world that has migrated permanently across international borders is relatively small (probably not more than 2 or 3 per cent). The "problem" of high-level migration arises when percentages become higher for particular nations or when migration flows are concentrated in particular fields where "shortages" are thought to exist. Second, the major *numerical* migration flow is from "developing" to "developed" nations. The latter presumably gain at the expense of the former, giving rise to cries of injustice. Third, in recent years the United States has been (and probably still is) the main migration destination (either directly or indirectly) of high-level international migrants. A shift may be in progress, but it is too early to alter the observation. Fourth, there are significant flows from developing nations to developed nations other than the United States, and there are flows among developing nations. The last-mentioned is probably the least well-documented.

In one of the best discussions of high-level international migration statistics to date, Brinley Thomas takes note of various flows and counterflows, classifying nations as follows: 1) advanced nations with a large net inflow (The United States, Australia); 2) intermediate (by which Thomas means that residence may be temporary) advanced nations with a large two-way traffic (the United Kingdom, Canada); 3) advanced countries with a large net outflow (The Netherlands, Norway, Switzerland); and 4) underdeveloped countries with a large net outflow (Greece, Iran, Turkey, and some Asian countries).[4]

How useful Thomas' classification is to a particular policymaker or researcher will depend on his purpose. It is generally instructive, however, incorporating as it does some notion of two-way flows. And the typology is illustrative of the need to differentiate high-level flows by area of origin and/or destination while viewing flows in relation to some measure of the economic resources at a nation's disposal, roughly divided by Thomas into the oversimplified categories of developed and underdeveloped nations. The reader should bear in mind that a net numerical outflow of migrants does not necessarily imply an economic "loss."

High-Level Migration to the United States

The percentage of high-level (in this case professional, technical, and kindred workers) to total immigrants entering the United States has increased dramatically—from approximately 1 per cent *circa* 1900 to somewhere between 10 per cent [5] and 22 per cent [6] today (depending on whether one uses all immigrants or immigrant workers as a base).

Whatever the percentage, it is higher than the existing percentage of high-level manpower as against total manpower in the United States labor force. From welcoming "your tired, your poor, your huddled masses yearning to breathe free," the United States seems to have moved toward a policy of welcoming the alert, the skilled, and the educated few yearning for employment.

Approximately one-fifth of all high-level immigrants to the United States in 1967 and 1968 were engineers and another one-fourth were in medical occupations. By way of contrast, social scientists constituted less than 2 per cent of the total high-level flow.[7]

From a slightly different perspective, we see that the percentage of high-level immigrants to total high-level manpower in the labor force within the United States is relatively low (or high, depending on perspective)—approximately 6 or 7 per cent. What is more important, however, is the fact that in some fields the percentage rises above 15 per cent, creating a strong dependency on foreign manpower.[8]

The high-level to total percentage of immigrants is about the same for the broad grouping into developing and developed nations. Within each category, however, there is wide variation. For instance, more than one-half of the Indian immigrants in 1967 were classified as high-level immigrants.[9] For Asia, there was a rapid rise following the change in immigration regulations in 1965—from less than 10 per cent in 1965 to almost 30 per cent in 1967.[10]

Among high-level immigrants, an increasing proportion have come from developing countries in recent years. More than one-half of all immigrant scientists, engineers, and physicians to the United States now come from developing nations. The increases have been highlighted as cause for concern. Although the proportion, by itself, has little meaning, it has been sighted as alarming evidence that the United States is unduly siphoning off talent from the developing nations.[11] To interpret the proportion one should take note of relative populations at migrant origins, of the relative numbers of high-level manpower available from each nation, and/or of the relative production of trained manpower. As we will see in chapter 4, when such comparisons are made, the developed-developing dichotomy does not appear to be a useful means of sorting out which nations are gaining or losing through migration. It is more appropriate to point to specific countries that are losing manpower.

Shifting distributions by country and occupation are related to shifts in the proportion of high-level immigrants classified as "trained" (from the paradigm of chapter 1, those trained at home before migrating to the United States for work) versus "untrained" (those migrating for study who then emigrate). As one might expect, most high-level migration from developed nations has been "trained" (over 95 per cent by one calculation) while a much smaller percentage of all immigration from developing nations falls in the "trained" category (approximately 60 per cent).[12] The distinction is based on tabulations of visas and visa adjustments and therefore must be interpreted carefully (see Footnote to Part I, pp. 76–88). The percentages tell nothing about the causal role of study abroad in the brain drain but are sometimes used to show that study in the United States causes nonreturn and that this is more often the case among students from developing than among students from developed nations. As the proportion of high-level migrants from developing countries (to total migrants) has increased, the importance of "trained" brain drain has decreased. Policy-makers and critics have turned their attention to foreign student non-return or "untrained" brain drain as we will see in more detail later in this chapter.

The Propensity to Migrate

To note relative percentages of national and occupational groups among high-level migrants does not provide us with an adequate indication of the propensity to migrate associated with each group. For insight into such propensity, comparisons with non-migrants from the same nations and/or occupational categories are needed.

Logically, the propensity to migrate varies among occupations. Demand in high- as well as low-level occupations and market structures differ by occupation and among countries for the same occupation. Career styles and patterns vary significantly among occupations; in some, advancement is almost inextricably linked to mobility—an extreme case being a diplomatic career—in others, movement is not a necessary precondition for advancement.[13]

There is a strong supposition, for instance, that the propensity to migrate is greater among physical and natural scientists, engineers and physicians, than among social scientists, educators, lawyers, or businessmen. The supposition is probably correct but there are few figures to prove it.[14] It must be remembered that social science is a late bloomer and that in many countries the total number of individuals who can be considered social scientists is very small. Hence the small number and percentage of social scientists migrating may still represent a relatively high propensity to migrate among modern social scientists, but because numbers are small the matter has received limited attention.

Somewhat better documented is the assertion that engineers are more apt to migrate than scientists.[15] Several reasons have been advanced to explain this phenomenon—one of the most interesting being that the respective occupations attract people with different sets of values; those choosing engineering rather than science are more likely to find migration necessary if they are to find a setting congenial to their value orientation, which is more material than intellectual. While the argument may hold for some settings, I think the reverse argument could be made: that the intellectual stimulation valued by scientists might be as lacking at home as material rewards for the engineers.

Medicine is probably the field that has received the most attention from researchers interested in international flows of high-level talent, and not without justification. There is a tendency for developing nations to "overproduce" graduates in this prestige field in relation to the economic demand for their services, and the percentages of local medical graduates that migrate are often very high.[16] Controlled price policies where socialized medicine is followed and concentration of graduates in large urban centers also increase the probability of medical migration. Both the United States and the United Kingdom are highly dependent on foreign personnel to fulfill their need for medical service. The high propensity of medical graduates to emigrate from developing nations to the United States may be directly linked to its seemingly limitless market and limited production of doctors.

But variation in the propensity to migrate, among the high-level migrants, is also related to education level or degree, even within particular occupational categories. It is estimated, for instance, that obtaining a doctorate about trebles the chances that a British scientist will migrate.[17] In moving to the doctoral level, an individual broadens the market in which he can sell his services. Also, a selection process is at work as people progress toward higher educational levels, a selection process that operates simultaneously along several lines yet to be sorted out. In spite of the above, there is no evidence to indicate that the relationship between level of education and the propensity to migrate is a simple, linear relationship. It is possible, for instance, that both B.A. and Ph.D. holders consistently have higher migration propensities than M.A. holders.

The conclusion drawn from Bayer's work (see chapter 1, p. 28) that individuals attending higher-quality educational institutions in the United States were more likely to migrate is supported by some evidence from international migration research. According to Wilson, to Rudd, and to the Jones Report (all dealing with British scientists),[18] and according to Grubel and Scott (dealing with foreign economists in the United States),[19] high-level migrants—at least those to the United States—are *on the average* better qualified than their counterparts in this country and probably better qualified, *on the average,* than their counterparts at home. On the other hand, there is evidence that the most talented nationals (with some obvious exceptions) tend to stay at home (and to return home after studying abroad). This is not necessarily a contradiction. The explanation may lie in movement of the "B+" talent—high-level and good, but not quite good enough to get one of the few top positions at home. There is, however, a vast range of abilities and backgrounds among migrants. The studies referred to above tend to deal with only an upper stratum of high-level migrants, defined narrowly in terms of high educational attainment, select occupational titles, or membership in a professional organization. A broader definition could change results. In medicine it is well established that many of the immigrants are second-rate doctors and often fill positions in second- and third-rate hospitals.[20]

The propensity to migrate, then, varies along several dimensions. To the foregoing disaggregation by type of occupation, level of schooling and quality of schooling, the standard variables of age, sex,[21] and race (or ethnic origin) should undoubtedly be added. Indeed, even a limited exploration of sub-categories suggests that aggregate treatments of high-level migration can lead to unjustified conclusions.

Migration Motives

Although it is possible, in theory, to approximate a hierarchy of importance among factors affecting the individual migrant's decisions, migration literature offers little to clarify the relative importance of specific factors in the decision to move (as differentiated from the probability that a move will occur discussed above). Pinpointing specific motives and sorting out objective from subjective "reasons" within the complex interplay of forces acting upon and within an individual is difficult in the extreme.

Even the grossest division into economic (which for most writers means monetary) and non-economic motives fails to produce clear results. Many writers would agree that ". . . the possibility of earning money is generally pre-eminent among the operating motives." [22] Others contend that migrants tend to rationalize their general feeling of insecurity and inadequacy into more specific economic factors,[23] or even more directly, that the real motivating forces are non-economic.[24]

The above emphasis on so-called economic motives is given here because an "economic" approach to migration decisions will be developed in later chapters. Many migration models assume the dominance of economic motives. Furthermore, the manipulation of economic incentives is frequently suggested as a (or even the) major means of stimulating or moderating migration flows.

The manner in which economic motives vary in strength with educational and occupational levels is not clear; it needs to be specified. It is probably true that ". . . as people get richer, their motives grow more varied and whimsical and the job of the social scientist [becomes] accordingly more difficult." [25] The same could probably be asserted with "more educated" substituted for "richer."

A sampling of studies probing the motives of high-level international migrants does not settle questions about the relative importance of economic and non-economic factors in decisions. Among Latin American physicians migrating to the United States, for instance, "lack of professional opportunity" was the most frequently mentioned factor influencing immigration. The components of "professional opportunity" listed in order of importance were: very low income, poor resources and facilities, and poor professional environment.[26] Among British scientists who come to the United States, one researcher pointed to "the possibility of the satisfaction of professional ambition" as the most important motive force. He suggested that with migrants satisfaction is linked to a need to achieve and is rooted in basic psychological drives rather than economic satisfaction.[27] However, other explanations are offered for the same movement: "For the young graduate or Ph.D. at the outset of his career [salaries in the United States] represent, in terms of purchasing power and standards of living, perhaps two to two-and-a-half or even three times those available in the United Kingdom";[28] or ". . . better opportunities and more salary seemed to be the dominant reason";[29] or ". . . because they are bored."[30]

Some high-level immigrants behave like "target workers," who migrate to work until they can accumulate a certain amount of savings, then remigrate.[31] Target migrants do not seek to "maximize" their earnings but monetary rewards determine their behavior. The high-level target worker may also link his target to attaining a particular level of experience that can then be taken home and converted into better earnings and/or professional achievement.

For many high-level migrants, the main motivation is political. The United States continues to profit from the influx of European Jews in the 1930s and 1940s. It is now profiting from Cuban talent. For others, social discrimination is important. Political and social motives can easily be translated into economic motives; political persecution and discrimination have their economic effects.

One could go on to cite numerous other considerations which enter into the decision to migrate, but little would be added. If any conclusion is suggested by monitoring the many statements of why the migratory elite voluntarily go or stay, it is that the economic factors, while present, are certainly not in themselves sufficient reason for permanent migration.

Although it is obviously crucial for policy-makers who wish to stanch the brain drain to identify motives so that appropriate remedies can be found, this task is more easily stated than carried out.

Closely related to the discussion of migration motives are attempts to predict the direction and volume of migration flows by looking at a variety of structural conditions at migrant origins or destinations which "push" or "pull" migrants.[32] Both economic conditions (such as labor market composition, salaries, employment rates) and non-economic conditions (such as climate or changes of government) have been explored for whatever help they might offer in predicting trends. These conditions are seldom strong predictors of migration, regardless of how they are measured.

Recent analyses of United States census data indicate that, for inter-regional flows of high-level individuals, both changes in the occupational structure [33] and expected lifetime earning differentials [34] are better gauges than income differences. The responsiveness of migrants to earnings seems to increase with educational level (but also to decline with age).[35] There is no indication however, that the relationship is a casual one. Earning streams will be examined in detail in Parts III and IV.

INTERNATIONAL MIGRATION FOR STUDY

To study abroad is to migrate. Presumably migration for study is temporary but it may also provide the springboard for more permanent migration. Thus background on the initial movement abroad is useful in understanding emigration through foreign student non-return.

Given the paucity of information and the enormity of the task, no attempt will be made to sort out the relative importance of ". . . educational, linguistic, religious and cultural tradition, proximity, financial support, ideology and tangible prestige [as they] appear to govern the flow of foreign students. . . ."[36] What we can do at this point is supply rough figures on student flows as provided by available statistics, and we can describe variations in the distribution of foreign students along several key dimensions.

No worldwide matrix of migration for study has been compiled; nor has there been a survey of foreign students that documents cross-nationally, for example, such a fundamental characteristic as age. Furthermore, available information, by country— such as foreign student enrollment, enrollment ratios and fields of study—is of uneven quality and must be treated cautiously.

At the beginning of the first development decade (school year 1959–60), there were approximately 200,000 students abroad enrolled in institutions of higher education, according to UNESCO's Ninth Annual Survey of foreign students.[37] In the same year, the United States (which appears as the dominant destination for migrating students as well as for "trained" high-level international migrants) was host to almost 50,000 foreign students, approximately one-fourth of UNESCO's conservative world estimate.[38] Midway in the decade (school year 1964–65) UNESCO's estimate had risen to approximately 290,000 students abroad,[39] of which more than 82,000 were studying in the United States.[40] By extrapolation, the number of university students abroad in 1969–70 should have reached at least one-half million. The United States hosted 135,000 students in that year.[41]

Although the absolute number of overseas students continues to increase, the rate of increase has declined in recent years.[42] Consequently, there has been a relative decline in study abroad as a percentage of total enrollment in higher education throughout the world, a percentage that has never been above 3 per cent.[43] The leveling off of study abroad ratios can be attributed to the rapid expansion of higher education "at home" during the early 1960s, particularly in developing countries. For example, between 1960 and 1965 the enrollment in higher educational institutions in Middle Africa rose by about 260 per cent, while the enrollment abroad of Middle Africans rose by only 66 per cent.[44]

But such global totals mask wide variations among both host and sender nations—variations at destination and origin. Host nations show a considerable spread in the percentages of foreign to total students (and by implication, in the percentage of total educational resources absorbed by foreign students). For instance, the United States and the Soviet Union, while hosting large numbers of students, are among the nations with the smallest ratios of foreign to total students, both with less than two per cent. Conversely, Switzerland fills more than one-fourth of its places with foreign students, even though the number of students is not great.[45] (See Appendix IV, column 6, for percentages for other nations.)

Some Necessary Distinctions

Cross-national comparisons of migration for study should also take account of the significant variation from one host country to the next in national origin of students, in field and level of study; and in degree of financial support provided locally. A thorough analysis of such variations has not been done, but several illustrations will make the point that focusing attention on national enrollment ratios is not a particularly meaningful exercise. Consider the fact that although less than 2 per cent of all students in United States universities are foreign students, the percentage at the graduate level is closer to seven. Recipients of doctorates from U.S. universities approach 15 per cent foreign and in some fields even more.[46] Comparisons of the United States with other nations should take these variations into account.

Or consider the differences between foreign student distributions in the United Kingdom and Switzerland, countries classified together in one cross-national analysis relating foreign study and development.[47] By comparison, the percentage of foreign students in Swiss universities in 1964–65 seems high, almost 30 per cent as against approximately 10 per cent in the United Kingdom. However, approximately 70 per cent of the students in the U.K. came from developing nations compared with only 25 per cent for Switzerland. And nearly 60 per cent of the U.K. foreign students were enrolled in scientific or technological courses versus less than 40 per cent in Switzerland.[48] Furthermore, UNESCO estimated that in 1963–64, the United Kingdom offered more fellowships in relation to the number of foreign students hosted than Switzerland—25 per cent and 4 per cent, respectively.[49] Whether the United Kingdom and Switzerland should be grouped together or whether one country should be ranked above the other when interpreting their role in migration for study will depend on the perspective brought to the analysis.

Distributions of foreign students by national origin, field and level of study, and by financial support not only differ from country to country, they also vary over time. At the global level it is difficult to discern recent trends in level of study or in sponsorship. One of the few shifts that can be identified is the declining number of medical students among those going abroad to study, a development to be watched with interest in view of the fact that medicine is a, if not the, major brain-drain field.

For individual host nations, shifts are clearer. In both the United States and the United Kingdom, for instance, clear trends toward science, toward study at the post-graduate level, and toward sponsored study are evident from 1955 to 1965.[50]

Variations Among Sending Nations

In the larger picture of trained and untrained migrations, we also need to identify to what extent particular nations depend on sending students abroad (or allowing them to migrate for study) as a means of developing their supply of high-level manpower. In nations where there are few institutions of higher education, there is dependency on foreign educational institutions. Student non-return under such circumstances will perforce account for a large portion of total high-level emigration. At the same time, foreign training may also be a major source, if not the major source, of high-level talent. Obvious as these facts may seem, they are often overlooked when brain-drain comparisons are being made between developed and developing nations. And they are overlooked by manpower planners whose projections are simply based on home-country enrollments and capacities. Study abroad may be viewed as an extension of a national system of education, but it is seldom considered from that perspective.

To obtain statistics about the percentages of foreign students enrolled in a particular country is much easier than to arrive at the number of students from the same country who are being educated abroad. In spite of home-country attempts to regulate and keep track of national students' international wanderings (through currency exchange regulations and visa requirements), estimates of students abroad made by countries of origin are extremely crude. Self-sponsored students are most likely to be omitted from official tabulations while sponsored students are counted, thus biasing totals. And individuals often use nonstudent visas to migrate even though their primary purpose may be to study abroad.

An alternative to counting students from each sending country as they leave for study is to count them in each of the various host countries and add up the enrollment figures. This alternative has the decided disadvantage inherent in relying on many different counting methods and definitions. Nevertheless the rather laborious and inadequate procedure along these lines adopted by UNESCO results in an approximation of the number of students abroad. When using the figures published in UNESCO's *Study Abroad* or *Statistical Yearbook* for cross-national comparisons, the method of their compilation must be kept in mind.[51]

When ratios are calculated which relate the number of nationals studying abroad at the third level (higher education) to the total number of nationals being trained at that level, nations tend to cluster according to broad areal groupings. (See Appendix IV, column 7.) European nations and most advanced "Western" nations including Japan generally train less than 5 per cent of their third-level students abroad. Norway, with more than 15, is a notable exception. Sub-Saharan nations, by contrast, tend to have large ratios—typically more than 25 per cent, sometimes reaching as high as 80 per cent. Latin American and Middle Eastern nations tend to fall within the 5 to 25 per cent range. (Figures for these countries are probably the most underestimated and they should be taken even less seriously than others.) Although typically grouped with African nations as "developing," countries of the Indian subcontinent and Asia show ratios that are usually below five. There is an effect of size.

In spite of the statistical qualifications, we can conclude from the above that the degree of dependence upon study abroad varies widely. Before trying to draw any further conclusions, such variations should be carefully scrutinized for underlying differences in patterns of sponsorship, field of study, and level of study among sending nations. To date, statistics are not available for such an exercise.

National, international, and periodic variations in foreign student flows will affect non-return and calculations of gains and losses to countries of origin and destination. But how? What, for instance, are the results of a shift toward graduate study abroad? Who bears the higher costs and reaps the greater benefits? Are graduate-level students more inclined to return home because they are more mature, possibly married to someone from home, and have more responsibilities? Or has their training advanced them beyond the point where they can be useful to their home country in their chosen field? How do home-country pressures that would moderate non-return change as changes occur in the numbers and types of students migrating for study?

What is the meaning of the changes in sponsorship pattern toward greater sponsorship? Are students more or less likely to remain abroad? Are host nations more likely to encourage non-return when they are heavily subsidizing foreign students than when they are not? (The 1965 and 1970 changes in U.S. immigration laws could be interpreted in that way.) Or are economic considerations overridden by a desire by host nations to retain international good will to the point that an extra effort is made to see that students return home? Does increased U.S. sponsorship bring with it a heightened desire to see foreign students return because the sponsorship is looked upon as foreign aid which, if not used in the country for which it was intended, is deemed ineffective? (That feeling persists in the United States in spite of the fact that non-return is relatively rare among those individuals trained abroad under U.S. technical assistance programs—but with such a statement we are jumping ahead.)

Several points emerge from the foregoing. Neither the absolute number nor the simple ratio of foreign students to total students enrolled can be taken as a sound basis for international comparisons. The need for a disaggregated approach is apparent. If economic gains and losses associated with foreign students are to be compared, we must ask specifically, "What costs and benefits are associated with foreign study in a particular field, at a particular level, in a particular country, at a particular time?"

FOREIGN STUDENT NON-RETURN—
THE UNTRAINED BRAIN DRAIN

In spite of what sometimes seems to be a surfeit of research dealing with foreign students, relatively few studies deal directly with their non-return or examine the economic impact of returnees and non-returnees. Until recently, research had been conditioned largely by the fact that foreign students were convenient subjects for sociologists and psychologists studying cross-cultural change, or had been dictated by a host country's official advisers who wanted to know what effect study "here" had on attitudes of foreigners toward "us" or upon "world understanding." [52] Although important and clearly related to return or non-return, these studies of "adjustment" or alienation or attitude change seldom supply insight into questions of non-return; they were not designed with such questions in mind.[53] They certainly supply few clues for measuring economic gains and losses through migration or for making decisions about the allocation of human resources,[54] the points emphasized here.

Return and remigration are often used to signify immigration *to the United States* after students have gone home following study. As used here the terms refer to remigration *home* following study abroad, and emphasize the fact that to study abroad is to migrate, and that the decision to remain or return home is not automatic. This definition also permits direct comparison of migration for study with other forms of migration.

The return of students from overseas study and the impact of foreign training on areas of origin has been dealt with in many "follow-up" studies. These studies are the closest approximation to research on the economic impact of study abroad that is found in the foreign student literature. Although the emphasis has often been correctly placed on *utilization* of foreign training rather than on the simple fact of return home and although conditions have been identified that favor utilization, it has not been rigorously defined.[55] In general, follow-up studies have not deeply probed into the question of non-return. For information, we must turn to the more recent and growing research that concerns itself more specifically with the subject. By examining the relevant literature, we are able to gain some insight into the magnitude and correlates of both return (by subtraction, as it were) and non-return.

From the many pre-1964 writings about foreign students, only two could be located which focused on foreign student non-return.[56] However, numerous other pieces of research prior to 1964 included incidental information about non-returnees [57] and several in-depth studies have recently appeared which focus on motives of non-returning students as well as on the factors predisposing them to remain abroad following study. From these studies, tentative conclusions and generalizations can be drawn about the magnitude and correlates of non-return and about motives of non-returnees.

The Magnitude and Rate of Non-return

There have been relatively few attempts to estimate foreign student non-return for students in countries other than the United States.[58] For the United Kingdom, it has been reported that of all foreign students graduating from universities in 1965–66, approximately 60 per cent returned home and another 6 to 9 per cent were thought to have gone to other countries, presumably leaving 31 to 34 per cent as non-returnees in the United Kingdom.[59]

Somewhat more detailed information is available for officially sponsored students in the United Kingdom. "In the last five years (1962–67?) only 61 (0.5 per cent) of the 12,000 students who have come to Britain under the Ministry of Overseas Development programmes of technical assistance have failed to return home." The same rate applies to Commonwealth Teacher Training Bursars and to British Council Bursars and Scholars. In the case of Commonwealth Scholarships for the four years from 1960 through 1963, 92.5 per cent (709 out of 766) were known to have returned home. The only field in which there was a significant number of non-returning students was postgraduate medical study.[60]

A Canadian survey determined that one-seventh of the foreign students trained in Canada in 1962 intended to remain in Canada.[61] And a recent United Nations report cites figures for African students remaining in France (suggesting that non-return is extremely high) and for Asian students wishing to remain in Australia (20 per cent).[62]

In the United States, while there has been no lack of estimates, there is little agreement about actual numbers of non-returnees. In fact, estimating the magnitude and rate of non-return carries a certain sporting challenge, given the underdeveloped state of official statistics. Several of the many estimates are brought together in Table 1.

TABLE 1—Estimates of non-return of foreign students in the United States, various years, various student populations, and various definitions of non-return

ESTIMATED PERCENTAGE	STUDENT POPULATION	YEARS	DEFINITION OF NON-RETURN	SOURCE
5.7	All foreign students	1962–66	Adjustment, Waiver of F, J, or H visa as determined from immigration records.	U.S. Dept of State, Council on Int'l Educational and Cultural Affairs, *Some Facts and Figures on the Migration of Talent and Skills* (Wash., D.C., 1967), p. 75.
3.8	All foreign students	1964–65	Intent to remain permanently, determined by a sample survey.	Operations Policy Research, Inc., *Foreign Students in the United States, A National Survey*, Vol. II (Wash., D.C.: U.S. Commission on Int'l Educational and Cultural Affairs, 1966), p. 413.
15.9	All foreign students	1964–65	Intent to remain permanently, determined from Institute of Int'l Education (IIE) census of foreign students.	See chapter 3, this volume.

TABLE 1—(*Continued*)

ESTI-MATED PER-CENTAGE	STUDENT POPULATION	YEARS	DEFINITION OF NON-RETURN	SOURCE
24.5	All foreign students	1967	Not specified.	United Nations, General Assembly, 23rd Sess., Nov. 5, 1968, *Outflow of Trained Personnel from Developing Countries, Report of the Secretary-General*, A/7294, p. 32.
2.7	J-visa holders	1962–66	Waiver of J visa.	U.S. Dept. of State, p. 65.
8.3	F-visa holders	1962–66	Adjustment of F visa.	*Ibid.*
1.0	J-visa holders	1964–65	Intent to remain permanently, from IIE census.	See chapter 3, this volume.
7.7	F-visa holders	1964–65	Intent to remain permanently, from IIE census.	See chapter 3, this volume.
51.0	All doctorate recipients	1964–66	Location of first job following degree.	National Academy of Sciences, National Science Foundation, *Doctorate Recipients from United States Universities, 1958–1966* (Wash., D.C.: Nat'l Academy of Sciences, Publication 1489, 1967).

37.0	Graduate Engineers, M.A. & Ph.D., Univ. of Cal., Berkeley	1954–65	U.S. residence in 1965 plus intent to remain permanently, determined by special survey.	Lynn Schell and Charles Susskind, *Exporting Technical Education* (New York: IIE, 1968), pp. 10 and 11.
46.0	All foreign students at Iowa Univ.	1950–60	Residence in U.S. in 1964, determined from immigration office records.	Wallace Maner, "More on Exchange or Immigration," *NAFSA Newsletter*, XVI, No. 8 (May 1965), p. 8.
1.0	U.S. Government-sponsored students	1962–66	Adjustment, Waiver of F, J, or H visa.	U.S. Congress, Senate Subcommittee on Immigration and Naturalization, Committee on the Judiciary, Hearings, *International Migration of Talent and Skills*, 90th Cong., 1st Sess., 1967 (Wash., D.C.: USCPO, 1968), p. 14.
9.0	Students sponsored by: Belgian-Amer. Foundation, Commonwealth Fund, Inst. of Int'l Ed, Rockefeller Found.	1920–50	Permanent residence in the United States, determined from addresses in organization files, in 1956.	Institute of International Education, *The Foreign Student, Exchangee or Immigrant*, New York, IIE, Commission on Educational Interchange, 1958, p. 3.
12.0	Students sponsored by the Amer. Assn. of Univ. Women, IFUW fellowships	1923–53	Permanent residence in the United States.	Ruth Tryon, *Investment in Creative Scholarship* (Washington: American Association of University Women, 1957), p. 105.

TABLE 1—(Continued)

ESTIMATED PERCENTAGE	STUDENT POPULATION	YEARS	DEFINITION OF NON-RETURN	SOURCE
18.0	Students sponsored by the National Inst. of Health	1956–60	Residence in the United States in 1962 plus intention to remain.	Kelly West, "Training for Medical Research: the World Role of the United States," *J. of Medical Education*, XXXIX (March 1964), p. 249.
25.0	Israeli students with F visas	1957–64	High probability of intended non-return.	P. Ritterband, "The Non-returning Foreign Student: the Israeli Case" (unpublished Ph.D. dissertation, Columbia Univ., 1968), Appendix A, p. 197.
36.0	Indian students	1964–65	Inclination "to think at one time of not going back."	Keshev Sharma, "Indian Students in the United States," *Exchange*, IV, No. 4 (Spring 1969), p. 52.
93.7	Indian engineering students (all levels, J-visa holders excluded)	1967	"Conversion to an immigrant visa expressed as a proportion of all those technically able to so convert."	J. R. Niland, "The Brain Drain of Highly Trained Engineering Manpower from Asia into the United States" (unpublished Ph.D. dissertation, University of Illinois, 1969), p. 42.

30.0	Canadian students	1964–65	Intention to remain permanently in the United States.	R. Pavalko, "Talent Migration: Canadian Students in the United States," *International Review of Education*, XIV, No. 3 (1968), p. 310. See chapter 7, this volume.
8.0	Peruvian students (males only)	1965–66	High probability of intended non-return.	Gregory Henderson, "Foreign Students: Exchange or Immigration?" *International Development Review*, VI (December 1964), p. 19.
67.0	Korean students	1947–61	No. of original students sent by Am. Foundation who could not be accounted for by definite return or by current student status.	
95.0	Chinese graduate students	about 1964–65	Not specified.	Joseph Platt, "Emigration of Scholars and the Development of Taiwan: Chinese-American Cooperation," *Development Digest*, IV (April 1966), p. 43.
30.0	Chinese students with J visas	?	Visa Waivers.	Cited by Paul Cook of the Council on Int'l Ed. and Cultural Affairs at the Region V Conference of the National Assn. for Foreign Student Affairs, International House, U. of Chicago, Feb. 25, 1967.

TABLE 1—(*Concluded*)

ESTI-MATED PER-CENTAGE	STUDENT POPULATION	YEARS	DEFINITION OF NON-RETURN	SOURCE
16.3	Chinese students (Taiwan and unspecified)	1964–65	Intent to remain permanently in the United States, determined from IIE census.	See chapter 3, Table 17 of this volume. Items 15 and 70 in the table have been combined.
13.4	Chinese and Formosan students at mid-west universities	1967	Intent (or hope) to remain permanently in the United States.	Tai Keun Oh, "The Role of International Education in Asian Brain Drain" (unpublished Ph.D. dissertation, University of Wisconsin, Madison, 1970, pp. 61–62.
46.9	Neurosurgical trainees	1950–65	Resident in the United States in 1968.	Joseph Evans, "Report on Foreign Neurosurgical Trainees," presented to the Adlai Stevenson Institute of Foreign Affairs (ASIIA) Study Group on Migration of Scientists and Physicians, Chicago, Illinois, April 4, 1968.

55.0	Pediatric trainees	1950–67	Immigrant pediatricians (total number trained minus those still in training).	A. David Rossin, "Brain Drain Project, April Report," *ASIIA Consortium News*, I, No. 3 (April 30, 1968), p. 18.
	Nuclear reactor technology trainees with:			
41.0	M.A. degree	1952–67	Resident in the United States in 1968.	*Ibid.*
78.0	Ph.D. degree			

Wide variations are evident, but it is also possible to guess the reasons by looking at differences in the student populations to which the estimates refer and at the diverse definitions of non-return that have been used. There are, for instance, differences in estimates for all foreign students in the United States indicated in the first four entries of Table 1 and associated differences in definition. Using visa adjustment gives a very different result from sampling intentions.

Given the broad variations in overall percentages as well as variations among sub-populations of foreign students, any attempt to deal with non-return at the aggregate level (for all foreign students) can be questioned. One need only compare the estimated rates of non-return for Chinese, Canadian and Peruvian students in Table 1, or note the high rate for doctorate recipients, to realize that non-return must be considered on a country-by-country basis and should take level of study into account. Table 1 also displays variations according to visa held, sponsor, institution attended, and field of study.

Many of the student populations in Table 1 can be disaggregated. If, for instance, Chinese post-graduate students are singled out from the Berkeley, Iowa, and "all doctorate" groups and compared with the figure of 95 per cent estimated by Platt for Chinese post-graduate students, there is substantial agreement. For Chinese engineering graduates from Berkeley, 1954–65, the rate of non-return was estimated by Schell and Susskind at 80 per cent (100 per cent at the Ph.D. level, 74 per cent at the M.A. level); [63] for Chinese students enrolled at Iowa University from 1950 to 1960, the estimated rate of non-return was 91 per cent (almost all students were at the post-graduate level); [64] and for Chinese doctorate recipients between 1958 and 1960, the non-return was calculated as 90 per cent.[65] If only Chinese students with exchange visitor visas are considered and non-return is defined by the proportion who obtain waivers, estimated rates are reduced considerably, as in the estimate by the Council on International Educational and Cultural Affairs cited in Table 1. On the other hand using visa adjustments as related only to those students who are "technically able to do so" produces an estimate of about 90 per cent for Chinese engineers,[66] a figure that is again close to Platt's estimate. If we incorporate all levels of study and all visa statuses, and use "intent" as the measure of non-return, the rate apparently drops (see chapter 3, Table 17 and the estimates from Oh's dissertation cited in Table 1). By including temporary non-returnees in the estimate Oh's figure rises from 13 to 81 per cent.[67] Such are the problems of estimating non-return even when country of origin is specified.

Correlates of Non-return

The several recent analyses of non-return need to be examined for possible patterns such as consistency in the personal and social backgrounds of non-returnees, in their conditions of study, in their employment expectations, and in their motives for studying in the United States.

From the following brief overview, it is evident that although simple correlates do appear in spite of diverse definitions and measurement methods, interpreting the correlates is difficult.[68] The overview serves to introduce empirical work to be presented in chapters 3, 4, and 7. Unfortunately the exploration of correlates is limited to foreign students in the United States. It is possible that an entirely different set of correlates is associated with migration following study abroad in other nations.

COUNTRY OF ORIGIN

In the past, the highest percentages of non-return (relative to the total number of foreign students in the United States from a country or area) have been from European nations and the lowest have been from African nations. Selected Asian nations also have high rates of non-return. Within areal groupings, there is substantial variation in rates from country to country. Non-return, if related to characteristics of the students' countries of origin, involves complex interactions between social, political, and economic features of one country as against another, as well as interactions in conditions of study. Simple cross-country comparisons are inadequate for defining such relationships.

The higher rates of non-return observed for European countries contradict U.S. government and U.N. observations, based on visa adjustment data, that the proportion of students from developing nations who stay is higher than that from developed nations.[69] There is no question that the absolute number of students from developing nations remaining in the United States has been greater than the absolute number from developed nations, but there have also been more foreign students in the United States from developing than from developed nations.[70] And it is also true that migration through non-return has constituted a larger part of the total high-level migration from developing countries. As explained in the previous section, this is partly due to national variation in the development of higher educational institutions in the countries of origin, but it is also a result of U.S. immigration policies which do not apply in the same manner to all countries. The student visa has provided a loophole for individuals who could not otherwise enter the United States. This will be dealt with in more detail in the Footnote to Part I.

More important, however, is the fact that the association between non-return and level of development is an artifact. When non-return is measured by relating the total number of non-returnees to the total number of university students in training at home and abroad, the association with level of economic development disappears (see chapter 4). There is not a clear connection between non-return, however measured, and social and economic conditions in the home country. Simply dividing nations into developed and developing nations for analysis of non-return, then, is not sufficient.

Visa, Field and Level of Study, and Sponsorship

Foreign students in the United States usually hold a non-immigrant visa—either a student (F) visa or an exchangee (J) visa—but some who may legitimately be considered students hold immigrant visas. If we do not distinguish by nation of origin or level or field of study, non-return is infrequent among J-visa exchangees; it is more frequent but still relatively low among F-visa students; it is high among immigrant-visa students. Given the requirements of these visas, the relationship is what we would expect to find (see Footnote to Part I).[71] However, when differences in average age, level of study, employment possibilities following study, and so forth, are considered, the difference between non-return among exchangees and students is minor. There seems to be a process of self-selection operating with respect to visa status, suggesting that proposals to change *all* visas to the tighter exchange visas in order to reduce non-return will be only marginally successful unless other variables influencing non-return also change.

The propensity to remain permanently in the United States appears to be slightly higher among medical and engineering students than among students in other fields, and there is substantial variation by subfield. If we leave out medical interns and residents, the difference between medicine and other fields is not as great as imagined. Agricultural students have a low rate of non-return.

Generally, both undergraduates and doctorate-level students are more apt to stay than those at the masters level. The relatively high emigration of doctoral students, who are presumably of greater "value" to their respective countries than less educated individuals, has led researchers to concentrate on this group even though they represent a comparatively small number of all non-returnees. The emphasis is justified, but often the research findings and consequent policy recommendations are indiscriminately applied to other students at other levels.

Sponsored students at all levels tend to return home, whereas those paying their own way are likely to remain abroad. This is not due to sponsorship *per se*, but to the fact that it provides control for the selection of students, contractual arrangements for return, and guaranteed employment.

PERSONAL CHARACTERISTICS, FAMILY AND SOCIO-ECONOMIC BACKGROUND

Older students are more apt to return home following study, other things being equal. Age reflects maturity, grounding in home culture, previous occupational involvement in the home country, and sometimes marriage to a home-country spouse.

Women marrying host-country nationals are less likely to return home than men. But the same characteristics, attitudes, and circumstances which increase the probability that a foreign student will marry a native also increase (independently) the probability of non-return. Indeed, marriage to a U.S. citizen is probably a less important correlate of non-return than commonly assumed.

Several studies have shown a relationship between social class and non-return; students from the lower end of the social scale in their home country are more apt to remain abroad. (However, at least one study throws doubt on this conclusion, finding no relationship between social class and non-return among Canadian students.[72]) The conclusion that students from a low socio-economic background are more apt to remain abroad parallels the more general tendency for the upwardly mobile to be mobile geographically as well. Members of ethnic and religious minorities also seem more predisposed than majority group members to migrate permanently.

Kinship ties are potentially strong forces for return in some nations and for some individuals, but may have the opposite effect when linked to academic failure or to the hope of bringing family members to the United States. In addition, students who have been sponsored for foreign study by family or village may wish to postpone the return to obligations resulting from such patronage.

EMPLOYMENT FOLLOWING STUDY

If an individual is employed in the United States during or following his period of study, it is only logical that his propensity to remain will increase, though little effort has been made to determine to what extent this is so. Nor have the benefits of on-the-job experience to returning students been studied. For some, practical training is simply another loophole allowing a longer stay. (It may be, as one author has suggested, a "Pandora's Box." [73]) For others, it is a period in which savings can be accumulated before returning home.

If an individual is guaranteed a job at home, he will probably return to it. This seems to hold even though the salary may be considerably lower than that he could earn in the United States and even though work conditions at home may be less desirable. Indeed, employment opportunity, defined in terms of an assured job in which skills acquired abroad can be used, may be the most important correlate of return.

There is no one simple association or set of associations that can infallibly predict non-return. Moving beyond prediction to an understanding of individual motives or the process by which decisions are reached, we find a knowledge of correlates helps but does not provide us with adequate explanations. To know correlates raises many but answers few questions about complex migrant motives and these are as hard to untangle as the motives of other migrants.

Motives of Non-returning Students

As with the earlier more general discussion of high-level migrant motives, this brief treatment of student motives will emphasize economic considerations. It is often assumed that economic factors (monetary or labor market conditions) dominate decisions to migrate but in fact this is less manifest with high-level than with unskilled migrants. Salaries are frequently mentioned by students as an important but seldom as the overriding factor in their decisions (see chapter 8).[74] Salaries, in any case, involve more than a simple comparison between actual money earned at home or abroad: there must be adjustments for relative purchasing power and differences in taxation, indirect subsidies and lifetime income prospects.

Another economic consideration is probability of employment, and whether this implies *any* job or a professionally satisfying one. Several surveys in which non-returning students were questioned about their motives show that better job opportunity (usually undefined or loosely defined) appeared most frequently as the deciding factor in migration.

The relationship between migration and individual perceptions of opportunity and of monetary rewards has not been clearly established. However, if individual perceptions of relative probability of employment in desired jobs at origin and destination could be included as adjustments to perceptions of comparative earnings, decisions that appeared to be economically "irrational" might then appear to be "rational." Incorporated in such a probability adjustment would be many non-monetary factors influencing probability of employment, each of which has economic implications.

SUMMARY

In a sense, this entire chapter constitutes a summary. Bits and pieces of the literature on high-level migration for employment and/or for study have been brought together, most of which dealt with migration to the United States. The chapter has been included to give the reader a feel for the literature and an understanding of the problems facing researchers as much as it has been to provide a documented overview of the magnitude and correlates of trained and untrained brain drains. From the overview, high-level international migration, as other types of migration, appears as a complex, multi-dimensional phenomenon requiring something more than the over-simplified treatment it is usually given. Disaggregation by country, field of study and/or employment, and by demographic characteristics of migrants is essential to our understanding the phenomenon. Unfortunately, however, lack of statistics and the tenuous nature of the global and national data that are available makes disaggregation to the desired level impossible, using standard sources.

From the available data, we can observe that only a small percentage of all high-level human resources has migrated for study and/or for work. The United States is a major destination for migrating talent. Migration for study is increasing absolutely, but is decreasing in relation to total university enrollments. Shifts toward study abroad at the graduate level in the more advanced nations and toward sponsored study are evident.

For knowledge of the brain drain other than the crudest approximations of magnitudes, we must turn to case studies of the trained and untrained components of brain drain. From the case studies, we surmise that non-return of foreign students and immigration of trained talent vary considerably both by country of origin and by destination. Medicine, science and engineering seem to be the fields in which most migration occurs. Among students, however, the differences by broad field are not significant. Although emigrants seem to be on the average, more talented than host nationals in similar fields, there is a wide range of ability. Foreign student non-return is often associated with holding an immigrant or student (F) visa, with self-sponsorship, with either undergraduate or Ph.D. study (vs. M.A.), with lack of guaranteed employment at home following study, with arrival in the U.S. at an early age, with low socio-economic status in the home country and/or minority status, and with marriage to a host country national. No one simple set of associations can be established;

interactions among the various correlates should be identified. From the associations, causal inferences are inappropriate. Similarly, inferring motives may not be justified. Longitudinal studies are needed and migrants in both groups, trained and untrained, should be compared with non-migrants.

NOTES

[1] See Wolfgang W. Scheuerer and John C. Shearer "Selected Bibliography, International Movement of High-level Human Resources (The 'Brain Drain'), by Sender Area" University Park: the Pennsylvania State University, 1967 (mimeographed); S. Dedijer and L. Svenningson, *Brain Drain and Brain Gain: A Bibliography on Migration of Scientists, Engineers, Doctors and Students* (Lund, Sweden: Research Policy Program, 1967); Education and World Affairs, *Selected Publications and Research Related to the International Migration of Professional Manpower,* Washington, January 1968; and Organization for European Cooperation and Development, *International Migration of Manpower* (Paris: Organization for European Cooperation and Development, 1969).

[2] Literally hundreds of articles and studies have appeared, for instance, since I published my review article in 1967, "Brain Drains and Brain Gains: Comments on the State of Research," *International Development Review,* IX, No. 4 (December 1967), pp. 4–9. Several recent reviews have been extensive. See United Nations, General Assembly, 23rd Session, November 5, 1968, *Outflow of Trained Personnel from Developing Countries, Report of the Secretary General,* A/7294 (New York: The United Nations, 1968). See also Committee on the International Migration of Talent, *The International Migration of High-Level Manpower* (New York: Praeger, 1970) published in connection with Education and World Affairs.

The research peak has, I am sure, been reached with the ongoing study at the Bureau of Applied Social Research, Columbia University, under the direction of William Glaser and sponsored by the United Nations. The study will involve 5 host countries (U.S., U.K., Canada, France, and Germany) and at least 15 sending countries. The sample is approximately 20,000 students.

[3] To illustrate the problem of measuring stocks vs. flows: it would be possible to measure the stock of foreign nationals from Country X who are resident in Country Y (given clear definitions) at two points in time, to subtract, and to obtain a figure totally unrelated to the number of individuals who had adopted permanent residence during the period. Those individuals counted at the first point in time could, in theory, have been entirely replaced by new and temporary migrants arriving in ever larger numbers. The first group might have had no permanent residents. A measure of turnover is needed.

Counterflows include return (remigration) after a period abroad (there is a problem of specifying the appropriate time period) of original emigrants; and counterflows include one-way migration in the opposite direction. Returnees and immigrants may bring valuable "know how" that is not possessed by emigrants. Although in- and out-migration may balance numerically, they may not balance qualitatively. Flows of corporation executives or technical assistance personnel from the United States to developing nations is one such counterflow. Such moves are often temporary, but continuous replacement results in what is, in effect, permanent migration. (See Bowman and Myers, pp. 894–97.) If returning emigrants are added to immigrants from other nations, Canada and the United Kingdom, while "losing" to the United States, are net "gainers" from the world.

Multiple moves are becoming more common. If migration statistics are to be useful, a means must be found for incorporating multiple moves.

[4] Brinley Thomas, "The International Circulation of Human Capital," *Minerva*, V, No. 4 (Summer 1967), pp. 479–506. Thomas is particularly alert to questions of counterflows.

[5] Bayer, *Social Forces*, XLVI, No. 4, p. 467. See also John R. Niland, "The Brain Drain of Highly Trained Engineering Manpower from Asia into the United States" (unpublished Ph.D. dissertation, University of Illinois, 1969), chapter 1. Niland gives an 11.5 per cent figure for 1967.

[6] Thomas, p. 482.

[7] U.S. Department of Justice, Immigration and Naturalization Service, *Annual Indicator of the In-migration into the United States of Aliens in Professional and Related Occupations, Fiscal Year 1967*. Prepared for the Council on International Educational and Cultural Affairs (Washington: U.S. Government Printing Office, 1968), p. 2.

[8] Bayer, *Social Forces*, XLVI, No. 4, p. 466.

[9] John R. Niland, *The Asian Engineering Brain Drain* (Lexington, Mass.: Heath Lexington Books, 1970), p. 3.

[10] U.S. Department of Justice, p. 2.

[11] U.S. Congress, House Committee on Government Operations, *The Brain Drain of Scientists, Engineers, and Physicians from the Developing Countries into the United States*, 90th Congress, 2nd Session, January 23, 1968, p. 2.

[12] *Ibid.*, pp. 2, 3.

[13] See, for instance, William F. Glueck, "The Economics of Executive Mobility," a paper presented to the Southern Social Science Association Meetings, Washington, D.C., 1968 (mimeographed).

[14] A follow-up study of Philippine university graduates shows that "those who studied education and law emigrated much less frequently (3–7 per cent) than did those who took liberal arts, engineering, or commerce (15–22 per cent)." Walden F. Bello, Frank Lynch, and Perla Q. Makil, "Brain Drain in the Philippines," in *Modernization: Its Impact in the Philippines*, ed. W. F. Bello and A. de Guzman (Quezon City: Ateneo de Manila University Press, 1969), p. 123.

[15] Grubel and Scott, *The Journal of Political Economy*, LXXXIV, No. 4; Paul Ritterband, "The Non-returning Foreign Student: The Israeli Case" (unpublished Ph.D. dissertation, Columbia University, Bureau of Applied Social Research, 1968), p. 94; and Stephen Hatch and Ernest Rudd, *Graduate Study and After* (London: Weidenfeld and Nicolson, 1968); or Ernest Rudd, "The Rate of Economic Growth, Technology and the Ph.D.", *Minerva*, VI, No. 3 (Spring 1968), p. 379.

[16] Harold Margulies and Helen Stephenson Bloch, *Graduates of Foreign*

Medical Schools Working in the United States of America (Cambridge, Mass.: Harvard University Press, 1969).

[17] Rudd, p. 370.

[18] James A. Wilson, "The Emigration of British Scientists," *Minerva*, V, No. 1 (Autumn 1966), p. 20; Rudd, p. 379; United Kingdom, Committee on Manpower Resources of Science and Technology, *The Brain Drain: Report of the Working Group on Migration* (London: HMSO, October 1967). In subsequent footnotes the last reference will be referred to as the "Jones Report."

[19] Herbert G. Grubel and Anthony Scott, "The Role of Foreigners in the U.S. Economics Profession," *American Economics Review*, LVIII, No. 1 (March 1967).

[20] Margulies, chapter 3.

[21] In Thomlinson, p. 227, the statement is made that "For both international migration and long-distance internal migration, the available evidence indicates a selectivity favoring males." However, Bayer notes the shifting proportions of men to women among immigrants to the United States. In 1910, the percentage of females stood at only 30, supporting Thomlinson's generalization, but by 1960, 56 per cent of all immigrants were female. Bayer, *Social Forces*, XLVI, No. 4, p. 467.

[22] Thomlinson, p. 225.

[23] Appleyard, p. 368.

[24] Petersen, pp. 277, 78.

[25] William N. Parker, "Comment on Rashi Fein's 'Educational Patterns in Southern Migration,'" *The Southern Economic Journal*, XXXII, No. 1, Part 2 (July 1965), p. 125.

[26] Kelly M. West, "Migration of Latin American Physicians to the United States," a report presented to the Advisory Committee on Medical Research of the Pan American Health Organization, May 1966 (preliminary draft).

[27] Wilson, p. 26.

[28] Jones Report, p. 21.

[29] Rudd, *Minerva*, VI, No. 3, p. 379.

[30] "Young Men Go West," *The Economist* (London), October 14, 1967, p. 193.

[31] Among Asians, the idea of accumulating a certain amount of capital before returning home apparently bulks large. (Niland, p. 77.)

[32] In discussing "push" and "pull" forces motivating moves, "the central question is not whether the forces that repel or those that attract are most powerful, it is, rather, how both of these forces can be moderated in a suitable way." (Pan American Health Organization, Migration of Health Personnel, Scientists and Engineers from Latin America, Scientific Publication 142 [Washington, D.C., September, 1966], p. 12.) On "A Differential Approach" rather than a use of pushes or pulls, see Enrique Oteiza, "A Differential Approach," *The Brain Drain*, ed. Walter Adams (New York: The Macmillan Company, 1968), pp. 120–134.

[33] C. Howard Davis, "Determinants of Mobility of College Educated Persons: 1955–60" (unpublished Ph.D. dissertation, Vanderbilt University, Department of Economics, 1967).

[34] Schwartz, p. 5.

[35] *Ibid.*

[36] M. Brewster Smith, "Foreign vs. Indigenous Education," *Post-primary*

Education and Political and Economic Development, Don C. Piper and Taylor Cole, eds. (Durham, N.C.: Duke University Press, 1964), p. 51.

[37] United Nations Educational, Scientific and Cultural Organization (UNESCO), *Study Abroad,* XIII (Paris: UNESCO, 1961), p. 643.

The UNESCO figures, whether in *Study Abroad* (Paris: UNESCO, 1948–), or in the *Statistical Yearbook* (Paris: UNESCO 1963–), should be treated skeptically: 1) The definition of "foreign student" and of "higher education" varies from country to country. 2) Collection and reporting techniques differ appreciably—some countries use detailed surveys to generate their statistics, others guestimate. 3) The UNESCO publications clearly indicate, country by country, the year for which figures were reported. The figures frequently pertain to periods as much as five years apart, making comparisons and totals diffcult to interpret. 4) Countries are omitted. Mainland China is excluded because it is not a member nation. The Philippines was omitted from the 1963 *Statistical Yearbook* and suddenly appeared in the 1965 *Yearbook* with a total of 50,000 foreign students, making it the second largest host country in the world according to UNESCO statistics.

UNESCO officials are aware of the difficulties and footnote liberally. Unfortunately, those who use the statistics tend to disregard the footnotes.

[38] Institute of International Education (IIE), *Open Doors* (New York: IIE, 1960), p. 6.

[39] UNESCO, *Study Abroad,* XVI, p. 512.

[40] IIE, *Open Doors,* 1965, p. 4.

[41] IIE, *Open Doors,* 1970, p. 5.

[42] Patricia Gachot, UNESCO *Features,* No. 597 (January 1970), p. 19.

[43] UNESCO, *World Survey of Education,* Vol. IV: *Higher Education* (Paris: UNESCO, 1966), p. 72. Using figures from the World Survey for 20 major host nations, the following were derived: 1950–54, 2.2 per cent; 1955–59, 2.4 per cent; 1960–62, 2.8 per cent. From the 1965 *Statistical Yearbook,* a ratio of 2.7 was estimated for the same countries in 1964/65. If the U.S. is excluded, ratios rise. For 1964/65, for instance, it would be 4.1 rather than 2.7.

[44] UNESCO, *Comparative Statistical Data on Education in Africa,* UNESCO-OAU/CESTA/Ref. 1, a document prepared for the Conference on Education and Scientific and Technical Training in Relation to Development in Africa, Paris, April 16, 1968. Gachot, p. 19, suggests the leveling trend may also be related to host country policies of limiting the availability of foreign student places and/or to developing nation fears that by sending students abroad they are promoting brain drain.

[45] Calculated from: UNESCO, *Statistical Yearbook,* 1966 (Paris: UNESCO, 1967), pp. 170–202 and 251–54. For raw data see Appendix V of this book. The calculation is: foreign student enrollment divided by total enrollment (foreign and national students included).

[46] Bayer, *Social Forces,* XLVI, No. 4, pp. 468–69.

[47] Organization for Economic Cooperation and Development (OECD), *Policy Conference on Economic Growth and Investment in Education,* Vol. V. (Paris: OECD, 1962). In the 1962 volume, OECD attempted to add meaning to the simple enrollment ratios by relating them to a measure of economic development. Three groups were identified: 1) Countries with high proportions of foreign students but low enrollment of nationals in relation to wealth (Austria, Switzerland, Ireland, the United Kingdom, and The

Federal Republic of Germany). 2) Countries in which foreign students form a moderate proportion of total students, but in which the proportion of national students in the population is in balance with national wealth (France, Canada, Belgium, the Netherlands). 3) Countries in which the proportion of foreign students is small in proportion to total enrollment and to national wealth (the United States, Norway, Denmark, Sweden). The OECD recognized the need to disaggregate. Statistics were presented for particular fields and it was noted that, for instance, higher ratios than those presented for the United States in general would pertain at the graduate level.

[48] United Kingdom figures were taken from the Association of Commonwealth Universities (ACU), *Commonwealth Universities Yearbook* (London: ACU, 1966), p. 2204. Swiss figures were taken from: Eidgenossischen Statistischen Amt, *Statistisches Jahrbuch der Schweiz*, 1965 (Basel: Birhauser Verlag, 1965), pp. 461, 466.

[49] UNESCO, *Study Abroad*, XVI, p. 513.

[50] Between 1954/55 and 1964/65 the percentage of foreign students who were studying at the graduate level changed from 39 to 48 in the United States and from 37 to 50 in the United Kingdom. In the same period, the percentage of self-sponsored students changed from 54 to 46 in the U.S. and from 65 to 52 in the U.K. The percentage of foreign students in the U.S. enrolled in the physical and life sciences increased from 12 to 18 per cent in that ten years. Calculations were made from IIE, *Open Doors*, and ACU, *Commonwealth Universities Yearbook*, various years. By 1970, the figures for the United States were 48 percent studying at the graduate level, 51 per cent self-sponsored, and 17 per cent in the physical and life sciences, indicating a slight reversal or a leveling out of the earlier trend.

[51] In the 1963 and 1965 editions of the *Statistical Yearbook*, estimates were presented for the number of students, by country of origin, in each of 15 major host countries. Together, the 15 nations hosted more than two-thirds of all students abroad in 1964/65. By adding up the students from Country X who were resident in each of the 15 countries, an approximate figure for students abroad from Country X could be obtained. The 1966 edition of the *Statistical Yearbook* did not present breakdowns by major host country but expanded the number of host countries considered. Students from Country X in over 50 countries were incorporated in the totals. Although most major host countries provide UNESCO with data on foreign students enrolled *by country of origin*, there are several major host country omissions, even in the 1966 edition, including the USSR, Argentina, Israel, and the Philippines. One can only guess at biases involved. An illustration: The Pan American Union Survey of the *Inter-American Exchange of Students and Professors* (Washington, D.C.: Pan American Union, 1966) included 1,087 Bolivians studying in Argentine universities. If accurate, the number would approximately double that reported by UNESCO for Bolivia and would increase the total Bolivian nationals enrolled at the third-level (whether home or abroad), by one-twelfth.

[52] See, for instance, Margaret Cormack, *An Evaluation of Research on Educational Exchange*, U.S. Department of State, Bureau of Educational and Cultural Affairs (Washington, D.C., 1962); and Barbara Walton, *Foreign Student Exchange in Perspective*, U.S. Department of State, Publication 8373 (Washington, D.C.: September 1967).

[53] An exception is Tamar Becker's recent study, "Patterns of Attitudinal Changes among Foreign Students," *American Journal of Sociology*, LXXIII, No. 3 (January 1968), pp. 431–42.

[54] This point is well illustrated by Wolfgang Scheuerer and John Shearer (comp.), "Selected Bibliography: The Contribution of Foreign University Training to Economic and Social Development by Host Area," prepared for the Carnegie Corporation by the Pennsylvania State University, Institute for Research on Human Resources and by the University of Chicago, Comparative Education Center (University Park, Pennsylvania: June 1967). (Mimeographed.)

[55] A pioneer study of returned students was done in 1955 by the Useems, who report in the *Western Educated Man in India* (New York: Dryden Press, Inc.) that ". . . less than 10 per cent of the returning Indian students ever have jobs in which they work full time in the field for which they have taken specialized training" (p. 82). Unfortunately, defining "utilization" by full-time employment in a particular field does not really tell whether returned students are contributing effectively to the economic development of their home country. A measure of productivity independent of type of employment is needed. And the propensity of foreign-trained Indians to change positions must be compared with the propensity of similar Indians trained at home. The 10 per cent figure might not be as alarming as it appears.

For an excellent summary of conditions under which returning foreign students seem to "utilize" their training, see Walton, pp. 10–13. For a summary of extensive studies following up U.S. government-sponsored "participant trainees," see Albert E. Gollin, "Foreign Study and Modernization: The Transfer of Technology Through Education," *International Social Science Journal*, XIX, No. 3 (1967), pp. 360–77.

[56] Grace Mary Scully, "An Exploratory Study of Foreign Students Who Do Not Wish to Return to their Home Country" (unpublished Ed.D. dissertation, Teachers College, Columbia University, 1956); Iraj Valipour, "A Comparison of Returning and Non-returning Iranian Students in the United States" (unpublished Ed.D. dissertation, Teachers College, Columbia University, 1961).

[57] For two such examples, see Richard T. Morris, *The Two-Way Mirror: National Status in Foreign Students* (Minneapolis: University of Minnesota Press, 1960); and, Louis P. Cajoleas, "The Academic Record, Professional Development and Return Adjustment of Doctoral Students from Other Lands: Study of Teachers College Alumni, 1946–1955" (unpublished Ph.D. dissertation, Columbia University, 1958).

[58] The previously cited study in progress at the Bureau of Applied Social Research, Columbia University, should produce relatively reliable estimates for non-return among foreign students in other nations than the United States.

[59] These figures were published in a note in *New Society* (March 7, 1968), p. 346. No source was given. However, the figures referred to are very similar to those quoted for graduates of the London School of Economics in Howard Glennerster, Althea Bennett and Christie Farrell, *Graduate School, A Study of Graduate Work at the London School of Economics* (Edinburgh: Oliver and Boyd, 1966), pp. 142–43. The main difference lies in the further breakdown of the residual 31–34 per cent into those who continue their studies, non-respondents, and others. When this is done, the authors con-

clude that the percentage of LSE graduates actually employed in England following study is only about 10 per cent (not the 31–34 per cent implied in the *New Society* article).

[60] The Ditchley Foundation, "Movement to the United Kingdom," a paper prepared for the Conference on the International Migration of Professional and Technical Skills with Special Reference to the Developing Countries, 16–19 February, 1968 by the Ministry of Labour, London, January 1968 (mimeographed), pp. 5, 6.

[61] Wilkinson, p. 149.

[62] United Nations, A/7294, p. 32.

[63] Charles Susskind and Lynn Schell, *Exporting Technical Education:* A Survey and Case Study of Foreign Professionals with U.S. Graduate Degrees (New York: Institute of International Education, 1968), p. 10.

[64] Wallace Maner, "More on Exchange or Immigration," NAFSA *Newsletter,* XVI, No. 8 (May 1965), p. 8.

[65] National Academy of Sciences, National Science Foundation, *Doctorate Recipients from United States Universities, 1958–1966* (Washington, D.C.: National Academy of Sciences, Publication 1489, 1967), p. 101.

[66] Niland, p. 23.

[67] Tai Keun Oh, "The Role of International Education in the Asian Brain Drain" (unpublished Ph.D. dissertation, University of Wisconsin, Madison, 1970), pp. 61–62.

[68] The main sources drawn upon in the following discussion are:
Robert G. Myers, "Study Abroad and the Migration of Human Resources" (unpublished Ph.D. dissertation, University of Chicago, Department of Education, 1967); Ronald M. Pavalko, "Talent Migration: Canadian Students in the United States," *International Review of Education,* XIV, No. 3 (1968), pp. 300–22; Paul Ritterband, "The Non-Returning Foreign Student: The Israeli Case" (unpublished Ph.D. dissertation, Columbia University, Bureau of Applied Social Research, 1968); Keshav Sharma, "Indian Students in the United States," Committee for the Comparative Study of New Nations, The University of Chicago (ditto); Charles Susskind and Lynn Schell, *Exporting Technical Education:* A Survey and Case Study of Foreign Professionals with U.S. Graduate Degrees (New York: Institute of International Education, 1968); and Barbara Walton, *Foreign Student Exchange in Perspective,* prepared for the office of External Research, U.S. Department of State, September 1967 (Washington, D.C.; U.S. Government Printing Office, 1969); Oh (see footnote 67); Niland (see footnote 9).

[69] U.S. Congress, House Committee on Government Operations, *Scientific Brain Drain from the Developing Countries* Report 1215, 90th Congress, 2nd Session, 1968, p. 14.

[70] See chapter 4.

[71] Approximately one-fifth of the immigrant visa holders responding to the IIE census said specifically that they did not plan to remain permanently in the United States.

[72] Pavalko, pp. 314–16.

[73] Josef Mestenhauser, "Practical Training, a Pandora's Box," NAFSA *Newsletter,* XVI, No. 8 (May 1965), pp. 1–3.

[74] The experience of foreign recruiters attempting to repatriate students supports the salience of employment assurance in decisions to return home. When recruiters have had the authority to sign individuals for specific posi-

tions, recruitment has been quite successful. On the other hand, recruiters who can only offer vague promises have not been as effective. Similarly, the Indian Manpower Pool seems to have met with only moderate success at best because it did not produce the jobs envisioned by early particpants.

See also Merriam F. Marshal, *Brain Drain Study at the Indian Institute of Technology, Kanpur* (Kanpur, India, July, 1969). High salaries were not necessary to induce talented individuals to return to work at IIT, Kanpur, suggesting that in some cases (where other benefits are high) competitive salaries (internationally) are not even necessary for inducing return.

A FOOTNOTE TO PART I

PROBLEMS OF DEFINITION

Several problems of definition (and associated measurement difficulties) have already been touched upon in the text and footnotes of chapters 1 and 2. I am reluctant to relegate the problems entirely to footnotes because they are critical and because there is a strong predilection to overlook or forget footnotes in our eagerness to get at "hard data." Hence this textual footnote.

When looking at student enrollment figures, for instance, it is altogether too easy to disregard whether or not the particular definition of "student" used includes or excludes "trainees" who are outside the formal educational system,[1] students in secondary and adult education as well as college and university institutions,[2] students participating on a part-time as well as full-time basis,[3] or students in short as well as long courses.[4] But the conceptual difficulties involved in deciding who ought to be classified as a student are relatively minor compared with those encountered when deciding who is or is not "foreign," with assigning a national affiliation, or with who should be termed an "immigrant" or a "non-returnee."

Two examples further illustrate the need to rescue problems of definition from the footnotes. The first is taken from the British *Jones Report* on brain drain, as reviewed in the press. In the published report, scrupulous attention was given to the fact that emigration totals from the United Kingdom included individuals who stated their intent to remain abroad *for at least one year* and to the fact that the total given did *not* represent a *permanent* outmigration. However, in popular reporting the statistics were quoted without the footnote and without mention that a sizeable proportion of the individuals included as emigrants were in fact students temporarily abroad for a period of more than one year or individuals temporarily employed abroad.[5]

The second illustration will be developed more fully later. Suffice to say at this point that by simply changing their definition of "foreign student" the Institute of International Education added approximately 13,000 students to their count of the total number of students in the United States in 1966–67. Although the IIE has carefully labeled the change, it has been missed by many readers who note the large jump in foreign student enrollments between 1965–66 and 1966–67.[6]

Assigning National Affiliation

Usually, one or more of the following is used to assign national origin or affiliation: 1) citizenship; 2) country of last residence; 3) place of birth; 4) place of education, either secondary (high school) or tertiary (university). Citizenship, last residence, and place of birth [7] are relatively straightforward means of identifying national origin and/or assigning national affiliation, though not entirely free from problems. Dual citizenship, early moves from the country of birth, and frequent changes of national residence complicate use, but seldom create major statistical distortions.

Defining national affiliation by locus of education is not straightforward but there is a rationale for using it, particularly place of *secondary* education. From a nationalistic viewpoint, the country that provides education is presumably entitled to reap the social benefits of that education and, the reasoning goes, if individuals migrate, these benefits are lost. Furthermore, the cumulative investment in an individual is not great until he reaches secondary school, at which time foregone earnings are added to direct educational costs to make potential losses greater. Using residence at the time of secondary education cuts out problems associated with movement in early childhood years that complicate use of either birthplace or citizenship. There are, of course, a few individuals who would be improperly classified because they have studied abroad at the secondary level.

But whether or not one accepts the idea of national claims on individuals educated at national expense, classification by education is useful for examining migration flows. Knowledge of the locus of education tells us something about the type, and perhaps about the quality, of education received as well as about national affiliation. That information is an aid to valuing migration.

Changing National Affiliation—When Does a Migrant Become a Non-returnee?

Let us assume we have a satisfactory way of operationalizing what the national affiliation of a migrant was prior to his coming to the United States. We are left with the problem of deciding whether migration is temporary or permanent. Unless migration is permanent, it is difficult to hold that a migrant has unequivocally "drained." A simple change of residence or movement to a location other than the place of birth, last residence, or secondary schooling says nothing about the intention to remain in the new location permanently. Let us look at changes of citizenship and visa, at length of time abroad, and at expressed intent to remain permanently as indicators of changing national affiliation, of permanent residence, and of brain drain.

A change of citizenship is a strong indication of intent to remain permanently in the United States. However, many migrants prefer to retain their former citizenship, even though they plan to remain abroad permanently or for a long time. Using change of citizenship, we would fail to identify large numbers of migrants who might otherwise be classified as permanent migrants; terms of the definition are too restrictive.[8]

Holding an immigrant visa or changing from a non-immigrant to an immigrant visa is another concrete indicator of a migrant's intention to remain abroad permanently. When discussing foreign student non-return, the U.S. government relies heavily upon tabulations of visa changes. Unfortunately, the meaning of a visa change is obscured for several reasons. First, a significant proportion of immigrant visa holders have returned home (particularly among those who are students). The immigrant visa and its accompanying status have been attractive to students and other migrants to the United States, offering the option of remaining *if* things work out well, yet without permanently breaking ties with the area of origin. Non-immigrant visas require the holder to return home (or change visa status). Among students, the immigrant visa has, in the past, also been sought because it has been free from the restrictions on employment that are attached to student and exchange visas, during and after the period of study.

Second, many non-immigrant visa-holders eventually become permanent residents,[9] regulations to the contrary.[10] Such individuals are part of a relatively large migration that does not enter migration statistics, or does so long after the fact, when an opportunity for changing visa status finally appears. To assume then, that all individuals who hold non-immigrant visas, including student and exchange visas, will return home or that they had return in mind when they arrived is questionable.[11]

The student visa has, in fact, been attractive to some would-be permanent migrants. Prior to 1965, it was relatively easy for individuals from countries which carried no immigration quota under the existing immigration law of the United States, to obtain immigrant visas and to enter the U.S. as immigrants even though they might be entering for educational purposes. (Western Hemisphere nations were non-quota nations.) Easy access to immigrant visas was also possible for student migrants from quota-surplus countries (such as England and Germany) for which the pre-1965 limit on immigrants was so large that it was seldom filled. On the other hand, students and non-students from quota countries (such as China, Korea, and Japan) were not able to obtain immigrant visas so readily because quotas were often extremely small (100 immigrants per year for China, for instance). Their only alternative was to come with another visa, usually a student

(F) visa or an exchangee (J) visa. It has been observed that "whenever there is great pressure from a particular country for immigration to the United States, people will use non-immigrant visas to get there with the hope of finding a loophole to stay." [12]

The Immigration Act of 1965 provided larger loopholes by abolishing quotas based on national origins, by putting acquisition of immigrant visas on a first-come, first-serve basis while moving highly skilled individuals up in the preference categories, and by liberalizing the adjustment procedures. Not surprisingly, there was a flood of visa adjustments among Asian students who had been waiting for their opportunity to change from student, non-immigrant status to immigrant status. The rash of visa adjustments in 1966 and 1967 does not necessarily indicate a sudden and drastic upswing in Asian students' desire to remain in the United States.[13] It did provide many of those who wanted to remain with a legal basis for doing so. Visa adjustments were not as prevalent among, for instance, students from the United Kingdom or from Latin American nations; there was less pressure.

The April 1970 amendment to the 1965 Immigration Act further complicates any attempt to index foreign student non-return by using visa adjustments.[14] The amendment allows certain exchangee visa holders to adjust their non-immigrant J-visa without first leaving the country for two years as previously required. The amendment was foreseeable because the 1965 law, in effect, discriminated against migration by most Northern Europeans in the high-level category who, not anticipating difficulties prior to 1965, had not bothered to obtain an immigrant visa and were far down in the list.[15] Once in the list, the force of numbers worked against them. Now Europeans have a loophole. The topic will be picked up again in chapter 9.

As an extreme example of distortions that can accompany the use of visa adjustment to index non-return (particularly in the early years for which figures are available), consider the Canadian case. In the two-year period from Fiscal Years 1962 to 1964, Canada appears in the statistics as having only three non-returning foreign students if visa adjustment is adopted as the indicator of non-return.[16] (Note the contrast with the 30 per cent figure in Table 1, calculated by using intent to remain as the basis for judging non-return.) The gross underestimate lies in the ease with which Canadians coming to the U.S. to study could obtain immigrant visas. In spite of such difficulties, the United States government continues to look to visa adjustment as the main indicator of the untrained brain drain and to make cross-national comparisons with the questionable statistics.[17]

If rates of foreign student non-return are calculated by using visa adjustment figures to define non-return, distortions can also occur because it is difficult to choose a proper base for calculating rates. Should, for instance, individuals from country X who adjust their status from student to immigrant in 1966 be compared with all students from that country who are enrolled in 1966, or is there a lag to adjustment, making the appropriate base 1965, 1964, or some earlier year?

If we assume that only students who have attained a B.A. (or perhaps even an M.A.) are technically eligible to adjust their visa (because they automatically fall into the preference category of high-level immigrants), then we should at a minimum remove all freshmen, sophomores, and juniors from the calculation. Comparing visa adjustments with eligible students thus leads to high estimates of non-return rates.[18]

Students not only wait several years before applying for an adjustment, they also wait for as much as two or three years before their adjustment request is granted—during which time they remain in the United States. A period of five or six years can very easily elapse between the time a student decides to remain and the time he becomes officially registered as a brain-drain statistic (i.e., when his adjustment is approved). In short, the difficulty of determining an appropriate base and the indefinite lag between entry and adjustment modify the significance that can be attached to non-return rates derived from visa adjustment figures.

Several circumstances suggest that the student visa will continue to serve as a loophole for individuals desiring to migrate to the United States. First, there is a ceiling on the number of highly qualified individuals who can enter the United States in one year. Second, there is considerable pressure against the upper limit, so that individuals applying directly for an immigrant visa from abroad must wait up to three years before they can migrate. A student or exchangee or trainee (H-visa) non-immigrant visa brings quicker results and, once in the United States, a request for adjustment can be filed. Until it is granted or rejected, the petitioner can stay. Third, the student visa allows foreigners to avoid the United States draft; an immigrant visa does not. Fourth, migration regulations for which "student status" becomes a dodge are not only imposed by the United States as a host country but also by countries of origin which do not wish to see their young emigrate. These same countries, however, may have more open regulations for those nationals who express their desire to study abroad. In short, the student visa will probably continue to function as a substitute immigrant visa for many "students." Finally, we need to know more about the trade-off between "trained" and "untrained" brain drains as related to availability of visas before taking legalistic definitions too literally. This theme will also be explored further in chapter 9.

A third means of defining permanent residence is to arbitrarily choose a time limit, beyond which migrating individuals are considered permanent, not temporary migrants. International migration statistics conventionally use a period of one year's residence abroad as an indication of permanent emigration.[19] Because students average more than one year abroad in studies, one year in residence is too short a period for differentiating permanent from temporary migrants among students. However, extending the time from one year to five or ten years would not solve the problem of classification; it would influence statistics, perhaps drastically without avoiding the essentially arbitrary nature of the chosen cut-off point.[20] Another difficulty with adopting length of time in residence to index permanent migration appears when calculating rates of migration and non-return. As with visa adjustment, the appropriate base figure is not obvious.

A fourth means of determining whether migration is permanent or not is to ask people about their intentions to remain or return. We are, of course, moving beyond available immigration statistics in suggesting such a definition, but a question of intended residence is included in the Annual Survey of Foreign Students in the United States which will be analyzed in chapters 3 and 4. And several case studies of non-return including the Peruvian student survey presented in chapter 7 use intent as an indicator of non-return.

Expressed intent carries the obvious difficulty that intentions can change over time. Longitudinal studies are needed to evaluate the accuracy of individual expressions of their intent to remain abroad. In chapter 3, more attention will be given to biases associated with the definition.

Clearly, combinations of the above means of determining when non-return occurs improve identification. If a migrant to the United States has an immigrant visa, has been in the United States for 10 years, and indicates his intention to remain, we can feel confident classifying him as a non-returnee.

Furthermore, by combining the indicators of national affiliation we can build migration sequences. We might, for instance, combine birthplace with location of secondary and university education, and with location of employment or intended employment. By dealing with sequences, we begin to overcome the problems of statistics collected at a point in time and we can begin to get a handle on migration patterns. National and international migration statistics do not now permit us to identify such sequences, with one exception—when birthplace and last residence differ. Educational background information is not obtained for migrants.

There is a source of information about high-level migrants to the United States that makes it possible to use locus of education to classify migrants. The National Science Foundation (NSF), when compiling its annual National Register of Scientific and Technical Personnel, obtains the following data: birthplace and date; locus of secondary education; dates, levels, and location of higher education; current employment by field; citizenship and visa status; and income. The data afford disaggregated comparisons between foreign individuals (defined by birth) trained outside the United States who then migrate (the trained-brain drain and category II of the migration paradigm) and those trained in the United States who remain for employment (the untrained-brain drain and category IV of the migration paradigm). Herbert Grubel has reworked the NSF information using a classification scheme combining birthplace, locus of high school, locus of highest educational degree, and locus of present employment (the U.S.).[21] He has used the classification to look in detail at characteristics of the foreign-born in one professional field, economics.[22]

The NSF classification is limited to the extent that it includes some temporary migrants. Also, because many foreign students do not enter professional life in the United States, the Register tells only part of the non-return story—no comparison can be made between non-returning and returning foreign students. The Register and the detailed reworking of basic data by Grubel nevertheless constitute one of the most promising sources now available for examining brain drain and for overcoming definitional problems indicated above. It allows disaggregation to a meaningful level and permits human capital values to be derived and compared using the age-income data collected.

AN ALTERNATIVE APPROACH TO DEFINING NON-RETURN

The definitions discussed above have all been based on a dichotomy of migrants into those who will return home and those who will not. A conceptually more satisfying but operationally more difficult measure of non-return is one which defines non-return along a continuum—either a probability scale or a time scale. Such a definition is difficult, if not impossible, to use if the only sources available are standard international migration statistics. In special studies, however, individuals can be asked to place themselves on a continuum indicating the probability of adopting permanent residence in the United States or elsewhere. Or the probability of non-return can be crudely approximated by combining various indicators of non-return, terming those who meet the most criteria as high-probability migrants and those who meet the fewest as low-probability migrants. Or a time scale might be set up by simply asking how long individuals have been abroad or how long they expect to remain abroad, or both. Instead of establishing an arbitrary cut-off point signalling non-return by classifying all who have been resident 3 years or more, let us, say, as permanent migrants, we can let time vary so that non-return falls along a continuum. (See chapter 7 for use of a non-return continuum to analyze non-return among Peruvian students in the United States.) A time continuum can be particularly useful in evaluating study abroad as associated with gains or losses through student migration. Time could also be used to talk of brain drain in terms of man-years, rather than in terms of men's lifetimes. Time is a critical variable in the decision models of chapter 6.

SUMMARY

In chapter 2 and in the Footnote to Part I, problems of definition were stressed for several reasons. First, there is a need to counter popular inferences about non-return tied to inappropriate definitions, particularly to non-return as defined by visa adjustments. Second, understanding definitional differences allows at least a partial unraveling of seemingly contradictory statements about brain drain and non-return. Finally, we need to break our set ways of defining problems and to overcome the increasing tendency to allow available data to dictate definitions rather than vice versa. I have suggested, for instance, that our definition of a migrant needs to be refined away from the simple dichotomy of migrant/non-migrant and that the distinction between a temporary and permanent migrant needs to be stretched to include intermediate conditions.

It will be many years before we remedy present data limitations or agree upon definitions. Meanwhile, a research strategy stressing case studies and the collection of original information seems desirable. More global analyses should incorporate alternative definitions and sets of assumptions. In brief, detailed description and analysis of high-level migration are in an infant stage.

NOTES

[1] The distinction is sometimes difficult to make. Are medical interns students? Should the 2,000 foreign students preparing for their law examinations at the Inns of Court in London be classified as students or as trainees? They are considered trainees. See Dunlop Fergus, *Europe's Guests: Students and Trainees* (Strasbourg: Council for Cultural Cooperation of the Council of Europe, 1966), p. 177.

[2] Should foreign students exclusively enrolled in language courses at universities be included as students while similar students in adult education programs outside a university setting are excluded? (See discussion of this question as it relates to Peruvian students in the United States in chapter 7.) Are university students abroad "brainy" while secondary students from other countries are not? Most statistics are restricted to students in institutions of higher education (for which definitions vary from country to country and sometimes within a country over time). British definitions of higher education, for instance, are much tighter than United States definitions. See the ACU, *Commonwealth Universities Yearbook*, 1965, p. 2339, as compared with the listing of institutions included in the IIE survey of foreign students in the United States (published each year in *Open Doors*).

[3] To illustrate the potential difference a part-time vs. full-time distinction can make, the author's population of Peruvian males studying in institutions of higher education in the United States was diminished by approximately 10 per cent simply by excluding part-time students that had been included in the IIE statistics. Only full-time students are reported in the United Kingdom. In Latin American and European nations, where an open university system is followed, the distinction is usually not made.

[4] See Fergus, p. 177.

[5] Jones Report, pp. 7, 8. For press treatments, see "British Peril in Brain Drain," *New York Times*, October 11, 1967, C. 9.; and "Brain Drain: The 'Right Solution,'" *The Times* (London), October 11, 1967, p. 3. In addition follow-up research shows that many graduates of British universities work abroad *temporarily* although for periods of more than a year. See Ernest

Rudd, "The Brain Drain and the Shortage of Scientists," *Higher Education Review*, I, No. 2 (1969), p. 68.

[6] Institute of International Education (IIE), *Open Doors, 1967* (New York: IIE, 1967), p. 1. Actually, the increase is not as great as indicated by the IIE. Some of the 13,000 non-returning individuals, all of whom were presumably excluded from previous surveys, were included in the past, depending on their visa. The actual increase associated with the definition change is approximately 9,500.

[7] Unlike other criteria, birthplace is unequivocal; there can be only one. In addition, it is appealing to those individuals who feel birth brings a claim on national resources and entails obligations to the nation, a most convenient stance when manpower is desired for development or military service. However, birthplace may differ from place of permanent residence, schooling, or citizenship. It is best used in conjunction with other criteria for assigning national affiliation.

[8] For example, only 8 per cent of the Chileans who were resident in the United States and who responded to a recent survey had acquired United States citizenship. The percentage planning to remain permanently in the United States was much higher. See, Sergio Gutiérrez Olivos and Jorge Riquelme Pérez, *La emigración de recursos humanos de alto nivel y el caso de Chile* (Washington, D.C.: Pan American Union, 1965), p. 27.

[9] See chapter 3, p. 122. Also, a Berkeley survey indicated that one-half of the students having immigrant visas planned to return home. The survey was reported in NAFSA *Newsletter*, XVII (January 1966) by Laurette Kirstein.

[10] F- and J-visas carry a legal (or moral) obligation to leave the United States following study. J-visa holders can remain for practical training for up to 18 months; then they are required to leave for a period of two years, after which they may migrate again to the United States. F-visa holders sign a statement on their I-20 form admitting them to the United States that says: "I seek to enter or remain in the United States *temporarily* and *solely* for the purpose of pursuing a full course of study at the school named on page 1 of this form." (Italics added.)

[11] In its Annual Report, the United States Immigration and Naturalization Service (INS) publishes statistics on the number of entrants to the United States with various kinds of visas. The INS figures are of limited utility in their present form; access is difficult and cross-tabulation with individual characteristics or conditions of study is not possible. In addition, INS has difficulty keeping track of individuals once they have arrived. Foreign students are an unusually mobile group and those who wish to avoid the INS are often able to do so. (See also footnote 17.)

[12] Robert B. Klinger, "Immigration and Non-Return," NAFSA *Newsletter*, XVI, No. 5 (February 1965), p. 2.

[13] In spite of previous evidence that the rate of adjustment by Asian students is highly elastic and in spite of observations such as Klinger's quoted in the text, the jump in Asian entrants following the immigration liberalization in 1965 seems to have been a surprise to some. See Walter F. Mondale, "The Cost of the Brain Drain," *The Atlantic Monthly*, CCXX, No. 6 (December 1967), pp. 67, 68. In 1957 and 1962, similar jumps occurred following temporary liberalization of adjustment procedures. (See also footnote 15.)

[14] See chapter 9 for additional discussion of the 1970 amendment.

[15] In 1967, over 80 per cent of the F-1 to immigrant adjustments and over 60 per cent of the J-1 waivers were by Asian students.

[16] Figures were obtained in correspondence with E. A. Loughran, Associate Commissioner, Immigration and Naturalization Service, Washington, D.C., May 17, 1965.

[17] Adjustment figures compiled since 1962 can now be found in the *Annual Report* of the Immigration and Naturalization Service and in their *Annual Indicator of the In-Migration into the United States of Aliens in Professional and Related Occupations* (Washington: USGPO, 1967–   ) prepared in conjunction with the U.S. Advisory Council on International Educational and Cultural Affairs. In the *Annual Indicator,* country of last residence is used to assign nationality; visa adjustment (or waiver in case of the J-visa) is the criterion for having changed to United States residence permanently. Adjustments are presented by country and occupational category for temporary non-immigrants holding an H-1 (alien of distinguished merit), H-3 (industrial trainee), J-1 (exchange visitor), or F-1 (student) visa.

[18] See Niland, p. 20, who removes all students not within a year of graduation from his calculation.

[19] For a good discussion of the international system of classifying migrants, see Brinley Thomas, *International Migration and Economic Development, A Trend Report and Bibliography,* UNESCO (SS.60/XI.6/A, Paris, 1961), p. 23.

[20] Shri Awasthi, for instance, has suggested a three-year period of residence as most appropriate. The three-year cut-off would probably result in a gross overestimate of non-return. See "Brain Drain from Developing Countries: An Exercise in Problem Formulation," *Manpower Journal* (New Delhi: Institute of Applied Manpower Research), II, No. 1 (April 1966), p. 92.

[21] Herbert G. Grubel, *Characteristics of Foreign-Born and Educated Scientists in the United States, 1966,* prepared for the National Science Foundation (Philadelphia: University of Pennsylvania, August 1968.)

In greater detail, the classification system set up by Grubel is outlined below. Category VI represents the trained brain drain; category V individuals are foreign student non-returnees.

MIGRATION SEQUENCES	COUNTRY OF:	BIRTH →	HIGH SCHOOL →	HIGHEST DEGREE →	EMPLOYMENT
I		U.S.	U.S. & Foreign	U.S. & Foreign	U.S.
II		U.S.	U.S.	U.S.	U.S.
		U.S.	Foreign	Foreign	U.S.
III		U.S.	Foreign	U.S.	U.S.
		U.S.	U.S.	Foreign	U.S.
IV		Foreign	U.S.	U.S.	U.S.
		Foreign	U.S.	Foreign	U.S.
V		Foreign	Foreign	U.S.	U.S.
VI		Foreign	Foreign	Foreign	U.S.
VII		No Answer	No Answer	No Answer	No Answer

[22] Grubel and Scott, *American Economic Review,* LVII, No. 1, pp. 131–45.

PART II

Non-Return Among Foreign Students in the United States

3

AN ANALYSIS OF FOREIGN STUDENT NON-RETURN USING THE INSTITUTE OF INTERNATIONAL EDUCATION FOREIGN STUDENT CENSUS, 1964–65

The most frequently quoted source of statistics concerning foreign students in the United States is the Institute of International Education (IIE) Annual Census of Foreign Students. The census has for several years included the question, "Do you plan to remain in the United States permanently?" allowing rough estimates of non-return among foreign students in the United States. However, prior to 1965, the answers to this question had not been formally processed by the IIE; hence this potential source of information about students' intentions to reside in the United States remained virtually untouched. Although simple counts of students responding "Yes" to the question produced crude estimates of the overall non-return rate, no cross-tabulations with conditions of study or individual characteristics existed. No cross-national comparisons had been made (and to my knowledge, none have been published since).

In view of the paucity of data concerning foreign student non-return and the current interest in the subject, it seemed worthwhile to exploit this unique source as far as possible.[1] In so doing, I encountered many of the problems of definition and measurement mentioned in chapter 2 and in the Footnote to Part I. I saw that the IIE census information, as published in *Open Doors,* while frequently cited, was seldom understood: clarification was needed. I am therefore including a brief description of the data source, both in its original form at IIE and as reworked to allow analysis of non-return.

THE INSTITUTE OF INTERNATIONAL EDUCATION ANNUAL CENSUS OF FOREIGN STUDENTS

Each year, the IIE polls more than 2,000 United States colleges and universities. In 1964/65, the year used for the following analysis, 2,556 institutions were queried. Census forms are sent to foreign student advisors at each of the polled institutions prior to the Fall registration, requesting them to obtain information from "all students who are citizens of countries other than the United States, irrespective of their type of visa, who are studying on the undergraduate or post-graduate level or equivalent." [2] The following information is requested:

Name of student
Full address in home country
Country of citizenship
Sex
Year of birth
Religion (optional)
Year college study began in the United States
Name of college or university
Whether enrolled at another university
Whether husband or wife accompanies
Major field of study
Academic status (Undergraduate, graduate . . .)
Sources of financial support
Type of visa
Intent to remain permanently in the United States

Cooperation with the census is voluntary, but returns have been remarkably high and remarkably complete.[3] The response rate for institutions in 1964/65 was approximately 90 per cent and information was accumulated for 88,719 individuals. The census undoubtedly represents the most complete data concerning foreign students in the United States available for the United States system of higher education. In spite of such thorough coverage,[4] some institutions (or parts of institutions) are missed.[5] And, within the polled institutions, some foreign students remain unnoticed or unlocated.

Furthermore, counts of students in September and October when the census is taken describe the number of students who enroll during an entire year. The IIE census may underestimate the total *yearly* population of foreign students by as much as 10 to 20 per cent.[6]

Excluded from the IIE survey are many individuals who might, by another definition, be considered students. Foreign student advisors were specifically instructed to exclude: high school or preparatory school students, trade school students without high school diplomas or the equivalent, foreign nationals whose primary purpose is teaching or advanced research but who might also be students, and foreign physicians serving as interns and residents in American hospitals. Also excluded are most industrial trainees, some student-visa holders who are studying in language schools not associated with an American college or university, some "exchange students" who are in institutions approved by the government but not included in the IIE listing, and all military trainees other than those at military academies. If these persons were regarded as students and if they could be located and included in the survey, the total number of foreign students alleged to be in the United States would rise substantially. On the other hand, IIE includes "special students" who are "non-matriculated," i.e. "not working for a degree and therefore receiving no credit for the courses taken." [7] Nevertheless, the definition of student used by the IIE is in general appropriate to its task; the number of higher education students excluded by definition is probably small.

Also excluded from the IIE totals are all individuals who do not meet the IIE definition of "foreign student." Prior to 1966/67, the definition was based on a combination of citizenship, visa status, and intention to remain permanently in the United States. Students with other than United States citizenship were *not* considered foreign if two conditions were met: (1) they held an immigrant visa (or if visa status was unknown), *and* (2) they also indicated their intention to remain permanently (by answering affirmatively the question, "Do you plan to remain permanently in the U.S.?"). These individuals, who will be referred to as "immigrant non-returnees," were excluded from the IIE's tabulation or presentation of data before 1966/67. The rationale for excluding immigrant non-returnees was simply that, as legal immigrants who had decided to remain, they no longer qualified as foreign. In 1964/65, 6,511 immigrant non-returnees were excluded.

The IIE basis for screening respondents was questionable (before the definition was changed in 1966) at the time of the 1964/65 census. First, a high percentage of respondents (36 per cent in 1964/65)[8] failed to provide the information needed to judge whether or not, by the IIE definition, an individual was in fact foreign. The result was an arbitrary decision to include in the census *all* individuals for whom visa and/or non-return information was incomplete, classing them all as foreign and thereby introducing a bias. If information had been complete, the number of students qualifying as "foreign" *by the 1964/65 IIE definition* would have been much smaller and the total number of foreign students enrolled as indicated in the IIE census would have been smaller.

Second, the IIE decided to include in the census students with F- or J-visas even though they indicated their intent to remain permanently in the United States. In 1964/65 there were approximately 3,000 such cases. Considering the ease with which visa adjustments could be made and considering the fact that former F- or J-visa holders who had already adjusted their visas were excluded, the decision to include the 3,000 students seems somewhat legalistic and inconsistent.

Apart from the inconsistencies introduced by arbitrary screening decisions, a good case could be made for treating all individuals studying in the United States who come from other nations as a group because they face similar problems, whether or not they plan to remain and regardless of their visa.

In order to remove the limitations imposed by the IIE definition of "foreign student" in terms of visa and intent and citizenship; and in order to analyze non-return, it was necessary to rework the 1964/65 IIE census data.[9] By reverting to a simple definition of "foreign student" based on citizenship (subsequently adopted by the IIE), it was possible to bring back in the 6,511 immigrant non-returnees who had been originally excluded. When the immigrant non-returnees were restored the working population of foreign students in the United States during the school year 1964/65 became 88,556.

Another step in preparing the 1964/65 data involved recoding visa information so that F-visa holders and J-visa holders could be identified. As visa status was being recoded, information concerning the intention to remain permanently was also taken from the original census forms and transferred to data cards. Because some individuals had clearly indicated that a "Yes" or "No" response could not be made to the question, "Do you plan to remain permanently in the U.S.?" an "undecided" category was added.[10]

Names and descriptions of the variables used in subsequent analysis of the updated IIE census are presented in Table 2. Note the several modifications of original variables. Before the reworked census data were analyzed, frequency distributions for the redefined foreign student population were run and compared with the frequency distributions as published in IIE's *Open Doors*.[11] From the comparisons, it was readily apparent that add-

TABLE 2—Description of variables used in the analysis of the Institute of International Education Annual Census of Foreign Students, 1964–65

VARIABLE NAME	DESCRIPTION
SEX	Male, Female
COUNTRY	Includes 230 "countries" listed by the IIE
COUNTRY (M1)[a]	Groups COUNTRY into 16 areas
AGE	Includes each age from 15 to 65
AGE (M1)	Groups AGE into 8 categories
FIELD	Includes 94 fields of study listed by the IIE
FIELD (M1)	Groups FIELD into 9 major categories
STATUS	Refers to levels of academic status, 5 categories
TIME	Refers to length of time since study began, year by year
TIME (M1)	Groups TIME into 5 categories
SPONSOR	Includes 5 separate and 15 combined categories
SPONSOR (M1)	Groups SPONSOR into 4 categories
SPONSOR (U.S. Gov't.)	Groups SPONSOR into U.S. government and all others
SPONSOR (For. Gov't.)	Groups SPONSOR into Foreign government and all others
SPONSOR (University)	Groups SPONSOR into U.S. university and all others
SPONSOR (Private)	Groups SPONSOR into Private and all others
SPONSOR (Self)	Groups SPONSOR into Self and all others
VISA	Includes F, J, Immigrant, Permanent resident, and Other
VISA (M1)	Combines Immigrant and Permanent resident of VISA
INTENT	Consists of Return, Non-return, and Undecided categories
INTENT (M1)	Combines Undecided and Return categories of INTENT

[a] (M) indicates a Modification of the originable variable.

ing the 6,511 immigrant non-returnees did little to change the distribution of students for variables presented by the IIE. This is in part a matter of the small number of additions relative to the size of the total population. The only instances where adding the 6,511 immigrant non-returnee cases changes by more than one per cent the proportion of students in a particular variable category are: Under "SPONSOR," the percentage of self-sponsored students increases relatively by 2 per cent, and under academic "STATUS," the undergraduates increase relatively by 2 per cent.

TABLE 3—Frequency distributions for foreign students in the United States, Fall 1964: VISA (M1), and INTENT[a]

CATEGORY	PERCENTAGE[b]	NUMBER[b]
VISA (M1)		
F (student)	70.0	48,926
J (exchangee)	13.4	9,380
Immigrant	11.3	7,890
Other[c]	5.3	3,695
All visas	100.0	69,891
INTENT		
Return	81.9	49,385
Non-return	15.9	9,614
Undecided	2.2	1,307
Total	100.0	60,306

[a] Calculated from: original census forms, Institute of International Education Annual Census of Foreign Students in the United States—1964–65. (Cited hereafter as IIE Census forms, Fall 1964.)
[b] The grand total for the census is 88,556. The percentage and number of non-respondents for each variable excluded from the calculations are:

NA VISA .... 21.1 per cent (18,665)
NA INTENT ...... 31.9 per cent (28,250)
[c] See footnote 10, chapter 3, for coding of VISA.

These increases suggest that immigrant visas and non-return occur slightly more frequently among self-sponsored undergraduates than among other SPONSOR and academic STATUS combinations.

Table 3 presents frequency distributions for two variables not included in *Open Doors* and critical to the following analysis: "VISA", and what I have labeled "INTENT" (as a reminder that the measure of non-return being used is the intent to remain permanently in the United States).

As the 7,890 figure for immigrant-visa holders indicates, not all immigrants in the reworked data came from the addition of immigrant non-returnees. In fact, more than 2,000 immigrant-visa holders were included in the original IIE tabulations. These were individuals who answered negatively or who did not answer the question of intended residence.

The Rate of Non-return

The present analysis focuses on the Non-return category of INTENT in Table 3. There are 9,614 individuals in this category, representing 16 per cent of all individuals indicating their intent. This percentage is higher than that usually derived from IIE data for foreign student non-return.[12] An element of both statistical juggling and of redefinition explains the higher percentage.

What may seem to be statistical juggling of intended non-return consists simply of excluding non-respondents from the percentage base. Since many individuals did not respond to the question of intended permanent residence, including or excluding them from tabulations can substantially affect the resultant figure. By leaving out non-respondents, the assumption is made that, if non-respondents had answered, they would have fallen into the categories of Return and Non-return in the same proportions as those who answered the question. There is evidence (developed in more detail below and in Appendix I) that non-respondents more closely resemble non-returnees than returnees. This presumption

has logical as well as statistical roots. If an individual is un
or if he feels somewhat guilty about his decision to sta
United States, he may avoid answering the question. I.
true, non-respondents should fall into the category of Non-return
more frequently than allowed for by assuming proportionate distribution. Exclusion of non-respondents, then, is likely to bias
estimates of non-return downward, and the 16 per cent figure can
probably be regarded as below the actual rate of non-return.

The effect of changing the definition of foreign student and re-
introducing immigrant non-returnees into the analysis can be
understood by comparing non-return rates for both definitions. To
simplify the comparison, the following notation is adopted:

N_i = "Immigrant non-returnees" (Non-returnees with immigrant visas or for whom there was no visa information).
N_s = "Student non-returnees" (Non-returnees with non-immigrant visas).
R_i = Returnees with immigrant visas or for whom there was no
   visa information.
R_s = Returnees with non-immigrant visas.

If the IIE definition in terms of citizenship, visa, and intent is
adopted, immigrant non-returnees (N_i) are left out of both the
numerator and denominator in the proportion. The rate of non-
return is:

$$\frac{N_s}{N_s + R_s + R_i} = \frac{3,068}{3,068 + 45,960 + 4,732} = 5.7\%$$

The interpretation which might be given to this estimated rate of
non-return is that it represents the rate at which foreign students
will seek to adjust their status to permanent residence. And indeed, non-return rates calculated from visa adjustments are
approximately of that magnitude.[13] In doing so, it is well to
remember that visa adjustments sometimes are made without an

accompanying commitment to remain permanently in the United States.

If foreign student is redefined simply in terms of citizenship, as it has been for this analysis, the rate of non-return becomes:

$$\frac{N_s + N_i}{N_s + N_i + R_s + R_i} = \frac{3,068 + 6,546}{3,068 + 6,546 + 45,960 + 4,732} = 15.9\%$$

This rate might be interpreted as the rate of intended non-return among all foreign nationals (regardless of visa) currently enrolled in United States institutions of higher education during the 1964/65 school year.

The main reason for presenting these simple calculations in detail is to illustrate how, by adopting different definitions, a basic statistic can be substantially altered, not to claim that either the 5.7 per cent or the 15.9 per cent figure is "right." The rate might have been altered further by excluding undecided individuals or treating them as non-respondents (in which case the two percentages would have been 5.8 per cent and 16.3 per cent, respectively). Or, by placing the undecided individuals with non-returnees (on the theory that those who are undecided will probably remain permanently), the percentages could have been raised to 7.5 per cent and 18.1 per cent respectively. With further speculation on the direction of bias introduced by dealing with intentions rather than behaviors and the direction of bias introduced by the large non-respondent group, it would not be difficult to justify a non-return rate exceeding 20 per cent.

Perhaps a more interesting and more legitimate way of looking at the INTENT figures would be to emphasize the percentage of foreign students who have actually indicated their intention to return (that is, who indicated they did not plan to remain permanently in the United States). Of the 88,556 total, a definite indication that residence would be outside the United States was given by only 49,385 individuals, or approximately 56 per cent. The remaining 44 per cent is a lumping together of all non-respondents, intended non-returnees, and undecided individuals. This percentage provides a kind of upper limit for the over-all percentage of non-return which can be hypothesized by using the IIE data; an upper limit, assuming that intention equals behavior.

The range of figures for foreign student non-return is, then, very broad. Such a range suggests that non-return figures given in summary form without qualification do not have much meaning. Although summary statistics are persuasive for policy purposes, they may be misleading. For instance, 8 of the 156 countries listed in *Open Doors* account for 51 per cent of the intended non-returnees (referring now to the original calculation of 15.9 per cent).[14] Canada and Cuba, which are quite special cases, together account for 26 per cent. In short, countries differ so markedly with respect to rate of migration, reasons for migration, and characteristics of migrants, that most discussion should refer to specific countries. Disaggregation beyond the country level and even more refined definitions of populations are desirable. It has been said by those whose business it is to persuade policy makers of the wisdom of a particular course of action that "One good summary statistic is worth a thousand detailed tables." Unfortunately this maxim, while politically expedient, perpetuates confusion and inhibits discriminating analysis.

One additional caveat is necessary before ending the discussion of global rates of non-return. The fact that there may be 5 per cent or 45 per cent clearly defined non-returnees among a population of clearly defined foreign students does *not* mean that having studied in the United States *caused* these students to remain. Nor does the fact that many students adjust visas prove that study experience in the United States caused them to take that action.

Before turning to more detailed examination of intended non-return, the effect of disaggregating the total population by sex will be examined, so that analysis can be more sharply focused.

Cross-tabulation by Sex

The percentage of male to total students for all countries combined is 77; the range among countries is from 98 (Saudi Arabia) to 45 (Philippines). Roughly, Africa and Middle Eastern countries have very high (over 90) male percentages among students in the United States. Latin American percentages tend to fall between 70 and 80. Asian variations are very wide. European nations are comparatively low in their percentage of males to total students.

It is tempting to generalize that the percentage of males among students in the United States is inversely related to the level of development of the country. The relationship is superficial, even at a global level, and it would be dangerous to apply the generalization to particular countries. Within broad geographical areas there is wide variation: 82 per cent of Norway's students are males, while Finland sends only 51 per cent males; Cambodia's 96 per cent is in notable contrast to neighboring Thailand's 71 per cent. Such variation suggests that any cross-country analysis should control for the variable SEX.

Sexes are also differently represented within FIELD of study. Engineering and agriculture are almost exclusively male fields, with 99 per cent and 95 per cent respectively, and business (86 per cent) is also a heavily male-dominated field. Following, in descending order of male dominance, are science (80 per cent), social science (73 per cent), medicine (62 per cent), humanities (59 per cent), education (54 per cent), and other fields (32 per cent). In relation to their 22 per cent representation in the total student population, females are over-represented in the humanities, education, and medicine. Their salience in medicine is explained by the large numbers of foreign women studying nursing at the undergraduate level.

Because the total percentage of females is not high and because they tend to concentrate in certain fields (35 per cent of all women are in the humanities, and only 2 per cent are in engineering and agriculture combined), there are some contexts in which focus on males is not only logical but necessary. Most discussions of non-return are carried on in the context of developing the underdeveloped. Emphasis is placed on the technical fields and on entrepreneurship. The humanities are considered to be less important in the economic and social development process. With few exceptions, males are the potential leaders and are in the technical and scientific fields, where they will make visible

TABLE 4—Distribution of VISA (M1) and INTENT within categories of SEX, foreign students in the United States[a]

Category	Male	Female	Total[b]
VISA (M1)[c]			
F (student)	71.2	65.9	70.0
Immigrant	10.0	15.8	11.3
J (exchangee)	13.7	12.5	13.4
Other[c]	5.1	5.8	5.3
All visas	100.0	100.0	100.0
Base N	53,720	16,068	69,891
INTENT[d]			
Non-return	15.0	19.0	15.9
Return	82.8	79.2	81.9
Undecided	2.2	1.8	2.2
Total	100.0	100.0	100.0
Base N	45,688	14,534	60,306

[a] Calculated from: IIE Census forms, Fall 1964.
[b] Male and Female do not equal Total because SEX was not determined for 140 respondents.
[c] See footnote 10, chapter 3, for coding of VISA.
[d] Excluded from the calculations are:

	Male	Female	Total
NA VISA	14,518	4,110	18,665
NA INTENT	22,550	5,644	28,250

contributions to their respective countries. In contrast, educated women are more apt to move out of the professional ranks by marriage. Consequently, the analysis of non-return that follows will be, for the most part, restricted to males. This rationale is supported further by noting that males are disproportionately represented in programs of government sponsorship and in graduate-level study (particularly at the doctoral level). (Also, males tend to stay slightly longer in the United States and to be, on the average, slightly older.)

Distributions of VISA and INTENT, presented in Table 4 vary for males and females. Females have a higher rate of non-return than males (19 per cent as against 15 per cent) and are more apt to be immigrant-visa holders (16 per cent as against 10 per cent). Because males predominate, the disproportionate rate of non-return among females only slightly affects the total percentage. Even this slight effect, however, takes on meaning if translated into absolute numbers; a change of only one per cent in the rate of non-return makes a difference of 682 individuals.

AN ANALYSIS OF INTENDED NON-RETURN AMONG FOREIGN STUDENTS IN THE UNITED STATES

The analysis of intended non-return is based on foreign students' answers to the IIE's question, "Do you plan to remain permanently in the U.S.?" Responses are analyzed here for 1964 only; there is no time depth to the analysis. Answers were coded (see footnote 10) into the following categories:

Non-return: The intention is to remain permanently in the United states.

Return: The intention is not to remain permanently in the United States and the assumption is that the individual will, therefore, return home.

Undecided: The respondent indicated that he had not made up his mind about permanent residence.

No Answer: The intention was not indicated or was ambiguous.

These categories combine to form the variable labeled INTENT.

Response Bias

But INTENT is one step from the fact: intention to act does not necessarily correspond to action. Some individuals who indicate in good conscience that they plan to remain in the United States or that they plan to return home may change their plans. Individual and national conditions change in ways that cannot be foreseen.

Although the direction of net bias is not certain, probably more individuals change their minds and stay than change their minds and return. The strong wording of the census question, which uses "permanently" as the standard against which intentions are to be judged, should keep changes from intended non-return toward return to a minimum. Uncertain individuals who wish to try the United States way of life for a short time are not likely to indicate an intention to remain. Presumably only those who are strongly committed to staying will indicate the fact. On the other hand, individuals who are unwilling to make a permanent commitment but who at least entertain the idea may decide to stay even though they did not indicate this intention in the IIE survey. Temporary non-return is not treated in this analysis.

In general, then, the bias is downward by using intentions to determine the rate of permanent non-return. There will be some variation in bias by country. When presenting aggregate statistics, the fact that there is a bias does not present an insurmountable problem as long as there is a good idea of the direction of the bias. If, however, the desire is to predict individual behavior from expressions of intent, the possibility of inaccuracy is immensely increased.

Another possible bias (which cannot be identified empirically) results from false answers. Students may not wish to respond truthfully for a variety of reasons, not the least of which would be their plan to remain permanently in spite of a signed agreement to return home or a visa status requiring exit. Because the IIE census has a quasi-public character, one could not blame an individual for concealing his true intentions if revealing them would conceivably lead to trouble later. In addition to legal obligations, individuals carry moral obligations to family or country that they know they may flout by remaining permanently. This may lead to an unwillingness to face squarely the fact that non-return is intended.

There is, of course, an alternative to the false answer—that is to leave the question unanswered. As indicated earlier, the No Answer category of INTENT constitutes a large percentage of the total (31 per cent), and the percentage varies by country.[15] Although non-response introduces a bias, it can be analyzed. In general, the distribution of non-respondents within each variable was closer to the distribution of non-returnees than returnees, suggesting a downward bias throughout. However, the resulting underestimates of non-return are probably greater for males than females, for engineering and humanities students than for students in other fields, and for graduate versus undergraduate study. (See Appendix I.)

Correlates of Intended Non-return

Using the IIE census data, we will examine cross-tabulations of non-return with field of study (FIELD), level of study (STATUS), sponsorship (SPONSOR), age (AGE), length of time since study in the United States began (TIME), and visa held at the time of the census (VISA). Depending on which way the tables are percentaged, one of two questions is being asked: 1) What is the distribution of non-return among categories of the variable, that is, what percentage of all non-returnees fall into each category of the variable? 2) How does INTENT vary between categories of the variable—what percentage of the students in each category of the variable are non-returnees?

NON-RETURN BY FIELD OF STUDY (FIELD)

Almost one-third of all non-returning male students are found in engineering (column 1, Table 5).[16] The percentage is slightly above the percentage of engineering students found among returnees (column 2), undecideds (column 3), or among the total population of male students (column 4). Similarly, there is a slight over-representation of business and humanities students among non-returning males while social sciences, physical and life

TABLE 5—INTENT by FIELD (M1): Distribution of categories of intended non-return across fields of study, foreign students in the United States, males only[a]

| | INTENT[b] | | | |
FIELD	Non-return	Return	Undecided	Total
Medicine	6.6	4.9	6.1	5.2
Social science	11.8	16.1	15.8	15.5
Science	16.8	18.5	20.2	18.3
Engineering	31.9	26.8	27.4	27.5
Agriculture	1.5	5.3	2.2	4.7
Business	10.4	9.8	9.0	9.8
Humanities	17.7	14.1	15.6	14.7
Education	3.2	4.1	3.3	4.0
Other	0.3	0.4	0.4	0.3
All fields	100.0	100.0	100.0	100.0
Base N	6,819	37,774	1,039	45,632

[a] Calculated from: IIE Census forms, Fall 1964.
[b] Excluded from the calculations are:
    NA INTENT only 21,891
    NA FIELD only 56
    NA INTENT and FIELD 659

sciences, agriculture, and education are slightly under-represented. Generally, however, the distribution by field of non-returning students is not dramatically different from the distribution by field of returnees, undecideds, or the total.

When the broad fields such as engineering, are broken down from the summary categories presented in Table 5 into the more detailed subject fields used by the IIE, the following subject fields contribute more than 4 per cent to non-return: electrical engineering (10 per cent), business (8 per cent), mechanical engineering (7 per cent), civil engineering (5 per cent), and chemistry (4 per cent). Definitions are, of course, loose. We cannot know, for instance, whether the majority of non-returning mechanical engineers were planning to be automotive mechanics or top-level space technologists; the mere fact that they were studying something they call mechanical engineering does not tell a great deal about non-returnees' plans.

Now let us approach the second question, "Within each field of study, what percentage of the students are non-returnees?" The question will be answered in two ways. First, fields will be listed from highest to lowest according to the percentage of the respondents in each field who said they were non-returnees. In this approach, we omit non-respondents (who are closer to non-returnees than returnees in their characteristics) and we do not count undecided individuals as non-returnees, even though many will in fact remain permanently. Thus the non-return figures (see column 1, Table 6) approximate a lower limit of the percentage non-return for each field.

The slightly higher rates of non-return in medicine and engineering fields (column 1 of Table 6) are in accord with most general observations about which fields have the highest rates of non-return. The high rate for humanities students is, however, surprising. That rate is linked to inclusion of intensive English-language programs in the humanities category. Note the low rate of non-return among agriculture students.

Using the more detailed IIE census classification of subjects,

TABLE 6—INTENT by FIELD (M1): The percentages of foreign students who intend to remain permanently and who do not intend to remain permanently in the United States, males only[a]

| | INTENT | | | |
FIELD	Percentage non-return[b]	Percentage return[c]	Base N, non-return[b]	Base N return[c]
Medicine	18.8	55.1	2,374	3,384
Humanities	17.9	50.9	6,707	10,491
Engineering	17.3	53.0	12,556	19,042
Business	15.8	56.0	4,488	6,586
Science	13.8	57.2	8,340	12,211
Education	12.2	60.5	1,807	2,406
Social science	11.4	60.5	7,063	10,080
Other	11.4	62.1	158	219
Agriculture	4.7	64.9	2,139	3,104
All fields	14.9	55.9	45,632	67,523

[a] Calculated from: IIE Census forms, Fall 1964.
[b] Excluded from the calculations are:
    NA INTENT only 21,891
    NA FIELD only 56
    NA INTENT and FIELD 659
[c] Excluded from the calculations are:
    NA FIELD 715

we can identify several fields in which the rate of non-return is high, more than 20 per cent: language (47 per cent), liberal arts (27 per cent), aeronautical engineering (26 per cent), accounting (26 per cent), psychology (23 per cent), and architecture (20 per cent). Electrical engineering, business, and mechanical engineering, which we previously saw accounting for large *numbers* of non-returnees, do not appear with particularly high *rates* of non-return.

Many students in language are intensive-English students who do not plan to do any additional university work. A larger-than-usual percentage already have immigrant visas. Their status as bona fide higher-education students is not clear, and they introduce a bias into rates of non-return calculated from the IIE census, particularly for students classified within humanities. Engineering non-returnees are not as apt to have immigrant visas as language students, suggesting that more engineers than language students develop their intention to remain in the United States after arriving. (That is, of course, not the same as saying that the percentage who change after arriving is particularly high for either group. We have no way of actually sorting out the timing of decisions from the data.)

The second way of approaching the percentage non-return within each field of study is to turn the question around and to ask what percentage of the students actually indicated in the census that they planned to return home. In so doing, we bring back in the non-respondents and the undecided students, and we tacitly group them with non-returnees. In Table 6, column 3, we see that 55 per cent of all medical students said they planned to return home. By assuming that all the other medical students will remain in the U.S., we approximate an upper limit for non-return, in this case 45 per cent. If we use percentage *return* to rank fields, we should find fields in the reverse order from our ranking when percentage *non-return* was used.

Looking now at the percentage return for each field of study as presented in column 3 of Table 6, we see that medicine, which has the highest rate of non-return (see column 1), does not have the lowest rate of return as we expected. Both humanities and engineering have lower rates of return than medicine. Therefore, the upper limit for non-return among humanities and engineering students is higher than for medical students, according to the IIE data. The reshuffling of rank order when return rather than non-return is used is of minor significance for FIELD.

NON-RETURN BY ACADEMIC LEVEL (STATUS)

Almost two-thirds of all non-returning male students are undergraduates according to the IIE data (see Table 7). The other non-returnees are either graduate students or "special" students, which means they are not registered in degree programs and that there is no way of telling whether they are studying at the undergraduate or graduate level. The 64 per cent figure for undergraduates among non-returnees is considerably higher than the percentage of undergraduates among returnees, undecideds, or the total. Since there is a tendency to underestimate non-return at the graduate level (see Appendix I), the predominance of undergraduates is somewhat exaggerated.

TABLE 7—INTENT by STATUS: Distribution of categories of intended non-return across academic levels, foreign students in the United States, males only[a]

| | INTENT[b] | | | |
STATUS	Non-return	Return	Undecided	Total
Special	3.8	6.6	2.3	6.1
Undergraduate	64.4	49.3	53.4	51.6
Graduate—unspecif.	1.2	1.2	1.2	1.2
Graduate—masters	16.1	25.4	18.7	23.9
Graduate—doctorate	14.5	17.5	24.4	17.2
All statuses	100.0	100.0	100.0	100.0
Base N	6,808	37,599	1,033	45,440

[a] Calculated from: IIE Census forms, Fall 1964.
[b] Excluded from the calculations are:
     NA INTENT only 21,234
     NA STATUS only 248
     NA INTENT and STATUS 1,316

Turning now to non-return within each academic level (see Table 8), we find undergraduates with the highest percentage non-return followed by graduates who did not specify masters or doctoral studies, followed by doctoral students, masters students, and special students. Although the difference between non-return percentages for doctoral and masters students is not great, it does support the commonly held notion that it is better to sponsor students for a terminal master's degree than for a doctoral degree if return is desired.

TABLE 8—INTENT by STATUS: The percentage of foreign students who intend to remain permanently and who do not intend to remain permanently in the United States, males only[a]

| | INTENT | | | |
| | NON-RETURN[b] | | RETURN[c] | |
STATUS	%	Base N	%	Base N
Undergraduate	18.7	23,488	58.3	31,801
Graduate—unspec.	15.9	529	8.1	5,367
Graduate—doctorate	12.6	7,801	63.1	10,401
Graduate—masters	10.1	10,860	66.4	14,415
Special	9.4	2,761	52.8	4,690
All statuses	15.0	45,440	56.7	66,674

[a] Calculated from: IIE Census forms, Fall 1964.
[b] Excluded from the calculations are:
NA INTENT only 21,234
NA STATUS only   248
NA INTENT and STATUS   1,316
[c] Excluded from the calculations are:
NA STATUS   1,564

When we look at return rather than non-return, we see that only eight per cent of the unspecified graduate students indicated they would return. In this group are a large number of students who did not answer the question about permanent residence or who were undecided. Special students also have a low rate of return, given their position at the bottom of the non-return ranking. I suspect many of the language students mentioned in the discussion of non-return by FIELD fall in the special category. Masters students are more likely to return than doctoral students who are more likely to return than undergraduate students. Because there is a bias in the data toward lower non-return among graduate students, the difference between undergraduate and graduate levels is probably exaggerated slightly.

NON-RETURN BY SPONSORSHIP (SPONSOR)

Many foreign students have more than one source of financial support. Consequently, sponsorship is divided into five categories, each corresponding to a major kind or group of sponsors (see Table 9). One-tenth of all non-returning male students received all or part of their financial support from the U.S. government while 90 per cent received no such assistance. The percentage figure of 10 per cent for non-returnees is lower than the percentage of returnees or the percentage of all students who were U.S. government sponsored. Relatively few of the undecided students were so financed. Non-returnees are also under-represented among those sponsored by foreign governments, by U.S. universities, and by private institutions (such as foundations or businesses). Only in the self-sponsorship category do we encounter an over-representation of non-returnees. Eighty-two per cent of the non-returnees were wholly or partially self-sponsored—that is, paid their own way. In the total population, only 64 per cent were self-sponsored.[17]

The fact that such a large percentage of non-returning students are self-sponsored poses a thorny policy problem. These individuals are not subject to the leverage that can be applied if scholarship aid has been given. They are free agents, and it will be difficult to influence them to return to their countries of origin. And we might raise the question, if they pay their own way, should they not be entitled to remain or return as they wish? The answer will depend in large part on what position is taken regarding the "debt" to society associated with upbringing and early education.

To note the above relationship of non-return to self-sponsorship and return to sponsorship does not, however, lead to a policy conclusion that more individuals should be sponsored, although this is a possibility—a country might reap a higher economic reward by helping sponsor overseas study and by thus gaining leverage on the student's return than by letting him pay his own way. The wisdom of drawing such a policy conclusion from the data de-

TABLE 9—INTENT by SPONSOR: Percentage of non-returnee, returnee, undecided, and total male foreign students in the United States who are partially or totally sponsored in five ways[a]

	INTENT[b]			
SPONSOR	Non-return	Return	Undecided	Total
U.S. government				
Non-U.S. government	89.5	85.6	94.2	86.4
U.S. government	10.5	14.4	5.8	13.6
All sponsors[c]	100.0	100.0	100.0	100.0
Foreign government				
Non-foreign government	97.6	88.8	96.7	90.3
Foreign government	2.4	11.2	3.3	9.7
All sponsors[c]	100.0	100.0	100.0	100.0
U.S. University				
Non-U.S. university	81.6	72.8	67.8	74.0
U.S. university	18.4	27.2	32.2	26.0
All sponsors[c]	100.0	100.0	100.0	100.0
Private				
Non-private	91.9	83.6	90.7	84.9
Private	8.1	16.4	9.3	15.1
All sponsors[c]	100.0	100.0	100.0	100.0
Self				
Non-self	18.0	40.1	20.9	36.4
Self	82.0	59.9	79.1	63.6
All sponsors[c]	100.0	100.0	100.0	100.0

[a] Calculated from: IIE Census forms, Fall 1964.
[b] Excluded from the calculations are:
    NA INTENT only 13,290
    NA SPONSOR only 1,129
    NA INTENT and SPONSOR ... 9,260
[c] Base N figures are:
    Non-return 6,473
    Return 37,056
    Undecided 1,030
    Total 44,559

pends, among other things, on the quality of self-sponsored individuals who are non-returnees about which no judgment can be made on the basis of the IIE data. If non-returnees are of low quality, inducing return by investing more heavily is obviously unwise.

The relatively high figure for non-return among government-sponsored students, shown in Table 10, is not consistent with the low figures usually quoted. It is explained by the fact that the United States government supports refugees who will be remaining permanently in the United States. For instance, among Cuban students with United States government sponsorship, 79 per cent (481) are non-returnees (if non-respondents are excluded from the calculation). These 481 individuals represent approximately 5 per cent of the total non-returnee population.

The figures for return tell a slightly different story than the non-return percentages in Table 10. Self-sponsored students have a

TABLE 10—INTENT by SPONSOR: Percentage of foreign students who intend to remain permanently and who do not intend to remain permanently in the United States, males only[a]

	INTENT			
	NON-RETURN[b]		RETURN[c]	
SPONSOR	%	Base N	%	Base N
Self	18.7	28,337	60.8	36,536
U.S. government	11.1	6,063	73.9	7,206
U.S. university	10.3	11,594	66.8	15,069
Private	7.8	6,709	73.8	8,246
Foreign government	·3.6	4,326	74.3	5,566
All sponsored[d]	14.5	44,559	64.1	57,849

[a] Calculated from: IIE Census forms, Fall 1964.
[b] Excluded from the calculations are:
NA INTENT only 13,290
NA SPONSOR only 1,129
NA INTENT and SPONSOR ... 9,260
[c] Excluded from the calculations are:
NA SPONSOR 10,389
[d] Multiple response allowed.

low return rate, as expected. Foreign governments are relatively more successful than others in getting students they have sponsored to return home, but their success is not significantly greater than that of U.S. government or private sponsors. By looking at *return,* we can see that sponsorship by a U.S. university is less likely to induce return home than sponsorship by the U.S. government, even though *non-return* among that group is not significantly different than among U.S. government sponsored.

Non-return by Age (AGE)

As Table 11 shows, non-return is disproportionately high for students between the ages of 18 and 21; almost 30 per cent of the non-returnees are in this age bracket as compared with only 22 per cent of all students and 21 per cent of the returnees. Non-

TABLE 11—INTENT by AGE (M1): Distribution of categories of intended non-return across age groupings, foreign students in the United States, males only[a]

	Intent[b]			
Age	Non-return	Return	Undecided	Total
15–17	1.6	0.9	1.4	1.0
18–19	13.3	6.8	6.0	7.8
20–21	16.4	13.7	14.3	14.1
22–24	21.8	25.7	22.8	25.1
25–29	26.6	32.4	36.7	31.6
30–34	11.9	13.5	11.8	13.2
35–39	4.7	4.6	4.4	4.6
40–	3.7	2.4	2.6	2.6
All ages	100.0	100.0	100.0	100.0
Base N	6,323	36,354	1,012	43,689

[a] Calculated from: IIE Census forms, Fall 1964.
[b] Excluded from the calculations are:
    NA INTENT only 16,559
    NA AGE only 1,999
    NA INTENT and AGE 5,991

returnees are also slightly over-represented in the 35 and older ages. The greatest *number* of non-returning students is in the 25 to 29 age group, but as we will see from Table 12, that age-group also has the lowest *rate* of non-return.

TABLE 12—INTENT by AGE (M1): The percentages of foreign students who intend to remain permanently and who do not intend to remain permanently in the United States, males only[a]

| | INTENT | | | |
| | NON-RETURN[b] | | RETURN[c] | |
AGE	%	Base N	%	Base N
15–17	24.1	428	52.4	593
18–19	24.8	3,388	56.4	4,408
20–21	16.8	6,175	61.9	8,059
22–24	12.5	10,952	63.5	14,726
25–29	12.2	13,817	59.7	19,698
30–34	13.0	5,772	59.2	8,284
35–39	14.6	2,028	58.2	2,895
40–	21.0	1,129	54.6	1,585
All ages	14.5	43,689	60.3	60,248

[a] Calculated from: IIE Census forms, Fall 1964.
[b] Excluded from the calculations are:
  NA INTENT only 16,559
  NA AGE only 1,999
  NA INTENT and AGE 5,991
[c] Excluded from the calculations are:
  NA AGE 7,990

The rate of non-return within age-group drops steadily (Table 12, column 1) as we move from the 18–19 category through the 20–21 and 22–24 groups to the 25–29 category. Then the rate rises with each category through age 40–plus. Return rates (column 3) show the mirror pattern, but the turning point is earlier, after the 22–24 category. The high rates of non-return among younger and among older students gives us the same "U-shaped" relationship found with academic status.

The high rates of non-return for younger students support what has long been a rule of thumb—that if return home is desired, students should not be sent abroad at too early an age. They should have a chance to be firmly grounded in their own culture; they should have a maturity which most younger students lack. But non-return rates are also relatively high for the oldest students. These rates cannot properly be compared with those for younger students for the older group is composed of students who have already been in the United States for several years. Many of the students that arrived in the United States at the same time as the older students have now gone home leaving among the older group many who will be non-returnees. This selective return as time passes distorts calculations of non-return rates. One way of overcoming the complication is to classify students by their age at the time they began U.S. study rather than by their present age. When that is done, the tendency for high rates of non-return to be associated with younger students is even clearer.[18] However, until age is cross-tabulated with such variables as sponsorship, visa, academic status, and so forth, it would be presumptive to attribute the higher non-return rates among younger students only to their age.

Non-return by Length of Time since Study Began (TIME)

Logically, it would seem that the longer an individual remains a student in the United States, the more apt he would be to remain permanently. It can be difficult to recoup costs of a prolonged United States education if employment in the home country is accepted. Also, it is commonly believed that the longer an individual stays, the more apt he is to become involved in a professional situation specific to the United States (or best pursued in the United States), to educate himself out of a job at home, or to succumb to United States affluence. Both the distribution of TIME within Non-return (see Table 13, and the distribution of INTENT within each category of TIME (see Table 14) support these presumptions.

Students in their first two years of study are proportionately

TABLE 13—INTENT by TIME (M1): Distribution of categories of intended non-return across categories of time since studies began, foreign students in the United States, males only[a]

TIME[c]	INTENT[b]			
	Non-return	Return	Undecided	Total
1	29.7	39.1	23.0	37.3
2	19.5	23.7	19.3	23.0
3–4	27.4	24.9	32.2	25.4
5–6	13.3	8.6	15.1	9.5
7+	10.1	3.7	10.4	4.8
All times	100.0	100.0	100.0	100.0
Base N	6,427	35,499	995	42,921

[a] Calculated from: IIE Census forms, Fall 1964.
[b] Excluded from the calculations are:
      NA INTENT only 11,372
      NA TIME only 2,767
      NA INTENT and TIME 11,178
[c] Years since study began.

TABLE 14—INTENT by TIME (M1): The percentages of foreign students who intend to remain permanently and who do not intend to remain permanently in the United States, males only[a]

TIME[b]	INTENT			
	NON-RETURN[c]		RETURN[d]	
	%	Base N	%	Base N
1	11.9	16,028	69.0	20,131
2	12.7	9,859	67.3	12,496
3–4	16.1	10,914	63.7	13,875
5–6	21.1	4,057	59.0	5,165
7+	31.6	2,063	49.8	2,626
All times	15.0	42,921	65.4	54,293

[a] Calculated from: IIE Census forms, Fall 1964.
[b] Years since study began.
[c] Excluded from the calculations are:
      NA INTENT only 11,372
      NA TIME only 2,767
      NA INTENT and TIME 11,178
[d] Excluded from the calculations are:
      NA TIME 13,945

under-represented among non-returnees, and those going beyond two years are over-represented (see Table 13). There is a steady increase in the rate of non-return as the length of time in the United States increases (see Table 14). Whether the stay is one or two years does not seem to make much difference. Extension from a two-year stay to a three- or four-year stay brings a somewhat greater jump in the non-return rate. However, the average number of years since study began is only slightly over two years. TIME, like AGE, is subject to problems of a shifting percentage base, as selective return occurs and the increases in later years therefore contain an upward bias of unknown magnitude. The steady increase of non-return with length of stay does not justify a causal interpretation. We know that length of stay is associated with non-return, but we do not know that *because* students take a longer period to complete their studies their propensity to remain permanently increases.

NON-RETURN BY VISA (VISA)

Only 11 per cent of all males answering the query on INTENT held immigrant visas, but 53 per cent of the non-returnees held immigrant visas, as seen in Table 15. Also over-represented among the non-returnees are those with visas labeled "Other." Unfortunately, this residual category was not well drawn; it includes both immigrants with irregular status (such as parolees and refugees) and assorted non-immigrant-visa holders (such as those with military, diplomatic, trainee, and temporary visitor visas). However, in general, the category falls in the immigrant class. Of the 615 male non-returnees with "other" visas, 433 are Cuban refugees. Another group of 40 individuals is from China or Hong Kong. In effect, the residual category seems to pick up non-returnees whose major reason for remaining is political.

Although the F- and J-visa categories are under-represented when non-returnees are compared with all males, it is surprising

TABLE 15—INTENT by VISA (M1): Distribution of categories of intended non-return across categories of visa held, foreign students in the United States, males only[a]

	INTENT[b]			
VISA	Non-return	Return	Undecided	Total
F (student)	36.6	76.4	71.4	70.3
Immigrant	52.8	2.8	21.7	10.7
J (exchangee)	1.0	16.9	1.9	14.2
Other[c]	9.6	3.9	5.0	4.8
All visas	100.0	100.0	100.0	100.0
Base N	6,401	35,722	1,000	43,123

[a] Calculated from: IIE Census forms, Fall 1964.
[b] Excluded from the calculations are:

      NA INTENT only 10,597
      NA VISA only 2,565
      NA INTENT and VISA 11,953

[c] See footnote 10, chapter 3, for coding of VISA.

that such a large number (2,406) did intend to stay even though a visa change would be necessary. Another 733 individuals in these two categories were undecided about remaining. F- and J-visa holders dominated the distribution of undecided individuals in the VISA categories.

More than one-third of the declared non-returnees are F-visa holders, but only 8 per cent of the F-visa holders are non-returnees (see Table 16). Taken alone, this rate of non-return is relatively modest. However, there is no way of knowing how many of the present immigrant-visa holders were formerly F-visa students.

According to the IIE census, non-return among J-visa holders is extremely low. And the J-visa seems to perform its task of inducing return as indicated by the extremely high 82% return figure. But in spite of the low non-return rate among J-visa holders, figures presented here do not provide a strong argument for one side or the other in the continuing debate over extension of

TABLE 16—INTENT by VISA (M1): The percentages of foreign students who intend to remain permanently and who do not intend to remain permanently in the United States, males only[a]

	INTENT			
	NON-RETURN[b]		RETURN[c]	
VISA	%	Base N	%	Base N
F (student)	7.7	30,333	71.3	38,267
Immigrant	73.3	4,614	19.0	5,348
J (exchangee)	1.0	6,121	82.2	7,351
Other[d]	29.9	2,055	50.5	2,754
All visas	14.8	43,123	66.5	53,720

[a] Calculated from: IIE Census forms, Fall 1964.
[b] Excluded from the calculations are:
    NA INTENT only 10,597
    NA VISA only 2,565
    NA INTENT and VISA 11,953
[c] Excluded from the calculations are:
    NA VISA 14,518
[d] See footnote 10, chapter 3.

the J-visa to all students as a means of insuring return home. First, there is no way of knowing the extent to which the legal requirement to return that the J-visa carries influenced the respondents' expressions of intent. Second, it may be that the strong relationship between J-visa status and return can be accounted for largely in terms of the conditions of study or sponsorship usually associated with the visa rather than in terms of the visa status, *per se*. Other evidence suggests that changing the visa requirement would have only a slight impact on non-return (see chapter 7).

SUMMARY

The overall rate of intended non-return among foreign students in the United States, defined in terms of students' citizenship and determined from the Institute of International Education Annual

Census of Foreign Students, 1964/65, is approximately 16 per cent.[19] This is probably a low estimate. Non-return for all females seems to be higher (19 per cent) than for all males (15 per cent). However, as is evident from the variation in non-return rates among several sub-populations of male students, global rates such as those cited for all students, all females, or all males, have very little meaning.

Among male foreign students, intended non-return varies only slightly with broad field of study; medicine, the humanities, and engineering are fields with the highest non-return rates. Significantly different is the low rate of non-return among agricultural students. Within the broad fields, there are major differences in non-return rates by subfields.

Undergraduate and doctorate-level students appear more likely to remain in the United States permanently than masters-degree students. Non-return rates are highest among students under 20 years of age and over 40. In intermediate ages, rates do not differ greatly. As is only logical, the longer a student has been in the United States, the more apt he is to remain permanently. The substantial and unknown biases operating for both age and length of stay as they are related to non-return make interpretation difficult. Finally, intended non-return is greater among self-sponsored students and immigrant-visa holders than among sponsored students and F (student) visa or J (exchangee) visa holders. The rate of non-return is very low among J-visa holders (1 per cent).

Causal inference from the above correlations is not justified. Associated conditions of study and associated patterns of student characteristics must be partialed out (as will be done in chapter 7 for one student group). And while the general scale of non-return rates within each of the classifications established appears to have value for making comparisons, the non-return rates should not be viewed as representing *the* rate of non-return for each category.

Omitted from consideration in chapter 3 has been discussion of variation in rates of non-return by country. The country variable is explored separately and in some detail in chapter 4.

NOTES

[1] The analysis also serves as a backdrop against which the analysis of Peruvian student non-return in chapter 7 can be viewed.

[2] Taken directly from the instructions mailed out by IIE.

[3] The variety of organizational structures among institutions participating in the census makes it almost impossible to standardize reporting procedures. In some cases there is no foreign student advisor specifically assigned to keeping track of foreign students. Some census forms are filled out directly by students, some by administrators, and some by secretaries copying information from registration records. It is not surprising that information is missing for many individuals, particularly in those cases where institutions filled out census cards for individuals. Still, the per cent responding is well within the respectable range accepted in most social scientific investigations, and the direction, if not the magnitude, of bias is known.

[4] Names of institutions surveyed have been obtained by the IIE from Part III (Higher Education) of the *Education Directory*, of the U.S. Office of Education: *Lovejoy's College Guide, Directory of Catholic Colleges and Schools* in the U.S.; reports of accrediting agencies; and previous surveys of the IIE.

[5] For instance, the author discovered that the relatively new Elbert Covell College of the University of the Pacific had been omitted in the 1965/66 IIE census. The University of the Pacific entry in the census was for only 13 foreign students, but the *Hearings on the International Education Act* listed 111 foreign students at Covell College, by name (U.S. Senate, Committee on Labor and Public Welfare, Subcommittee on Education, *Hearings on S.2874, International Education Act*, 89th Congress, 2nd Session, 1966, p. 585).

[6] An underestimate of 10 to 20 per cent is indicated by the author's work and by Paul Ritterband's recent study of Israeli non-returnees.

[7] IIE; *Open Doors,* 1965, p. 14.

[8] Not answering on visa were 3,596 individuals (4.1 per cent); not answering on intent were 13,181 individuals (14.9 per cent); not answering on both visa and intent were 15,069 (17.0 per cent).

[9] The critical appraisal, reworking of data, and analysis of non-return could not have been done without the cooperation of the Institute of International Education. What is presented in the following pages is not necessarily in accordance with the opinions of the IIE and any errors in reworking and interpreting the data are my responsibility.

[10] *Visa* categories used in the recoding were:
No Answer (included ambiguous and multiple answers)
Students (included: F; F-1; F-2; I-20; I-20A; I-94; and "student")
Exchangees (included: J; DS-666; P-I, P-II, P-III followed by a number; G-I, G-II, G-III followed by a number; "exchange visitor"; "exchange student")

Immigrants (included: Any visa letter K through Z; "immigrant"; "emigrant"; first preference; I-151; Bill number; "permanent," "resident," or combination; "permanent work")

Other (included: Any visa letter A through I (excluding E); NATO; MAAG ID card; Waiver; Special; Diplomat; Passport; Parolee; Docket Supervision; ITO; Tourist; exile refugee; service; military)

Intent to remain permanently was taken from the question, "Do you plan to remain in the U.S. permanently? Yes___ No___." If an individual wrote in "I am not sure" or "Undecided" or placed a question mark, he was placed in the undecided category on Intent.

[11] For the new frequency distributions as compared with the IIE *Open Doors* distributions, see Myers, "Study Abroad and the Migration of Human Resources," Appendix IV.

[12] See, for instance, *The Foreign Student: Immigrant or Exchangee? A Statement Prepared by the Committee on Educational Interchange Policy,* Institute of International Education (New York, May 1958), p. 3.

This pamphlet gives a figure of 10 per cent for IIE-sponsored individuals. The figure has been generalized to all foreign students and has served as a rule-of-thumb for several years.

[13] The eight countries and their percentages are: Canada (13.9), Cuba (12.5), Germany (5.2), The United Kingdom (5.0), Iran (4.4), China Republic (3.9), India (3.4), and China-unspecified (3.1). Base N equals 9,614.

[14] According to the figures presented in the Immigration and Naturalization Service's *Annual Indicator,* Fiscal Year 1968, p. 39, the rate of adjustment was 6.4 per cent (adjustments to admissions; H-1, H-3, J-1, and F-1 visas combined) for the four year period 1964–1968.

[15] Countries with over 40 per cent not answering the question of intended residence are: British West Indies, 84 per cent (Base N = 25); Rumania, 82 per cent (27); China-unspecified, 66 per cent (1,716); U.S.S.R., 61 per cent (28); Hungary, 56 per cent (101); Yugoslavia, 53 per cent (162); Poland, 50 per cent (126); Israel, 47 per cent (1,271); Argentina, 46 per cent (521); United Arab Republic, 45 per cent (1,122); Haiti, 42 per cent (169); Iceland, 42 per cent (106); Cuba, 42 per cent (1,874); Belgium, 42 per cent (194); Italy, 41 per cent (550); Austria, 41 per cent (132); West Germany, 41 per cent (1,375); France, 40 per cent (607); and Switzerland, 40 per cent (231).

[16] If females had been included, the humanities would have jumped dramatically to become the field with the most non-returning foreign students. Over 40 per cent of the female non-returnees were studying in the humanities.

[17] The reader will notice that when the percentage of students sponsored by the U.S. government (10.5) is added to the percentages sponsored by foreign governments (2.4), U.S. universities (18.4), private organizations (8.1) and self (82.0), the total is well over 100 per cent. Some individuals have more than one source of funds.

[18] 30,112 students answered the questions about age *and* length of stay *and* permanent ersidence. Using slightly different age categories from those adopted in my analysis, Richard Levich calculated the following rates of non-return by age when U.S. study began: age 18 or below, 27; ages 19/20, 20; ages 21/22, 13; ages 23/24, 11; ages 25/26, 10; ages 27/28, 10; ages

29 and above, 12. Richard Levich, "An Analysis of Expected Loss from Foreign Student Non-Return," unpublished paper, Chicago: The University of Chicago, Department of Economics, May 1969, p. 15.

[19] Of the 121,300 students included in the IIE census of 1968/69, 34 per cent did not answer the question of permanent residence. Of those who did answer, 23 per cent said they intended to remain, a significant increase over the 16 per cent figure for 1964/65. See IIE, *Open Doors*, 1969, p. 10.

4

CROSS-NATIONAL COMPARISONS OF FOREIGN STUDENT NON-RETURN

The number and percentage of students abroad who decide to remain abroad varies from country to country, and behind the academic rationale of wanting to discover the reason for this is a normative question as to the extent to which nations are "losing" or "gaining" because of non-return, both absolutely and relatively. One approach to both sets of questions is a macro approach, utilizing cross-national comparisons. The broad-brush treatment of cross-national comparison has the virtue of simplicity but carries the ever-present dangers of over-simplification and possible distortion. The degree of credence afforded macro studies is partly a matter of taste and partly a matter of the manner in which the macro-analysis is carried out.

In this chapter, several methods will be used to look at non-return cross-nationally. First, countries will be compared using an index of non-return calculated by relating the number of non-returnees to the total number of students in the United States (determined from the IIE foreign student survey). Next an index of manpower loss will be developed relating the number of non-returnees (again from IIE data) to the total number of nationals being trained in the home country, in the United States and in third countries. Finally, emigration through non-return will be juxtaposed with the ability of a country to absorb high-level manpower, as represented by the relationship between per capita income and student enrollments at the third level.

A CROSS-NATIONAL COMPARISON, USING AN INDEX OF INTENDED NON-RETURN

CALCULATING THE INDEX

A variety of foreign student non-return rates could be calculated for each country with IIE census data, depending on the definition of foreign student adopted and on the assumptions made about the distribution of non-respondents to the question of permanent residence. (See Appendix I.) The same caveats discussed in chapter 3 for global rates of non-return pertain to estimating rates for individual countries. But, defining "foreign student" in terms of citizenship, as has been done for this analysis, poses more of a problem at the country level than it does in the aggregate, where the primary distinction is only United States or non-United States citizenship. Problems of third-country residence enter. In this analysis, a Chinese citizen who was resident in Indonesia (or elsewhere) before studying in the United States is counted as Chinese. Following the IIE, the particular problem of two Chinas has been handled by dividing the population into two groups: Taiwanese and Chinese—unspecified. Except for this distinction, no attempt is made to incorporate residence into the country definition.

Non-response is handled by assuming that non-respondents will be distributed proportionately among the return, non-return, and undecided categories of INTENT. This procedure adjusts for the differential bias introduced by variation in the magnitude of non-response from country to country. The undecided category might have been similarly treated, but because there is no indication of the direction undecided individuals are most apt to go in making their decision to remain permanently or return, and because the category is small, they are included in the tabulations as part of the rate base. In effect, this groups all undecided individuals with returnees. The conservative nature of this procedure is consistent with the general tendency for rates of non-return to be under-estimated.

The rate of non-return which serves as the index of intended non-return is calculated as follows:

$$\frac{\text{Non-return}}{\text{Non-return} + \text{Return} + \text{Undecided}}$$

The actual rates of non-return calculated in this manner for each country are apt to be less accurate than the rank order of rates. A rate presented here should not be interpreted as *the* rate of non-return for a particular country. In order to compare rates, however, it is only necessary to make the assumption that differen-tial bias from non-response has been adequately taken into ac-count by excluding non-respondents and to assume that the remaining bias is relatively constant across countries. The second assumption is necessitated by the potential discrepancy between expressed intention and eventual behavior. It seems plausible to assume that people do not vary significantly from country to country in the degree to which they give inaccurate answers.[1] The fact that individuals have the option not to respond makes this a plausible assumption, but there will, of course, be exceptions.

RANKING THE COUNTRIES

Table 17 presents a listing of countries [2] arranged by rate of non-return among male students. Please keep in mind that the IIE data are for 1964–65. Several patterns are apparent from a simple inspection of the table:

1. The countries with the highest rates of non-return are those within the Communist bloc of nations; of the top twelve countries, nine are definitely in the Communist political camp. Many of the individuals from these nations are, in fact, political refugees, and it is this rather than residence in a Communist nation which no

ranking of countries by an index of non-return among
students in the United States, 1964, males only[a]

RANK	COUNTRY[b]	PERCENT-AGE NON-RETURN	TOTAL MALE STUDENTS	No ANSWER	BASE N (TOTAL—NA)
1	Estonia	100.0	8	5	3
2	Portuguese Guinea	100.0	1	0	1
3	Latvia	95.8	35	11	24
4	Rumania	80.0	27	22	5
5	Hungary	79.6	101	57	44
6	Stateless[c]	76.8	249	98	151
7	Cuba[d]	75.3	1,874	783	1,091
8	Lithuania	75.0	10	2	8
9	Poland	60.3	126	63	63
10	British West Indies	50.0	25	21	4
11	Czechoslovakia	50.0	19	11	8
12	Bulgaria	50.0	10	6	4
13	Netherlands	43.5	453	163	290
14	Germany	38.3	1,357	550	807
15	China (unspecified)[e]	35.5	1,716	1,133	583
16	Yugoslavia	35.5	162	86	76
17	Ireland	35.4	244	83	161
18	Italy	33.8	550	227	323
19	Haiti	30.6	169	71	98
20	Austria	29.5	132	54	78
21	Macao	28.6	11	4	7
22	United Kingdom	27.1	1,802	624	1,178

[a] Calculated from: IIE Census forms, Fall 1964.
[b] Excluded from the calculations are:
    NA Country 4
[c] Stateless are those who indicated no citizenship. They are not the same as No Answer individuals.
[d] Includes a large percentage who are refugees.
[e] Chinese citizenship was indicated but was not specifically attached to Taiwan or to the People's Republic.

TABLE 17—*Continued*

Rank	Country[b]	Percent-age Non-return	Total male students	No Answer	Base N (Total−NA)
23	Denmark	26.9	129	51	78
24	Finland	25.8	107	41	66
25	Bolivia	25.7	248	65	183
26	Swaziland	25.0	8	0	8
27	Luxembourg	25.0	7	3	4
28	Portugal	24.6	102	33	69
29	El Salvador	24.5	188	41	147
30	Switzerland	23.9	231	93	138
31	Western Samoa	23.8	31	10	21
32	Norway	22.6	405	122	283
33	French Oceania	22.2	16	7	9
34	Malta, Gozo	22.2	11	2	9
35	Spain	21.7	357	131	226
36	Argentina	21.6	521	238	283
37	Dominican Republic	20.6	165	58	107
38	Bermuda	20.3	67	8	59
39	British Honduras	20.0	47	7	40
40	Bahrain	20.0	5	0	5
41	France	19.9	607	245	362
42	Mexico	18.8	1,145	303	842
43	Belgium	18.6	194	81	113
44	Sweden	18.6	179	55	124
45	Guatemala	18.0	206	50	156
46	Honduras	17.9	145	39	106
47	Iran	17.8	3,445	1,313	2,132
48	Leeward Islands	17.5	63	23	40
49	Netherlands Antilles	17.3	68	16	52
50	Barbados	17.0	79	20	59
51	Fiji	16.0	58	8	50

TABLE 17—*Continued*

Rank	Country[b]	Percent-age non-return	Total male students	No Answer	Base N (Total—NA)
52	Panama	15.9	406	91	315
53	Canada[f]	15.8	7,978	2,157	5,821
54	Peru	15.7	613	193	420
55	Greece	15.5	1,296	501	795
56	Hong Kong	15.4	2,376	808	1,568
57	Tonga	15.4	54	15	39
58	Colombia	15.2	1,020	395	625
59	Ecuador	15.0	324	104	220
60	Nicaragua	14.4	236	56	180
61	Syria	14.3	424	159	265
62	Surinam	14.3	16	9	7
63	Costa Rica	14.1	219	63	156
64	Ceylon	14.0	76	26	50
65	Jordan	14.0	645	203	442
66	Uruguay	13.6	58	14	44
67	Chile	13.3	387	146	241
68	Israel	13.0	1,271	594	677
69	Cyprus	12.7	131	52	79
70	Taiwan	11.7	3,428	1,016	2,412
71	Windward Islands	11.5	69	17	52
72	Iraq	11.4	846	274	572
73	Burma	11.3	110	39	71
74	Union of South Africa	11.2	351	119	232
75	Korea	11.0	2,067	752	1,315
76	Lebanon	10.8	665	200	465
77	British Guiana	10.7	277	44	233
78	Trinidad	10.2	446	84	362
79	Bahama Islands	9.5	85	22	63
80	Paraguay	9.4	47	15	32
81	Turkey	9.1	889	353	536
82	U.S.S.R.	9.1	28	17	11

[f] Includes one individual from Newfoundland.

TABLE 17—*Continued*

Rank	Country[b]	Percent- age Non- return	Total male students	No Answer	Base N (Total—NA)
83	Philippines	8.8	1,144	373	771
84	Venezuela	8.8	1,040	314	726
85	New Zealand	8.7	176	61	115
86	Brazil	8.2	528	172	356
87	Iceland	8.0	43	18	25
88	Japan	7.6	2,473	861	1,612
89	Australia	7.5	554	166	388
90	United Arab Republic	7.5	1,122	505	617
91	India	7.2	6,136	1,991	4,145
92	Jamaica	7.1	756	177	579
93	Malaysia[g]	6.8	415	98	317
94	Mozambique	6.7	19	4	15
95	Saudi Arabia	5.6	566	140	426
96	Vietnam	5.4	235	69	166
97	Kuwait	4.8	215	70	145
98	Angola	4.4	25	2	23
99	Tunisia	4.4	72	27	45
100	Rhodesia	4.3	186	22	164
101	Morocco	3.9	73	22	51
102	Ghana	3.7	256	66	190
103	Laos	3.7	32	5	27
104	Thailand	3.6	1,168	323	845
105	Liberia	2.9	235	60	175
106	Pakistan	2.9	980	232	748
107	Indonesia	2.8	635	167	468
108	Pacific Islands	2.7	119	8	111
109	Somalia	2.5	99	20	79
110	Ethiopia	2.3	226	52	174
111	Cambodia	2.2	202	21	181
112	Libya	2.1	72	24	48
113	Afghanistan	1.9	146	38	108
114	Guinea	1.8	87	30	57

[g] Includes "Malayan Federation" respondents (5).

TABLE 17—*Continued*

Rank	Country[b]	Percent- age Non- return	Total male students	No Answer	Base N (Total—NA)
115	Sudan	1.7	174	54	120
116	Nigeria	1.6	1,256	298	958
117	Zambia	1.6	77	13	64
118	Congo— Leopoldville	1.4	90	20	70
119	Sierra Leone	· 1.3	96	19	77
120	Tanzania	1.0	234	41	193
121	Ryukyu Islands	0.9	128	14	114
122	Kenya	0.4	662	111	551
123	Uganda	....	189	43	146
124	Cameroon	....	86	16	70
125	Algeria	....	81	32	49
126	Malawi	....	77	9	68
127	Nepal	....	75	15	60
128	Togo	....	37	8	29
129	Ivory Coast	....	17	5	12
130	Zanzibar	....	17	2	15
131	Malagasy Republic	....	16	2	14
132	Congo— Brazzaville	....	15	7	8
133	Gambia	....	12	2	10
134	Yemen	....	12	1	11
135	Basutoland	....	11	1	10
136	Aden	....	9	1	8
137	Mauritius	....	9	2	7
138	Dahomey	....	8	1	7
139	Martinique	....	6	2	4
140	Mali	....	6	1	5
141	Burundi	....	5	0	5
142	South West Africa	....	5	1	4
143	Qatar	....	4	1	3
144	Upper Volta	....	4	1	3

TABLE 17—*Concluded*

Rank	Country[b]	Percent-age Non-return	Total male students	No Answer	Base N (Total—NA)
145	Tibet	....	3	0	3
146	Bechuanaland	....	3	0	3
147	French West Africa	....	3	3	0
148	Rwanda	....	2	0	2
149	Seychelles	....	2	2	0
150	Niger	....	2	0	2
151	Chad	....	2	1	1
152	French Equatorial Africa	....	2	2	0
153	Gabon	....	1	0	1
154	Monaco	....	1	1	0
155	Indochina	....	1	0	1
156	Guadeloupe	....	1	0	1
157	Bhutan	....	1	0	1
158	Trucial Oman	....	1	0	1
159	Latin America (unspecified)	....	1	1	0
160	Africa (unspecified)	....	1	1	0

doubt underlies non-return. This perspective makes the presence of the category Stateless among the top twelve listings plausible. Nor is it difficult to imagine non-return associated with political refuge from Portuguese Guinea. Of the top twelve countries for male non-return, this leaves only the British West Indies as seemingly out of place (for which notice the high percentage nonresponse and the small base number).

In addition to a heavy loading with Western European nations, the second group of twelve countries listed includes four which resemble those in the first set above. Yugoslavia falls in the Communist group. Haiti is a police state from which political refuge might be desired. China (unspecified) and Macao, it may be

hypothesized, are heavily loaded with politically displaced or dis-
enchanted individuals. (Such speculations, however, move beyond these data.)

2. Countries with high rates of non-return tend to be European.
Eighteen of the top 24 countries are European (Eastern European and Balkan nations as well as Western Europe and Scandi-
navian states). Unless Turkey (ranked 81st) and Iceland (ranked
87th) are considered European, the lowest European nation in
the list is Greece, ranking 55th, with a non-return rate of 15.5.
The next lowest is Sweden, ranking 44th, with a non-return rate
of 18.6. With the exception of Turkey and Iceland, European nations fall in the top one-half of the ranking, or, adding Greece to
the exceptions, in the top one-third. Consequently the ranking
supports the repeated statements that "brain drains" are largely
from the "advanced European" nations.

A great deal of attention has been given to the United Kingdom's flow of talent to the United States. Less has been said about
the flights of German talent; however, Germany appears higher
on the list than the United Kingdom. It may be that the German
figure is partially accounted for by either "German" students
whose residence was other than Germany (that is, who moved
from Germany at an early age) or by children of refugees from
East Germany or Eastern Europe whose roots in Western Germany were not deep.[3]

The appearance of France so high in the list is somewhat surprising. A general presumption has been that non-return among
French students is low, which is true in relation to United Kingdom or German non-return, but not when compared with all
nations.

3. Progressing beyond the top twenty-four countries, the pattern becomes less clear. In the second group of twenty-four countries, European nations continue to appear frequently (there are
nine, including Malta as European), and Latin American countries begin to appear regularly (there are nine). In addition, this

set includes the first sub-Saharan country (Swaziland), the first two Middle Eastern states (Bahrain and Iran), and three Pacific Islands. Of these last seven, only Iran has a large number of students in the United States.

4. Generally, Latin American and Caribbean countries are higher in the list than Asian or African countries, especially Haiti (ranked 19th) and Bolivia (ranked 25th); in view of the political and economic situation, this high rate is not surprising. The persistent complaint that Argentina loses large numbers of high-level individuals to the United States is supported by the figures presented here.[4]

5. Non-European but "Western" developed countries fall lower in the list than European nations. Canada, with a rate of 15.8 (ranked 53rd), New Zealand, with a rate of 8.7 (ranked 85th), and Australia, with a rate of 7.5 (ranked 89th) are relatively low in the scale.

6. Several countries which are reputed to have high rates of non-return fall quite low in the list. Taiwan, with a rate of only 11.7 (ranked 70th), Korea, with a rate of 11.0 (ranked 75th), the Philippines, with a rate of 8.8 (ranked 83rd), and India, with a rate of 7.2 (ranked 91st), are all lower than might have been expected. In fact, Far Eastern countries generally place lower in the ranking than hypothesized by the author. This may be a reflection of the limited validity of INTENT as a measure of non-return. It might be a reflection of the stereotypic desire to keep up appearances, which in this case means maintaining the fiction of return home. It might also be a reflection of the tendency of Foreign Student Advisors and others to look at absolute rather than relative numbers of non-returning students when judging non-return. The four countries last mentioned all send large numbers of students and rank near the top in total number of non-returning students.

The statistics presented here do little to illuminate the return rate for Chinese students. Neither the Taiwanese rate nor that for Unspecified China can be defended as being particularly meaningful. It is interesting, however, that the IIE procedure of separating the two produces such a discrepancy in rates.

Middle Eastern nations also fall lower in the list than might be expected. The only one that appears to follow the anticipated pattern is Iran; while high among Middle Eastern nations and in absolute numbers of non-returnees, it is well down in the ranking. Israel's non-return rate of 13 is probably an underestimate; notice the high rate of non-response among Israelis.

7. African countries typically have non-return rates below 5. The only exceptions are Swaziland, with a rate of 25.0, South Africa, with a rate of 11.2, and Mozambique, with a rate of 6.7.

The interested reader will undoubtedly examine the ranking of countries to see how particular countries stand in relation to his own preconceptions. However, the individual rates are less important than their relative standing. Although one may question the validity of the absolute rates of non-return for individual countries, the main purpose in establishing the index was to be able to make cross-national comparisons.

CROSS-NATIONAL COMPARISONS

As a consequence of the above, it was logical to presume that, with European nations at the top of the list and African nations at the bottom, the non-return index would correlate nicely with conventional country indexes of economic development. With the Communist political bloc at the top and the new African nations loading the bottom, there was a similar expectation for matching a political indicator with non-return (although the particular political indicator of relationship was not obvious).

These logical presumptions were checked by making a series of scattergrams, plotting the index of non-return against various economic and political indicators.[5] Economic indicators used were: per capita Gross National Product, percentage of total population who are wage and salary workers, and percentage of the labor force engaged in agriculture.[6] The relationship between non-return and these economic indicators is very loose. For instance, the zero-order correlation between non-return and per-capita income was .59 ($R^2 = .35$) for the 96 countries included. The correlation was pushed upward by a tight fit at the lower income levels, giving way to a much broader scatter of non-return rates among countries with higher per capita incomes. (See Appendix II for countries used and for income levels.)

Consistently deviant were Haiti, Yugoslavia, and Bolivia, with high non-return rates but low indexes for economic development; and New Zealand and Australia, with a low rate of non-return but relatively high positions on the scales of economic development.

The political indicators explored were taken from a factor analysis by Banks and Gregg [7] of the political indices in Banks and Textor's *A Cross-Polity Survey*.[8] Banks and Gregg grouped political systems according to five factors which they labeled polyarchic, elitist, centrist, personalist, and traditional. The only factor that seemed to provide a logical hypothesis for the present analysis was the one labeled "elitist." Loading high on the elitist factor were "recently independent states," where "relatively small 'modernizing elites' are attempting to bring about rapid and radical social change in the face of impressive cultural resistance of an essentially 'parochial' character that remains as a carry-over from the colonial period." [9] At the other end of the elitist scale were nations with fairly well-established systems in which change is not radical and swift (and in which there is presumably less political opportunity). The hypothesis guiding exploration of this particular index was that non-return would be highest where change was slowest and where there was presumably less opportunity for political involvement. The correlation between elitism, so defined, and non-return rates was relatively high: $-.75$ ($R^2 = .56$) for 105 nations. New African nations load heavily on elitism and have low rates of non-return; European nations and higher rates of non-return are at the other end of the scale. (See Appendix II for countries and factor loadings.)

Several other variables were checked for possible relationship to non-return. Presumably nations with the most highly developed educational systems would be the highest exporters of talent. They are not only able to train more people in the prerequisite skills for study abroad but they are also apt to have educated individuals to fill the high-level positions at home. To check this assumption, non-return rates were correlated with the Harbison and Myers composite educational index which purports to rank countries by the degree of their human resource development.[10] No clear relationship emerged. The zero-order correlation was .49 (R^2 = .25) for 66 countries. (See Appendix II for countries and composite education index values.)

It was further hypothesized that non-return would be highest for those countries having the highest general rate of immigration to the United States. If student non-return parallels immigration, then non-return is not as unique a form of migration as it might seem to be. Associated with this hypothesis is the possibility that student non-return is related to the pulling power represented by prior migration. A sample scattergram of non-return by total immigration suggests that non-return rates are not related to gross immigration. (See Appendix II for 1955–1964 immigration figures.) [11]

When a check was made to see how the index of non-return compared with visa adjustment, so often used as an alternative definition of non-return,[12] there was no relationship. However, a similar comparison using a Spearman rank correlation for 38 non-Latin American countries was done by Michel Hervé, and resulted in a coefficient of .77. When only quota countries are considered, the relationship between the non-return index and visa adjustment does seem to hold, lending credence to the general validity of the index.[13]

Regression Analyses

To check for more complex relationships, 64 countries for which data were available were selected from the original 158 countries.

(See Appendix III for a listing of countries included.) The following study conditions and country characteristics were used in multiple regression analysis against non-return as the dependent variable:

Conditions of study:

1. The percentage of undergraduate male students in the United States from each country
2. The percentage of self-sponsored male students in the United States from each country
3. The percentage of F-visa male students in the United States from each country
4. The percentage of male students over thirty years of age in the United States from each country [14]

Country characteristics:

5. Per capita income
6. A composite educational index
7. Political elitism [15]

Education (E), income (I), and political elitism (P) indexes were treated as dummy variables. In addition, income and education were cross-tabulated, and each interaction was treated as a dummy in a joint education-income variable (EI). Table 18 presents the variables, the number of cases for each dummy variable, the multiple R^2 for each regression run, the F value, and the regression coefficients of the various items in each equation.

Zero-order correlations for these 64 countries are presented in the final column of Table 18. Education, income, and political indicators each correlate with non-return, but the correlations are not high, as might have been predicted from the scattergrams.

Zero-order correlations for conditions of study by non-return were also run for all 158 countries, providing a check on the sample of 64. From a comparison of the two sets of correlation coefficients (see Table 19), it is evident that choosing countries

TABLE 18—A summary of regression results, non-return by selected country characteristics and conditions of study, 64 countries[a]

VARIABLE NAME	N	REGRESSION NUMBER							
		(1)	(2)	(3)	(4)	(5)	(6)	(7)	(8)
		CARDINAL VARIABLES							
STATUS	64								
SPONSOR	64								
VISA	64								
AGE	64								
NON-RETURN	64								
EDUCATION	64								
INCOME PER CAPITA	64								
POLITICAL ELITISM	64								
		DUMMY VARIABLES[b]							
Education (E)$_1$	17	....		....			....		....
E$_2$	16	5.72		0.04			2.32		− 1.76
E$_3$	18	18.93		4.67			12.83		− 1.40
E$_4$	13	14.46		− 4.59			7.66		− 8.53
Inc. per cap. (I)$_1$	13		....	....				....	....
I$_2$	22		9.13	8.06				6.10	6.31
I$_3$	16		23.78	22.10				19.22	20.48
I$_4$	13		20.02	22.77				14.22	20.49

142

	N	(1)	(2)	(3)	(4)	(5)	(6)	(7)	(8)
E_1I_1	10				....				
E_1I_2	7				7.79				
E_2I_1	13				− 0.48				
E_2I_2	10				6.78				
E_2I_3	3				26.02				
E_3I_2	5				15.01				
E_3I_3	10				28.78				
E_3I_4	3				17.65				
E_1I_3	3				7.72				
E_1I_4	10				20.47				
Pol. elitism $(P)_1$	33					14.49	10.47	9.24	9.54
P_2	18					....	....	....	....
P_3	6					− 0.86	1.34	3.31	4.09
R^2		.195	.263	.289	.330	.190	.254	.306	.333
F		4.85	7.18	3.86	2.95	7.15	3.96	5.12	3.43
Constant		8.51	4.94	4.93	5.05	10.67	6.75	2.90	2.83

[a] Calculated from: IIE Census forms, Fall 1964. See Appendix II for listing of countries.
[b] See Appendix III for description of variables.

TABLE 18—Continued

		REGRESSION NUMBER							MEAN	ZERO-ORDER CORRELATION
VARIABLE NAME	N	(9)	(10)	(11)	(12)	(13)	(14)	(15)	(16)	(17)
					CARDINAL VARIABLES					
STATUS	64		0.22				0.20	0.13	47	.07
SPONSOR	64			0.32			0.48	0.61	37	.45
VISA	64				− 0.23		− 0.49	− 0.59	57	−.35
AGE	64					0.30	0.39	0.40	27	.26
NON-RETURN	64								18	
EDUCATION	64								—	.30
INCOME PER CAPITA	64								—	.39
POLITICAL ELITISM	64								—	−.40
					DUMMY VARIABLES[b]					
Education (E)$_1$	17								28	−.35
E$_2$	16								23	−.12
E$_3$	18								25	.32
E$_4$	13								23	.16
Inc. per cap. (I)$_1$	13								20	−.39
I$_2$	22								34	−.17
I$_3$	16								22	.33
I$_4$	13								23	.23

144

Variable[b]									
E_1I_1	10	...	...	...	...	...	...	16	−.33
E_1I_2	7	6.25	4.69	0.37	7.49	5.11	2.93	12	−.11
E_2I_1	13	− 0.80	3.61	−10.70	3.66	− 2.42	− 4.18	5	−.17
E_2I_2	10	0.59	0.76	− 5.71	5.51	− 3.20	− 3.10	14	−.15
E_2I_3	3	24.59	20.68	12.98	28.54	22.95	9.70	5	.17
E_3I_2	5	10.19	14.44	4.13	15.49	1.36	4.92	18	.04
E_3I_3	10	22.04	23.86	13.51	23.66	14.84	4.92	12	.35
E_3I_4	3	7.73	9.43	2.83	10.62	2.70	1.54	5	.06
E_4I_3	3	− 2.20	2.86	− 5.78	5.06	−14.65	− 3.45	5	.07
E_4I_4	10	12.95	15.08	5.57	17.48	7.18	6.01	19	.21
Pol. elitism $(P)_1$	33	12.74	13.33	14.16	6.96	14.14	4.80	52	.44
P_2	18	...	...	...	...	...	...	28	−.27
P_3	6	4.70	4.36	8.76	2.16	0.22	− 0.80	20	−.24
R^2		.401	.433	.493	.449	.459	.751		.674
F		3.16	3.25	4.13	3.46	3.60	9.68		30.53
Constant		2.23	− 9.29	− 5.33	2.16	− 1.28	3.93		11.83

a Calculated from: IIE Census forms, Fall 1964. See Appendix II for listing of countries.
b See Appendix III for description of variables.

145

TABLE 19—Correlations between non-return and selected variables for 158 countries and for 64 countries[a]

ITEM	ZERO-ORDER CORRELATIONS	
	158 Countries[b]	64 Countries[c]
STATUS	.226	.071
SPONSOR	.442	.450
VISA	.040	−.350
AGE	.295	.258

[a] Calculated from: IIE Census forms, Fall 1964.
[b] See Table 17 (excluded are French Equatorial Africa, Africa, and Latin America).
[c] See Appendix II for listing of countries included.

primarily on the basis of available data, as done for this analysis (and as done by Harbison and Myers,[16] whose choices for the educational index heavily influenced this sample) leads to a bias. The correlation between VISA and non-return is strikingly affected by working with the 64-country sample rather than with all 158 countries. The larger number includes many small countries omitted from the 64-country sample. Consequently, percentages for non-return, VISA, and so forth may be more erratic for these small countries than for the larger nations because of the small base numbers from which the former percentages were computed.

Included in the sample of 64 countries are 77.5 per cent of the non-returning males and 75.3 per cent of the total male foreign student population in the United States. A different sample of countries might lead to different conclusions; certainly caution must be exercised in generalizing to the larger group.

The results of the regression analyses of the 64 countries can be briefly summarized:

1. Neither education, nor income, nor political elitism alone accounts for a large percentage of the variance (see Table 18, regressions 1, 2, and 5).

2. The effect of using the interaction of education and income is minor; explanatory power is only slightly greater than when the

two are combined without attention to interaction effects (regressions 3 and 4).

3. When the education-income interaction and political elitism are taken into account (regression 9), 40 per cent of the variation in non-return across the 64 countries is explained.

4. If either STATUS or SPONSOR or VISA or AGE is added singly to education-income and political elitism, the addition has relatively little effect on the predictive power (regressions 10, 11, 12, and 13). However, when all are added at once (regression 14), the multiple R^2 reaches .75, indicating that three-quarters of the variance has been accounted for. The fact that STATUS, SPONSOR, VISA, and AGE in combination, but without education, income, and political elitism, result in an R^2 of .67 suggests that these are the dominant elements in the regression and that the effect of controlling for the country characteristics is slight.

5. Further evidence of the dominance of the conditions of study comes from a comparison of partial correlations with and without introducing country characteristics (see Table 20). While only STATUS (with the lowest coefficients) increases its partial correlation when controls are added, none of the study-condition variables drops below a partial r of .5 in the 64-country analysis. Although the fact that these partials hold up so well indicates the dominance of study-condition variables, it does not provide a clear description of the manner in which this dominance works. It may be that the study conditions incorporate elements of education, income, and political elitism.

6. The coefficients for a dummy variable in the regression equations represent predicted differences in amount of non-return attributable to that dummy variable when controlling for other variables with which it has been combined. By looking at the manner in which these coefficients are maintained or washed out, it is possible to obtain an idea of how the net effect of membership in the particular class changes as other variables are introduced. For instance, the net effect of membership in the first class of political elitism (P_1, Table 18) holds up quite well until

TABLE 20—A comparison of partial correlations, non-return by STATUS, SPONSOR, VISA, AGE, and STUDENTS, with and without controlling for education, income, and political elitism[a]

	PARTIAL CORRELATIONS		
	64-COUNTRY ANALYSIS[b]		158-COUNTRY ANALYSIS[c]
ITEM	Variables 1, 2, 3, and 4, with Education, Income, and Politics added	Variables 1, 2, 3, and 4, without other controls	Variables 1, 2, 3, 4, and 5, without other controls
1. STATUS	.273	.192	−.175
2. SPONSOR	.593	.742	.470
3. VISA	−.640	−.739	−.067
4. AGE	.504	.515	.194
5. STUDENTS[d]	*	*	−.096

[a] Calculated from: IIE Census forms, Fall 1964.
[b] See Appendix III for listing of countries included.
[c] See Table 17 (excluded are French Equatorial Africa, Africa, and Latin America).
[d] STUDENTS, which has a negligible effect, was not included in the regression runs with 64 countries.

VISA is introduced, as in regression 12, or until all conditions of study are introduced, as in regression 14. The effect of political elitism can also be seen by examining the way in which its categories vary with respect to each other. In regression equations 12 and 14, the effect of political elitism, as indicated by the difference between coefficients, seems to have been swamped by other variables. Again, the interpretation is not obvious. It is possible that the conditions of study pick up a considerable amount of what is included in political elitism, hence substitute for it and modify its apparent significance. However, an individual is a member of a political system prior to obtaining a visa or a particular type of sponsorship. The causal sequence would logically run from the country characteristics through the conditions of study to non-return even though the conditions appear most important. In the particular case of the reduced net effect of political elitism when VISA is introduced, it is logical to assume a connection between VISA and political elitism. If this is so, it seems to hold only when education and income are introduced as controls; the zero-order correlation between political elitism and VISA is only .159.

The zero-order correlation between political elitism and non-return is substantially increased if a larger number of countries is used, if a log scale is applied to non-return, and if political elitism is not arbitrarily divided into dummy categories. Note the coefficient of .40 in column 17 of Table 18 as compared with the .75 zero-order correlation reported earlier for 105 nations (p. 139).

Looking at the large cells of education-income interaction (dummy E_2I_2; dummy E_3I_3; and dummy E_4I_4) in relation to each other gives an idea of the way in which the interaction factor operates. Again, differences are reasonably constant across regression equations 4, 9, 10, 11, and 12 until all four conditions of study are added simultaneously (regression 13). Then the difference between E_2I_2 and E_3I_3 drops from approximately 18 (in regressions 4, 9, 10, 11, 12, and 13) to approximately 8 (in regression 14). The difference between E_3I_3 and E_4I_4 drops from approximately 8 to approximately 4, clearly indicating a reduction in the net effect on non-return of the education-income interaction when conditions of study are introduced.

7. As might be expected, SPONSOR and VISA are dominant among the conditions of study, indicated both by their zero-order correlations and by their effect on regression coefficients.

Although this exploration of multiple relationships has been brief, it suggests that correlates of non-return are difficult to identify clearly. While the zero-order correlations for political elitism and income variables indicate that it might be fruitful to pursue cross-national correlations in more detail, the regression analysis suggests that a more fruitful approach to non-return may lie in examination of study conditions and what is behind them.

NON-RETURN IN BROADER PERSPECTIVE:
AN INDEX OF MANPOWER LOSS

In the foregoing exercise, a familiar method of dealing with non-return has been employed. It is common to hear that "X" per cent of the Taiwanese or Korean students in the United States remain in the United States or that the percentage of Taiwanese students who remain is much higher than, for instance, the Ghanaian students. But it is well to pause and to ask why the particular means of relating foreign student non-returnees to total foreign students from each country is so often used and, more specifically, to ask what the resulting ratio is supposed to indicate.

What can be surmised from the non-return rate is, assuming accuracy of the measure of non-return, that if a country allows individuals to go abroad for study, it can probably expect "X" per cent to remain abroad permanently. However, relating the total number of non-returnees to the total number of foreign students from a particular country does not necessarily indicate either the relative seductive power of the United States for students of different national origins or their relative discontent with their home country. Nor does a relatively high non-return ratio necessarily imply that promoting study abroad is an unwise policy; it may mean that if a lower non-return rate is desired, the circumstances under which study abroad occurs and the type of individuals who are often chosen for study abroad may have to be changed.

Presumably the higher the non-return ratio, the less profitable study abroad is as a strategy for developing the home country; the associated "loss" is relatively greater. This may be true when comparing a country with itself at two points in time and assuming that study conditions, student characteristics and employment circumstances do not change. However, when making cross-national comparisons; a higher percentage of non-return among students from England than from Iran may not indicate a greater relative loss to England than to Iran. The question of loss remains open. To illustrate, suppose a nation has 40 individuals studying engineering in the United States, *all* of whom intend to remain permanently in the United States. The non-return rate of 100 per cent appears ominous. Indeed, it seems that unless the rate could be lowered drastically or unless the circumstances surrounding study abroad could be changed, to adopt study abroad as a strategy for training talented manpower would be pure folly. But suppose also that these 40 non-returning students represent only a small fraction of the total engineering manpower of the home country; that there are, for example, at least 10,000 qualified or qualifying engineers at home, some of whom are unemployed. Then, "loss" does not appear as great.

Contrast the above with another hypothetical situation in which 40 individuals from a second country are studying engineering in the United States, of whom 4 decide to remain. The lower rate of non-return for Country 2, 10 per cent, does not appear nearly as ominous as the 100 per cent for Country 1. However, assume further that in the second case, the non-returnees are 4 of only 1000 qualified or qualifying home country engineers, and that there are job openings at home. In which case is the "loss" greater? Furthermore, it is not at all improbable that in the case of Country 1, the bulk of the non-returning students would be engineers unable to obtain employment at home (for whatever reason), while Country 2 non-returnees might be talented employables.

The above again suggests the need for a broad perspective. It appears advisable to relate the untrained brain drain, represented by the number of non-returning students, to an indicator of total national manpower available as well as to the total number of students abroad. By so doing, one presumably arrives at a more accurate indicator of relative national gains and losses associated with non-return.

One method that has been used in an attempt to assess the

relative importance of emigration (trained and untrained), based on an indicator of available manpower, has been to compare the number of immigrants to the United States with the number of graduates from institutions of higher education in the home country. Sometimes, the comparison is made within specific occupations.[17] The approach can be useful, or it can produce distortions.

If a large percentage of all high-level manpower is being trained *abroad,* a comparison with *home* graduates is not particularly appropriate. By using the comparison of non-return to home-country production of graduates, it would be possible for a country to be losing more individuals than it is producing because those being trained outside the country are not included in the graduate total. At postgraduate levels and in scientific fields, many nations find themselves heavily dependent on foreign study. Developing nations train large percentages abroad at all levels; in sub-Saharan African nations, an average of 40 per cent of all students are trained abroad.[18] On the other hand, European nations seldom train more than 5 per cent abroad. Cross-national comparisons that do not take into account varying dependence on foreign training can therefore be misleading.

Another problem arises when comparing non-return figures based on *total enrollment* with the number of *graduates.* When dealing with non-returnees who have just completed their degrees in the United States (as done by the National Science Foundation in their analysis of doctorate recipients), the comparison with home-country graduates is appropriate. However, when using a source such as the Institute of International Education Survey or similar broad-ranging surveys, the more logical base is total student enrollment at the third level; in such surveys, the number of non-returnees is determined from among students at all levels of study and is not restricted to those who are graduating.

With the above in mind, an index has been developed relating the number of foreign student non-returnees in the United States (as determined from the IIE survey) to the total number of nationals enrolled at the third level in the home country and abroad (including those enrolled in countries other than the United States). For lack of a better designation, the index will be referred to as the index of manpower loss.

The manpower loss index can be visualized by referring to, and slightly modifying, the education-migration paradigm presented in chapter 1, Figure 1. In Figure 5, locus of study abroad

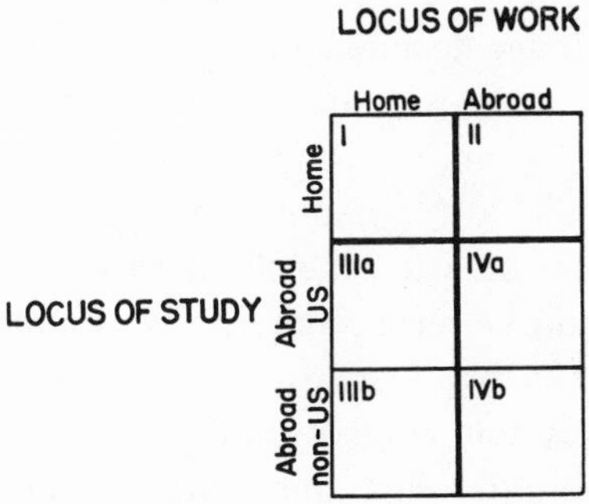

FIGURE 5—Migration Paradigm: A Modification

has been divided into study in the United States and study elsewhere abroad. Non-return among students *in the United States* is represented by the number of students in cell IVb and is the numerator of the index of manpower loss. For purposes of calculating the index, the six cells of Figure 5, taken together, are defined as the entire population of nationals enrolled at the third levels of education at home and abroad. Following their education, some of these students will remain at home (cell I) or return home (IIIa) and (IIIb), entering the national work force. Other students will migrate (II) or remain abroad following their study (IVa and IVb). Theoretically all students now in training could enter the home work force, in which case II, IVa and IVb would be equal to zero. Whatever the numbers in each cell, their total constitutes the denominator of the index of manpower loss.

The index of manpower lost through non-return of students in the United States, then, is represented by:

$$\frac{IVb}{I + II + IIIa + IIIb + IVa + IVb} \times 10{,}000$$

In standardized form, the index can be interpreted as follows: Of every 10,000 nationals being trained at the third level, X (the index number) are being trained in the United States *and* plan to remain there permanently following their study.[19]

Note that the index denominator includes individuals who may eventually migrate but who are presently being trained at home (I) or in a third country (IVa); the numerator does not.[20] If figures were available for non-return among students in third countries and for the rate of emigration of home-trained individuals, they could be incorporated in the numerator to indicate the total amount of brain drain, both trained and untrained. In the index, as it is computed, I and IVa are set equal to zero. Focus, then, is on the untrained brain drain of *U.S.-trained* individuals.

The index does not incorporate offsetting national gains that might result from immigration or from non-return of foreign students being hosted by each of the countries. These additions would offset, in part, or entirely, the numerical manpower loss of many nations.

Enrollment figures were obtained from the *UNESCO Statistical Yearbook, 1966*. The figures are subject to all the problems associated with UNESCO data that were mentioned in chapter 2; they must not be taken too literally. To obtain the total enrollment of nationals at the third level, the total third-level enrollment in the home country was adjusted, first by subtracting the number of non-nationals hosted, and then by adding the number of nationals studying overseas. (See Appendix IV.)

To estimate the number of students from each country who planned to remain in the United States, Institute of International Education data from the 1964/1965 survey of foreign students were used. The number of non-returnees was estimated for the total population of students, both male and female (this is in contrast to the focus on males in the previous section).[21] This was necessary in order to make a valid comparison with UNESCO data.

Ranking and Interpreting the Rank

In Table 21, nations have been ordered according to the index of manpower loss. In contrast to the ranking by percentage non-return earlier in this chapter, the index seems to be topheavy with developing rather than developed nations, particularly Latin American and Middle-Eastern nations. In the top 25, only Canada and Norway are among the group of nations generally labeled as developed nations. Israel and Ireland are marginal.

If the ordering in terms of manpower loss is compared with the ordering of the same 78 countries on the index of non-return, the difference is striking. A Spearman rank correlation for the two rankings is only .53.[22] Two nations appear in the top ten on each listing (Haiti, El Salvador) and only 11 of the top 25 nations in the index of manpower loss are also among the top 25 in percentage of non-return (Haiti, Iran, El Salvador, Honduras, Nicaragua, Ireland, Bolivia, Norway, Guatemala, Colombia, Greece). Seven of the 11 repeaters are Latin American countries, most of which are in the Caribbean area.

Generally, the position of nations in the ranking by manpower loss accords more directly with frequently voiced impressions about the relative importance of non-return than does rank order on the index of non-return. For instance, Taiwan, reputed to experience large drainage through student non-return, moves toward the top of the listing. Also rising in rank are Iran, Hong Kong, Jamaica, Ethiopia, Somalia, Nigeria, Kenya, Israel, and Lebanon. On the other hand, France drops drastically, much more in line with the notion that brain drain from France is slight.[23] Austria, Germany, and the Netherlands drop significantly in the list, much more so than the United Kingdom. Other nations

TABLE 21—A ranking of selected nations in terms of Manpower Loss[a] through foreign student non-return, study in the United States only, about 1964/65

Rank	Index Number	Country	Rank	Index Number	Country	Rank	Index Number	Country
1	314	Hong Kong	27	34	Iceland	53	9	Portugal
2	311	Jamaica	28	34	Switzerland	54	8	Ceylon
3	298	Haiti	29	34	United Kingdom	55	8	Libya
4	189	Iran	30	31	Sierra Leone	56	8	Vietnam
5	174	El Salvador	31	27	Ethiopia	57	7	Argentina
6	139	Honduras	32	24	Malaysia	58	7	Belgium
7	138	Mozambique	33	22	W. Germany	59	7	Morocco
8	117	Nicaragua	34	21	Syria	60	6	Afghanistan
9	109	S. Rhodesia	35	20	Korea	61	6	Australia
10	106	Saudi Arabia	36	19	Tanzania	62	6	Burma
11	100	Liberia	37	19	Chile	63	6	Cambodia
12	87	Ireland	38	18	Ghana	64	6	U.A.R.

13	69	Bolivia	39	18	Nigeria	65	5	France
14	67	Lebanon	40	17	Austria	66	4	New Zealand
15	62	Israel	41	17	Guinea	67	4	Sudan
16	61	Costa Rica	42	16	Denmark	68	3	India
17	58	Somalia	43	16	Netherlands	69	3	Tunisia
18	56	Guatemala	44	13	Sweden	70	2	Japan
19	56	Taiwan	45	11	Luxembourg	71	1	Pakistan
20	55	Jordan	46	11	Thailand	72	0	Algeria
21	55	Norway	47	10	Finland	73	0	Burundi
22	52	Colombia	48	10	Kenya	74	0	Cameroon
23	50	Canada	49	10	S. Africa	75	0	Dahmey
24	50	Ecuador	50	10	Spain	76	0	Ivory Coast
25	40	Greece	51	10	Turkey	77	0	Madagascar
26	38	Iraq	52	9	Italy	78	0	Uganda

[a] Manpower Loss is indexed as the number of U.S.-trained non-returning foreign students per 10,000 nationals being trained both at home and abroad (in all countries). Non-return was determined from the Institute of International Education Annual Census of Foreign Students and Total enrollments were estimated from the *UNESCO Statistical Yearbook, 1966*. For original figures and the method of calculating the index, see Appendix IV.

which fall in the listing are Italy, Denmark, Finland, Portugal, Spain, Argentina, Sweden, Belgium, New Zealand, Japan, and Burma.

Not conforming to the position often assigned to it in foreign-student and governmental folklore is India. Even if the IIE non-return rate for Indian students is quadrupled on the assumption that the rate is a gross underestimate and raised from 7 to 30 per cent, the *index* of manpower loss would only be 15, which would not even move India into the top half of the ranking.[24]

The index of manpower loss was plotted against per capita income, the Banks and Gregg index of political elitism, and the Harbison-Myers composite education index. Correlation coefficients for the comparisons are presented in Table 22, together with correlation coefficients for the same countries, using the index of non-return instead of the manpower loss index.

From Table 22, it is evident that the manpower loss is not

TABLE 22—Zero-order correlations, non-return and manpower loss indexes by selected country indexes, 78 countries

COUNTRY INDICATORS[c]	INDEX					
	MAN-POWER LOSS[a]		NON-RETURN RATIO[b]			
			ALL (M + F)		MALES ONLY	
	Regular	Log	Regular	Log	Regular	Log
Income per capita	−.100	−.015	.256*	.324**	.230*	.305**
Log income	−.009	.057	.486**	.617**	.457**	.592**
Political elitism	−.203	−.101	−.614	−.757**	−.599**	−.748**
Education index	−.243	−.261	.361**	.520**	.328**	.490**

[a] For calculation of the non-return ratio, see chapter 4, p. 129.
[b] For calculation of the manpower loss index, see chapter 4, p. 154.
[c] For countries included and details of the country indicators, see Appendix III.
[d] * indicates significance at the .05 level; ** indicates significance at .01.

significantly related to the economic, educational and political indicators used. By contrast, the non-return indexes display relatively high zero-order correlations, whether calculated for all students or for males only, both with and without transforming the index to a logarithmic scale.

Looking at non-return of foreign students as related to the total national manpower being trained at the third level presumably clarifies questions of relative national losses through non-return. Although this method progresses one more step beyond simple consideration of absolute numbers, no adjustment has been made for national variation in absorptive capacity. Political, social and economic structures differentially inhibit individuals of comparable ability from nation to nation, allowing them to make greater or lesser contributions to the development of their nation on return home. Furthermore, no attempt has been made to relate the production of high-level manpower to total population. In short, it may be that a nation is, for any of several reasons, over- or under-producing high level manpower in relation to the ability of the nation to utilize the manpower. There is nothing in the index of manpower loss, based only on enrollment totals, that adjusts for the national ability or willingness to absorb talent produced.

NON-RETURN AND THE NATIONAL ABILITY TO ABSORB MANPOWER

In an insightful piece of research, Michael Hervé has used the same data sources dealt with above (UNESCO and IIE) to explore foreign student non-return cross-nationally as it relates to the effective demand for high level manpower.[26] Hervé's procedure is a surprisingly simple one. He first sets up an equation representing the "best fit" between the number of students per 100,000 population and per capita income for 102 nations. The equation approximates a statement of national ability to absorb students. Given the per capita income of a country, it was then possible to predict an expected enrollment. Hervé compared expected enrollments with actual enrollments for each country included and labeled countries as surplus or deficit, depending on whether actual enrollment exceeded or fell short of expected enrollment.

Nations in which the excess of actual over expected student enrollments was at least as large as the expected enrollment are listed in Table 23. If the percentage excess allowed is reduced from 100 to 30 per cent, the following nations would also have been included in the listing: Singapore, Peru, New Zealand, Uruguay, Pakistan, Costa Rica, Panama, Thailand, Bolivia, Greece, and Ecuador. On that basis, Hervé notes that, "Most of the excess countries outside Latin America are also the countries often mentioned in connection with the brain drain to the United States: India, Korea, the Philippines, Taiwan, the U.A.R., Syria, Lebanon, and Greece." [27]

It is logical to expect emigration from countries in which there is an overproduction of high-level manpower. And it seems less appropriate to emphasize the loss of manpower when there is an excess than it does when there is a deficit. On the other hand, deficit countries that are also countries of substantial emigration, as in the case of Iran, would appear to be experiencing a loss of talent through non-return. Hervé labels such nations "crisis" countries; although apparently able to absorb (economically) more manpower than is being trained, nationals continue to emigrate.[28]

According to Hervé's figures, all sub-Saharan nations for which an estimate of income and enrollment was available are deficit countries with a deficit that is at least as large as the actual enrollment figures in the home country (sometimes as high as 10 times the actual amount). Hervé does not take into account the fact that a large percentage of the actual enrollment of students from the sub-Saharan nations is overseas enrollment. He agrees[29] that deficits computed for these nations would be cut considerably if study abroad could have been taken into account, when

TABLE 23—Countries showing a "surplus" or "deficit" of student enrollment in relation to the "effective demand" for students[a]

COUNTRIES SHOWING AT LEAST 100 PER CENT SURPLUS (ACTUAL OVER PREDICTED ENROLLMENT)		COUNTRIES SHOWING AT LEAST 100 PER CENT DEFICIT (PREDICTED OVER ACTUAL ENROLLMENT)	
COUNTRY	PER CENT SURPLUS	COUNTRY	PER CENT DEFICIT
Philippines	488	Sub-Saharan	
Lebanon	232	nations	All over 300
Syria	210	Luxembourg	1,329
Korea	200	Laos	1,300
U.A.R.	188	Saudi Arabia	1,000
China	144	Cyprus	850
Argentina	132	Afghanistan	550
Japan	123	British Guiana	475
India	115	Haiti	400
Puerto Rico	100	Cambodia	275
		Algeria	267
		W. Germany	217
		Morocco	191
		Jordan	138
		Libya	138
		Tunisia	138
		Norway	133
		Nepal	117
		Malta	115
		Malaya	109
		Iceland	107
		Jamaica	107
		Indonesia	100
		Iran	100

[a] Calculated from Michel E. A. Hervé, "International Migration of Physicians and Students: A Regression Analysis," Washington, U.S. Agency for International Development, Office of Program and Policy Coordination, April 1968 (mimeographed). Appendix I, columns 3 and 4. Surplus and deficit are defined by the manner in which actual enrollments differ from predicted enrollments as determined from a regression equation relating the number of students per 100,000 population to per capita income. If actual enrollments exceed predicted enrollments, there is said to be a surplus.

setting the original equation relation between per capita income and *total* enrollments.

If deficit countries are related to their respective rates of non-return, several candidates for crisis countries appear other than Iran: West Germany, Haiti, Luxembourg, and Norway.

Hervé carried his analysis one step further, hypothesizing that the number of non-returning students should be a function of the total number of students in the United States and of the surplus or deficit conditions at home. For 78 countries, he found that ". . . the main explanation for non-return is to be found in the random factor: the number of non-returnees is essentially a function of the number of students in the U.S. In general, the surplus or deficit at home did not seem to be a factor in the decision not to return." [30] When Latin American countries were treated separately, however, ". . . the hypotheses that surplus or deficit at home affected the decision to return was found to be verified." [31]

In his analysis, Hervé utilizes a very specific criterion by which the relative loss of nations from student emigration can be judged. He has not attempted to value migrants in terms of the cost of their training or in terms of their potential contribution to the home country. Logically, such valuations and the conditions of excess or surplus identified by Hervé should hang together. However, the existence of such a relationship has not been established nor does it *necessarily* follow that conditions of supply and demand for high-level manpower will be related to migration decisions or to the value of migrants. They might be more closely related to conditions of supply and demand for higher education.

SUMMARY

Cross-national comparisons have been used to put the untrained brain drain in perspective. Relative losses through non-return were defined in several ways: 1) relative to the total number of foreign students in the United States, 2) relative to the total manpower supply in training at home and abroad and 3) relative to the effective demand for high-level manpower in the home country determined from the relationship between enrollment per 100,000 population and per capita income. The three indexes produced very different country rankings and the strength of the relationship between non-return and such country indicators as per capita income, political elitism, and educational development was strongly affected by which index of non-return was chosen. No consistent set of relationships emerged. The mild zero-order correlations between the rate of non-return (number 1 above) and various country characteristics disappeared when the index of manpower loss was substituted. Furthermore, variation in conditions of study and student characteristics by country seemed, in regression analyses, to be more important than the characteristics of the country of origin in determining who would remain and who would return home following study in the United States.

The separate analyses were hampered by inadequate statistics. Although more accurate statistics might alter rankings even further, it is doubtful that relationships between non-return and country indices would be greatly improved. Interactions among the country characteristics and between country characteristics, conditions of study, and individual characteristics would have to be sorted out. As stressed throughout chapters 1 and 2, further disaggregation by level and field of study is required before more definite conclusions can be drawn from the analysis.

Reviewing the three analyses of relative loss, one is struck, however, by the recurrent positioning of at least three countries near the top of all non-return rankings. Haiti, Iran and Norway seem to be losing talent, no matter what perspective is applied.

Little imagination is required to speculate about the reasons for Haitian non-return. An extremely closed society, a strong-handed dictatorship and chronic underdevelopment characterize Haiti, making it a less than desirable working locale for all but a small group of talented Haitians. In a sense, many of the Haitian non-returnees could be considered political refugees even though they do not technically or legally qualify as such. Although a number of nations score as low or lower than Haiti on many of the most common development measures, most show signs of development while Haiti remains relatively stagnant, constrained rather than pushed by the ruling elite. In addition, Haiti is much closer to the United States than most other nations at similar level of development; the United States is a logical migration destination.

Iran has also been a country with political problems. Nepotism is deeply rooted.[32] The high non-return for Iranian students occurs in spite of relatively high economic growth in recent years. The Iranian government has taken a variety of steps to try and stop the outflow of talent (military exemptions have been granted for those who are now abroad and would like to return, inexpensive flights home are made available, a counselor for foreign students presumably keeps track of and tries to retrieve students, but apparently without much success). Indeed, until major changes occur within the structure of the society itself it is unlikely that the Iranian brain drain will slacken. It will be interesting to see what happens over the next 10 years in this crisis country.[33]

The Norwegian case is radically different from either Haiti or Iran. Norway is a reasonably stable polity and boasts a relatively open society. Per capita income of the residents is high on the world scale. Until recently, however, expansion of the Norwegian system of higher education proceeded very slowly. Instead, the government apparently chose to allow many students to pursue their education abroad at higher levels and has even assisted them by making loan funds available. This seems to have been done realizing that a substantial proportion of students would remain abroad. Nevertheless, the view may have been sound economically, saving the cost of constructing and maintaining expensive facilities at home and of attempting to keep educational output from outdistancing economic opportunity (in which case migration might have occurred anyway, but after Norway had incurred the expense of training emigrés). Whether economically sound or not, the Norwegian policy stands in contrast to the more common nationalistic complaints that emigration of the talented is, by definition, a loss. In addition, Norway is making its contribution to the world and to its own citizens by giving them the option to migrate. Loan funds are not now tied to return (but they do provide some leverage for return and they do carry an obligation for repayment). It might be argued that Norway, wisely or not, is one of a very few nations in the world in a position to take such an international approach to the allocation of manpower. The Norwegian situation will undoubtedly change as the system of higher education continues to grow.

In addition to the three nations appearing high on all three indexes, there are several other nations that appear well up on two indexes. Ranking high on both the non-return and manpower loss indexes, though not high deficit countries, are: Bolivia, Colombia, Ecuador, El Salvador, Greece, Guatemala, Honduras, Ireland, Jordan, the Netherlands, and Nicaragua. Seven of the 11 are Latin American nations, of which 4 are Central American republics, suggesting propinquity as a factor in the migration. The 4 Central American republics and Jordan were slight deficit nations and the others were balanced or surplus countries by Hervé's definition. Hong Kong, Taiwan, and Israel should probably be included in this group. All 3 fall just below the arbitrary cut-off of 15 per cent that was used by the author to designate countries high on the non-return index. Furthermore, all 3 have large percentages of non-respondents on the question of intended non-return.

West Germany and Luxembourg are ranked high on the non-return index and are high deficit nations while falling below the top one-third on the manpower index. West Germany is not far below the arbitrary cut-off point on the manpower index and might easily have qualified with Haiti, Iran and Norway as high in all 3 categories.

Several other nations have relatively low rates of non-return but rank high on the manpower index while appearing as deficit countries: Jamaica, Liberia, Saudi Arabia and Mozambique.

The United Kingdom merits special mention because of its high non-return rate and because so much attention has been given there to the brain drain. The country ranks just below the one-third mark on the manpower index and it is a mild deficit country. While lending credence to U.K. brain-drain complaints, the rankings also lend themselves to the conclusion that the complaint is not as justified with respect to non-returning students as it is for many other nations. The untrained brain drain from the United Kingdom is less important than the trained brain drain.

Finally, the reader is asked not to overrate the significance of the cross-national comparisons presented in chapter 4. He should be particularly cautious not to select results to buttress arguments about the size of the untrained brain drain to the United States. The foregoing analyses are not particularly relevant to the task of estimating the absolute magnitude of brain drain to the United States from any one country or of estimating the associated loss. Taken together the statistical manipulations may stimulate hypotheses relating to the variation in non-return among nations. One of the firmest conclusions that can be drawn from the analyses is that viewing non-return and associated losses only in terms of the so-called rate of non-return is not sufficient.

In spite of including an index of so-called manpower loss as a complement to non-return rates, the problem of identifying *economic* gains and losses through foreign student non-return has been skirted. None of the relative measures of non-return used in the chapter included a valuing of non-return that is related to costs and benefits of study abroad and non-return. In using the concept of effective demand, Hervé sought an economic explanation for non-return. His technique does not allow a calculation of aggregate gains and losses nor does it allow comparison of education-work alternatives. The problems and possibilities associated with economic valuation of emigration through non-return are discussed in Part III.

NOTES

[1] For instance, individuals from a country which suffered a political over-throw (after the IIE census was taken) may have changed their intentions, thus increasing the probability of inaccurate answers from that country.

[2] Country, nation, and state are used loosely in the exposition to refer to political divisions which may or may not be fully recognized countries or nations in the usual sense of the word. The divisions are largely dictated by data.

[3] The disruption of World War II still seems to be reflected in migration patterns. When working with the original census cards, the author noted, but could not check statistically, that the migration from Latin America to the United States for study and the non-return among Latin American students seemed to be disproportionately linked with an indication of Jewish religion on the census forms. (This item was not coded and was optional.) It would not be surprising to find that a sizable percentage of the Latin American brain drain associated with study abroad is simply composed of children of German refugees who left in the 1930s and 1940s and went wherever they could at the time. Now they would like their children to make another move to improve their lot.

[4] For instance, see Enrique Oteiza, "Emigration of Engineers from Argentina: A Case of Latin American Brain Drain," *International Labour Review,* XCII, No. 6 (December 1965), pp. 445–61.

[5] The methodology follows that adopted by Mary Jean Bowman and C. Arnold Anderson, "Concerning the Role of Education in Development," *Old Societies and New States,* ed. Clifford Geertz (New York: The Free Press of Glencoe, 1963), pp. 247–79.

[6] For per capita Gross National Product, figures were taken from Bruce M. Russett *et al., World Handbook of Political and Social Indicators* (New Haven: Yale University Press, 1964), pp. 149–54; for wage and salary percentages, from *ibid.,* pp. 28–31; for percentage labor force in agriculture, from *ibid.,* pp. 175–79.

[7] Arthur S. Banks and Philip M. Gregg, "Grouping Political Systems: Q-Factor Analysis of A *Cross-Polity Survey," The American Behavioral Scientist,* IX, No. 3 (November 1965), pp. 3–6. For a description of the factorial procedure, see p. 3.

[8] Arthur S. Banks and Robert B. Textor, *A Cross-Polity Survey* (Cambridge, Mass.: M.I.T. Press, 1963).

[9] Banks and Gregg, *The American Behavioral Scientist,* IX, No. 3, p. 3.

[10] Frederick Harbison and Charles A. Myers, *Education, Manpower, and Economic Growth* (New York: McGraw-Hill, 1964), pp. 45–48.

[11] U.S. Immigration and Naturalization Service, *Annual Report, 1964* (Washington, D.C.: U.S. Government Printing Office, 1964), p. 48.

[12] Visa adjustment figures were obtained through personal correspondence

with E. A. Loughran, Associate Commissioner, Management, U.S. Immigration and Naturalization Service, Washington, D.C., May 17, 1965.

[13] Michel E. A. Hervé, "International Migration of Physicians and Students: A Regression Analysis," Washington, D.C., U.S. Agency for International Development, Office of Program and Policy Coordination, April 1968 (mimeographed).

[14] Calculated from the original census forms of the Institute of International Education Annual Census of Foreign Students.

[15] See Appendix VI for the treatment of these variables.

[16] Harbison and Myers, p. 33.

[17] See, for instance, Grubel and Scott, The Journal of Political Economy, LXXIV, No. 4, p. 374; and the Reuss Committee Report, p. 8.

[18] Angus Maddison, Foreign Skills and Technical Assistance in Economic Development (Paris: Organization for Economic Cooperation and Development, 1965), p. 54.

[19] The index does not include those non-returnees who do in fact return home for a short period before remigrating to the United States for permanent residence.

[20] Some idea of the importance of third-country training for each nation can be obtained by comparing the overseas enrollments taken from UNESCO sources. (See Appendix IV, column 3.)

[21] First, non-return percentages were calculated for each country by relating the number of non-returnees to the total number of students responding to the question of non-return. Each national percentage was then applied to the total number of students from the nation, thus distributing non-return among the non-respondents and providing an adjusted estimate for the total number of non-returnees. As suggested in the previous chapter, this procedure probably results in an underestimate in most cases.

[22] This includes six nations in the identical positions at the bottom of the list because they have a value of zero on both. If the six are excluded the rank correlation falls below .50. A product moment correlation produces a coefficient of only .228, suggesting that the two dimensions are distinct.

[23] See, for instance, Robert Mossè, "France," The Brain Drain, ed. Walter Adams (New York: Macmillan Company, 1968), pp. 157–165.

[24] It has been suggested that the low Indian index may be related to third-country migration by Indian students—many to England. However, according to UNESCO, more than half of the Indian students abroad are studying in the United States and it is doubtful that the Indian index would rise dramatically if third countries were included. An effect of size is also at work.

[25] The Nigerian conflict renders the non-return rate relatively meaningless for that country at the present time.

[26] Hervé, entire paper.

[27] Ibid., IV–2.

[28] Ibid.

[29] But Hervé observes that the high correlation between per capita income and enrollments per 100,000 population would probably not decrease as a result of incorporating students enrolled abroad. Hervé, personal correspondence, September 30, 1968.

[30] Hervé, IV–6.

[31] Ibid.

[32] Habib Naficy, "The 'Brain Drain': The Case of Iranian Non-Returnees." Report presented at Conference of the Society for International Development, March 17, 1966, Washington, D.C. Iranian Embassy, 1966 (mimeographed).

On the Iranian brain drain, see also: Mohamad Borhanmanesh, "A Study of Iranian Students in Southern California" (unpublished Ph.D. dissertation, The University of California at Los Angeles, June 1965); Iraj Valipour, "A Comparison of Returning and Non-returning Iranian Students in the United States" (unpublished Ed.D. dissertation, Teachers College, Columbia University, November 1961); Khodadad Farman-Farmaian, *The Problem of Brain Drain, A Profile of its Factors* (Teheran, the Central Bank of Iran, January, 1969); and W. A. Copeland, "The Pahlavi-Pennsylvania Contract," *International Development Review*, X, No. 3 (September 1968), pp. 21–23.

[33] Professor Marvin Zonis of the University of Chicago provides excellent background on Iranian study abroad and non-return in his "Higher Education and Social Change in Iran: Problems and Prospects, Prepared for the Conference on Iran in the 1960's: A Consideration of Problems and Prospects," Columbia University, November 7–9, 1968). He notes that the higher-education system is now being "modernized" as well as expanded, but that revolutionary changes await parallel changes in the larger society.

[34] As indicated in Table 2, approximately 15 per cent of all Norwegians trained at the third level are trained abroad. The percentage has dropped from about 30 per cent in the last decade.

PART III

Education and Migration: An Economic Perspective

5

ESTIMATING AGGREGATE GAINS
AND LOSSES OF HUMAN CAPITAL
THROUGH MIGRATION

As the title of Part III implies, a choice has been made to consider the "value" of foreign study and of non-return in economic terms. Other perspectives are also important, but an economic perspective has been chosen for several reasons:

(1) National complaints about losses through emigration are often couched in economic terms, but often with seemingly little understanding of what is implied by the facts and figures presented or by the values assigned. Similarly, proposals for making compensating international payments to loser nations presuppose an accurate accounting technique and a valid basis for calculating economic gains and losses.

(2) Even within the economic realm, there is considerable disagreement about what constitutes an economic gain or loss through migration and about how the gain or loss should be measured. Without attempting to resolve the controversy or to eliminate the contradictions, it should be possible to point out the key issues and the varying assumptions that carry analysts in different directions.

(3) The economic concepts of human capital, as applied to migration, need to be clarified and extended. The present approach often appears to be more a publicity gimmick than a

serious analytical tool. The weaknesses and strengths of the main
methods for valuing migratory flows in terms of human capital
(using costs or using present values) need to be looked at more
closely.

Paralleling what has been noted for research and writing about
foreign students and about migration the literature of economics
prior to about 1960 contained little that could be considered
directly relevant to the economic assessment of high-level migration, study abroad, or foreign student non-return. While the
international movement of "brainy" manpower had been neg-
lected by economists, "brawny" manpower had received considerable attention, theories of labor migration had been evolved
and some impressive empirical work had been done.[1]

There are probably several reasons why high-level or skilled
manpower was not differentiated in earlier work: tools from
economics were not yet honed for such an examination; the concepts of "human capital" had not penetrated economics sufficiently to be incorporated into migration [2] or international trade
models; [3] high-level international migration had not yet achieved
the status of an Issue; and statistics were lacking which separated
labor into unskilled and skilled or non-professional and professional or uneducated and educated. More important, however,
is the fact that until recently most migration was indeed migration
of unskilled or semi-skilled workers with so-called high-level migrants forming a small proportion of the total. The shifting
educational and occupational composition toward the skilled and
the educated has been clearly documented—causing Brinley
Thomas to remark as early as 1961 that:

> The accent is no longer on mass movements but on qualitative fac-
> tors, transfer of skill, and particularly the migration of relatively scarce
> "human resources." [4]

Since 1960, economists have made rapid progress on both
theoretical and empirical fronts, but problems of measurement
and methodology still present formidable obstacles to the eco-

nomic analysis of high-level migration. In addition, a number of key issues remain unresolved—and may, in fact, be impossible to resolve because they are firmly based in contradictory definitions, assumptions, and/or philosophical positions. It is not the purpose of this chapter to attempt resolution nor to argue strongly for one versus another of the many viewpoints; several approaches to the same problem may be equally valid. For the moment it is enough to mention several choices that must be made when estimating economic gains and losses through migration. The listing alone should serve to alert readers to the dangers inherent in the summary statistics so frequently seen in popular writings about the brain drain.

Whether a net gain or loss is thought to be associated with migration depends on the unit to which gains or losses are thought to pertain (individual, enterprise, nation, world) and on the definition of the relevant unit. (Is a "nation," for example, comprised of all individuals who remain within national borders following emigration, either including or excluding new immigrants, or does it refer to all former citizens or national residents regardless of their current location and without reference to national borders?) [5]

Sometimes linked to choice of definition, but also independent of it, is the critical choice of an appropriate criterion for judging gains or losses. Whether a nation is thought to gain or lose depends upon whether emphasis is placed on economic growth (usually maximization of Gross National Product), on social welfare (usually inferred from what happens to per capita incomes of the relevant population), on income distribution (among either individuals within a nation or among nations, and measured either by a narrowing of the income range or by shift from one group to another), or on the loss of the flow of savings and taxes. The utility of one versus another of these measures depends on the purpose behind the measurement. [6]

Depending on what criterion is adopted, choices may also have to be made between a static or a dynamic outlook (which may involve a decision to project an economic system into the future either as it is at present or as it probably will be according to the best guesses that can be made).

Whether a gain or a loss is associated with migration may depend on whether one accepts actual income (or an appropriate estimate thereof) as a reasonable proxy for productivity (i.e. whether a person is paid his true marginal product); on the degree to which the effect of migration on the operation of other factors of production is thought to be important (i.e. whether there are "external" economies or diseconomies that are not represented in the gains or losses registered through the market—for instance, missing leadership or an imbalance between skilled and unskilled workers); on whether those who migrate are supposed to have a higher rate of savings than those who remain, in which case the rate of investment would decline; on whether one accepts the position that a migrant takes along not only his education (for which the home country paid) but also his fertility, making it unnecessary for those who remain to provide education for the emigrant's children; on whether emigrants are thought to draw on the public purse for welfare benefits in proportion to, or in excess of, the tax revenue they provide; and on whether one accepts the notion that contribution to national welfare can come from emigrants residing outside the home country. Finally, estimates will differ according to whether one adopts a long-run or a short-run emphasis.

To date, the most controversial yet perhaps the most thought-provoking theoretical work on international flows of human capital by economists has been that of Harry Johnson and of Grubel and Scott.[7] Their theoretical base in the economics of international trade and their international perspective lead to an orentation toward free flow of goods and people among nations. From their neo-classical economic assumptions and their emphasis on social welfare indexed by per capita income effects, they develop a well-reasoned argument that unrestricted flow of men among nations for study and work is in the best economic interests of the world.

Countering them are Thomas, Aitken, Patinkin, Shearer and others.[8] From an essentially nationalistic orientation, these writers note benefits from difficult to measure economic "externalities."[9] They present their arguments in dynamic terms, criticize the free-market, marginal-analysis assumptions of Johnson and others, and emphasize the effect of high-level migration upon both Gross National Product and the redistribution of capital among individuals and nations. They conclude that high-level migration, particularly from low-income nations, leads to wider gaps between rich and poor, to a retardation of economic development and to a worsening of the world economic situation.

Other economists stress the value of more than one set of criteria and more than one approach in estimating gains and losses associated with international migration.[10] And it has been suggested that the balance between gains and losses, as well as the methods used to estimate them, should depend on the particular circumstances encountered at migrant origins and destinations.[11] If one accepts the possibility of multiple approaches to gains and losses, it would be easy to agree with Kindleberger's statement that "economic analysis is unclear whether emigration helps or hurts a country."[12]

While recognizing that many shifts occur as economies adjust in response to human capital moves,[13] I have chosen to deal here only with the gains and losses of human capital *per se*. A full accounting is not attempted. Gains and losses, then, will be discussed in terms of the human capital value that is added to or subtracted from total productivity, implying a goal of maximization of Gross National Product. One major purpose of restricting the discussion in this manner is to explore the degree to which conventional assessments of human capital gains and losses are sensitive to assumptions about the capacity and character[14] or the experience composition of migrant streams. Gain and loss may be distorted *even* when the goal of GNP maximization and its associated assumptions are accepted as reasonable. Furthermore, application of human capital concepts within a productivity-maximization framework may be positively (as opposed to normatively) applied to developing hypotheses about migration behavior.

HUMAN CAPITAL MEASURES AND MIGRATION [15]

Neither human capital concepts nor their application to migration can be termed new. The idea of embodied human capital appeared in England before Adam Smith [16] and several applications to migration were made in the nineteenth century.[17] However, extensive use of the concept did not come until after World War II, as economists discovered that injections of physical capital were not always sufficient to bring about economic development and as econometric models failed to account for growth in traditional terms—without including the human factor.[18]

Current acceptance of the salience of human capital measures stems largely from pioneer work by T. W. Schultz, who based his estimates on educational costs.[19] A parallel methodology has developed from the work of Becker,[20] Mincer,[21] and Bowman,[22] among others, who have emphasized internal rates of return or discounted present values rather than replacement costs in assessing human capital values, taking into account the timing and sequences of costs, income flows and alternatives.

There is no need to review here the general literature of the economics of education and of human capital formation; [23] nor to enter the debate about the human-capital approach.[24] However, a more detailed examination of recent applications to migration is in order, indicating perspectives and techniques that can be adopted, and pointing to problems and potentialities involved in human capital approaches to migration.[25]

Although the most appropriate use of human capital concepts

as applied to migration is not to determine aggregate gains and losses, this is the application most frequently encountered today and it will be discussed first. Two main alternatives for making such estimates will be examined and several specific empirical attempts to determine aggregate gains or losses through migration will be discussed. The more appropriate application of human capital concepts within decision models and as a source of hypotheses about behavior is reserved for chapter 6.

COST VALUATIONS OF INTERNATIONAL MIGRATION

A relatively simple and commonly utilized method of valuing migration flows in economic terms is to estimate the cost of "producing" (or replacing) those who have migrated. According to this method, national gains are realized if a nation acquires through migration, and at a cost saving, human capital formed elsewhere. National losses are incurred when a nation pays for the formation of human capital that others then acquire cost-free.

Usually, an average cost figure is calculated for a "typical" migrant representing the average amount of training (and sometimes experience) of a particular stream of migrants; the cost figure is then applied to all migrants. As an example, the following has been excerpted from a U.S. government report on the brain drain:

If an average cost figure of $20,000 is used, the 1967 scientific emigration to the United States of 7,913 persons represents an investment loss in one year of more than $150 million by the developing countries.[26]

Elements included in the cost figure of $20,000 were not specified in the foregoing. It is difficult to make a judgment about the statement on that point alone. Assuming for the moment the general validity of a cost approach, the method of determining costs must be examined before blindly accepting such an estimate. Sometimes costs are thought of only in terms of direct educational costs. This results in a gross underestimate of human capital value. At present, however, cost estimates often include the opportunity cost incurred by individuals and societies when the decision is made to forego work and hence earnings in order to continue the process of education. As has been frequently pointed out, foregone earnings probably account for more than half of the cost associated with pursuing higher education.[27] There is an additional cost element that is sometimes incorporated into human capital estimates—what it cost to raise and maintain a child in the period before the child could enter the labor force. How to estimate this remains an open question. One method of dealing with the problem of maintenance is to make one estimate incorporating it and one leaving it out.

A second and perhaps more difficult matter that must be raised is whether the appropriate costs of training and foregone earnings are based on data from the area of origin or of destination. In the quoted passage, the cost figure of $20,000 apparently represents the cost in the United States of bringing an individual to the educational level of the migrant on arrival (or at the time an adjustment to immigrant status is made). If one is speaking in terms of gains to the United States, that procedure seems appropriate. If, however, one is speaking of the loss to the countries of origin, as the U.S. government report does, the use of United States training cost figures can be questioned. Indeed, in the latter situation, estimating what is *embodied in* individuals as measured by the cost of their training may be irrelevant; the United States market may be able to absorb and utilize the embodied skills, but the home country may not be able to, regardless of the cost involved.

Whether we are considering U.S. gains or home-country losses, however, the calculation is complicated by the fact that many immigrants arrive via the foreign student non-return route. Non-returnees will have incurred large portions of their educational costs in the United States. Whether or not students pay their own way, a large portion of the costs is borne by the United

States prior to the time of immigration. Logically, then, the "average" cost figure for either a cost-free gain to the United States or a loss to the country of origin would be a gross over-estimate.

Two Illustrations

1. THE COST TO THE UNITED STATES OF INTERNATIONAL EDUCATIONAL EXCHANGE

Setting these questions aside for the moment, let us consider two specific cost assessments of the human capital of migrating students. The first is an assessment by Grubel and Scott [28] of the gain (or loss) to the United States of hosting foreign students,[29] taking into account that (1) the U.S. spends money to educate many students from other countries who will return home without making any direct economic contribution to the United States; (2) many foreign students who have brought with them training acquired at the expense of other nations will remain in the U.S.; and (3) many U.S. students are educated abroad at the expense of other nations. Although most current debate, both practical-political and academic, centers on measuring putative losses of sending nations, the Grubel and Scott assessments are made from the perspective of the receiving nation—the United States.

Using figures from the IIE Annual Census of Foreign Students, Grubel and Scott derived estimates for costs incurred by the United States in the course of providing education to foreign students. They made adjustments in the cost figure, allowing for variation in sponsorship patterns among foreign students (assuming 40 per cent of the students were self-sponsored) and for cost differences between graduate and undergraduate study. All fields of study were treated in a similar manner, and simplifying assumptions were made about age on arrival, prior education, duration of study, and transportation costs.

Against these cost estimates was set the value of the gain

(saving in costs) to the United States of acquiring non-returning foreign students. Ten per cent of the total foreign student population were assumed to be non-returning (at both graduate and undergraduate levels). The non-returnees were valued at what it would have cost the United States to "produce" the equivalent in the country. Two methods were used. The first estimate was made by adding to prior educational costs the cost associated with earnings foregone in order to study from age 14 to age 20 (the average age of arrival). The second method was to combine prior educational costs with an estimate of maintenance cost—that is, what it cost to bring up the child to age 20. The two estimates were presumed to be lower and upper limits respectively of the capital value of foreign students staying in the United States. These were approximately $17,300 and $24,000 respectively (which makes the $20,000 figures cited earlier appear reasonable).

Combining the above benefit from non-return with an estimate of what the U.S. saves by training U.S. students abroad, Grubel and Scott concluded that, depending on which of the methods for valuing non-return was used, the *net* average cost to the U.S. per annum of training foreign students between 1954 and 1964 had been either − $18 million or + $16 million. "Whichever of the two figures for the final U.S. balance one considers to be more appropriate, the importance of both estimates is that the resource cost of the program is very small indeed." [30]

The choice of 10 per cent as the appropriate non-return rate affects the validity of the final estimate of gains to the United States through foreign student non-return, but does not affect the methodology. Similarly, the values assumed for age, prior education, duration of study and transportation may be questioned, but changing numbers would not alter the method. Raising this non-return rate to 20 per cent and juggling the other figures would not substantially affect the conclusion drawn. A more direct methodological question, however, involves the assumption that non-returning foreign students of a particular age will add to the United States economy in relation to what it would have cost to educate them in the United States. This assumption implies that 20 years of education and experience in a foreign country is equivalent to 20 years of education and experience in the United States. In general, the assumption is justifiable, and non-returnees are probably as capable, on the average, as United States students with similar education. The degree to which problems of language and other cultural difficulties might hamper the non-returnee will depend on the occupation and the individual.

2. U.S.-CANADIAN EDUCATIONAL EXCHANGE

The second estimate was made by Wilkinson.[31] To estimate educational costs he, like Grubel and Scott, included direct educational costs, opportunity costs of student time (foregone earnings), and maintenance costs. He used Canadian cost figures to do the costing for both the non-returning U.S. students in Canada and for Canadian students remaining abroad. There was no breakdown by field of study and no apparent need to differentiate amounts of prior schooling. The cost of upbringing to age 14 was added and an adjustment was made for sponsorship variation.

When valuing and comparing student flows specifically between Canada and the United States, Wilkinson introduced a non-return rate of 5.7 per cent, derived from a 1961/62 Canadian survey of foreign students, for non-returning United States students in Canada. He speculated that the figure for Canadian students in the United States is at least 5.7 per cent, in which case, according to his estimates, Canada is a net loser of human capital. (But Canada is a net gainer vis-à-vis the rest of the world because 14.3 per cent of all foreign students in Canada indicated their intent to remain following their study.) [32]

The work of Grubel and Scott and of Wilkinson provides one workable methodology for evaluating gains and losses associated with study abroad. Such approximations provide a general idea of the magnitude of the "problem." [33] Their calculations, however, may be more worthwhile from a propagandistic viewpoint than they are representative of "true" human capital value.

Before leaving the examples, several points should be emphasized: in both cases, the authors disaggregate the student population but not beyond splitting students by level of education; only home country figures were used and a simple dichotomization into returnees and non-returnees was made without considering variations in the length of study abroad. Further attention will be given to these points below.

PRESENT VALUE ESTIMATES AND INTERNATIONAL MIGRATION

To measure the human capital value of a migrating individual in present value terms is to ask what he can be expected to contribute to society during the remainder of his lifetime, as figured by what society will pay for his services—his earnings. The emphasis of a present-value approach is on the *utilization* of, rather than the resources embodied in, human capital. [34]

Once appropriate estimates for expected future earnings are determined, year by year, the procedure for calculating present values is relatively simple. The projected earnings expected each year until death (or sometimes retirement) can be discounted back to the present and the discounted values for each year can be summed. Thus the earnings stream is represented as a single dollar figure and allowance is made for the fact that a dollar available today is worth more over one's lifetime than a dollar acquired later in life. Unfortunately, the choice of the appropriate estimating procedure and the appropriate discount rate is not as easy as the calculation. Estimates are sensitive to both choices. [35] Typically, the figures for expected future earnings are derived from census data indicating what an average individual earns currently at each age and with a certain amount of educational attainment. In effect, a cross-section of the present is projected into the future. (This will be illustrated later in this chapter.) Other methods are, however, available for estimating future earnings.

REPLACEMENT COST VERSUS PRESENT VALUES

If the market equilibrium conditions of theoretical economics existed, valuing human capital at replacement cost or at discounted present values would give the same result. But to assume equilibrium conditions evades the question; under the existing circumstances, the two methods do yield different results.

Measuring human capital in cost terms as a way of assessing the resources that have gone into the making of a man is quite different from using cost valuations to assess gains and losses through migration. The most serious distortions are likely to occur when replacement cost estimates exceed present value. For instance, the cost of educating a doctor who is emigrating from the capital city of a Latin American country to the United States (or of educating his replacement) may be much higher than the actual value of his services in the Latin American market. This may in fact be one factor which led him to migrate.

If a trained individual emigrates, he takes with him his productivity (and his earnings) from the moment he migrates. If there is a lag between the time of his leaving and the time a trained replacement becomes available, the interim loss of productivity should be considered as part of the loss attending the emigration.[36] Using replacement cost would not pick up this human-capital loss. Where lead-times for training are long, this difference can be substantial unless a process of continuous replacement is figured into the training system.[37] Consider also the replacement cost of training a new engineer, age 20, versus training a new engineer, age 40. The costs might be quite similar, whereas the present value of the lifetime earnings stream for the former would be greater.

On the other hand, if present-value calculations depend on cross-sectional data, and if the cross-sectional cut is made at a point of boom or bust, the profile of the relative earnings across occupations (or across countries) will not be representative and will certainly change; demands for particular levels of skill (and specializations within levels of skill) do differ through time and between localities. In that case, cost may be a more accurate proxy for some "true" present value than the present value determined from a distorted pattern of relative earnings. Indeed, Wilkinson felt that "variations from year to year in demands for people with varying amounts and types of schooling would alter present and future occupational groups and hence individual and total discounted values." [38] The importance of demand differentials will depend on whether occupational categories are broadly or finely defined and whether analysis emphasizes occupations particularly subject to cyclical fluctuations. For broad categorizations there is little problem.

CHOOSING APPROPRIATE EARNINGS STREAMS

If present values are accepted in principle as useful human capital measures for valuing migrants and for analyzing migration decisions, all that remains is to define the conceptually appropriate lifetime-earnings streams from which present values should be calculated. In this chapter this will be done for one-way migration. Remigration will be introduced in the following chapter.

The expected earnings of a person considering a move can be approximated, from both individual and social perspectives, by establishing what "similar individuals" on the average are earning in the area of origin or in the area of destination. If similar individuals are properly chosen and their earnings are known, then expected earnings, upon which the rational decision to move will be based, will presumably equal or closely approximate actual earnings, thus providing an accurate indicator of migrating human capital.[39]

The accuracy of earnings estimates will depend, then, on the choice of characteristics defining similar individuals for whom earnings are known. Restricting consideration for the moment to cross-sectional earnings, is it possible to delineate a meaningful reference population without retreating to the individual level? Suppose, for example, that it were possible to determine age-earnings profiles within sex-race-educational attainment-occupation categories. Would this be enough?

The following hypothetical case illustrates that choice of the appropriate earnings streams involves even more than the above critical disaggregation. In areas A and B, respectively, there are two groups of individuals who are matched on sex, race, age, educational attainment, and occupation. Assume that the average present value of future earnings for group A is higher than for group B, even when cross-sectional earnings are adjusted for possible market differences between the two areas and for differentials in expected growth rates. Given this fact, migration should be from B to A if the decision to move is economically rational (and if the difference in values more than covers the costs of moving and relocation). However, it is not difficult to imagine circumstances prompting a move in the opposite direction—in what appears to be an irrational manner. Consider, for instance, a skilled worker trained in A, where training is of higher quality and more up-to-date, and where there are more opportunities to use the new talent in a job situation. He will have an advantage over similar individuals in B who share his characteristics but lack his quality of training and experience. His salary expectations may, in fact, be higher in B than in A, and he may move.

More concretely, incomes of white males with the same years of schooling are higher in the North than in the South (except at college levels). Yet in spite of lower average income, people move into the South, suggesting that the Southern in-migrant is not typical of the area into which he is moving. It is possible that some of the difference might be accounted for in terms of age or occupation. It is also possible that important non-economic elements play a part and cause persons to move even though it appears to be to their economic disadvantage. If, however, it is assumed that an individual will not normally migrate unless his potential discounted earnings stream in the new area is going to be at least as high as that of the area of origin, and then if a perverse migration occurs even within race-age-sex-schooling categories (as seems to be the case), the fallacy of using present values of average individuals at destination within such categories is underlined.

The fact that a migrant from one area can command higher earnings than similar individuals in another area suggests that further differentiation is needed before appropriate human capital values can be determined. It also suggests that previous location, particularly location of education, may be an important differentiating variable. Furthermore, the procedure for assigning human capital values while using the same earnings streams for *both* immigrants to an area and for natives in the area appears questionable, and is dictated largely by practical considerations. An example of this procedure and of the difficulties inherent in choosing appropriate earnings streams when estimating aggregate human capital gains or losses can be seen from Rashi Fein's study of interregional migration within the United States.[40]

Fein was interested in determining the net human capital gains or losses through migration to various regions of the United States. Working only with males, he broke down migrant flows by age, race and educational attainment within each major geographical area (as defined by the United States census). Focusing on the South, he then computed net in- or outflows for each age-race-education category. To get estimates of social net capital gains or losses associated with migration, he multiplied net flows by average discounted values of Southern age-earnings streams (discounted at 5 per cent) for each race-education category. These subtotals were then summed to give the overall net gain or loss to the region. Present values became, in effect, weightings for the various demographic categories. Fein's procedure preserved the disaggregation by sex, age, race, and schooling, making allowance for life-time earnings differentials that are linked to these characteristics. However, the distinction between characteristics of immigrants and emigrants was unfortunately lost in this procedure for valuing human capital.

The potential importance of taking market differences into account can be illustrated by making some simple calculations related to Fein's work. The distribution of schooling among 1955–60 out-migrants from the South as a whole is very close to the distribution of schooling among 1955–60 migrants into the South. Assume an average present-value figure of $40,000 for income streams of white male Southerners leaving the South and of $50,000 for white male migrants from other regions into the South. Compare (Table 24) the net human capital gain when in-

TABLE 24—Alternative estimates of net human capital gains from migration for the United States South, 1950–1960

	NUMBER MIGRATING[a]	PRESENT VALUE (PER MIGRANT)	TOTAL VALUE (MILLIONS)	NET HUMAN CAPITAL GAIN (MILLIONS)
Out-migration	554,900	40,000	22,196	. . . .
In-migration:				
a. Valued at destination	579,100	40,000	23,164	968
b. Valued at origin	579,100	50,000	28,955	6,759

[a] The figures for numbers migrating in and out of the South, exclusive of the intra-South migration, are taken from William N. Parker's comment on Rashi Fein's article (see footnote 40), in the *Southern Economic Journal*, XXXII, No. 1, Part II (July 1965), p. 126, Table I.

migrants are valued at destination and at origin; both relative and absolute increases are substantial. Raising or lowering present migrant values would change numbers but not the argument. From the perspective of the South, Fein's method (valuing both streams at Southern values) sets a minimum for net gains, while

valuing both in- and out-migrants at their respective origins sets
a maximum.

SCHOOLING, EXPERIENCE AND HUMAN
CAPITAL GAINS AND LOSSES

It seems, then, that until data are available that further distinguish among migrants, there can be no firm answers concerning
the most appropriate lifetime-earnings stream to use. However, it
is possible to speculate which of the streams, at origin or at destination, most accurately represents an individual's expected earnings and his productive contribution. Such speculation is keyed to
the fact that knowing location provides extra information about
individuals. Location can act as a proxy for differences in quality
of schooling, environmental experience, and job experience.[41]

In line with the particular interest in study abroad and non-
return, but with broader implications, the two factors tied to
location receiving most attention here will be differences in quality of schooling and differences in experience—both on-the-job
experience and more general experience.

Differences in quality of schooling by region and the manner
in which they affect income has been difficult to document.[42]
In spite of wide intraregional variations, however, broad interregional differences can be identified. Scores on the Armed
Forces Qualification Test, cross-tabulated by educational attainment within geographical areas, clearly point to differences in the
quality of schooling.[43] On an international plane, educational differences can be dramatic, particularly when comparison is between an advanced Western nation and a less developed African,
Asian, or Latin American country.

Tying location to experiential learning is more difficult. Learning from experience begins before employment and occurs outside the schools. There is ample evidence that youth from rural
communities start at a disadvantage when they come to the city;
the extent of the disadvantage varies with the nature of the rural

area.[44] Similarly, international migrants encounter many disadvantages in a new cultural setting. A measure is needed of this disadvantage as it is reflected in earnings. Knowing where an individual had his secondary schooling would provide information concerning his location during critical years of experiential learning as well as identify his formal schooling geographically.

Learning on the job is a major component in the formation of human competencies.[45] There can be no doubt that work opportunities and, with them, opportunities for learning on the job vary substantially from one place to another. This is glaringly obvious if one looks across nations. It is sufficiently evident within the United States, even when an adjustment is made for age, sex, and prior schooling. There is a strong presumption that knowledge of the location in which men have acquired their work experience will improve statistical predictions of their competencies in much the same way that knowledge of the location of schooling would.

How far a migrant's previous experiential learning may be transferable to his new setting is another matter. Undoubtedly there is selectivity in such transferability; he can move into the new environment carrying his experience with him only to the extent that the new environment gives scope for its use.

This transfer of experience may contribute to differentiation of labor markets between natives and in-migrants or between natives trained at home and natives trained abroad, especially in the middle and higher occupational brackets. It is a reasonable generalization that unless a man can take enough of his acquired competencies with him to ensure earnings at least as high as those he would receive in the present location, he will not move—at least not if he already has a substantial investment in such competencies and there is a demand for them in the present location. (This must be taken into consideration when judging foreign student non-return.)

These comments concerning effects on potential earnings associated with location of schooling and experience can be systematized by setting up a rough typology of schooling-work combinations as between two regions, A and B (which might be two regions within the same country or which might be two countries). Within any age- sex- race- education- and, ideally, prior occupation-grouping we could further classify migrants who moved from place A to place B, according the timing of their move, using, for instance, five moments (or events) in the migrants' life histories: birth; schooling (location at graduation?); first employment; a subsequent employment (say 10 years later?); and employment after age 40. Using these, the following could be distinguished:

1. Those born in A, but who migrated to B for schooling and work. (Sequence $1 = A \rightarrow B \rightarrow B \rightarrow B \rightarrow B$)

2. Those born in A and schooled in A, but who migrated to B as soon as their formal schooling was completed and who have worked only in B. (Sequence $2 = A \rightarrow A \rightarrow B \rightarrow B \rightarrow B$)

3. Those born in A and schooled in A who remained to work for some time in A, but moved to B before they were 40, continuing to work in B thereafter. (Sequence $3 = A \rightarrow A \rightarrow A \rightarrow B \rightarrow B$)

4. Those born in A and schooled in A who worked in A to at least the age of 40, migrating to B after that age. (Sequence $4 = A \rightarrow A \rightarrow A \rightarrow A \rightarrow B$)

We could, of course, add an all-A sequence (no migration), and we could build in remigration.[46]

For each of the above, what would be the most conceptually appropriate earnings stream as between earnings in the area of origin, A, and of destination, B?

1. The first category of individuals might be expected to have an age-earnings profile very close to or even the same as comparable lifetime B residents of the same race, sex, age, years of schooling—and perhaps prior occupation—because all schooling and work experience is in B.

2. Those in the second category were schooled in A, but their entire work experience is in B. Profiles of their average earnings would be expected to fall somewhere between those of lifetime

residents of A and B, but closer to the latter. Deviations from average B earnings streams would increase with greater regional differences in average quality of schooling[47] and with greater regional differences in the out-of-school environment of the migrant's adolescent years (which can be approximated by splitting into urban and rural as well as attaching to location). Also related to this, though partially independent of it, is the extent to which migrants from A enter labor markets in B that are distinct from those in which lifetime residents of B sell their services.

3. Migrants in category 3 should also, on the average, have future income streams falling somewhere between those of lifetime residents of A and of B. The older they are at migration and the more experience they bring with them, the closer one might expect them to be to the lifetime residents of their area of origin. Here (as also in case 2), if migrants to B work in branch organizations which have head offices in and are operated by individuals from A, their earnings streams should approximate A-type earnings. This is merely an extreme of differentiated labor markets—islands of A located within the geographical boundaries of B. On the other hand, the younger the migrant the larger the part of his experience he will accumulate in B (segregation of labor markets aside), and the more clearly will his future income stream approach the B pattern.

4. If the movement to region B comes after age 40, it is possible that earnings in B will be similar to those in A, where schooling and work experience were obtained. Non-economic locational preferences for B aside, the A income potential should in fact give a minimum estimate of earnings streams in B. It is assumed that a rational person established in a career in A will not move after age 40 unless he can earn at least as much in his new location virtually from the start. Although there are exceptions, there is sufficient empirical evidence to show that after age 40, most men are recouping investments in themselves rather than making new ones, intuitive reasoning quite aside.[48]

In the above, no attention has been given to two obvious factors that affect productivity and earnings streams of any given population of migrants: ability and attitudes toward work. It can reasonably be assumed that the ability distribution for a given age, race, sex, education category of the population will not differ much among countries or regions. This does not, however, guarantee that the average ability of migrants is no different from that of non-migrants, once disaggregation has established homogeneity of population subgroups in other critical respects. The saving feature of assuming that they are equal is the critical disaggregation presupposed; there can be no presumption that within each population subcategory mobility will be correlated either positively or negatively with ability.[49] Differences in attitudes toward work are a problem that will simply be ignored for the present. It should be noted, however, that both ability and attitudes can be objectively assessed. It is probable that the locational proxy which picks up differences in experiential learning includes an element of attitudinal difference and that attitudes would be partially incorporated in this way.

MAKING THE CONCEPT OPERATIONAL

While the above discussion points to problems in choosing appropriate earnings streams for use when calculating human capital values and suggests conceptual bases for dealing with these problems, it does little to make the suggested concepts operational.

The United States census contains the minimum disaggregations of sex, age, school attainment, race, and current occupation by broad geographic area and by income. However, there is no breakdown that separates out migrants in each of these cells. Ideally, one would also like to have migrants' location of birth and of schooling, as well as occupation prior to migration and location at the time of migration. While multiple cross-tabulations of this sort are not out of the question for regional analysis using United States census data, it will be many years before similar data are available for other countries.

The above discussion, based on the assumption that earnings averages are meaningful, may hold for the United States but does it have validity in less developed countries? Not only are censuses less complete but market conditions are less competitive than in the United States. Earnings streams have been used to determine rates of returns to education in various developing nations and, as will be seen in the example below, even to estimate gains and losses associated with foreign study. But little attention has been given to the validity of the earnings data which have come from such diverse sources as tax files, job advertisements and responses to special questionnaires administered to samples of individuals in various occupations. In all the examples of which I am aware, the data are for a point in time and take on a static, cross-sectional character.

When using earnings profiles in countries where recruitment to jobs is only loosely associated with productive ability of individuals, interpretations of results must be cautious. Furthermore, it is possible that earnings distributions may be discriminatory and therefore disaggregation will not adequately moderate the differences and averages will lose meaning. For instance, in a particular country lawyers may earn very high salaries or very low salaries, with very few individuals falling in between, creating a bimodal distribution that may be tied as much to "political pull" as to ability or training.

Another operational problem that should be mentioned is the problem of comparing earnings streams across national borders. An adjustment must be made for differences in purchasing power of migrants' earnings at origin and destination. Although differences in the standard of living exist to a certain extent among regions of the same country, comparisons are not complicated by currency differences.

These operational problems are not insurmountable. They will be discussed in more detail in Part IV. Having pointed to potential problems associated with present value evaluations (and having, I hope, also established the potential utility of present-value measurement as an analytical tool in the study of migration), let us look at an illustration of the method.

THE PRESENT VALUE OF FOREIGN STUDENT NON-RETURN: AN ILLUSTRATION

Rather than apply the present-value method to determining U.S. gains associated with foreign student non-return, let us take an example in which the calculation is attempted from the viewpoint of a sending country.[50]

The human capital loss to India associated with student non-return from the United States has been estimated in present-value terms by Gopal Dorai.[51] From advertisements by the Union Public Service Commission announcing employment opportunities and salaries in India, he calculated present values of expected earnings streams for United States-trained Indians employed in India. Separate calculations were made using discount rates of 5 per cent, 10 per cent and 15 per cent. Dorai adjusted the totals for unemployment among foreign-educated Indians and he separated, where possible, undergraduates from postgraduates.

For the overseas undergraduate, Dorai calculated present values of $43,427, $33,324, and $14,200 respectively at the 5%, 10% and 15% discount rates. For a postgraduate the amounts were $55,819, $30,410, and $20,307 respectively. To estimate the capital value of non-returning foreign students, i.e. the social loss to India for the period 1958–66, Dorai multiplied each present value estimate by the number of non-returnees in each year, assuming first that all students were undergraduates and then that all were postgraduates.

The results for the 5 and 15% discount rates are shown in the column of Table 25 labeled "total capital values."

From the Dorai example, it is evident that the rate of discount used makes a significant difference in the total estimated loss. The amounts involved may seem large, particularly the 1966 value, reflecting a large jump in non-return following the new immigration

TABLE 25—Estimated capital values at age 25, non-returning Indian students who have studied in the United States, 1958–66, in dollars[a]

YEAR	NUMBER OF NON-RETURNING FOREIGN STUDENTS[b]	TOTAL CAPITAL VALUES[c]			
		UNDERGRADUATES		GRADUATES	
		at 5%	at 15%	at 5%	at 15%
1958	96	4,168,992	1,363,200	5,358,624	589,449
1959	74	3,213,598	1,050,800	4,130,606	454,366
1960	69	2,996,463	979,800	3,851,511	423,666
1961	86	3,734,722	1,221,200	4,808,434	528,048
1962	114	4,950,678	1,618,800	6,363,366	699,970
1963	434	18,847,318	6,162,800	24,225,446	2,664,799
1964	158	6,861,466	2,243,600	8,819,402	970,134
1965	140	6,079,780	1,988,000	7,814,660	859,613
1966	1,015	44,078,405	14,413,000	56,656,285	6,232,191
1958–1966	2,186	94,931,422	31,041,200	122,028,334	13,422,236

[a] Taken from: Gopal Dorai, "Economics of the International Flow of Students: A Cost-Benefit Analysis," Wayne State University, Department of Economics, 1967 (mimeographed).

[b] For the years, 1962–1966, the number of non-returning Indian students was taken as the number of students who adjusted their status to immigrant in each year. For the remaining years, 1958–1961, student non-return was calculated by applying the ratio student-to-immigrant-visa-adjustments/total immigrants, determined for years 1962–1966, to the figure for total immigrants in the earlier years. This procedure was necessary because information on student visa adjustments was not available for years before 1962. The problems of using this means of determining non-return are set out in chapter 2.

[c] The present values used to obtain the total capital value estimates are:

Undergraduates: $43,427 (at a 5 per cent discount rate)   Graduates: $55,893 (at a 5 per cent discount rate)
$14,200 (at a 15 per cent discount rate) $20,307 (at a 15 per cent discount rate)

It should be noted that Dorai took his estimating procedure one step further. Assuming that what is lost to India is only that part of future earnings that would have been saved and invested, he multiplied all human capital values by .11, a figure representing the rate of saving among Indians. This gave him his final estimate of social loss.

197

legislation of 1965. However, it should be pointed out that in 1967 the total number of scientific, engineering and medical manpower emigrating from India has been estimated at only 2 per cent of the total output of scientists, engineers, and physicians in India in that year.[52] Unemployment among the educated in India is not a myth. In short, the absolute values of estimated human capital gain or loss must be put in perspective in much the same way as absolute numbers of migrants must be before they acquire meaning.

SUMMARY AND COMMENT ON ESTIMATING AGGREGATE HUMAN CAPITAL GAINS AND LOSSES THROUGH MIGRATION

The application of human-capital principles to estimating gains and losses through migration requires more complex analyses than have previously been done. Migrant populations must be disaggregated into more homogeneous groups and greater attention must be given to a variety of personal characteristics, including locus of schooling and experience, before attaching human capital values. Gross rather than net flows should be assessed. In most cases, present values rather than costs are the more appropriate human capital measure.

Because these preferred procedures make severe demands on existing sources of data, they have seldom been employed in conventional assessments of gains and losses. Although inventive compromises have been used to make estimates for both international and internal human capital flows, aggregate estimates may nevertheless be misleading. If one incorporates remigration (as will be done in the following chapter), the accuracy of most current estimates of aggregate gains and losses must be even further questioned.

In spite of the obvious conceptual and empirical difficulties surrounding the calculation of aggregate gains and losses through migration, serious suggestions have been made that nations gaining high-level manpower, as measured in human capital terms, should compensate losing nations for their losses. Such suggestions presuppose not only an accurate accounting system of who goes where, when, and for how long, but also presuppose a correct and agreed-upon measure for setting absolute values on migratory flows. Neither exists at present.

Major questions also remain concerning the relationship between international flows of physical capital and of human capital. The two are similar but different, and the extent to which they can be considered to offset each other has not been established. It is not clear, for instance, that remittances should be figured as a direct offset to human capital flows on a one-to-one basis, no matter how the human capital values are calculated. Nor is it clear that human capital values of migrating individuals and the monetary value of foreign aid, large parts of which involve physical capital, should be compared directly, as is frequently done.

In view of the above, attempts to measure human capital gains and losses for the purpose of balancing international flows of goods and services by making compensatory payments seem ill-advised.[54] For a nation to legally inhibit the in- or out-movement of individuals on the basis of such aggregate measurements would also seem ill-advised. Similarly, establishing the "debt" owed to his home country by an emigrant on the basis of human capital assessments seems inappropriate. Such policy questions receive fuller treatment in chapter 9.

What purpose, then, is served by calculating aggregate gains and losses other than a propaganda one (which could be positive)? As such calculations are incorporated into social decision models, their utility will become clearer. As will be apparent in chapter 6, a more appropriate application of human capital concepts to migration lies in the analysis of private and social migration decisions.

NOTES

[1] A good discussion of earlier work may be found in Brinley Thomas, *International Migration and Economic Development, A Trend Report and Bibliography*, United Nations Educational, Scientific, and Cultural Organization (SS.60/XI.6/A), Paris, 1961.

[2] In the nineteenth century, however, estimates of human capital gains and losses were made for the United States, England, and Germany. Both replacement cost and present-value methods of measurement were used. See Friedrich Kapp, "Immigration and the Commissioners of Emigration in the State of New York," in *Historical Aspects of the Immigration Problem: Selected Documents*, ed. Edith Abbott (Chicago: The University of Chicago Press, 1926), pp. 370–78; and Richmond Mayo-Smith, *Emigration and Immigration* (New York: Scribner's Sons, 1892), pp. 105–21.

[3] For instance, solution of the Leontief paradox (that U.S. trade was labour-using and capital-conserving instead of the reverse—as predicted by international trade theorems) awaited better identification of the human capital component in production.

[4] Thomas, p. 61. A similar view is expressed in F. Musgrove, *The Migratory Elite* (London: Heinemann, 1963).

[5] Mary Jean Bowman, "Principles in the Valuation of Human Capital," *The Review of Income and Wealth*, XIV, No. 3 (September 1968), pp. 217–46.

[6] *Ibid.*, p. 242; Also, see Anthony Scott, "The Human Capital Approach to International Migration," a paper prepared for the Conference on Research in Income and Wealth, The University of Wisconsin, November 15–16, 1968, p. 27.

[7] See the following three works by Harry Johnson: "Economics of the 'Brain Drain': The Canadian Case," *Minerva*, III, No. 3 (Spring 1965), pp. 299–311; "The Cosmopolitan Viewpoint," in *Brain Drain*, ed. Walter Adams (New York: Macmillan, 1968), pp. 69–91; and "Some Aspects of Brain Drain," *Pakistan Development Review*, VII (Autumn 1967), pp. 379–411.

See also Herbert G. Grubel and Anthony Scott, "The International Flow of Human Capital, the Brain Drain," *American Economic Review*, LVI, No. 2 (May 1966), pp. 268–74. With "Discussion" by Burton Weisbrod, *ibid.*, pp. 277–80.

[8] Brinley Thomas, "International Circulation of Human Capital," *Minerva*, V, No. 4 (Summer 1967), pp. 479–506; with "Comments" by H. G. Johnson and A. D. Scott, *Minerva*, VI, No. 1 (Autumn 1967), pp. 105–16 and a "Reply" by B. Thomas, *Minerva*, VI, No. 3 (Spring 1968), pp. 423–27.

John Shearer, "In Defense of Traditional Views of the 'Brain Drain' Problem," *Exchange* (Fall 1966), pp. 17–25.

Alan Patinkin, "A Nationalist Model," in Adams, pp. 92–108.

[9] An externality refers to a contribution made by an individual "to the welfare or productivity of others in the country of his residence over and above what the individual is paid for doing, and for which he could not be paid in a competitive market for his services. . . ." Furthermore an externality "is

peculiar to him personally and in his professional capacity," Johnson, in Adams, pp. 77–8.

[10] Xenophon Zolotas, *International Migration and Economic Development* (Papers and Lectures Series, No. 21, Athens: Bank of Greece, 1966).

[11] Bernard Okun and Richard W. Richardson, "Regional Income Inequality and Internal Population Migration," *Economic Development and Cultural Change,* IX, No. 2 (January 1961), pp. 128–43.

[12] Charles P. Kindleberger, "Emigration and Economic Growth," Banca Nazionale del Lavoro *Quarterly Review,* XVIII (September 1965), p. 235.

[13] Zolotas, pp. 11–23.

Migration is accompanied by effects on the flow of money, on patterns of consumption and investment, and by demographic effects. For treatment of remittances, see Tadeusz Stark, "The Economic Desirability of Migration," *The International Migration Review,* I (Spring 1967), pp. 7–9, or Robert H. Eldridge, "Emigration and the Turkish Balance of Payments, "*Middle East Journal,* XX, No. 3 (Summer 1966). For the economic effect of immigration on consumption and investment, see E. J. Mishan and L. Needleman, "Immigration: Some Economic Effects," *Lloyds Bank Review,* LXX (July 1966), pp. 33–46. For demographic effects, see J. Isaacs, *Economics of Migration* (London: Paul Kegan and Co., Ltd., 1947).

[14] Mayo-Smith, p. 105.

[15] This section draws heavily from an article written as a collaborator with Mary Jean Bowman titled "Schooling, Experience, and Gains and Losses Through Migration," *Journal of the American Statistical Association,* LXII (September 1967), pp. 875–98.

[16] E. A. J. Johnson, "The Place of Learning, Science, Vocational Training and Art in Pre-Smithian Thought," *Journal of Economic History,* XXIV, No. 2 (June 1964), 120–44.

[17] See Footnote 2.

[18] Edward F. Denison, *The Sources of Economic Growth in the United States and the Alternatives before Us* (Committee for Economic Development Supplementary Paper No. 13; New York, 1962).

[19] T. W. Schulz, *The Economic Value of Education* (New York: Columbia University Press, 1963).

[20] Gary Becker, *Human Capital* (New York: Columbia University Press, 1964).

[21] Jacob Mincer, "On-the-Job Training: Costs, Returns, and Some Implications," *The Journal of Political Economy,* LXX, No. 5, Part II (October 1962), pp. 50–79.

[22] Mary Jean Bowman, *The Review of Income and Wealth,* XIV, No. 3, p. 222.

[23] Information on the subject can be found in Mark Blaug, *Economics of Education, A Selected Annotated Bibliography* (London: Pergamon Press, 1966), and Mary Jean Bowman, "The Human Investment Revolution in Economic Thought," *Sociology of Education,* XXXIX, No. 2 (Spring 1966), pp. 111–37.

[24] Criticism and rebuttal are plentiful. See, for instance, Mark Blaug, "The Rate of Return on Investment in Education in Great Britain," *Manchester School* (September 1965), pp. 205–62; H. Villard, "Discussion of Becker's Underinvestment in College Education," *American Economic Review,* Papers and Proceedings, L, No. 2 (May 1960), pp. 375–78.

There are several assumptions in the more puristic variants of human capital investment theory that are frequently challenged:

The theory assumes operation of a free-market society in which there is near-perfect mobility, near-perfect knowledge, perfect competition, free choice, and no discrimination in labor markets. In such a system wages and salaries are accurate indicators of economic productivity.

People are economically rational. Therefore non-monetary and psychic benefits such as security, status, and climate preferences are not included in decisions.

All education is viewed as an investment. No allowance is made for education as a consumption item.

All costs and benefits of education accrue to the decision maker; there are no "spill-over" effects.

If applied to social decisions, human capital investment theory operates at the margin, indicating the direction in which investment should move but not providing an indication of the degree of movement.

The empirical simplifications that evoke most criticism are:

Men are assumed to have equal native ability.

Current cross-sectional data are adequate for projecting future earnings.

The assumptions are less restrictive applied to private human capital investment decisions than to social decisions. Privately-expected earnings can replace socially-determined earnings. The private expectations presumably include individual adjustments for market imperfections, ability, and future economic changes anticipated, as individually *perceived*. Still assumed, however, is knowledge allowing proper perception.

A concept can be useful even though all assumptions do not mirror reality. In this case, the most important assumption underlying application of the human capital concept is that, if conditions were met, society would be economically better. Accepting this, the imperfect reality we live in can be compared with a better system, and points of deviation can be identified. Social decisions are made from a viewpoint. A better economic system may be only one goal. Application of the human capital concept, as application of all economic theory, seeks to provide clues for approaching the economically rational, which is not the same as saying that economic rationality must predominate. It provides one standard by which alternatives can be judged.

Also worth considering is the fact that analysis can control for many of the factors, such as ability or social class, which are assumed to have no influence on earnings but which in reality do. Furthermore, non-monetary benefits and spill-overs can be negative as well as positive. And, although market imperfections are present, the push and pull of the market is felt, perhaps strongly enough to justify the assumptions made. Finally, people may not profess to be economically rational, but they may act *as if* they were making rational investment decisions, whether or not they think they are.

Part of the present research is devoted to pushing back the limits imposed by the assumptions of human capital investment theory when theory is operationalized.

[25] For a more general evaluation of the human capital approach of alternative techniques used, see: Mary Jean Bowman, "Human Capital Concepts and Measures," *Economics of Higher Education,* ed. S. Mushkin (Washington, D.C.: U.S. Government Printing Office, 1962), pp. 69–92; W. G. Bowen, *Economic Aspects of Education. Three Essays* (Princeton, N.J.: Industrial

Relations Section, Princeton University, 1964), pp. 3–38; and B. W. Wilkinson, *Studies in the Economics of Education* (Occasional Paper No. 4; Ottawa: Department of Labour Economics and Research Branch, 1965), chapter I.

[26] *Scientific Brain Drain from the Developing Countries: Twenty-third Report by the Committee on Government Operations* (Washington, D.C.: U.S. Government Printing Office, 1968), p. 5.

[27] T. W. Schultz, *The Economic Value of Education* (New York: Columbia University Press, 1963).

[28] The contrast between theoretical and empirical treatments of brain drains can be striking, as shown by Grubel and Scott's estimates of human capital associated with migration. In their theoretical work they emphasize the diverse effects of out-migration on social welfare of the country of origin, defining social welfare as per capita incomes of all initial residents, whatever their place of residence after migration. (Grubel and Scott, *American Economic Review*, LVI, No. 2, pp. 268–74). They discard the more commonly used addition to Gross National Product as a social standard. However, Grubel and Scott do not attempt direct empirical assessments in such a framework; the practical difficulties are manifold. Instead, they turn to measures of additions to, or subtractions from, total productivity. Using a cost approach, they emphasize gains to countries of destination rather than losses to countries of origin. They have worked with migrating scientists and engineers, economists and foreign students. See the following: "The Immigration of Scientists and Engineers to the United States," *The Journal of Political Economy*, LXXXIV, No. 4 (August 1966), pp. 368–78; "The Characteristics of Foreigners in the U.S. Economics Profession," *American Economics Review*, LVII, No. 1 (March 1967), pp. 131–45; and "The Cost of U.S. College Exchange Programs," *The Journal of Human Resources*, I, No. 2 (Fall 1966), pp. 81–98.

[29] *Ibid.*, p. 98.

[30] *Ibid.*

[31] Bruce W. Wilkinson, *Studies in the Economics of Education*, p. 19.

[32] Bruce W. Wilkinson, "Some Economic Aspects of Education in Canada," (unpublished Ph.D. dissertation, Massachusetts Institute of Technology, 1964), p. 149. Wilkinson also made detailed estimates for non-student migrant flows. He first divided the migrant population into broad occupational categories; he then estimated the average number of years of schooling for each category and applied appropriate cost figures for each amount of prior schooling. An adjustment was made for money and personal effects which migrants transported at the time of the move.

[33] Anthony Scott, p. 54.

[34] Mary Jean Bowman, "Schultz, Denison, and the Contribution of 'Eds' to National Income Growth," *The Journal of Political Economy*, LXXII, No. 5 (October 1964), pp. 450–64.

[35] To discount the earnings for year n, one simply divides the anticipated earnings (Y) by the value $(1 + r)^n$ where r equals the discount rate—usually the rate of interest one might expect to get on an alternative investment. The present value of a future income stream can be represented, then, by:

$$\sum_{1}^{n} \frac{Y}{(1 + r)^n}$$

The intricacies of choosing an appropriate discount rate will not be discussed here. A standard practice is to vary the discount rate, using a maximum value, a minimum value and an intermediate value. Nor will allowance be made for personal time preference functions which enter the discounting procedure. For a discussion of the choice of "reservation rates" see Valerien Harvey, "Economic Aspects of Teachers' Salaries," (unpublished Ph.D. dissertation, Department of Education, the University of Chicago, 1967). See also Martin J. Bailey, "Formal Criteria for Investment Decisions," *The Journal of Political Economy*, LXVII, No. 5 (October 1959), pp. 476–88; J. Hirschleifer, "On the Theory of Optimal Investment Decisions," *ibid.*, LXVI, No. 4 (August 1958), pp. 329–52; and, M. S. Feldstein and J. S. Fleming, "The Problem of Time-Stream Evaluation: Present Value versus Internal Rates of Return Rules," *Bulletin of Economics and Statistics*, XXVI (1964), pp. 79–85.

[36] This loss is apart from the loss that might occur as a result of his making other factors of production temporarily unusable.

[37] However, if human capital is being produced in oversupply in order to allow continuous replacement, there is a built-in cost—the cost that society is willing to pay to avoid temporary disruptions.

[38] Wilkinson, *Studies in the Economics of Education*, p. 19.

[39] If earnings within the disaggregated categories are determined from cross-sectional data, the qualifications must be entered where there is a growing economy, these expectations will include adjustment for anticipated growth, taken into account by adjusting cross-sectional earnings (Becker, chapter 4, uses such adjustments). In this chapter and the next, the simplifying assumptions are made that the cross-sectional earnings of "similar individuals" can be adjusted for growth as well as for changes in demand which might cause expected and actual earnings to diverge. In chapter 8, an alternative to the cross-sectional method is used in which adjustments for growth are incorporated in a different manner.

[40] Rashi Fein, "Educational Patterns in Southern Migration," *The Southern Economic Journal*, XXXII, No. 1, Part II (July 1965), pp. 106–24.

[41] These factors can be particularly important in considering migration for education and migration following study. Presumably many persons study abroad to obtain a higher-quality education than would be possible at home. Presumably this education should put them in a favored position when they return, in relation to local individuals who are similar in other respects. If home-country average earnings for similar individuals were adopted as the expected earnings and as a measure of the contribution which would be made on return, an underestimate would probably result. By such standards, one might predict non-return. In this chapter, however, the argument is restricted to one-way migration.

[42] Finis Welch, "The Determinants of the Return to Schooling in Rural Farm Areas, 1959," (unpublished Ph.D. dissertation, Department of Economics, The University of Chicago, 1966).

[43] Bernard D. Karpinos, "The Mental Qualification of American Youths for Military Service and Its Relationship to Educational Attainment—A Differential Evaluation," U.S. Department of the Army, Office of the Surgeon General, Medical Statistics Agency (Washington, D.C., 1960). (Mimeographed.)

[44] The critical importance of community characteristics in determining

differences among schools in distributions of achievement has been well documented. See, for example, H. T. James, J. Alan Thomas, and Harold J. Dyck, *Wealth, Expenditure and Decision-Making for Education* (U.S. Department of Health, Education, and Welfare, Cooperative Research Project No. 1241; Stanford, Calif.: School of Education, Stanford University, 1963); Charles Benson *et al.*, *State and Local Fiscal Relationships in Public Education in California*, A Report of the State of California Senate Fact Finding Committee on Revenue and Taxation (Sacramento, Calif., March 1965).

[45] If Mincer's estimates are accepted, over a lifetime, investments in learning on the job typically exceed investments in schooling in the United States today. Mincer, *The Journal of Political Economy*, LXX, No. 5, Part II, p. 73.

[46] Note the similarity between the classification of migrants established here and that used to classify high-level migrants by Grubel working with National Science Foundation data. (See the "Footnote to Part I", p. 84.)

[47] This makes the further assumption that migrants embody the same average schooling quality when compared with non-migrants in the area of origin.

[48] A fifth category, which is really a special case of the fourth, has quite different implications. Suppose an individual born in A, schooled and with his work experience in A, possesses a skill that has become obsolete after age 40 (or somewhat earlier). In this case the migrating individual has suffered a severe "human capital loss." He has little or no learned competence to apply in either A or B, and his expected earnings stream cannot be measured by an average in either area.

[49] See, for example, Donald J. Bogue, "Internal Migration," *The Study of Population*, ed. Philip M. Hauser and Otis Dudley Duncan (Chicago: The University of Chicago Press, 1959), pp. 504–5; Brinley Thomas, "International Migration," *ibid.*, p. 525.

[50] Using present values Bruce F. DeVine of the Claremont Graduate School is working on alternative estimates to those offered by Grubel and Scott. DeVine feels on the basis of preliminary work, that the Grubel and Scott measures grossly underestimate the U.S. gains. He suggests that the capital value of students, when calculated in present value terms, is probably at least double that arrived at by Grubel and Scott, and that "the U.S. is a net beneficiary through the Foreign Student Exchange Program to the tune of 5–10 per cent of the amount spent annually by this country for bilateral economic assistance." (Personal correspondence, March 25, 1969).

Present value calculations have also been used by Richard Levich in "An Analysis of Expected Loss from Foreign Student Non-Return," unpublished paper (Chicago: The University of Chicago Department of Economics, May 1969). Levich controls for age on arrival and field of study. Earnings streams are derived from National Science Foundation data. Costs are calculated in several ways. The "probable gain" to the U.S. is extremely sensitive to the assumptions made. However, gains from admitting younger foreign students are generally greater than admitting older ones. Although the U.S. spends more to educate them, the probability that they will remain is higher, offsetting the fact that they are "worth" less than the older students. (Levich's calculations do not take into account a critical interaction between age at entry and sponsorship.)

[51] Gopal Dorai, "Economics of the International Flow of Students—Cost-Benefit Analysis" (unpublished Ph.D. dissertation, Department of Econom-

ics, Wayne State University, 1968). Dorai's main purpose in calculating the present values was to examine the private decision to migrate, using a decision model similar to that presented in chapter 6. His estimate of aggregate loss to India was secondary. To make his comparison, a conversion from rupees to dollars was necessary. In converting rupees, Dorai made an adjustment reflecting purchasing power differences between India and the United States using the United Nations *Retail Price Comparisons for International Salary Determinants.*

[52] M. Blaug, P. R. G. Layard, and M. Woodhall, *The Causes of Educated Unemployment: The Indian Case* (London: Allen Lane, The Penguin Press, 1969), chapter 6. On Indian Emigration see also the following publications by the Institute of Applied Manpower Research in New Delhi: IAMR Report No. 2/1968 (Migration of Indian Engineers, Scientists and Physicians to the United States) and IAMR Report No. 4/1970 (the "Brain Drain" Study, Phase I: Analysis of Ordinary Passports Issued During 1960–1967).

6

DECISION MODELS FOR MIGRATION-EDUCATION ALTERNATIVES

MIGRATION AS A PRIVATE INVESTMENT

In a seminal article written in 1962, Larry Sjaastad looked at migration primarily as a form of private, rational decision-making —as a private investment that entails costs and engenders increments to lifetime earnings streams.[1] To oversimplify, people discount expected earnings streams to put present values on themselves for alternative courses of action: migrating or remaining in the same location. In theory, people will move if they can increase their present value by an amount greater than the cost of moving. This added value might be attained if, by moving, a person finds a better market for his existing skills, upgrading himself within his occupation, or if migration provides an opportunity for him to change occupations, thereby acquiring a new skill and increasing his remuneration. Sjaastad emphasized occupational change in attempting to account for observed age patterns in such migration.

Costs, according to Sjaastad, include direct costs of moving and earnings foregone while moving, while searching for employment, and while training for a new position. Returns are the expected additional income prospects at the area of destination over those at the place of origin.

Sjaastad's primary concern was with the efficiency of migration as a process of resource allocation. He argued that much of the seemingly non-rational response or lack of response to economic incentives to move is really a matter of measurement methods which look at net rather than gross figures. He also noted the general failure to disaggregate populations sufficiently before associating them with differential opportunities and earnings. In order to identify statistically the potential earnings streams of migrants at places of origin and destination, Sjaastad suggested that comparisons be made among more homogeneous sub-groupings, specifying particular age-occupation classifications. His suggestion has been picked up in the comments in chapter 5.

The basic model applied by Sjaastad may be formulated as:

$$\sum_{t=a}^{n}\frac{Y_t - X_t - C_t}{(1+r)^{t-a}}$$

where: Y_t = earnings expected at destination in year t
X_t = earnings expected at origin in year t
C_t = costs associated with the move occurring in year t
a = year in which migration is anticipated

If the above expression has a positive value, migration should occur.

Psychic costs and benefits are incorporated into the discussion by Sjaastad, who notes that while psychic costs could explain the existence of earnings differentials larger than that implied by money and opportunity costs of migration, ". . . these excessive differentials would not represent resource misallocation. The optimal allocation of resources must take tastes as given, and will vary if people prefer familiar over strange surroundings." [2]

MIGRATION AND A RATIONALE OF COMMUNITY INVESTMENTS IN EDUCATION

In his treatment of migration, Weisbrod took up a very different tack, even though he started from the same base in human-investment theory as Sjaastad and, like Sjaastad, computed human capital in present value terms.[3] Weisbrod set up a model in which the community is treated not only as an aggregative entity that receives benefits and incurs costs, but also as a decision-making unit analogous to the individual decision maker of micro-economic theory. The decision on which he focused is local investment in schooling. He was concerned with how migration affects benefits accruing to the community from investments in education, and hence with how it affects the cost-benefit balances that determine rational investment decisions. He argued that rational community behavior in this context leads to under-investment on a national scale because of spill-over effects—external benefits of a community's investments that accrue to other communities.

In Weisbrod's analysis, the relevant population which makes up the decision unit, the community, is not congruent with the relevant population to whom benefits are thought to accrue. The latter is also labeled the community but does not include migrants; benefits to migrants that accrue after they have migrated are not thought to be benefits to the community, even though such individuals are part of the community at the time initial investment decisions are made. The problem of choosing a relevant population is thus brought into focus and the somewhat unrealistic application of decision models that may result is evident.

Another point that should be considered and that bears on Weisbrod's hypothesized underinvestment is that education can be used by a community as a means of attracting migrants. This alternative, leading to what appears at first glance to be over-investment, is at least as logical a policy for stationary community members to follow as that of underinvesting for fear they will lose their more itinerant associates.

A careful study of Weisbrod's method for computing spill-overs points up the problems involved in assigning values to human capital flows. Working from incremental income streams associated with varying levels of educational attainment through high school graduation, he assumed, for instance, that the relevant income for valuing both *in-* and *out-*migrants of a given age, race, and sex are the same. All those who migrate to and from the community (Clayton, Missouri), are valued at local (non-South) rates, regardless of their origin or the location of their previous education. This empirical compromise dictated by data limitations is discussed by Weisbrod at some length and I have already dealt with it in chapter 5.

MIGRATION AND REMIGRATION

The models and empirical work of Sjaastad and Weisbrod, as well as that of Fein, were based on the assumption that migration is permanent. One of the more obvious results of this common tendency to treat migration as though it were a once-and-for-all affair may be faulty assessments of brain drains or brain gains, an additional reason for the cautious acceptance of aggregate figures emphasized in the preceding chapter. Losses and gains accompanying remigration are clearly of a different magnitude than those attending initial migration, but in some cases remigration offsets previous loss. Evaluation depends on whether the remigrants are college students returning home, prodigal sons, disappointed jobseekers, retrained workers, retiring elders, or political "outs" who are now "in." In short, it depends on how the human capital value of remigrants differs from what it was when they first migrated, whether they were trained, how long they stayed abroad.

A basic weakness of one-way migration simplifications is their disregard for the duration of migration. There is a continuum from brief periods away at school or on a short-term job assignment to permanent residence abroad. To disregard temporary migration is to disregard important linkages among educational investment, on the job learning and migration which, when coupled with regional differentials in quality and availability of schooling and experiential learning, can provide extremely important channels for the transfer and local acquisition of know-how. Developing countries are faced with important choices as to how this know-how and qualified manpower can best be obtained. How many and what kinds of individuals should be sent for study and/or work experience abroad, and for how long? How many can be expected to return? Would it be more "rational" to import outside experts on a temporary basis? How can these choices be evaluated from the points of view of the receiving and sending nations or regions? What is the incentive system or decision process that will lead people out and back? What strategies are possible for inducing higher rates of return home among those subsidized for study or training abroad (or for that matter in another region of the same country)?

Human investment decision models specifically incorporating remigration sequences provide a systematic method for dealing with the above questions. With these questions in mind, decision models are presented, from both the individual and social viewpoints, which allow comparison of educational investments for different sequences and timing of migration and remigration. Individual decision models have social significance as well; understanding the individual decision calculus can provide a basis for predicting behavior and for attempting to influence it. Individual models are presented first and then transformed into social decision models by replacing individually expected earnings with socially expected earnings or realized productive contributions, and by applying probability values to allow for different assumed rates of remigration and emigration.

In accordance with the discussion in chapter 5, these models assume disaggregations by sex, age, race, educational attainment, and occupation. Relevant earnings streams are those of an average individual within each category. The models focus on choice with respect to locus, duration, and sequences of schooling and experiential learning. In accord with the theme of this study, examples will be drawn primarily from decisions relating to foreign study. However, the models can be generalized to internal migration.

Theories and models need not be judged only in terms of their relative power of prediction in empirically defined situations. They are conceptual tools which organize thought by abstracting from reality. Such abstraction is the primary purpose of the present chapter. Consequently, the models assume that earnings streams can be identified which correspond to each of the many possible alternatives, although in practice this may not be possible. On the other hand, the models could have been generalized to incorporate non-monetary and psychic as well as monetary benefits, but this has not been done in order to keep the model at least potentially operational.

The following notation is used:

a—age at the first decision point relating to migration
b—date of actual or intended out-migration
m—age at return from residence abroad
n—retirement age
R_t—expected earnings in the year t at the place of origin prior to (or in absence of) any migration
D_t—expected earnings abroad in the year t
Y_t—expected earnings in the year t at the place of origin for migrant returnees ($t > m - a$)
C_t—direct cost in the year t of schooling or training in the area of origin
K_t—direct cost in the year t of schooling or training abroad
Z_t^o—direct cost of out-migration incurred in year t
Z_t^h—direct cost of return migration incurred in year t
r—external discount rate
V—present value of future income streams
j—superscript denoting a particular individual or homogeneous group

INDIVIDUAL DECISION MODELS

At the outset, models for three simple migration sequences are presented, one of which is really a base line model in which no migration occurs.[4] The three sequences presented correspond to sequences established in the migration paradigm of chapter 1.[5]

1. Present value in a situation of no migration:

$$V_1{}^j = \sum_{t=a}^{n} \frac{R_t - C_t}{(1+r)^{t-a}} \qquad (1)$$

2. Present value in a situation of immediate and permanent migration:

$$V_2{}^j = \sum_{t=a}^{n} \frac{D_t - K_t - Z_t{}^o}{(1+r)^{t-a}} \qquad (2)$$

3. Present value in a situation of immediate but temporary migration:

$$V_3{}^j = \sum_{t=a}^{m-1} \frac{D_t - K_t - Z_t{}^o}{(1+r)^{t-a}} + \sum_{t=m}^{n} \frac{Y_t - Z_t{}^h}{(1+r)^{t-a}} \qquad (3)$$

An individual has many choices within each of the three sequences. To illustrate the complexity of the alternatives, consider the base sequence (1) and picture a high school graduate deciding about his future.[6] The graduate must weigh going to work immediately against spending 1, 2, 5, or more years in school, during which his earnings are low or zero. He must weigh schooling now against schooling later. He is faced with a variety of institutional settings in which he might obtain his education. Each of the above choices is presumably associated with a distinctive set of possible cost streams (C_t) and with a distinctive set of potential future earnings profiles (R_t).

Each schooling choice can be associated with a set of alternative occupational and job choices characterized by varying amounts of experiential learning. These additional alternatives operate in conjunction with schooling to determine yearly earnings (R values) that can be expected.

The high school graduate may choose between positions with higher learning potential which pay little at first but will bring higher pay later, and positions which pay well at first but hold little or no promise of earnings increase in the future.[7] So long as the present value of the deferred earnings pattern exceeds the present value of the other stream, using a discount rate greater than the individual's reservation rate, he will choose the deferred earnings.[8] The relation of experiential learning to earnings stream differences and the place of experiential learning in the models are less observable than the effect of schooling. Schooling obviously involves foregone earnings: most students do not work or they have earnings far below what they might have if employed full time. And schooling also carries direct costs—books, tuition, fees—that are only too evident to all who have paid them at one time or another. However, costs of experiential learning to an individual are opportunity costs embedded in the earnings streams and are usually less conspicuous even when they are cumulatively substantial.

From the above it is apparent that even within sequence 1 there are potentially a very large number of schooling and experience combinations from which to choose, each with its earnings stream and associated costs. The possibilities multiply even more when migration is introduced as in sequence 2 and when remigration is allowed, as in sequence 3.

In theory, one could identify the costs and earnings streams for varying combinations within each of the above sequences, selecting the one with the highest present value. However, many combinations can be immediately discarded as unpromising ones. Furthermore, in practice, any one individual will be constrained by his native ability, his interests, his financial situation, behavior of acquaintances, sources of information, and the like. The possibilities actually considered by him may be reduced to the most promising and feasible ones, even to choices among two or three specific alternatives for which costs and benefits are weighed and compared.

Although the emphasis will be on comparisons among migration sequences, that is, among sequences tied to location, comparing alternatives within each sequence may be an equally important use of the models. It is possible that all the most feasible alternatives fall within one sequence. If study abroad under several conditions of study resulted in increases in present value, one might ask how earnings on return (Y), earnings while abroad (D), and direct costs of study abroad (K) will differ if study is at a better or a poorer university, if study leads to a degree or does not, if on the job training is substituted for formal study or if it is added in the period following study, if study is in one as against another specialty, or if study is for longer as against shorter periods of time.

Four examples illustrate the models operating within different constraints.

1. If the decision to be made is simply whether to invest in study outside the area of origin or not, without allowing the option of non-return, the relevant comparison would be between present values, V_1 and V_3. This might be the case when an individual feels constrained to work in his home country (by family, by feeling of nationalism, by agreement made with his sponsor). If V_3 is greater than V_1, then the rational alternative, within the constraint, would be to study abroad. Conversely, if V_1 is greater than V_3, then the most rational investment is to remain at home for training.

2. If the decision to be made is simply whether to migrate or not, then the relevant comparison would be between V_2 and V_1. This might be the case when, for instance, commitment to a particular profession was the major constraint and permanent location would be determined by the best offer in the profession, regardless of geographical location. If V_2 is greater than V_1, then migration should occur. A special case of this type of decision is that in which education has been completed at home and there are no further direct costs anticipated for training. The C_t and K_t terms drop out of the model and the comparison is

simply between the two discounted earnings streams, with an adjustment for the cost of moving. This is Sjaastad's basic model.

$$V_2 - V_1 = \sum_{t=a}^{n} \frac{D_t - R_t - Z_t^o}{(1+r)^{t-a}} \qquad (4)$$

3. A third type of comparison would be necessary if the decision centers on whether or not to migrate after a period of training abroad. V_2 and V_3 would be compared: if V_3 is larger than V_2, then the decision would be to stay abroad. Such a situation could arise where an individual committed to a particular vocational course felt that foreign training was best in his field and that it must be obtained, but that location following his training was an open question. Or this might be the case of an individual who could not obtain entrance to a local university and had to migrate for his education.

This third comparison is most relevant to the case study presented in Part IV, in which individuals have already decided to study in the United States. Since they have already migrated for study, their expectations and decisions really begin with time m rather than time a (or at some time between m and a). Their basis for decision may now be different from what it was when the original decision to study abroad was made. Information about United States salaries is more available, they are more mature, and family situation may have changed or nationalist feelings may have been dissipated during their stay.

4. If the original decision is not made within constraints on either location of study or location of work following study, then comparisons would be made among all three sequences, (1), (2), and (3). The highest present value would determine the choice by rational individuals.

It is useful to think beyond constraining factors to what individual decisions might be if constraints were removed. Would it make a difference, for instance, if individuals were supplied with information or had certain legal restrictions removed?

The three main sequences represented in (1), (2), and (3)

could be expanded. For instance, an individual might also consider remaining in the home area for some period $(b - a)$ before going abroad. Later, he would still have the option of staying abroad or returning. A decision of this sort might revolve about whether to do undergraduate work at home or abroad before doing graduate study abroad, and/or emigrating, and/or returning.

The present value of the decision to remain temporarily in the area of origin, then migrate permanently, would be expressed:

$$V_4{}^j = \sum_{t=a}^{b-1} \frac{\overset{\text{Gould}}{R_t - C_t} \overset{+}{} \sum_{t=b}^{n} \frac{\overset{\text{Coin Hug}}{D_t - K_t - Z_t{}^b}}{(1+r)^{t-a}}}{(1+r)^{t-a}} \tag{5}$$

The present value of the decision to remain temporarily in the area of origin, to migrate temporarily, then return to the area of origin, would be expressed:

$$V_5{}^j = \sum_{t=a}^{b-1} \frac{\overset{\text{Coin Home}}{R_t - C_t}}{(1+r)^{t-a}} + \sum_{t=b}^{m-1} \frac{\overset{\text{Coin X}}{D_t - K_t - Z_t{}^o}}{(1+r)^{t-a}} + \sum_{t=m}^{n} \frac{\overset{\text{Coin region}}{Y_t - Z_t{}^h}}{(1+r)^{t-a}} \tag{6}$$

Another modification or expansion of the models would be that which allows an individual to return to the country of foreign training after having returned home following his study. This type of decision might enter the calculations of an individual who had the option of taking a scholarship requiring him to return to the area of origin following training, but for a limited period such as twice the time spent studying abroad.

These models could be generalized to admit unlimited numbers of moves, of learning situations, and of successive cost-benefit relationships. Also, the external interest rates used could be varied to allow for shifts in relevant criteria or reservation rates.

ADJUSTMENTS

Adjustments for the probability of employment and for mortality have not been included in the models as presented above. It is assumed that an individual does not consider the possibility of dying before retirement and that even if he did, the difference in mortality rates for adults is slight across countries or regions and would not usually have much effect on relative present value estimates in different locations.[9]

Employment opportunity or, to look at it negatively, unemployment probability, is a different proposition. It is possible that employment prospects will differ enormously in certain fields from region to region or country to country. A Paraguayan nuclear physicist might be able to obtain any number of positions in his occupation in the United States but be unable to find employment in Paraguay. If he insists on working in his field, his income stream would total zero at home and there would be no doubt about where he would locate. A more moderate example would be that of an agricultural engineer who might be more highly paid in the United States *if* he gets a job, but who is virtually assured of a job when he returns home, albeit a lower-paying job. It is conceivable that the job insurance would attract him home.

While calling attention to the possible need for adjustment, unemployment is not formally introduced into the models. The manner in which ordinary unemployment enters the model would depend on the source of earnings statistics. If average earnings through time of a "homogeneous" group are calculated without including the unemployed, adjustment would be necessary. If, however, average earnings of the homogeneous group serving as the individual's reference in making his decision include the zero earnings of unemployed, the adjustment is already incorporated in the earnings stream. It is assumed that the earnings stream figures in the models include this adjustment.

In addition to the adjustment for uncertainty of employment, there is the more complicated matter of decision in the face of uncertainty about income, even though employment is anticipated. The models presented abstract from uncertainty or (alternatively) assume behavior coordinate with maximization of mathematical expectations.

The models require another adjustment where earnings streams for two areas are compared. Purchasing-power parity is a concept with which economists have struggled for many years without satisfactory resolution. Official exchange rates are seldom appropriate earnings adjustments. The often used "market basket" is inaccurate when similar items such as a car or a maid have different social as well as monetary values across cultures.

Grubel and Scott have ably summarized the difficulties of identifying an appropriate earnings stream:

> Upon close inspection it can be seen that in order to arrive at an estimate of the differences in real incomes between two countries an individual has to go through a complicated calculus involving his personal time preferences for work, his age and family status in relation to his income, the relative price of commodities, tax rates, government services, climate and institutional characteristics of the job.[10]

SOCIAL DECISION MODELS AND MIGRATION PARAMETERS

Shifting to a social viewpoint, for instance that of a regional or national body which is deciding whether or not to subsidize study outside its area, necessitates a redefinition of parameters. It does not require a change in notation or a change in the basic form used in the individual models. Costs and returns are now those to society. For example, all educational services such as teacher time, physical facilities, and so forth, are real social costs, even though subsidies may reduce or eliminate such costs to the individual. The lifetime streams are gross rather than net earnings. As with individual models, mortality and unemployment adjustments are assumed to be allowed for the earnings streams. Adjustments for growth, market distortions, uncertainty, "real income" differences, and non-monetary costs and benefits are still pertinent at the social level. Appropriate identification of Y, K, and Z then turns the individual decision models into marginal social cost-benefit models.

Changing to a social perspective requires more than a redefinition of the parameters in the family of models. An adjustment must be made for the loss of social product which occurs during the period of migration. The method for making such an adjustment is not clearly defined, depending upon whether or not we decide to treat all output while abroad as lost to the area of origin. If we decide that an individual must be physically present in order to add to the product of an area, permanent migration, from this viewpoint, involves an unambiguous and total loss to the area of origin. In the models, total loss to the area of origin will be assumed for the time spent abroad. However, modification of the models to include possible counterflows that do not depend on residence (and about which we have little empirical evidence) will be noted.

An assumption of these models is that economic value can be measured in terms of additions to Gross National Product. The alternative measure of per capita income suggested by Grubel and Scott is also defensible. The two approaches should complement rather than replace each other.

The following notation must be added:

α_t—the probability that an individual who has migrated for training will return before age t

$1-\alpha_t$—the probability that an individual who has migrated for training will not return before age t

λ_t—the probability that an individual who has not migrated for training will migrate before age t

$1-\lambda_t$—the probability that an individual who has not migrated for training previously will not migrate before age t

i—a superscript denoting a particular combination of formal study conditions (including length of time of study) and of job training.

TRAINING AT HOME AND MIGRATION

In order to establish a base line against which other alternatives can be compared, the probability that an individual studying at home will migrate following his study should be introduced as an adjustment to the human-capital value derived from such education. This can be done simply by adapting sequence (1), redefining parameters, and introducing the probability of emigration as follows:

$$V_6{}^j = \sum_{t=a}^{n} \frac{R_t(1 - \lambda_t) - C_t}{(1 + r)^{t-a}} \tag{7}$$

$V_6{}^j$ represents the discounted present social value of an average individual in group j as of age a, adjusted for the probability that migration will occur following study and assuming that mortality and unemployment adjustments are included with the R_t figures.

The parameter, λ, pertains only to out-migration. It is likely that as age increases, the probability of migration decreases so that, as a function of t, λ rises but at a declining rate. For any t, the cumulative migration probability, λ_t, will also depend on the age of decision a and on the amount of training received after age a. To incorporate these considerations, a period of training, $(m - a)$, is defined, with which the set of probabilities, $\lambda_t{}^{a,m}$, can be associated. Separate present values can be associated with each decision point, a, and with each period of time, $(m - a)$. These values depend on the costs, earnings streams, and migration probabilities associated with combinations of a and m. The present value may be represented as:

$$V_7{}^j{}_{a,m} = \sum_{t=a}^{n} \frac{R_t{}^{a,m}(1 - \lambda_t{}^{a,m}) - C^{a,m}}{(1 + r)^{t-a}} \tag{8}$$

It is difficult to predict the dependence of λ on $m - a$, for it probably depends simultaneously on several other factors such as the particular level and field of training as well as on the job opportunities in that field. Additional superscripts could be added to R_t and C_t for level of training, for field of study, for location of study (within the area), for mix of formal study with on the job training, all of which would produce variations in λ_t as well as in R_t and C_t. In order to simplify for expositional purposes, all such variations as well as variations in length of time abroad can be included in one superscript, i. The summary equation for the sequence associated with training at home, adjusted for the probability of subsequent migration, becomes:

$$V_8{}^{i,j} = \sum_{t=a}^{n} \frac{R_t{}^i(1 - \lambda_t{}^i) - C_t{}^i}{(1+r)^{t-a}} \tag{9}$$

As with individual decisions, the number of possible schooling and experience combinations will be very large. Again, there will be constraints limiting actual choices. In addition to the individual constraints there will be social constraints; training must be in a field considered vital to the national interests, for example.

As with the individual models, the emphasis here is on choices *between* migration for training and training at home. However, as with private models, the process of maximizing the investment within either the training-at-home or training-abroad sequence may be a useful application of the social decision models. For instance, given a putative manpower shortage in a particular field for which training is only available abroad, how does one select the individuals and study conditions that will provide the greatest relative benefit in fulfilling the presumed need?

TRAINING ABROAD AND MIGRATION

In the case of training abroad, out-migration has already occurred, but it may be either temporary or permanent. How will the value of the out-migrant to his country of origin vary with the length of time spent abroad before returning and with the activity in which the migrant engaged while abroad? Permanent migration is actually a special case of temporary migration in which the age of return, m, equals the retirement age, n (the point at which this particular set of models terminates). There are no earnings in the country of origin (Y_t) or return costs ($Z_t{}^h$) and the probability set for return, α_t, equals zero throughout. Because permanent migration is a special case, one model can deal with both temporary and permanent migration.

As in the private models, the set of probabilities depends on the number of years of training, $m - a$, on the age at which training begins, a, on the mix of formal education and training on the job, on the level of training, and so forth.

Splitting the equation into two parts to represent the period of training, $m - a$, and the period following training, the summary equation for the present value to the country of origin associated with a training abroad sequence is:

$$V_9{}^{i,j} = \sum_{t=m}^{n} \frac{Y_t{}^i(\alpha_t{}^i) - Z_t{}^h(\alpha_t{}^i)}{(1+r)^{t-a}} - \sum_{t=a}^{m-1} \frac{K_t + Z_t{}^o}{(1+r)^{t-a}} \qquad (10)$$

Any part of costs for training or travel borne by other than the area of origin would be deducted from the K and Z values. If, for instance, the United States government or a foundation sponsors a student entirely, removing the Z and K values from the equation, the present value reduces to the value of the discounted earnings stream on return, adjusted for the probability of return.

For each period of training ($m - a$) there will be a different set of migration probabilities (α_t) and of associated earnings streams (Y_t). The probability set, α_t, is likely to be a declining function of ($m - a$). The rate at which α_t declines will be one of the critical elements in the process of maximizing returns from study abroad. If the rate of non-return ($1 - \alpha_t$) increases rapidly with increased time abroad ($m - a$), the profitability of a longer training period may be offset by the increased loss from emigration, placing a considerable constraint on the types of training that may be sought abroad. Similar considerations pertain to maximization by formal-informal mix of schooling, type of training, location, and so forth.

Let us now assume that maximization has occurred within each of the sequences (training at home and training abroad), either as a result of comparing many alternatives and picking that one with the highest present value or as a result of choosing from among the few possibilities left after constraints were placed on choice. Optimization of the social investment choice between study abroad and study at home, then, consists simply of comparing the two maximized present values, V_8 and V_9.

Another way of looking at the comparison would be to present the parameters for both choices together in an inequality. The advantage of doing this is that comparisons could be made between training alternatives at home and abroad which are not necessarily the maximum investment alternatives in either case. Alternatives will overlap—the "best" alternative at home may have a higher present value than average training abroad, but a lower present value than the best training abroad. The inequality would be:

$$\sum_{t=a}^{n} \frac{Y_t{}^i(\alpha_t{}^i) - R_t{}^i(1 - \lambda_t{}^i)}{(1+r)^{t-a}} - \left[\sum_{t=a}^{n} \frac{K_t - C_t}{(1+r)^{t-a}} + \sum_{t=a}^{n} \frac{Z_t{}^o + Z_t{}^h(\alpha_t{}^i)}{(1+r)^{t-a}} \right] \gtreqless 0 \tag{11}$$

If the earnings increment from study abroad is greater than the increment in direct training cost associated with such study plus the combined costs of moving to and from the location, and when adjustment has been made for the loss through migration which would occur, and assuming the appropriate discount rate, *then* the rational social alternative would be, at the margin, as of time *a*, to invest in training abroad.

Stated differently, if the value of the inequality (11) is greater than zero, the rational social decision, between the two choices and at the margin, is to opt for investment in training abroad. If (11) equals zero, society is indifferent. If (11) has a value less than zero, investment in study abroad is not economically warranted.[11]

The inequality (11) could also be used to examine the effect of fluctuating probabilities of non-return. How large could the rate of non-return be before the model would show a negative value? An exploration of this type could show the extent to which efforts aimed at curbing non-return are worthwhile. The probability of return can be influenced through selection policies and incentives. However, the cost of these efforts may outweigh their results.

Another practical, important issue is whether and how long students sent overseas should be allowed or encouraged to stay after completing their formal schooling in order to acquire experience. The solution will depend, in part, on how much "wastage" from increased probability of non-return offsets the potential increase in benefits from practical training.[12]

The policy alternative facing many planners is whether to import talent or to train local people abroad. While the short-run policy of importing has certain advantages, the longer-term balance sheet is not so clear. Before weighing these alternatives, the model can be brought to bear on alternatives in the purchase of services of foreign experts such as a one-man long-term contract, a sequence of short-term contracts to several people, or a system of two-year rotations between individuals. This application has been formulated elsewhere.[13]

SUMMARY

In chapters 5 and 6, several methods and applications of human capital concepts to migration have been discussed. There are at once common elements and sharp distinctions in problem foci, in theoretical frameworks applied, and in the kinds of compromises made by using incomplete and sometimes inappropriate sets of data. It is evident that the analysis of migration in terms of human capital investment is opening over a broad front, and is moving beyond simple counting and cross-tabulation of migrant characteristics toward a more meaningful assessment of migration.[14]

In part, sophisticated application of human capital principles fails because the prior problems of delineating populations as discussed in Parts I and II have not been solved. Nevertheless, it is evident that application of human capital concepts to migration holds promise, primarily as a means of conceptualizing and analyzing empirically both individual and social investment choices.

In chapter 6, the importance of sorting out remigration in assessing gains and losses was emphasized and remigration was incorporated into a series of private and social decision models. Several applications of the models were suggested.

Chapters 5 and 6, though critical of recent applications by others and though presenting a methodological scheme designed to overcome those criticisms, do not come to grips with the more practical difficulties involved in making the methodology operational. This will be done in chapter 8.

NOTES

[1] Larry Sjaastad, "The Costs and Returns of Human Migration," *The Journal of Political Economy*, LXX, No. 5, Part II (October 1962), pp. 80–93.

[2] *Ibid.*, p. 85.

[3] Burton A. Weisbrod, *External Benefits of Public Education* (Research Series Report No. 105; Princeton, N.J.: Industrial Relations Section, Princeton University, 1964).

[4] The models used here are part of a family of such models for analysis of investment in human resources. Their relation to Gary Becker's "internal rates of return" is evident. However, for the present purpose, Becker's "internal rate of return" is less appropriate and less flexible than comparison of present values taking an assumed external discount rate. Use of the "internal rate of return" method entails unnecessarily restrictive assumptions. (See also footnote 7 below).

[5] Those choosing sequence 1 would be "non-migrants"; sequence 2, "non-returnees"; sequence 3, "returnees," according to the paradigm of chapter 1.

[6] Though this complexity is further compounded by various kinds and

degrees of uncertainty, the common practice of abstracting from uncertainty is followed here. This simplification is necessary for expositional purposes, but should not be taken to imply that effects of uncertainty and ignorance are unimportant either in individual behavior or in social policy-making. Some attention to uncertainty is given when discussing adjustments to the model. (See also footnote 7 below.)

[7] This description of choices, and the use of present value comparisons, does not require assumption with respect to year-to-year choices of alternatives or constancy of internal rates of return to successive self-investments such as Mincer used (*The Journal of Political Economy*, LXX, No. 5, Part II, p. 53). For some remarks on Mincer's as one of a broader set of models that varies the length of a contract term, see Mary Jean Bowman, "The Costing of Human Resource Development," *The Economics of Education*, Proceedings of the 1963 Conference of the International Economics Association, ed. E. A. G. Robinson and J. E. Vaizey (London: Macmillan and Co., 1964), pp. 421–50. A few aspects of decision-making with respect to human resource formation under uncertainty are also included in that article.

[8] On reservation rates, see Valerien Harvey, "Economic Aspects of Teachers' Salaries" (unpublished Ph.D. dissertation, Department of Education, The University of Chicago, 1967), p. 35.

[9] Where, or if, there are extreme differences in shapes of life income streams, identical mortality adustment could still have differential effects on present values, but such situations are rare.

[10] Herbert Grubel and Anthony Scott, "The International Flow of Human Capital: The Brain Drain" (Department of Economics, The University of Chicago, 1966), p. 23. (Mimeographed.)

[11] Again, it should be pointed out that the model, as presented does not incorporate the multitude of economic effects associated with human capital migration that are not directly transfers of human capital. For instance, the change in remittance flows that might accompany migration does not appear. Such adjustments could be included by addition of several terms representing the principal adjustments, or they could be grouped in a catch-all term representing all indirect effects (net). The following has been suggested by Mary Jean Bowman. Let W_{qs} = the social welfare effect of the choice $V_q{}^{ij}$ over V^{ij} where the subscripts q and s refer to particular migration (or non-migration) sequences.

Simplifying to take $\qquad\qquad \hat{V}_{qs} = \hat{V}_q{}^{ij} - \hat{V}_s{}^{ij},$

we have: $\qquad\qquad\qquad \hat{W}_{qs} = \hat{V}_{qs} + \hat{U}_{qs}$

where U_{qs} is the net indirect repercussions over and above $(+ \text{ or } -)$ the direct human capital estimate, $\hat{V}_{qs}$. One can then ask what is in $\hat{U}$.

[12] Niland explores this issue in detail. See particularly chapter 6.

[13] Bowman and Myers, pp. 894–97.

[14] See the following, for instance, in addition to those mentioned in chapters 5 and 6, for applications of the human capital concept to migration: Frank T. Bachmura, "Latin American Brain Drainage," in *The Movement Toward Latin American Unity*, ed. Ronald Hilton (New York: Frederick A. Praeger, 1969), pp. 426–44; Hans-Joachim Bodendorfer, "The Mobility of Labor and the Theory of Human Capital," *The Journal of Human Resources*, II, No. 4 (Fall 1967), pp. 431–48; Samuel Bowles, "Migration as Investment:

Empirical Tests of the Human Investment Approach to Geographical Mobility," (Cambridge, Mass.: Harvard University, Program on Regional and Urban Economics, July 1969); Peter J. Hill, "The Economic Impact of Immigration into the United States," (unpublished Ph.D. dissertation, The University of Chicago, 1970); and Samuel Levy, "Research Proposal: International Migration of Human Capital: The Case of Physiicans" (Detroit, Wayne State University, College of Liberal Arts, Department of Economics, 1967).

PART IV

A Case Study of Non-Return Among Peruvian Students in the United States

7

THE MAGNITUDE AND CORRELATES
OF PERUVIAN NON-RETURN

In a sense, the choice of Peru and Peruvian students for this case study was incidental: any one of many other nations might have been chosen. The research as originally planned was designed to explore non-return from a particular viewpoint (economic) and to test a methodology (see chapter 8) rather than to provide a policy for a particular nation. Policy implications resulting from the research are a by-product. Furthermore, choice was not governed by a desire to generalize empirical findings beyond the country chosen to a particular geographical or supposedly culturally homogeneous area.

Peru is not a "typical" developing nation or a "typical" Latin American nation. Although Peru is similar in many respects to the South American republics of Colombia, Ecuador and Bolivia, it is also unique in many respects. Too often Latin American countries are lumped together indiscriminately, an error I wish to avoid. Generalization from the Peruvian data, then, is not warranted, but findings can be used to formulate hypotheses about non-return in other countries sharing some of Peru's characteristics and problems. On a broader plane, the Peruvian case can appropriately be used to help support or to challenge shaky generalizations derived from previous cross-national research or from other case studies.

Among the salient reasons for choosing Peru were the following:

1. In the five-year period prior to the study (1960–65), economic conditions in Peru had been favorable. Peru had not only been able to attract substantial amounts of foreign capital [1] for developing its diverse and abundant national resources, but the country had also enjoyed relative economic stability and a relatively high rate of sustained economic growth.[2]

The conditions allowed one to ask whether, given a favorable economic climate, migration of human resources still occurred.

2. The Peruvian economy functioned as a mixed economy, including and encouraging a large private sector. There was relatively little governmental ownership, and although the economy was presumably controlled by a traditional oligarchy conditions were changing.[3] In the early 1960s a technological elite [4] was taking its place alongside the "forty families." Whether new opportunities were perceived by most Peruvians studying in the United States or only by a selected few was a matter for research. Did anticipation of continued change influence the decision to remigrate or remain following study abroad? The extent to which existing market imperfections were reflected in individuals' migration decisions was at least as interesting.

3. It was not difficult to emigrate from Peru nor, prior to 1965, to obtain an immigrant visa to the United States, since Peru was a former non-quota country. This relative freedom to move approximates a condition assumed in many economic decision models—that individuals are able to move in response to economic differentials. It effectively moderates a potential constraint on the operation of an economic model such as that of chapter 6.

4. From 1960 to 1965, study in the United States played an increasing role in conscious attempts to build up Peruvian institutions. Many students had been sponsored to study in the United States for this reason, but unsponsored as well as sponsored Peruvian students were present in the United States in substantial numbers, providing an interesting possibility for contrast.

5. The number of Peruvian students in the United States was large enough to make an analysis statistically feasible as well as worthwhile. In 1965, Peru ranked third of the twelve South American countries with students in the United States, after Venezuela and Colombia; of all countries, Peru ranked twenty-seventh. In addition, foreign study accounted for at least 20 per cent of all third-level education by Peruvians.[5] At the graduate level the percentage was probably higher.

6. At the time, Peru was not officially concerned about a brain drain.[6] This might seem to be a reason for excluding Peru from consideration, but exploring questions of non-return in a relatively uncharged atmosphere was thought desirable. In chapter 4 (see p. 132 Table 17, line 54) the non-return rate for Peru was estimated at 15 per cent. On the one hand, one might ask whether the lack of concern about this relatively high percentage was caused by general unawareness, or whether the drain, though substantial in numbers, had little economic effect. On the other hand, one might feel that the drain was relatively small, in which case emphasis could be placed on the decision to return home rather than on non-return. In the long run it may be more important to know why people return home than why they remain abroad.

7. Familiarity with Peru after two years' residence provided a basis for building a relevant research design. It also provided access to the student population being questioned.

Focusing as it did only on students and student migration decisions, the research excluded most Peruvian migrants to the United States, and did not speak to the larger question of the total flows of Peruvian and extra-Peruvian manpower in and out of Peru. In addition, it was restricted to Peruvian students *in the United States*. One writer suggested that Peruvians studying in the United States constitute only 20 per cent of the total overseas student population.[7] Three estimates for Peruvian students abroad are compared in Table 26. A more complete analysis of the option to study abroad as exercised by Peruvians would have compared

TABLE 26—Peruvian students abroad, selected countries, various years

	SOURCE		
COUNTRY	UNESCO[a]	PAU[b]	MINISTRY[c]
Austria	2		
Belgium[d]	11		
Canada[d]	25		
Czechoslovakia	10		
France	57		
West Germany	102		
Italy	32		
Japan	15		
Spain[d]	664		4,500
Switzerland	24		
United Kingdom	15		
United States	766	766	6,100
Argentina		2,649	8,200
Bolivia		40	3,900
Brazil		19	3,000
Colombia		1	
Costa Rica		1	
Chile		42	
Ecuador		4	
Mexico		23	
Uruguay		4	
Venezuela		1	
Totals	1,723	3,550	25,700

[a] United Nations, Educational, Scientific, and Cultural Organization, *UNESCO Statistical Yearbook*, 1965 (SS.66/XIV.10/AF; Paris, 1966), Table 18, Education at the third level: foreign students, by country of origin, in 15 selected countries, around 1964, pp. 306–13.

[b] Pan American Union, *Survey of the Inter-American Exchange of Students and Professors* (Washington, D.C., 1966), Tables I and II, Number of foreign students in institutions of higher education, academic year 1965–66, by country of origin and where studies were carried out, pp. 25–57. Only 44 of 200 universities responded to this survey. These are, therefore, only the roughest of estimates.

[c] Based on figures supplied by the Ministry of Foreign Affairs of Peru, as quoted in *El Comercio* (Lima, Peru), September 24, 1963.

[d] UNESCO figures for these three countries were from 1963 surveys. All other UNESCO figures are from 1965 surveys.

students in Argentina, Spain, Bolivia, Brazil, Chile, France, and Germany, to name a few of the countries drawing Peruvian students, but this is beyond the scope of this study. Although study in the United States covers a relatively small percentage of total Peruvian study abroad, the United States has a substantial proportion of Peru's graduate student population.

DELINEATING THE POPULATION

The base population for the case study consisted of: (1) all Peruvian (2) males (3) enrolled on a full-time basis (4) in institutions of higher education (5) within the United States (6) as of March 1, 1966.

(1). A student was considered Peruvian if his citizenship at the time of study was Peruvian. By this definition, an individual with Peruvian citizenship, but living in the United States with an immigrant visa, was still considered Peruvian. His national status alters only by procuring United States citizenship (or citizenship of another country). Such a definition lies between that which might be made by the Peruvian government, "Once a Peruvian, always a Peruvian," [8] and that which suggests that the act of securing an immigrant visa is, in itself, sufficient to signal a shift of national status. The rationale for including Peruvian citizens who have immigrant visas was tied to the nature of the immigrant visa and to the study's focus on non-return.

By this definition, an individual indicating his *intent* to remain in the United States permanently was considered Peruvian until he had actually acquired United States citizenship, and former Peruvians holding United States citizenship at the time of the survey were excluded from the study.

Using a change in citizenship to distinguish Peruvians from non-Peruvians leaves an ambiguous area: dual citizenship. The two types of dual citizenship encountered were: persons whose parents were not Peruvian but who were born in Peru, and persons who had one Peruvian parent and one parent of another nationality. It was not possible to set one rule for including or excluding individuals with dual citizenship; each case was considered individually. In general, a person was included if it was evident that the Peruvian part of his citizenship held meaning for him, either because he had spent a substantial part of his life in Peru or because he viewed himself as Peruvian.

(2). The study was restricted to males because the total number of females was not great enough to allow separate analysis. Moreover, female students are of secondary interest in the context of non-return, for with few exceptions they play a minor role in professional life in Peru. As students in the United States, they tend to be concentrated in Catholic women's colleges or secretarial schools. To include them would have unecessarily complicated the study and diverted interview time more profitably devoted to males.

(3). Enrollment on a full-time basis was defined by the question: "Are you enrolled for at least 12 semester credits or do you spend at least 45 hours per week in class, studying, researching, and/or writing your thesis?" The distinction between part-time and full-time students could not be made before mailing questionnaires.

Restricting the population to full-time students resulted in a narrow interpretation of "student." However, my main interest was in those whose primary role was that of student. (If an individual is not devoting the major part of his time to studying, he should be classified first in his work role and only secondarily as a student.) Although part-time students were excluded from most analyses, the information from their returned questionnaires was coded and will be incorporated into discussions where relevant.

Emphasizing full-time study accords with student visa (F-visa) terms (see Footnote to Part I, fn. 10). However, our definition is broader than that of the Immigration and Naturalization Service in that it includes immigrant-visa holders on the same basis as student-visa holders.

(4). A liberal interpretation was given to "institution of higher education," and some technical and commercial schools enrolling students who were required to have completed high school were included. The schools were those defined by the Institute of International Education as institutions of higher education for its annual census.[9]

(5). The United States was defined to include Alaska and Hawaii but not Puerto Rico, the Canal Zone, or other territories.

(6). In order to identify the current Peruvian student population, it was necessary to bring the IIE listing up to date. Enrollment as of March 1, 1966, was adopted rather than enrollment in Fall 1965—the period during which the IIE survey was taken—because turnover occurs from semester to semester. The considerable change which occurred as a result of the updating process is discussed in Appendix V.

OBTAINING THE DATA

In April and May 1966, questionnaires were sent to 729 Peruvian males thought to be studying in institutions of higher education in the United States. An attempt was made to include all Peruvian male students in the survey. Names were obtained from the Institute of International Education (IIE) Annual Census of Foreign students, from Foreign Student Advisors and from the Peruvian students themselves. The process is detailed in Appendix V. Fifty-nine of the 729 questionnaires [10] were returned with "addressee unknown"; of the 670 individuals who received the questionnaire, 522 responded; of these, 476 were full-time students.

Interviews were also conducted with a non-random sample of 208 Peruvian students, 187 of whom were full-time students responding to questionnaires. The interview population is described and discussed in chapter 8 in conjunction with the economic approach to student decision-making.

To determine how representative of the population of male

Peruvians the respondents were, respondents and non-respondents were compared with respect to the only solid piece of information available for all names on the mailing list: institutional affiliation. When institutions were typed by mode of organization and instruction (university, four-year college, junior college, technical institution, professional school and other), by control (public, private–non-sectarian, and private-religious), by size (under 1,000, 1,000–4,999, 5,000–9,999, and 10,000 or more), and by "quality" (high, medium, and low)[11] no significant difference was found between respondents and non-respondents.

Distributions of traits among respondents were also compared with distributions of traits among all Peruvian males in the IIE Census, 1964/65.[12] There was no significant difference between the two populations in distribution of academic status, sponsorship categories, or visas, but there was a significant difference in field of study. In relation to the IIE 1964/65 group, respondent students were slightly over-represented in engineering, medicine and business and under-represented in the social sciences and the humanities. With the exception of field, then, the respondents seemed to constitute a reasonably unbiased sample of Peruvian male students studying in institutions of higher education in the United States in 1966.

DESCRIPTION OF THE POPULATION

In spite of substantial variation among individuals and institutions attended, the population of male Peruvian students (as represented by the 476 respondents) lends itself to some generalization. A profile of the students is presented in Table 27. From the profile it is evident that the "average" student in early 1966 was young, single, self-sponsored and studying at the undergraduate level under a student (F) visa. Study was generally in fields other than the traditional subject areas of law and medicine. Generally, the duration of time in the United States had been less than two years.

TABLE 27—A profile of male Peruvians studying full-time in universities in the United States, Spring 1966[a]

	PERCENTAGE	BASE N[b]
1. Age—25 or younger	75	471
2. Marital Status—unmarried	82	475
3. Academic status—undergraduate	70	473
4. Sponsorship—self-sponsored	60	476
5. Visa—student (F) visa	60	456
6. Field of Study—		
Engineering	37	466
Business administration	19	466
Science	11	466
Agriculture	11	466
Medicine	5	466
Other	17	466
7. Length of study in U.S.—more than 2 years	38	470
8. Prior university training—Peru or elsewhere	43	476
9. High school attended—private	60	454
10. Father's education—some university	51	440
11. Mother's education—some university	16	440
12. Father's occupation—professional, technical or managerial	68	432
13. Father's income—in excess of US$10,000	36	391
14. Servants—more than 2, living in	36	435
15. Father's birthplace—outside Peru	20	446
16. Religion—other than Roman Catholic	18	429
17. Residence—coastal Peru	96	455
Lima	80	455

[a] Calculated from Peruvian Student Survey of Attitudes and Expectations, 1966, Questionnaire 1 (Q-1).
[b] There were 476 students in the working sample. The difference between 476 and the Base N used for each item indicates the non-response for that item.

Although there were variations within the group, the general socio-economic level was well above the average for Peru. Of the students' fathers, half had had some university education,[13] two-thirds were in professional (including technical or managerial) occupations,[14] one-fourth had incomes in excess of US$10,000 per year.[15] The skewed distribution suggests that the students at the lower end of the socio-economic scale are probably more accurately classed as lower-middle-class than as lower-class Peruvians. The concentration of residence in coastal Peru, the relatively large percentage of fathers born outside the country and the relatively large percentage of non-Roman Catholic students also indicate that Peruvians training in the U.S. in 1966 were not typical of the larger population of Peru.[16]

PATTERNS AND CORRELATES

From various cross-tabulations of student characteristics and conditions of study, patterns emerge. Traits tend to cluster within categories of sponsorship and according to an index of socio-economic status. The sample was simply dichotomized into sponsored students (government, foundation, business, or religious sponsorship) and unsponsored students (i.e., self-sponsored). Socio-economic status was established by doing a principal components analysis using items 9 through 14 in Table 27. The resultant factor loadings were used to arrange individuals into five equal groups.[17] Table 28 shows the relationship between sponsorship and socio-economic status. (For convenience, socio-economic status will be referred to henceforth by the abbreviation SES.)

As might be expected, individuals who were unsponsored were more apt to be high-SES individuals who could afford to study abroad on their own. There is less reason to expect that sponsored students should be concentrated in lower-SES categories; both low- and high-SES students are eligible for sponsorship. Those with high-SES background might be expected to have a relative advantage over others in terms of previous training and connections. Nevertheless, there was a concentration of sponsored students in low-SES categories. Partial explanations may lie in the methodology used in establishing SES, in the fact that sponsors

TABLE 28—Socio-economic status by sponsorship categories, Peruvian students in the United States, 1966[a]

SES	UNSPONSORED		SPONSORED	
	%	#	%	#
1 (High	28.4	82⎫ I	7.0	13⎫ III
2	22.1	64⎭	16.5	31⎭
3	20.8	60	19.3	36
4	15.9	46⎫ II	26.2	49⎫ IV
5 (Low)	12.8	37⎭	31.0	58⎭
Total[b]	100.0	289	100.0	187

[a] Calculated from: Peruvian Student Survey, Q-1.
[b] χ^2 is significant at the .01 level, indicating that difference in SES among sponsorship groups is greater than chance.

chose to select individuals from lower status backgrounds, and in the fact that individuals from lower-SES backgrounds gravitate toward institutions such as universities or governmental jobs where awards are most frequently available.

From the cross-tabulation, four sponsorship-SES groups can be delineated. Contrasts are clearer if restricted to the top two and bottom two categories of socio-economic status within each category of sponsorship, omitting temporarily the middle-SES category. The four groups to be described below are marked in Table 28 and labeled by Roman numerals. A comparison of the four groups is set out in Table 29.

Group I students (Unsponsored–High-SES) are almost all young undergraduates with student visas. They are more apt to be studying business administration than students in any other group. Engineering is also popular, followed by agriculture. Agriculture students in Group I are typically from coastal hacienda families and usually studying at a university such as California Polytechnic at San Luis Obispo. Following study, a majority expect to be in business or in a high administrative position. In line with chosen fields of study, engineering and agriculture are the other main occupational choices. Engineering seems to be studied

TABLE 29—Comparison of four groups of male Peruvian students in the United States, selected characteristics (in percentages)[a]

	UNSPONSORED		SPONSORED	
	Hi SES (I)[b]	Lo SES (II)	Hi SES (III)	Lo SES (IV)
1. Age—25 or younger[c]	97	75	77	60
2. Acad. status—undergrad	90	93	43	28
3. Visa—student (F)	84	57	50	38
4. Field—				
Engineering	30	56	35	31
Business administration	35	17	12	4
Science	2	12	12	25
Agriculture	15	5	9	14
Social sciences	8	2	23	10
Other	10	8	9	16
5. Occupational Expectation—				
Engineering	16	36	18	16
Business administration	54	28	25	7
Science	1	4	5	5
Agriculture	13	3	5	4
Education	4	13	32	53
Social science	3	9	10	6
Other	9	7	5	9
6. Previous job in a Peruvian university	0	0	23	36
7. Propensity to remain in the United States—				
Low	71	46	73	78
Medium	26	36	20	15
High	3	18	7	7

[a] Calculated from: Peruvian Student Survey, Q-1.
[b] For derivation of groupings, see Table 28.
[c] The base numbers, by group and variable are as follows:

Group/Variable	1	2	3	4	5	6	7
I	144	144	139	144	140	146	146
II	83	82	82	82	72	83	83
III	44	44	42	43	44	44	44
IV	107	107	104	105	105	107	107

Non-response can be obtained by subtracting the base numbers from the totals for each group: I = 146; II = 83; III = 44; IV = 107.

more as a path to administrative employment than as preparation for professional engineering; while 30 per cent are studying engineering, only 16 per cent say they expect to become engineers.

Group II students (Unsponsored–Low-SES) are not so uniformly age 25 or under or so uniformly student visa holders as are Group I students, but they are still predominantly young undergraduates with student visas. Almost all those *not* holding a student visa in Group II hold immigrant or tourist visas. These individuals are studying engineering in larger percentages than found in other groups; more than one-half of these lower-SES students are in engineering. Business administration is not so popular as it is for Group I students, but it is still more popular than in either group of sponsored students. Science is studied more frequently than among the higher-SES students in Group I. This tendency for lower-SES students to be more inclined toward science is also present when the comparison is made between Groups III and IV. It is logical that they should be attracted to the more achievement-oriented fields.

About two-thirds of the Group II students in engineering expect to pursue a professional career as an engineer. Note that the expectation of a business or administrative career is lower and the expectation of a career in education is higher in Group II than in Group I. The tendency again is toward achievement-oriented fields.

Groups III and IV are sponsored students. In general, sponsored students are older, more apt to be studying at the graduate level, and less apt to hold a student visa than unsponsored students. These tendencies are more pronounced for lower-SES students (Group IV) than for higher-SES students (Group III). Whereas those students in Group II without student visas usually hold immigrant or tourist visas, students in Groups III and IV most frequently hold an exchange visitor (J) visa which requires return to Peru.

In contrast to unsponsored students in Groups I and II, a much smaller percentage of Group III and particularly Group IV stu-

are found in business administration. In Group IV, a significantly higher percentage of students are in science. Group III
is more heavily loaded toward the social sciences than the other
groups.

None of the students from Groups I and II were previously
employed in the Peruvian university system; one-fourth of all
Group III students and one-third of all Group IV students were
so employed before studying in the United States. Sponsors
clearly favor the universities in their recruiting. This fact helps to
explain the high percentage of individuals who indicate they
intend to pursue a career in education—in this case, university-
level teaching. Group IV students stand out in this respect.

When students sponsored by the U.S. government are separated from other students, even sharper patterns emerge. Most
of the U.S.-sponsored students are J-visa holders, older than 25,
and in fields other than business or engineering (particularly in
science and agriculture). They are often recruited from university
faculties and are returning to their universities following study.

From the above, it appears that foreign study is serving different purposes for different groups of individuals. One might expect
these differences to be linked to non-return in a systematic
fashion. In Table 29, the propensity to remain in the United
States has been included to give the reader a preview of that
which follows. Clearly, non-return is most frequent among the
unsponsored-low-SES students of Group II.

PERUVIAN STUDENT NON-RETURN

As noted in earlier chapters, analysis of non-return requires
something more than a simple dichotomization into non-returnees
and returnees. In the present analysis, non-return is defined by a
continuum along which the probability can be located that an individual will remain permanently in the United States. To make
the definition operational, the continuum is divided into six categories. (No attempt is made to assign specific probability values

to the six categories.) Individuals for whom permanent United States residence is virtually certain are in the top category (NR1), and those for whom return to Peru is virtually certain are in the bottom category (NR6).

In assigning individuals to the six categories, two questions of "intent" were cross-tabulated, one indicating intended short-term residence, but including the possibility of permanent residence abroad, and one indicating intended long-term (permanent) residence (see Table 30, footnotes b and c). The set of categories presented in Table 30 was derived from this cross-tabulation.

TABLE 30—A scaling of the propensity to migrate permanently to the United States (A Non-return—Return Continuum)[a]

CATE-GORY	PERMANENT RESIDENCE[b]	SHORT-TERM PLANS[c]	SUB-TOTAL	TOTAL	%
NR1	UNITED STATES	Stay permanently in the U.S.	16	16	3.4
NR2	UNITED STATES	Probably stay in U.S. permanently	3		
	UNITED STATES	Probably stay in U.S. temporarily	1		
	UNITED STATES	Stay in U.S. temporarily[d]	5		
	UNITED STATES	Return to PERU[d]	3		

[a] Calculated from: Peruvian Student Survey, Q-1.
[b] Permanent residence was based on the question:
  Where do you intend to settle permanently?
  Possible responses were:
    In Peru; In the United States; In a third country; I am not sure.
[c] Short-term plans were indicated by the question:
  What do you plan to do when you finish studying in the United States?
  Possible responses were:
    I intend to leave the United States immediately; I intend to remain temporarily in the United States; I intend to remain in the United States permanently; My plans are indefinite, but I hope to leave immediately; My plans are indefinite, but I hope to remain temporarily; and My plans are indefinite, but I hope to remain permanently.
[d] These answers do not necessarily contradict the long-term plans. They represent plans to leave the United States and then remigrate.

TABLE 30—*Continued*

CATE-GORY	PERMANENT RESIDENCE[b]	SHORT-TERM PLANS[c]	SUB-TOTAL	TOTAL	%
	Undecided	Probably remain permanently in U.S.	10	22	4.6
NR3	Undecided	Probably stay in U.S. temporarily	18		
	Undecided	Stay in U.S. temporarily	42	60	12.6
NR4	Undecided	Return to PERU	17		
	No Answer	Undecided	4		
	No Answer	Probably stay in U.S. temporarily	33		
	No Answer	Stay in U.S. temporarily	7	61	12.8
NR5	No Answer	Probably return to PERU	3		
	No Answer	Return to PERU	1		
	PERU	Probably stay in U.S. temporarily	7		
	PERU	Stay in U.S. temporarily	115		
	PERU	Probably return to PERU	5	131	27.5
NR6	PERU	Return to PERU	186	186	39.1
		Total	476	476	100.0

Two methods of validating the continuum were used. First, placement of particular individuals in non-return categories was compared with interviewers' judgments about the probability of non-return.[18] At the extremes, there was no disagreement between interviewers and the placements made. There were no instances when interviewers thought an individual who was placed by cross-tabulation in NR5 or NR6 (highly probable return) would remain. There were no cases in which interviewers thought an NR1 (highly probable non-return) individual would return to Peru. However, in NR2, three of the twenty-two individuals were judged by the interviewers as probably returning to Peru, in spite of their high placement on the scale of permanent residence in the United States. In the middle categories, NR3 and NR4, the area of greatest indecision, interviewers found thirteen individuals they thought would be permanent United States residents. Eleven were in NR3 and two were in NR4, which is as it should be. Coupling these judgments with the fact that no such individuals appeared in NR5 or NR6 gives at least surface validity to the continuum.

The second method of checking the continuum was to cross-tabulate categories of non-return with other logical indicators of intended non-return (Table 31). In general, percentages decrease with progression from NR1 to NR6 on the continuum, indicating that the probability of permanent residence is decreasing. The method used to evolve the continuum is thus upheld. Particularly indicative are the decreasing percentages of individuals who intend to apply (or have applied) for United States citizenship.[19]

The percentage of immigrant-visa holders is high in NR5, explained primarily by the fact that this category includes many who will work temporarily in the United States before returning to Peru. The fact that a student has a United States wife or fiancé does not necessarily mean he will remain. Percentages generally decrease through the six category divisions, but not in as regular a manner as with citizenship or visa. Holding dual citizenship and having family in the United States do not relate to the established categories; on the other hand, they do not show striking patterns contradicting the continuum.

Length of time of residence in the United States, which provides an alternative means of scaling non-return, is incorporated only indirectly into the continuum. Those who indicated they would remain temporarily in the United States are placed in intermediate categories of the continuum. However, there is no attempt to distinguish the exact period of anticipated residence. Students might be ranked according to the total period antici-

TABLE 31—Categories of non-return by logical indicators of non-return[a]

NON-RETURN CONTINUUM	INTENDS TO APPLY FOR U.S. CITIZENSHIP		CURRENTLY HOLDS AN IMMIGRANT VISA		HAS U.S. WIFE OR FIANCÉE		IMMIGRATED TO U.S. BEFORE STUDY BEGAN		HOLDS DUAL CITIZENSHIP: U.S.-PERU		FAMILY IS CURRENTLY IN THE U.S.		BASE N
	%	#	%	#	%	#	%	#	%	#	%	#	
NR1	75.0	12	56.3	9	37.5	6	18.8	3	0.0	0	0.0	0	16
NR2	36.4	8	36.4	8	9.1	2	9.1	2	0.0	0	4.5	1	22
NR3	5.0	3	26.7	16	13.3	8	5.0	2	3.3	2	10.0	6	60
NR4	3.3	2	8.9	5	1.6	1	3.3	2	1.6	1	3.3	2	61
NR5	1.5	2	16.8	22	4.6	6	0.8	1	1.5	2	0.8	1	131
NR6	0.0	0	4.3	8	3.3	6	0.0	0	0.0	0	1.1	2	186
Total	5.7	27	14.3	68	6.1	29	2.3	11	1.1	5	2.5	12	476

[a] Calculated from: Peruvian Student Survey, Q-1.

248

pated between their arrival in the United States and their departure following study and job experience. Such a ranking would be somewhat distorted by variation of time spent in the United States (1) before, (2) during, and (3) after United States study. The anticipated date of departure would, at best, be an approximation—probably a less accurate judgment than the estimate of permanent residence used to establish the non-return continuum. Therefore, an allowance would have to be made for the certainty with which these estimates were made. In spite of its drawbacks, this scaling could be useful. In fact, if the model presented in chapter 6 is to be of maximum utility, it must identify or make some assumptions about the length of time abroad for each of the three periods mentioned above.

Clearly, temporary residence in the United States is an important dimension of non-return. In addition to the 16 students definitely planning to remain permanently in the United States and the 12 who will probably remain permanently, there were 164 who definitely plan a temporary stay and another 59 who will probably remain temporarily (refer back to Table 30). These 223 individuals are 48 per cent of the population being studied. Of the 223, 147 indicated their plans during temporary residence, and all but 10 planned to work. Of the 137 planning to work, 65 indicated they planned to remain for more than two years following study.

For the cross-tabulations of non-return by study conditions and background characteristics, scaling by length of United States residence will not be included. In chapter 8, in applying human capital models to individual decisions, the time element will be considered.

THE MAGNITUDE OF PERUVIAN
STUDENT NON-RETURN

The number of high-probability non-returnees among the Peruvian students is small. Only 16 individuals fall into category

NR1, and another 22 students are in NR2. If analysis were predicated on a dichotomization into returnees and permanent residents, the most logical cutting point would be after NR2, and the rate of non-return would be $38/476 = 8$ per cent. If, instead, the entire continuum were considered and adjustments were made for interviewers' judgments, the highly probable non-returnees would increase to 48 (10.1 per cent). Because interviewers contacted only about one-third of the students, it is likely that more would have been judged non-returnees if more interviews had been conducted. Both the 8 and the 10.1 per cent are probably conservative estimates of the population who will remain permanently in the United States, but an exact rate or upper limit of non-return cannot be set. If, to those planning to stay permanently, we were to add all students planning to remain temporarily for at least two years, the rate of non-return would be approximately 20 per cent. The 15.7 per cent obtained for Peruvian males from the analysis in chapter 4 (Table 22) does not seem unreasonable as an estimate of permanent non-return in light of the above.

Problems of dichotomization and of using intent to define non-return have been discussed in chapter 2. The present analysis avoids dichotomization by adopting the six-category scale. In most of the following tables, however, the six categories will be collapsed to three for clarity of exposition. The continuum remains. Categories NR1 and NR2, containing students with a high probability of *Non-return* are combined at one of the continuum. In the middle, NR3 and NR4 constitute an *Undecided* group of students among whom the probability of remaining is neither high nor low. At the opposite end are students with a low probability of remaining in the United States or, conversely, with a high probability of *Return* to Peru as indicated by their position in NR5 or NR6. Subsequent tables will carry the labels Non-return, Undecided, and Return.

PATTERNS AND CORRELATES OF PERUVIAN
STUDENT NON-RETURN

To parallel the discussion of IIE data presented in chapter 3, the following variables will be cross-tabulated with categories of the non-return continuum: field of study, academic status, sponsorship, visa, age, and length of time since study began in the United States. Additional background and study variables will then be introduced: educational background, location and type of institution attended in the United States, religion, socioeconomic status, and reasons for studying in the United States. Finally, employment expectations and reasons for studying in the United States will be explored.

Non-return and Field of Study

The proportion of students with a high probability of *non-return* (NR1 + NR2) is highest within the fields of science (19.6 per cent) and medicine (10.3 per cent) (see Table 32). At the opposite end of the continuum, high probability of *return* (NR5 + NR6) to Peru is most characteristic of agricultural students (80.3 per cent) and least often found among medical students (24.1 per cent).

Medical students are conspicuously concentrated in the middle category of the continuum. In fact, all but 2 of the 38 medical students in the NR3 + NR4 category are concentrated in NR3, the category in which all individuals specifically stated they were undecided about their residence (see Table 30). There is a strong presumption that many of these medical students will stay in the United States. Many are looking ahead to internship and specialization in United States hospitals. Having developed their specialty and having been out of touch with Peru for an extended period, it will be difficult to return and establish themselves in a position commensurate with their training and knowledge. It

TABLE 32—Peruvian student non-return, by field of study and by academic status (in per cent)[a]

| | THE NON-RETURN CONTINUUM[b] | | | | |
ITEM	Non-return (NR1 + NR2)	Undecided (NR3 + NR4)	Return (NR5 + NR6)	TOTAL PER CENT	BASE N
Field of study					
Medicine	10.3	65.6	24.1	100.0	58
Social science	4.8	30.9	64.3	100.0	42
Science	19.6	11.8	68.6	100.0	51
Engineering	8.3	17.9	73.8	100.0	156
Agriculture	7.2	12.5	80.3	100.0	56
Business	1.3	25.3	73.4	100.0	79
Humanities	5.3	26.3	68.4	100.0	19
Education	0.0	20.0	80.0	100.0	5
Total[c]	7.9	25.3	66.8	100.0	466
Academic status—undergraduate					
Freshman	3.7	34.7	61.6	100.0	107
Sophomore	11.5	28.1	60.4	100.0	96
Junior	6.6	31.2	62.2	100.0	61
Senior	10.6	28.8	60.6	100.0	66
Total[c]	7.8	30.9	61.2	99.9	330
Academic status—graduate					
M.A., M.S.	6.4	12.8	80.8	100.0	94
M.D., Ph.D.	12.6	15.6	71.8	100.0	32
Other	5.9	11.8	82.3	100.0	17
Total[c]	7.7	13.3	79.0	100.0	143

[a] Calculated from: Peruvian Student Survey, Q-1.
[b] See Table 30, pp. 245–46 for derivation of categories.
[c] Excluded from the calculations are:
    No answer on Field   — 10
    No answer on Academic Status — 3

has been estimated that approximately 70 per cent of the Peruvians studying medicine abroad return to Peru.[20] As shown in Table 32, this is not an unrealistic rate to apply to the United States, but the possibility of error is high; if all undecided cases in NR3 decided to remain in the United States, this would reduce the return rate to only 28 per cent.

Non-return and Academic Status

The probability of return to Peru is generally higher among graduate than among undergraduate students (see Table 32, column 3). Although the percentage of students with a high probability of returning to Peru is somewhat lower for doctoral-level students than for other graduate students, the percentage is higher than corresponding percentages at each undergraduate level. This supports similar findings in other studies, although small numbers prevent solid conclusions about the different rates of non-return among levels of study.

As might be expected, percentages in the undecided category generally decrease with level of education; individuals who are at a more advanced stage in the educational system are usually more certain of their career goals and are usually under greater pressure to make decisions even when not as certain of their career as they would like to be. The higher percentages of return for graduate students reflect this difference. The greater rate of sponsorship at the graduate level may also be the cause of higher return probability among graduate students. Similarly, the fact that most medical students are self-sponsored might account for the slightly lower return rates among doctoral-level students.

Non-return and Sponsorship

Self-sponsored students are less apt to return home than students sponsored by the United States government (see Table 33). Students sponsored by other organizations are intermediate. The role of sponsorship in return and non-return will be elaborated below.

Non-return and Visa

The success of sponsored programs in inducing return is also suggested in Table 33, this time in the small number of J-visa holders who are apt to migrate. At the non-return end of the continuum there is little difference between F- and J-visa holders.

At the return end, however, the difference is more pronounced. Perhaps the most surprising finding, however, is the relatively high percentage of immigrant-visa holders indicating probable return to Peru. As mentioned previously, it was not difficult, prior to 1965, to get an immigrant visa, and Peruvians often exercised this option, coming as immigrants even though planning to study. In addition to allowing students to work more hours per week, the immigrant visa allowed entrance to the United States without prior acceptance by a United States university, which an F visa requires. Requests for university admission could then be made in person and after a brief period of adjustment to the United States. With the new immigration legislation and the Vietnam war, the immigrant visa has not only become harder to obtain (for particular types of immigrants including semi-skilled or unskilled students), but it is also less attractive because it carries a draft obligation.

Non-return and Age

Younger Peruvian students are found more often in the middle categories of the non-return continuum (see Table 33), and less often at both extremes. The same arguments about career certainty and career pressure apply to younger versus older students as applied to undergraduate versus graduate students.

Non-return and Length of Time Since Study Began

As expected, the proportion of high-probability non-returnees increases as the number of years since study began increases (see Table 33); conversely, percentages in the return category decrease. The greatest changes in rates of return and non-return seem to come after three years residence abroad. We must interpret with caution, however. An open class (four or more years) and small numbers do not allow us to determine whether the changes occurring after three years represents a leveling off or whether the rapid increase in non-return continues. But more important is the fact that we are dealing with a shifting popula-

TABLE 33—Peruvian student non-return, by sponsorship, by visa, by age, and by length of time since study began (in per cent)[a]

| ITEM | THE NON-RETURN CONTINUUM[b] | | | TOTAL PER CENT | BASE N[c] |
	Non-return (NR1 + NR2)	Undecided (NR3 + NR4)	Return (NR5 + NR6)		
Sponsorship					
Self-sponsored	9.3	30.5	60.2	100.0	289
U.S. government sponsored[d]	0.0	9.5	90.5	100.0	63
Other[e]	8.8	21.8	69.4	100.0	124
Total	8.0	25.4	66.6	100.0	476
Visa					
F (student)	5.0	25.4	69.6	100.0	283
J (exchangee)	4.8	11.9	83.3	100.0	84
Immigrant	25.0	30.9	44.1	100.0	68
Other	14.3	52.4	33.3	100.0	21
Total	8.3	25.0	66.7	100.0	456
Age					
25 and under	7.4	28.2	64.4	100.0	350
Over 25	9.9	16.5	73.6	100.0	121
Total	8.1	25.3	66.7	100.1	471
Length of time since study began					
Less than one year	5.8	22.8	71.4	100.0	171
One but less than 2 yrs.	7.2	26.2	66.6	100.0	126
2, but less than 3 yrs.	8.2	25.9	65.9	100.0	85
3, but less than 4 yrs.	11.6	25.6	62.8	100.0	43
4 or more years	15.6	31.1	53.3	100.0	45
Total	8.1	25.4	66.5	100.0	470

[a] Calculated from: Peruvian Student Survey, Q-1.
[b] See Table 30, pp. 245–46 for derivation of categories.
[c] Excluded from calculations are:

No answer on Sponsorship — none
No answer on Visa   —   20
No answer on Age   —   5
No answer on Time   —   6

[d] Includes individuals who have United States government sponsorship in combination with other forms of sponsorship.
[e] Includes sponsorship by universities, foundations, business and religious organizations, the Peruvian government, and international agencies.

tion base. After three years, many of the students who will go home have already done so; it is only logical for the rate of non-return to be higher among those who remain than it was among the entire population at the time of arrival. Clearer inferences must await a larger sample and a longitudinal study.[21] And the interaction of time with such variables as level of study and obtaining a job offer in the United States must be examined.

Non-return and Institution Attended

Presumably, location and type of institution could influence the rate of non-return. Quite clearly, the only broad geographic area in which there are significant numbers of high-probability non-returnees is the West Coast (see Table 34). This does not mean that students are induced to remain in the United States by conditions on the West Coast. It is as likely that students who plan to remain permanently go to the West Coast on arrival as it is that they become enamored of the area after a period of study there. When interviewing in California (which is probably closest to Peru in climate of all states in the United States), I encountered several Peruvian students who had decided to stay in spite of negative feelings which had developed since arriving.[22]

In general, non-returnees tended to be at lower-quality institutions. Non-return is not associated with any particular size of educational institution. Over 80 per cent of the students at higher-quality institutions definitely planned to return to Peru.

Non-return and Educational Background

The cross-tabulation of selected secondary schools with non-return is not particularly revealing, except for the lower percentage of returnees among graduates of Leoncio Prado Military Academy (see Table 35). The difference is even more pronounced if NR6 is isolated; only 23 per cent of the category are sure they will return to permanent residence in Peru. Many Leoncio Prado graduates plan to remain temporarily in the United States or are undecided about their future course; consequently, it would not

TABLE 34—Peruvian student non-return, by location, size, and quality of educational institution attended[a]

	THE NON-RETURN CONTINUUM[b]				
ITEM	Non-return (NR1 + NR2)	Undecided (NR3 + NR4)	Return (NR5 + NR6)	TOTAL PER CENT	BASE N
Location[c]					
New England	5.5	16.7	77.8	100.0	18
Middle Atlantic	8.3	22.3	69.4	100.0	36
East North Central	3.8	26.9	69.3	100.0	52
West North Central	4.1	10.1	85.8	100.0	49
Southeast	5.6	29.2	65.2	100.0	72
E. and W. South Central	5.6	29.6	64.8	100.0	71
Mountain States	7.0	32.6	60.4	100.0	43
West Coast	14.1	26.0	59.9	100.0	135
Total	8.0	25.4	66.6	100.0	476
Size[d]					
Under 1,000	6.3	31.2	62.5	100.0	32
1,000—4,999	8.5	24.8	66.7	100.0	117
5,000—9,999	8.2	24.8	67.0	100.0	97
10,000 or larger	7.5	25.8	66.7	100.0	225
Total	7.9	25.7	66.4	100.0	471
Quality[e]					
High	8.1	10.8	81.1	100.0	37
Medium	4.9	27.0	68.1	100.0	270
Low	12.1	32.8	55.1	100.0	58
Total	6.3	26.3	67.4	100.0	365

[a] Calculated from: Peruvian Student Survey, Q-1 and interviews.
[b] See Table 30, pp. 245–46 for derivation of categories.
[c] Categories are the same as those adopted by the U.S. census.
[d] Institutions were typed according to size as indicated by Burckel, *College Bluebook*. Five institutions could not be typed.
[e] Institutions were typed for quality according to Astin's scaling, *ibid*. The 111 institutions which could not be typed were distributed as follows: NR1, 6; NR2, 9; NR3, 10; NR4, 15; NR5, 37; NR6, 34.

TABLE 35—Peruvian student non-return, by secondary school background[a]

	THE NON-RETURN CONTINUUM[b]				
ITEM	Non-return (NR1 + NR2)	Undecided (NR3 + NR4)	Return (NR5 + NR6)	TOTAL PER CENT	BASE N
Selected secondary schools					
U.S. or Canadian high schools	5.6	33.3	61.1	100.0	18
English-speaking high schools in Peru[c]	4.8	25.0	70.2	100.0	84
Guadalupe[d]	9.1	24.3	66.6	100.0	33
Leoncio Prado Military Academy[e]	8.6	34.3	57.1	100.0	35
Other	8.8	25.0	66.2	100.0	284
Total[f]	7.9	26.0	66.1	100.0	454
Public—private					
Public	12.5	22.8	64.7	100.0	184
Private	4.8	28.2	67.0	100.0	270
Total[f]	7.9	26.0	65.1	100.0	454
Religious—non-religious schools					
Religious	3.8	26.8	69.4	100.0	186
Non-religious	10.9	25.5	63.6	100.0	258
Total[f]	7.9	26.1	66.0	100.0	444

[a] Calculated from: Peruvian Student Survey, Q-1.
[b] See Table 30, pp. 245–46 for derivation of categories.
[c] Includes the American School of Lima, Santa María, Markham, and San Andrés.
[d] Nuestra Señora de Guadalupe is commonly regarded as among the best if not *the* best, public high school in Peru.
[e] A military academy in Callao, the port city of Lima.
[f] Excluded from the calculations are:
      NA Selected secondary schools 22
      NA Public—private (not typed) 22
      NA Religious—non-religious (not typed). . 32

be surprising if a higher percentage of the Prado graduates remained than is picked up by the non-return category.[23]

There are significant differences in non-return between public and private high school graduates and between religious and non-religious school graduates. It is logical that those who are from a private school background (which is sometimes a religious school background as well) would be more apt to return home because these individuals are typically from "better" families with better opportunities and connections.

Non-return and Religion

Non-Catholics have only a slightly higher propensity toward non-return (see Table 36). However, in the undecided and return categories, a clear difference between Catholic and non-Catholic students emerges. Non-Catholics are more concentrated in the middle categories; apparently they are more prone to migrate but are not committed.

TABLE 36—Peruvian student non-return, by religion[a]

| | THE NON-RETURN CONTINUUM[b] | | | | |
RELIGION	Non-return (NR1 + NR2)	Undecided (NR3 + NR4)	Return (NR5 + NR6)	TOTAL PER CENT	BASE N
Roman Catholic	7.2	22.8	70.0	100.0	361
Other	10.2	41.0	48.8	100.0	78
Total[c]	7.8	26.0	66.2	100.0	439

[a] Calculated from: Peruvian Student Survey, Q-1.
[b] See Table 30, pp. 245–46 for derivation of categories.
[c] Excluded from the calculations are: NA Religion...37.

Non-return and Socio-economic Status

By itself, SES relates moderately to non-return, and the propensity to remain in the United States is higher for the lower-status individuals. When SES is combined with sponsorship (see Table 37), non-return rises rapidly with decline in SES among unsponsored students and varies only slightly among sponsored students.

Table 37 lends significance to the descriptive groupings elaborated earlier in the chapter: sponsored, unsponsored-low SES, and

TABLE 37—Peruvian student non-return, by SES[a]

| | THE NON-RETURN CONTINUUM[b] | | | | |
SES[c]	Non-return (NR1 + NR2)	Undecided (NR3 + NR4)	Return (NR5 + NR6)	TOTAL PER CENT	BASE N
		Total			
1 (High)	3.1	25.3	71.6	100.0	95
2	5.3	24.2	70.5	100.0	95
3	8.4	28.1	63.5	100.0	96
4	8.4	28.4	63.2	100.0	95
5 (Low)	14.7	21.1	64.2	100.0	95
Total	8.0	25.4	66.6	100.0	476
		Unsponsored			
1 (High)	2.4	24.4	73.2	100.0	82
2	4.7	28.1	67.2	100.0	64
3	11.7	33.3	55.0	100.0	60
4	10.9	41.3	47.8	100.0	46
5 (Low)	27.0	29.7	43.3	100.0	37
Total	9.3	30.5	60.2	100.0	289
		Sponsored			
1 (High)	7.7	30.8	61.5	100.0	13
2	6.5	16.1	77.4	100.0	31
3	2.8	19.4	77.8	100.0	36
4	6.1	16.3	77.6	100.0	49
5 (Low)	6.9	15.5	78.6	100.0	58
Total	5.9	17.6	76.5	100.0	187

[a] Calculated from: Peruvian Student Survey, Q-1.
[b] See Table 30, pp. 245–46 for derivation of categories of the non-return continuum.
[c] For description of the SES index, see Appendix VI.

unsponsored-high SES. The highest propensity toward non-return occurs in the unsponsored-low SES group reaching a rate of 27 per cent for the fifth SES category.

Non-return and Marital Status

Knowing that non-returnees are more apt to have United States wives than returnees (see Table 31) does not mean that marriage to a United States woman *causes* permanent migration as is often assumed. It may be that the same characteristics and conditions that lead to migration lead to marrying an American girl. Unfortunately, the small number of Peruvian students (twenty-nine) with U.S. wives precludes detailed analysis, but some evidence can be offered to suggest that marriage *qua* marriage is not a major factor in Peruvian student non-return. Of the twenty-nine students with U.S. wives (6 per cent of the total population of Peruvian male students), eight students indicated their strong intention to remain (NR1 or NR2), nine were less definite about residence (NR3 and NR4), and twelve said they would return to Peru (NR5 or NR6). Although 8/29ths, a relatively high 28 per cent, seemed destined to remain (versus 30/447ths or only 6 per cent for the other students), it is equally significant that 72 per cent do not intend to remain. Further, if one looks specifically at the eight non-returnees with U.S. wives, only one (12.5 per cent) is from a high SES background (i.e., falls in the upper two categories of the SES index) in spite of the fact that eleven of the twenty-nine (38 per cent) are from high SES backgrounds. Thus, if marriage causes non-return, it may be only in combination with lower social status at home, in which case the marriage cannot logically be labeled *the* cause of non-return.

Non-return and Job Assurance

Students were asked the question, "Do you have employment assured in a specific job when you finish your studies in the United States?" [24] A strong relationship emerges: ten per cent of the students with no job assurance were non-returnees and only 57 per cent planned definitely to return, whereas only one per cent of those with assured jobs were non-returnees and 86 per cent planned definitely to return to Peru (see Table 38).

Job assurance turns out to be a fairly powerful variable. As we can see from Table 38, there is very little difference between migration propensities of sponsored and unsponsored students

TABLE 38—Peruvian student non-return, by employment assurance and sponsorship[a]

	THE NON-RETURN CONTINUUM[b]				
SPONSORSHIP	Non-return (NR1 + NR2)	Undecided (NR3 + NR4)	Return (NR5 + NR6)	TOTAL PER CENT	BASE N[c]
	Total				
Sponsored	4.9	18.0	77.1	100.0	183
Unsponsored	7.9	30.3	61.7	99.9	277
Total	6.7	25.4	67.8	99.9	460
	No Job Assured				
Sponsored	8.2	24.7	67.1	100.0	85
Unsponsored	10.9	36.8	52.2	99.9	201
Total	10.1	33.2	56.7	100.0	286
	Job Assured				
Sponsored	2.0	12.2	85.7	99.9	98
Unsponsored	0.0	13.2	86.8	100.0	76
Total	1.1	12.6	86.4	100.1	174

[a] Calculated from: Peruvian Student Survey, Q-1.
[b] See Table 30, pp. 245–46 for derivation of categories.
[c] Excluded from the calculations are: NA Job Assurance—6. Also excluded are ten individuals with assured jobs in the United States of which five were in the NR1 + NR2, three were in NR3 + NR4 and two were in NR5 + NR6.

when non-return is examined within categories of job assurance. If students have been guaranteed jobs on return, there is virtually no difference in their propensity to remain in the United States (two per cent for sponsored vs. zero per cent for unsponsored) or to return to Peru (86 per cent for sponsored vs. 87 per cent for unsponsored). Sponsorship is closely linked to assurance of a job and it is that assurance rather than the sponsorship, per se, that looms large in getting people back to Peru. Only 67 per cent of the sponsored students without a job guarantee say they will definitely return as compared with 86 per cent of the sponsored students who have a job waiting.

Although those students with jobs assured at home tend to go back, this does not mean that a job offer to those planning to remain abroad would necessarily induce return. The effect of such a policy would have to be judged by a longitudinal survey. But 37 per cent of the unsponsored students without assured jobs seem to be undecided about returning or remaining, whereas only 13 per cent of the unsponsored students with jobs fall in the less committed NR3 and NR4 categories. While age and career patterns may explain some of the difference, it is plausible to think that there would be some value in recruiting abroad for positions at home; and that assuring jobs would decrease the propensity to remain in the United States.[25] What kind of jobs would need to be offered at what salaries are different questions.[26] Whether the substantial cost of recruiting would be offset by the benefits derived is yet another point to be considered.

Another relationship that can be profitably reexamined, bringing in job assurance is that between visa and non-return. An assumption is often made that requiring all foreign students to hold an exchange (J) visa would substantially raise the rate of return home. However, it is legitimate to ask using the Peruvian data, whether it is the J-visa that influences return or the circumstances accompanying the J-visa. Generally, we find that most exchange visa holders are older, U.S. government-sponsored individuals who have had experience in a particular job and institution, and who have a job assured upon return—usually in the institution from which they came. F-visa holders do not have the same characteristics or job expectations; they are much less apt to have a job assured.

When non-return is compared across categories of visa, controlling specifically for whether or not a job has been assured, it clear that assurance of a job alters the relationship between visa and non-return (Table 39). Looking first within the part of Table 39 dealing with "job assured," we see that the non-return percentage is between zero and two, regardless of the visa held, and the return percentage is between 83 and 88. Now, turning to cases in which no job is assured, we find that J visa-holders are more likely to return (78 per cent) than students in any other visa

TABLE 39—Peruvian student non-return by visa and job assurance[a]

| VISA | THE NON-RETURN CONTINUUM[b] | | | TOTAL PER CENT | BASE N[c] |
	Non-return (NR1 + NR2)	Undecided (NR3 + NR4)	Return (NR5 + NR6)		
	Total				
F (student)	4.0	25.5	70.4	99.9	274
J (exchangee)	4.8	12.0	83.1	99.9	83
Immigrant	20.3	32.8	46.9	100.0	64
Other	16.7	50.0	33.3	100.0	18
Total	7.1	25.0	67.9	100.0	439
	No Job Assured				
F (student)	5.6	32.2	62.2	100.0	180
J (exchangee)	11.1	11.1	77.8	100.0	27
Immigrant	23.2	35.7	41.1	100.0	56
Other	25.0	66.7	8.3	100.0	12
Total	10.5	32.4	57.1	100.0	275
	Job Assured				
F (student)	1.1	12.8	86.2	100.1	94
J (exchangee)	1.8	12.5	85.7	100.0	56
Immigrant	0.0	12.5	87.5	100.0	8
Other	0.0	16.7	83.3	100.0	6
Total	1.2	12.8	86.0	100.0	164

[a] Calculated from: Peruvian Student Survey, Q-1.
[b] See Table 30, pp. 245–46 for derivation of categories.
[c] Excluded from calculations are:

NA Visa $= 22$
NA Job $= 5$
NA Visa and Job $= 1$

Also excluded are nine individuals who answered visa and job assurance questions but who had jobs assured in the United States.

category. However, comparing J with F visa students we find among the J visas a higher rate of non-return (11 per cent as against 6 per cent). The largest difference between J and F categories is among the undecided students. If a large portion of the undecided F visa group decide to remain in the U.S., then it might be argued that the J visa does work, by comparison, for those who study abroad without guarantee of employment on return. If most undecided students with F visas return to Peru, the visa will have had little effect on non-return. In addition, a small case base prevents firm conclusions about non-return or return among jobless exchangees.

Until longitudinal information is available clarifying the relationship between visa status and non-return, a word of caution seems justified to those who would indiscriminately require exchangee visas of *all* students, thinking that such measures would make a significant inroad on non-return.[27] Such caution is in addition to the more frequent objection to restriction of free movement by *requiring* return home.

Non-return and Stated Reasons for Study in the United States

In Tables 40 and 41, reasons for migrating to study in the United States are ranked in order of frequency mentioned and are related to non-return following study. Several of these reasons have already been touched upon when discussing the validity of the non-return continuum earlier in the chapter.

The only specific reasons that stand out with high percentages of non-return are the two dealing specifically with migration. Together, these reasons were mentioned by only 16 students. Failure to get into a Peruvian university was associated with a 10 per cent non-return rate. We can speculate that such non-returning students are either disgruntled by being rejected in the competition for Peruvian university places or are students of low ability for whom jobs will not be available in Peru.

Of more direct interest among the reasons, however, are the economic reasons included in the list. Likelihood of non-return is not distinctively high among students citing job opportunity or earnings as reasons for coming to study in the United States (Table 40). However, job opportunity (but not earnings) was prominent among reasons cited by those students who are most

TABLE 40—Peruvian student non-return and reasons for study in the United States (percentages within reasons)[a]

REASON	The Non-return Continuum[b]			Total PER CENT	BASE N
	Non-return (NR1 + NR2)	Undecided (NR3 + NR4)	Return (NR5 + NR6)		
Increase job opportunity	8	27	65	100	257
Training superior in the U.S.	7	26	67	100	228
No similar training in Peru	8	24	70	100	178
Desire to understand culture	9	26	66	101	158
Increase earnings	8	26	66	100	151
Gain prestige	8	24	68	100	148
Learn English	5	25	70	100	146
Travel	5	26	69	100	113
Parents decided	10	30	60	100	105
Peruvian universities crowded	10	32	58	100	96
Given grant	4	15	81	100	75
Establish independence	7	38	54	99	73
Other[d]	5	32	63	100	62
Disliked Peruvian education	5	47	48	100	19
Family was already in the U.S.	8	67	25	100	12
Immigrated before study	45	45	9	99	11
Considering emigration	60	20	20	100	5

[a] Calculated from: Peruvian Student Survey, Q-1.
[b] See Table 30, pp. 245–46 for derivation of categories.
[c] Multiple response allowed.
[d] Could not be classified into any of the listed categories and sufficiently diverse that a new category was not warranted.

likely to remain here (see Table 41). Economic motivations of returning and non-returning students will be discussed more fully in chapter 8.

TABLE 41—Peruvian student non-return and reasons for study in the United States (percentages, within category of non-return)[a]

	THE NON-RETURN CONTINUUM[b]		
REASON	Non-return (NR1 + NR2)	Undecided (NR3 + NR4)	Return (NR5 + NR6)
Increase job oppor- tunity	53	57	53
Training superior in the U.S.	42	50	48
No similar training in Peru	37	35	41
Desire to understand culture	37	33	33
Increase earnings	32	32	32
Gain prestige	29	30	32
Learn English	21	30	32
Travel	16	24	25
Parents decided	26	26	20
Peruvian universities crowded	26	25	18
Given grant	8	9	20
Establish independence	13	23	13
Other[c]	8	17	13
Disliked Peruvian education	3	7	3
Family was already in the U.S.	3	6	4
Immigrated before study	13	4	3
Considering emigration	8	1	1
Base N[d]	38	121	317

[a] Calculated from: Peruvian Student Survey, Q-1.
[b] See Table 30, pp. 245–46 for derivation of categories.
[c] Could not be classified into any of the listed categories and sufficiently diverse that a new category was not warranted.
[d] Multiple response allowed. Hence percentages do not total 100. Base N for total = 476.

SUMMARY AND A WORD OF CAUTION

From the foregoing cross-tabulations of the non-return index with student characteristics and conditions of study it is evident that Peruvian student non-return is only weakly related to field of study and to academic status. Slightly stronger relationships are found between the intention to remain in the United States and both the type of sponsorship and type of visa held. Unsponsored students are more prone to remain whereas sponsored students, particularly U.S. government-sponsored students plan to return. Immigrant or tourist visa holders are much more apt to remain in the United States than student (F) or exchangee (J) visa holders. Non-return is also mildly related to socioeconomic status (inversely), to marriage to a U.S. wife, to quality education (inversely), and to religious background (higher among non-Catholics). Job assurance shows a relatively strong association with return to Peru.

There is considerable interaction among the above variables. For instance, when sponsorship and SES are crossed, non-return is found to be highest among unsponsored, low-SES students. However, the unsponsored, low-SES students are also quite apt to be without assurance of a job in Peru, young, studying at the undergraduate level, possessors of a visa other than a J visa, budding engineers, and enrolled in a lower-quality United States institution. Job assurance interacts with both visa and sponsorship to moderate the relationships with non-return.

To view non-return as related to only one variable at a time, then, can be misleading; caution must be exercised in interpreting simple marginal tabulations. To know which student background characteristics and conditions of study correlate with non-return does little to *explain* non-return. With this background, we may now turn to consideration of migration decisions.

NOTES

[1] "It is a measure of the confidence in Peru felt abroad that foreign capital continues to enter at an increased rate; this confidence is also demonstrated by the successful sale on the New York market of US$15 million in Peruvian 9 per cent bonds. The external debt on December 31, 1965 rose by 38 per cent, or US$17 million, to US$429 million." ("General Confidence in Peru," *Peruvian Times,* XXVI, No. 1358 [December 30, 1966], 12. Reprinted from the World Banking Supplement of *The Statist,* London, December 2, 1966.)

[2] From 1960 to 1965, the average annual increase in Gross National Product was 6.6 per cent. Per capita GNP increased at an average rate of 3.6 per cent. *Cuentas nacionales del Perú, 1950–65* (Lima: Banco Central de Reserva, 1966), p. 7.

See also Rosemary Thorp, "Inflation and Orthodox Economic Policy in Peru," *Bulletin of the Oxford University Institute of Economics and Statistics,* XXIX, No. 3 (August, 1967), pp. 185–210.

[3] François Bourricaud, *Structure and Function of the Peruvian Oligarchy,* Studies in Comparative International Development, Vol. II, No. 2; (St. Louis: Social Science Institute, Washington University, 1966).

[4] Alvin Cohen, "The Technology/Elite Approach to the Development Process: Peruvian Case Study," *Economic Development and Cultural Change,* XIV, No. 3 (April 1966), pp. 323–33.

[5] The total university population for 1964 was estimated at 50,027 (Oficina Nacional Inter-universitaria de Planificación, "Configuración descriptiva de la universidad peruana," Lima, June 1966). If study abroad is estimated at what seems a reasonable figure of 15,000 (see Table 26), then the percentage of foreign students to total is 23 per cent.

[6] By 1968, however, official attention was being given to the flight of Peruvian talent, see *Informe Económico Anual: Sector Educación* (Lima, Instituto Nacional de Planificación, 1968).

[7] Fernando Romero, *Educación y desarrollo económico* (Lima: Banco Central de Reserva del Perú, 1963), p. 384, quoting *El Comércio* (Lima, Peru), September 24, 1963. The *El Comércio* report was based on figures supplied by the Department of Organizations for International Cooperation of the Peruvian Ministry of Foreign Affairs.

[8] The Peruvian government does not take this extreme position in its legal requirements. Peruvian citizenship is withdrawn if a Peruvian acquires citizenship or serves in the military of another country. However, a Peruvian returning to Peru after having served in the United States military (as required by his United States immigrant status) can revalidate his citizenship. The extreme position of "once a Peruvian, always a Peruvian" is implied if arguments about recouping lost Peruvian talent include recouping of individuals who have adopted United States citizenship.

[9] One major difficulty interfered with using the IIE's listing of institutions of higher education as the basis for defining higher education and for delineating the population of Peruvian students. An examination of the IIE census forms for 1965 showed sixty Peruvian students at New York University. Upon inquiring into this large number, it became evident that only

three students were actually enrolled at NYU; the others were at the New York University Language Institute. Most of the latter were part-time students; all were exclusively involved in learning English at the Institute and were not taking other courses. Of these fifty-seven students at the Language Institute, none had been recommended for further study at the university. In short, the level and focus of these individuals seemed incompatible with most definitions of higher education. Consequently, this group was excluded from the study. Otherwise it would have been necessary, in order to be consistent, to locate and include intensive English programs in a variety of other settings that were clearly outside the college and university system of the United States. For instance, in San Francisco, the John Adams Annex of John Adams Adult School showed twenty-two Peruvians studying English in April 1966. Under certain circumstances, this school grants F-visas, and students can study on a full-time basis. The average age of all students at the school was twenty-three, putting them in the higher-education age group (interview with the Registrar, May 4, 1966). The John Adams educational program, a mixture of "Americanization" and adult education courses, fulfills an important function and enrolls significant numbers of foreign students and of Peruvians. One San Francisco Peruvian told the author that there must be "five hundred Peruvians studying at John Adams Adult School." Though exaggerated, this estimate indicates that the numbers of fringe-area "students" is large. Similar gross estimates were made for Cambria and Belmont schools in Los Angeles. It would be interesting, in another study, to identify language training institutes of various kinds and look at them in detail as they relate to the question of non-return and brain drain.

Excluding intensive English students at the NYU Language Institute also raised the problem of treating other centers for learning English that were in college or university settings. For instance, included in the IIE census were individuals who were partially or exclusively involved in intensive English programs at the University of Miami (Florida), the University of Kansas, the University of San Francisco, Winooski College, and Michigan State University, to name a few. There was not time to visit each center, and there was no good way of sorting out individuals before mailing questionnaires. Consequently, all were included with the idea that further screening might be necessary after questionnaires had been received. It was decided that "intensive English" students would be excluded unless taking their English concurrently with some other academic work at the college or university level. A combination of English and other courses totaling twelve semester hours would be viewed as legitimate full-time student work.

[10] An example of the questionnaire is included in Myers, "Study Abroad and the Migration of Human Resources," Appendix XII.

[11] Institutions were categorized by organization, control, and size according to information from Christian E. Burckel, The College Bluebooks, Book I, Vol. I, American Institutions of Higher Education, 11th ed. (Yonkers, N.Y.: The College Bluebook, 1965). Institutions were roughly categorized by "quality" using the index prepared by Alexander W. Astin, Who Goes Where to College? (Chicago: Science Research Associates, Inc., 1965), pp. 57–83.

[12] The comparison involves an assumption that there was no change in the distribution of characteristics and study conditions among students on the IIE list between Fall 1964, and Spring 1966, when the survey was taken.

Furthermore, there is an assumption that the IIE distribution is close to the "true" distribution of characteristics among Peruvian students.

[13] Less than 2 per cent of the economically active population as enumerated in the 1961 Peruvian Census of Population had had at least one year of university education. Approximately 12 per cent claimed secondary education. (República del Perú, Instituto Nacional de Planificación, in cooperation with the Organization for Economic Cooperation and Development, *Desarrollo económico y social, recursos humanos y educación* [Lima: Instituto Nacional de Planificación, June 1966], Anexos 3–10, Table IV.)

[14] According to the Peruvian Census of 1961, approximately 5 per cent of the economically active population can be classified as professionals, technicians, directors, or administrators. Among 12 per cent are white-collar workers in office, or sales positions. (República del Perú, Instituto Nacional de Planificación, Dirección Nacional de Estadística y Censos, *VI Censo nacional de población: 1961.* Vol. IV: *Características económicas,* p. xix.)

[15] Estimates of professionals' salaries in Peru are difficult to obtain and are seldom accurate. To give some perspective, however, the 1961 census indicates only 0.4 of 1 per cent of the economically active population with incomes over 20,000 soles per month (approximately US$10,000 per year). For professionals, technicians, managers, administrators, the percentage is only slightly higher: 1.3 per cent (calculated from *ibid.,* pp. 286–88, Table 118). In a recent survey done in Arequipa, the second largest city of Peru, only 2 per cent of the economically active population was earning more than 10,000 soles (US$375) per month. (See República del Perú, Ministerio de Trabajo, Servicio del Empleo y Recursos Humanos, Centro de Investigaciones Sociales por Muestro, *Características socioeconómicas de la población de la ciudad de Arequipa, encuesta de hogares* [Lima, November 1966], p. IV–14, Table 6-A.)

See aslo salary estimates derived in the following chapter.

[16] The percentage of foreignborn in Peru is less than 1 per cent. In Lima, it is slightly higher—almost 3 per cent. (República del Perú, Instituto Nacional de Planificación Nacional de Estadística y Censos, *VI Censo nacional de población: 1961.* Vol. II: *Migración, nacionalidad legal, estado conyugal, religión, fecundidad,* p. iii.

The percentage of non-Roman Catholics in Peru is 1.9 per cent. (*Ibid.,* p. xxiii.)

[17] Keep in mind that the socio-economic index is an artificial construct and that the entire Peruvian student population was, on the average, high in the Peruvian social system. It was difficult, for this reason, to know how to appropriately label the categories of the five-category scale. Although there are very few students who could be considered to have "lower" class backgrounds, the index does seem to discriminate.

[18] Interviewers took their cues from expressed preferences, from the manner in which respondents handled questions of income projections, from the presence or absence of strong attachments which interviewed students might have developed in the United States, and so forth. However, these were subjective impressions, and the author did not wish to enter them as other than a check on questionnaire responses; there is no guarantee that they are accurate. Approximately one-third of the total population was interviewed, setting limits for the check.

[19] This category includes dual citizenship, which accounts for the two NR5 cases.

[20] Thomas L. Hall, *Health Manpower Planning: The Peruvian Case Study,* (Baltimore: Johns Hopkins Press, 1969), pp. 276–77. The estimates were based on a tabulation of foreign medical graduates of Peruvian nationality and on degrees validated in Peru. United States-trained doctors were not fully represented in the survey.

[21] I am presently involved in following up a sub-sample of the 476 students (four years after the original survey) to see whether students have changed their minds about returning home, to see whether the length of stay in the U.S. was prolonged and to see whether training is being utilized.

[22] There was a tendency for some students to feel that they were unjustly classed with California's large Mexican migrant labor population.

[23] Typically, the Leoncio Prado graduates were adventurous, *mestizo* or Oriental, lower-middle-class Peruvians with immigrant visas, studying in lower-quality schools, often on a semester-to-semester basis and with varying academic success. There were of course, exceptions to this generalization.

[24] Ten individuals who had jobs assured in the United States were excluded from the tabulations. Had they been included the relationship between non-migrant return and job assurance would have been even more striking.

[25] For a preliminary (and somewhat superficial) study of recruiting efforts by U.S. firms with branches in Latin America, see Henry M. Steiner and Ivan Arauco (Recruiting Latin American Students in the U.S. for U.S. Firms Operating in Latin America: A Preliminary Investigation" (Austin, Texas, University of Texas, Graduate School of Business, August 1969). Mimeographed.

[26] For instance, the Latin American Scholarshp Program in American universities (LASPAU) has made a determined effort to choose Peruvian students carefully and to obtain institutional agreements prior to departure guaranteeing employment on return. Presently, however, budgets are tightened and job assurance is reduced. Consequently, there is concern among those who administrate LASPAU that, in spite of their careful efforts, some students will remain in the U.S.

[27] For a detailed discussion of immigration visa regulations and nonreturn among Israeli students, see Paul Ritterband, "Law, Policy, and Behavior: Educational Exchange Policy and Student Migration," *The American Journal of Sociology* LXXVI, No. 1 (1970), pp. 71–82. Ritterband notes how visa "washes out" in the analysis of non-return.

8

THE DECISION TO MIGRATE—
AN ECONOMIC APPRAISAL

A social scientist studying migration is virtually forced to adopt a point of view from the outset; migration is a complex phenomenon. The viewpoint will, of course, color the work done, but it need not invalidate it. Perspective is necessary, each analysis, from its own angle, forming part of a larger whole. I have adopted an economic approach, focusing on expected earnings as they relate to migration and migration decisions.

The focus on expected earnings is conditioned in part by the desire to "value" migration and to apply models developed in chapter 6. But at least as important is the search for clues to the significance of earnings (which can be manipulated) in migratory decisions. Except when building an economic model representing the "ideal," it is not enough to assume that all decisions are economically rational. On the other hand, the fact that individuals play down the importance of earnings in their decisions is not reason enough to disregard them. Sorting out the manifest and latent components of decisions is tricky indeed.

Most individual decisions have economic consequences, directly or indirectly. Anticipated consequences may be incorporated intuitively into the decision calculus. Although it is a rare person who will, for a specific decision, actually compute expected mone-

273

tary gains and losses for alternatives, it is my hypothesis that most individuals act *as if* they had done such computations.[1] If this is true, it implies either that monetary incentives can be manipulated to influence behavior or that economic factors form a necessary but not sufficient condition for action. In the latter case, manipulation of monetary incentives alone would not influence behavior, but it would constitute a necessary precondition for precipitating behavioral change through additional non-economic incentives.

The following illustrates simultaneously the non-economic and money-related components involved in a decision. One Peruvian student, describing fellow Peruvian students he thought would be most likely to remain in the United States, said, "They came originally because they dreamed of Hollywood and meeting beautiful girls and owning a big car." A decision built on such a fantasy is not rational in the sense of being based on an intellectual inquiry; nor is it an economically rational decision based on perfect information and resulting in maximization of the individual's position. However, the decision may, nevertheless, be both reasonable and economic when viewed *post hoc*. The girl and car are symbols of social and economic success; of a success that, for those being described, was not attainable at home. Although exaggerated, the symbols are based on real differences. To the extent that they do represent real economic and social differences between Peru and the United States (for a particular individual), myth mirrors reality, and symbols are not as economically irrational a basis for decision as might appear at the outset.

The fact that people may not be fully aware of economic components underlying their decisions does not make the economic aspects any less important. It does make it difficult to sort out the importance of economic motivations vis-à-vis other considerations. To what extent are the stated motives (whether economic or non-economic) really dominant? What part do rational economic thinking and earnings-maximization play in the decision to study abroad? My hypothesis is that economic considerations are more important than individuals are willing to admit, that they are labeled unimportant when a standard of economic security or the maximum alternative has already been established, and that, generally, people do act in an economically rational manner even though they do not admit it. To check these presumptions, two sets of considerations labeled as important in making decisions will be examined briefly: 1) reasons for study in the United States and 2) considerations in choosing a particular place to work and live.[2] Then, attention will be directed to comparison of earnings-estimates in alternative education-employment situations in accordance with the argument developed in chapter 6.

REASONS FOR STUDY ABROAD

When students were asked directly about their reasons for studying abroad and were allowed to choose several reasons, over one-half checked "increase job opportunity" and one-third mentioned "increased earnings." These are the most obviously "economic" alternatives among the reasons listed (see Table 41, chapter 7). There was virtually no association between reasons and the propensity to return home. However, when students were asked to select the *one most important* reason, opportunity and earnings were chosen by relatively few (Table 42). When recalling the reasons at the time of their original decision to study abroad, nine per cent of the students mentioned increased job opportunity, two per cent mentioned earnings. When asked what the most important reason was as they saw it at the time of the survey, students were more apt to mention opportunity (17 per cent) or earnings (8 per cent). Apparently, the importance of economic considerations grows with time.

At best, the above results of direct questioning are ambiguous

TABLE 42—"The most important reason" cited by Peruvian students for studying in the United States, at the time of the original decision and at present (percentages)[a]

	ORIGINALLY[b]		AT PRESENT	
REASON	RANK	%	RANK	%
No similar training in Peru	(1)	24.2	(2)	18.4
Training superior in the U.S.	(2)	22.6	(1)	29.9
Peruvian universities crowded	(3)	9.6	(10)	1.4
Increase job opportunity	(4)	8.7	(3)	16.5
Other[c]	(5)	5.4	(6)	6.1
Given grant	(6)	5.1	(8)	2.8
Parents decided	(7)	4.9	(14)	0.2
Desire to understand culture	(8)	3.8	(5)	7.5
Gain prestige	(9)	3.6	(7)	3.8
Establish independence	(10)	2.9	(9)	2.4
Increase earnings	(11)	2.2	(4)	8.0
Travel	(12)	1.8	(12)	0.7
Family was already in the U.S.	(13)	1.6	(14)	0.2
Disliked Peruvian education	(14)	1.6	(12)	0.7
Learn English	(15)	1.2	(11)	1.2
Immigrated before study	(16)	0.7	(14)	0.2
Considering emigration	(17)	....	(17)	....
Total		99.9		100.0
Base N[d]		447		423

[a] Calculated from: Peruvian Student Survey, Q-1.
[b] Students gave answers in retrospect. The study is not longitudinal.
[c] Answers in this category could not be classified into any of the listed categories and were sufficiently diverse to preclude a new category.
[d] Excluded from the calculations are:
  NA "Originally" 29
  NA "At present" 53

concerning the relative importance of so-called economic motives for migration. Ambiguity enters not only because results are different according to whether one looks at response frequency or at the most important choices, but also because other responses have an economic component hidden in them. The desire for training not available in Peru could be economically motivated.

From the direct questioning, then, it would be difficult to argue convincingly that economic considerations were dominant in the complicated decision matrix of Peruvian students migrating to the United States for study.

CONSIDERATIONS IN DECIDING WHERE TO WORK AND LIVE

More closely related to the question of non-return and to the results of study abroad are student assessments of important considerations in deciding where to work and live following study. Students were asked, "Which of the following are very important to you in deciding where you will live and work? (Check as many as apply to you.)" A listing of considerations is presented in Table 43, ranked by frequency mentioned when no limit was placed on the number that could be selected. The same table shows what percentage of the respondents chose each consideration as most important in deciding where to work and live. As with the reasons for study abroad, economic considerations (earnings) and job opportunity are first choices of a relatively small percentage of the population. As before, direct questions about the importance of economic factors do not demonstrate the predominance of economic motivations.

That economic considerations are not far below the surface, however, is suggested by the fact that when students were asked what they thought would lead *others* to remain in the United States, 53 per cent thought economic considerations were most important and another 26 per cent mentioned job opportunity (see final column of Table 43). We have no way of knowing to what extent respondents are really projecting their own feelings while talking about "others."

Another demonstration that economic factors are important, but not dominant, particularly for non-returnees, comes from comparing Tables 44 and 45 which present cross-tabulations of

TABLE 43—Important considerations cited by Peruvian students in deciding where to work and live[a]

CONSIDERATIONS IN DECIDING WHERE TO WORK AND LIVE	FREQUENCY MENTIONED[b]	MOST IMPORTANT	MOST APT TO LEAD OTHERS TO RESIDENCE OUTSIDE PERU
Help development	58.8	25.7	1.7
Family ties	56.5	17.1	0.7
Use professional skills	54.2	15.5	3.9
Job opportunity	54.0	14.2	26.2
Culture of the people	41.8	6.7	1.7
Economic considerations	39.9	7.1	53.0
Nationalism	34.0	5.1	0.7
Professional recognition	33.6	4.2	2.2
Improve social standing	23.3	1.1	6.3
Geography	18.1	0.4	0.5
Political preference	6.5	0.2	2.7
Religion	5.7	0.7	0.2
Other[c]	4.2	2.0	0.2
Total[d]	....	100.0	100.0
Base N	476	451	413

[a] Calculated from: Peruvian Student Survey, Q-1.
[b] Students were asked to check as many as applied. Thus the column percentages total well over 100 per cent.
[c] Could not be classified into any of the listed categories and sufficiently diverse that a new category was not warranted.
[d] Excluded from the calculations are:
    NA "Most important" 25
    NA "Most apt to lead to residence outside Peru" 63

non-return by choice of important considerations in deciding where to work and live. In Table 44, when only the most important consideration is included, economic considerations are not prominent but job opportunity is. In Table 45, when the *two* top considerations were tabulated together, the importance of economic considerations for non-return is raised considerably (with multiple response, approximately 40 per cent of the non-returnees checked economic considerations).

TABLE 44—Peruvian student non-return and the "most-important" consideration in deciding where to work and live[a]

	THE NON-RETURN CONTINUUM			
CONSIDERATIONS IN DECIDING WHERE TO WORK AND LIVE	Non-return (NR1 + NR2)	Undecided (NR3 + NR4)	Return (NR5 + NR6)	TOTAL
Help development	5.6	10.2	34.2	25.7
Family ties	11.1	5.9	22.2	17.1
Use professional skills	27.7	21.2	11.8	15.5
Job opportunity	30.5	22.9	8.7	14.2
Economic considerations	5.6	13.6	4.7	7.1
Professional recognition	....	9.3	2.7	4.2
Culture of the people	13.9	9.3	4.7	6.7
Nationalism	....	1.7	7.0	5.1
Other reasons[b]	5.6	5.9	4.0	4.4
Total[c]	100.0	100.0	100.0	100.0
Base N	36	118	298	451

[a] Calculated from: Peruvian Student Survey, Q-1.
[b] See Table 42.
[c] Excluded from the calculations are:
    NA "Most important consideration"..... 25

Several other interesting patterns emerge from the cross-tabulations in Tables 44 and 45. A desire to help in the development of a country, a nationalistic commitment, and family ties increase as the probability of return increases. Use of professional skills, job opportunity, and economic considerations are much more important for non-returnees than for returnees. Economic considerations are more frequently mentioned by individuals in NR3 + NR4 than in other categories when only one choice is allowed, as in Table 44.

There are clear associations between sponsorship and SES on the one hand, and the importance of factors in deciding where to work and live on the other (see Tables 46 and 47). Sponsored students are much more likely to espouse nationalism and to state the importance of helping their country to develop. (Virtually all such individuals fall into NR5 and NR6). They are interested

TABLE 45—Peruvian student non-return and "most important" considerations in deciding where to work and live, when first and second choices are allowed[a]

CONSIDERATIONS IN DECIDING WHERE TO WORK AND LIVE	THE NON-RETURN CONTINUUM		
	Non-return (NR1 + NR2)	Undecided (NR3 + NR4)	Return (NR5 + NR6)
Help development	5.6	32.2	50.3
Family ties	13.9	22.9	40.6
Use professional skills	41.7	34.7	23.8
Job opportunity	38.9	33.9	20.1
Economic considerations	38.9	26.3	14.1
Culture of the people	27.8	17.8	10.4
Professional recognition	16.7	17.8	11.7
Nationalism	....	4.2	16.1
Other reasons[b]	8.3	5.1	9.7
Total	....	....	....
Base N	36	118	298

[a] Calculated from: Peruvian Student Survey, Q-1.
[b] See Table 42.
[c] Multiple response allowed.

in putting acquired skills to use, but they deem job opportunity and economic considerations less important. The most striking differences related to SES are in the importance of putting professional skills to use and in family ties. The professional path is an important means of rising socially and economically in a rigid social structure. Consequently, it is not surprising to note the primary importance attached to it by those at the lower end of the SES scale.

To summarize, development is important to sponsored individuals who are highly likely to return; family ties are important to unsponsored, higher-SES individuals (ties often mean a family business as well as pure family loyalty), and the use of professional skills is important to sponsored students who are required to return and also to unsponsored students falling in the middle or at the non-return side of the non-return continuum.

TABLE   46—Sponsorship and "most important" considerations cited by Peruvian students in deciding where to work and live[a]

CONSIDERATIONS IN DECIDING WHERE TO WORK AND LIVE	SPONSORSHIP	
	Unsponsored	Sponsored
Help development	21.0	32.6
Family ties	21.8	11.0
Use professional skills	12.2	20.4
Job opportunity	17.4	8.8
Economic considerations	9.2	3.9
Culture of the people	7.4	5.0
Professional recognition	4.1	5.0
Nationalism	3.3	7.7
Other reasons[b]	3.6	5.6
Total[c]	100.0	100.0
Base N	271	181

[a] Calculated from: Peruvian Student Survey, Q-1.
[b] See Table 42.
[c] Excluded from the calculations are:
   NA Considerations 24

Individuals low in the SES scale are more likely to state the importance of professional skills. Job opportunity is deemed more important by unsponsored students and those with a higher probability of non-return. Its relatively high position among "Non-returning and Undecided" individuals suggests that providing jobs might be an appropriate strategy to attract individuals home. Economic considerations are not a stated primary concern of a large percentage of students but seem to be important secondary considerations, particularly among those most prone to permanent residence outside Peru.

The question remains, however, to what extent students act (or in this case intend to act) *as if* economic considerations were dominant rather than secondary. For further insight, earnings estimates will be examined.

TABLE 47—SES and "most important" considerations cited by Peruvian students in deciding where to work and live[a]

CONSIDERATIONS IN DECIDING WHERE TO WORK AND LIVE	SES				
	1 (HIGH)	2	3	4	5 (LOW)
Help development	23.9	35.1	9.6	27.5	30.9
Family ties	22.8	16.5	26.5	15.4	7.4
Use professional skills	4.3	11.0	19.3	23.0	20.2
Job opportunity	9.8	17.6	20.5	9.9	12.8
Economic considerations	11.9	2.2	9.6	6.6	5.3
Culture of the people	14.1	4.4	2.4	7.7	3.2
Professional recognition	3.3	5.5	3.6	6.6	3.2
Nationalism	6.6	4.4	2.4	1.1	10.6
Other reasons[b]	3.3	3.3	6.1	2.2	6.4
Total[c]	100.0	100.0	100.0	100.0	100.0
Base N	92	91	83	91	94

[a] Calculated from: Peruvian Student Survey, Q-1.
[b] See Table 42.
[c] Excluded from the calculations are:
    NA Considerations 24

APPLYING THE DECISION MODELS

The Interview and Q-2 Samples

Earnings estimates were obtained from interviews and from a second questionnaire (Q-2) mailed to first-round respondents who were not interviewed. Of the 207 interviews, 188 were usable; that is, they were with full-time students and were reasonably complete. One hundred and twenty Q-2 questionnaires were returned out of the 330 sent out.

The non-random interview sample and the relatively low questionnaire response rate resulted in minor biases.[3] The biases do not preclude using the sample to apply models developed in chapter 6; nor do they prevent a discussion of earnings estimation. However, caution should be exercised in generalizing the findings to the population at large.

The Estimating Procedure[4]

Rather than relegate to an appendix the method for obtaining estimates of expected earnings, a somewhat detailed account is presented in the text. As suggested earlier, one of the challenges for those who would measure human capital in terms of discounted earnings is the challenge of arriving at a meaningful estimate of future expected earnings.

Individuals were asked to project what they thought they would earn for three situations:

1. If they had not come to the United States to study;
2. If, following their present study, they returned to Peru;
3. If, following their present study, they remained in the United States permanently.

The first alternative, which, in comparison with each of the other two, was to have provided information concerning the decision to study abroad, has been discarded. The students had been asked to project themselves back to Peru at the time of their original decision, and to imagine that they had come to the opposite decision (not to come to the United States). It was felt that this was an unrealistic request and could not yield satisfactory answers. Consequently, focus is on expected earnings following study.

The interviewed students were asked to make earnings estimates for themselves assuming work in Peru and assuming work in the United States. Estimates were for the first and fifth years following study, for the year of maximum earnings, and for retirement. Students were asked to indicate their age at each estimation point.

Projecting to retirement proved extremely difficult; the time horizon for most students seemed to be approximately ten years. Consequently, a modification was introduced in the questionnaire: estimates were requested for the first, fifth, and tenth years following study and for age fifty. It seemed to be easier for individuals to make estimates for a specific age than to guess at the age of maximum salary. Retirement was dropped.

The following instructions were given:

> When estimating salary (or income from independent practice), do not include additional income you may expect from sources outside your employment. Include in your estimates all yearly increments to a base income and include benefits such as housing if they are provided by the organization for which you expect to work. Assume that you will be employed and that there is no change in the purchasing power of the *sol* or the dollar.

Asking individuals to exclude additional income was directed toward screening out income from stocks, bonds, and property.[5] It meant, however, that individuals anticipating two jobs occasionally excluded the income from the second job, even though it was a productive contribution and might be related to the primary employment. The result is a probable underestimate in earnings for some persons.

The assumption of no change in the purchasing power of the Peruvian *sol* was an attempt at standardizing the process of anticipating earnings; otherwise some might have included varying degrees of mild inflation while others would not. This does not mean, however, that an individual would be making an estimate without taking the future into account. Anticipated growth rates, for instance, could still be incorporated in individual estimates.

Some students were unwilling to give estimates; some were unable to. The percentage of responses for the different age points is presented in Table 48 for interviewed students and for questionnaire respondents. (The respondents will be called Q-2 respondents in the remainder of the discussion.)

From Table 48 it is evident that the time horizon was not much more than five years for many individuals, although the ten-year estimates and age-fifty estimates were made for Peru by more than 60 per cent of the respondents and the ten-year estimate for the United States was made by more than one-half of the Q-2

TABLE 48—Percentage of students in the Peruvian Student Survey making earnings estimates for various points in time[a]

| | INTERVIEW | | | | Q-2 | | | |
| | PERU | | U.S. | | PERU | | U.S. | |
CATEGORY	%	#	%	#	%	#	%	#
Starting salary	81.9	154	90.4	170	86.6	103	77.3	92
5-year estimates	61.2	115	68.1	128	77.3	92	60.5	72
10-year estimates	——	—	——	—	72.3	88	53.5	64
Maximum	52.1	98	44.1	83	——	—	——	—
Age 50	——	—	——	—	63.0	75	46.2	55
Base N	——	188	——	188	——	119	——	119

[a] Calculated from: Peruvian Student Survey, Interviews and Q-2.

respondents. As might be expected, students were generally more able to make estimates for Peru than they were to make estimates for the United States. The one exception seemed to be that interviewed individuals were aware of United States starting salaries.

There were many reasons why students were reluctant to make estimates; in fact, one reason why interviews were carried out was to ascertain such factors. In some cases, the reluctance was due to uncertainty because no clear vocational choice had yet been made, pending the outcome of a course (or courses) of study. Until the student was sure of academic success, he could not commit himself to an associated vocation. When vocational and educational objectives were clear and academic outcome was no obstacle, employment was not necessarily assured, and estimates involved employment assumptions. Some students were struggling to decide whether they should return to the family business or strike out on their own. Others were not at all sure they would be able to get a job in their field at the level they wished. For many, indecision centered about whether or not they would be able to obtain a position with an American company in Peru when studies were completed. It was hoped by many, particularly engineers, that they would be able to work for a North American company in Peru for several years to gain the experience and capital necessary to set up their own consulting firm or business.

In general, students anticipating self-employment had a difficult time making estimates—particularly those planning a business career rather than a professional career. They correctly noted that what they would pay themselves did not necessarily represent their productive contribution to the business, particularly in early years when they were plowing earnings back into the company rather than taking them out in salaries. In most such cases, individuals resorted to something like "This is about what I think I would need to get from my business in order to live reasonably."

The effect of investment decisions on income estimates varied not only among vocations and among individuals, but also affected an individual's estimates for the United States and Peru. Plowing back earnings might be much more relevant to his estimates for Peru, where he expected to make his own investment decisions and to set his own earnings, but not at all relevant for the United States, where a salaried position in a large corporation was anticipated.

Even when education, vocation, and employment were assured and were in a field other than business, there was some difficulty in making estimates. For instance, university professors working within a set salary framework can nevertheless vary their earnings by moving through the salary scale at a faster or slower pace, by taking on extra administrative duties at the university, or by taking extra jobs on the outside. The present estimates did not reflect consultant fees that university professors might expect to earn as a result of their association with the university. For instance, faculty members at the Agrarian University have not been pushed toward becoming "exclusive dedication" professors, the understanding being that they should be able to take advantage of income possibilities outside the university. Nevertheless, many are required to be "full-time" professors.[6]

Those planning government employment were also anticipating fixed salary schedules, but there is always the chance that positions will change hands as ministers or governments change. Job assurance in government can prove ephemeral.

For each age and even within projected age-occupation categories, salary predictions ranged widely. As an example, the estimates for engineers at selected ages in Peru are presented in Table 49.

TABLE 49—Earnings estimates made in 1966 by Peruvian students anticipating engineering careers in Peru following study in the United States, at selected ages[a]

Age	Earnings range[b]	Median earnings[b]
25	5,000– 18,000	12,000
30	6,000– 50,000	16,000
35	12,000–100,000+	19,000

[a] Calculated from: Peruvian Student Survey, Interviews and Q-2.
[b] Estimates of earnings are in Peruvian soles and are monthly estimates.

The wide range of salary estimates for a given age and given occupation, even among individuals at similar educational levels, can be interpreted either as wild and unrealistic fluctuations or as a reflection of the broad individual differences present in the population studied. To guard against wildly unrealistic estimates, interviewers requested two estimates from students for each year (age). The first estimate was made assuming that conditions were favorable; the second was made if students felt there was a reasonable possibility the favorable conditions would not be present. Most students did not exercise the second option or made a second estimate that was close to the first (a difference of 1,000 or 2,000 soles per month). When two estimates were given for one point in time, they were averaged to obtain one earnings estimate. If the difference between a student's two estimates for one age was so great as to exceed the average of two, the estimates were discarded as meaningless.[7]

The range of earnings within age, education and occupation does represent diversity, even within the select student population. The presence of such diverse estimates, assuming that the estimates have some relation to reality, underscores the need for a disaggregated approach in valuing migration. The relative contributions of the various students on return to Peru will differ greatly. The importance of non-return as a loss to Peru will depend on those relative potential contributions of the non-returnees.

COMPARING EARNINGS ESTIMATES FOR EMPLOYMENT IN PERU AND IN THE UNITED STATES

Adjusting Estimates for Differences in Cost-of-Living

In oversimplified form, the hypothesis governing the present economic analysis of migration behavior is that people will choose to settle where earnings are perceived to be the highest. The hypothesis assumes a complicated comparison which could be made in a variety of ways. Not the least of the complications in international comparisons of earnings is the problem of purchasing-power parity among nations (see chapter 6, p. 218). Instead of using the official exchange rate or cost-of-living adjustment or a "market basket" approach, individuals were asked the following question to ascertain an appropriate adjustment ratio for purchasing power in the United States and in Peru:

If you earned $10,000 per year in the United States (a little more than $800 per month), you could live at a certain standard of living with that amount. But what would you have to earn in Peru (in soles per month) to live equally well by Peruvian standards?

Phrasing the question in this way allowed individuals to take account of variations in values from one culture to another (for example, maids versus washing machines). In a crude way, it built in tastes and preferences by allowing individuals to weigh their own market basket comparisons. It also allowed for individual perceptions of differences that are as important in assessing motivations as "actual" differences. At the individual level, one can raise questions about the accuracy of such estimates, but in this context, there is little question about the appropriateness of the method used. However, individual adjustment ratios were also averaged to produce a general cost-of-living adjustment figure such as could be obtained from a standard index, a procedure that is not so obviously appropriate. This procedure produced an estimate of 16,400 soles per month and an adjustment ratio of approximately .75, by which United States estimates converted to soles at the exchange rate should be reduced if they are to be compared to the Peruvian estimates. Estimating a cost-of-living adjustment in this manner weights the conversion more in terms of Peruvian than in terms of United States consumption patterns. Other indices, including the exchange rate, tend to weight in a reverse manner, imposing U.S. patterns. And the adjustment as made here takes into consideration the social class composition of the particular population being studied.

It is instructive to compare the above method with that used by Stanley Braithwaite, in his excellent article, "Real Income Levels in Latin America." [8] Braithwaite points to the problems involved in trying to use exchange rates for inter-spatial comparisons and notes that he has

. . . endeavoured to circumvent these difficulties by adopting the often discussed "purchasing power parity" approach whereby national accounts data are converted into a common monetary denominator (in this case, the U.S. dollar) expressed in "real" or quantitative terms, which as far as possible eliminate inter-spatial differences.[9]

Market basket weightings were determined separately for both U.S. and for Latin America and a combined weighting was used

—a geometric mean of the two. For all Latin American countries except Venezuela and Panama, Braithwaite found that the official exchange rate underestimated the dollar values in Latin America, relative to the United States. For Peru, he calculated that the real per capita product in 1960 at the official exchange rate was $207, but using the purchasing power equivalent it was $338. The ratio of the two, .61, is somewhat below the .75 ratio obtained by averaging the Peruvian student ratios. The discrepancy between these two adjustment figures is not great and the direction of the discrepancy makes sense. The tastes and preferences of the particular Peruvian population being discussed here were decidely upper class and were probably closer to U.S. tastes than for the population in general. If only lower-class students had been included, the adjustment figure would have been at or below .61.

This cost-of-living adjustment is critical in a discussion of economic motivations. As pointed out by Braithwaite, the weighting (toward the U.S. or toward Peru) can make a difference. In some

TABLE 50—Comparative income distribution of Chilean migrants to the United States before and after migration, as of 1963[a]

LAST SALARY IN CHILE		FIRST SALARY IN THE UNITED STATES	
Monthly salary[b]	Percentage of persons receiving salary	Monthly salary	Percentage of persons receiving salary
151–180	27	Under 200	3
181–200	21	201– 300	25
201–300	27	301– 400	32
301–350	14	401– 500	14
351–450	8	801–1,000	10
Over 450	3	1,001–1,500	1
		1,501–2,000	1
		Over 2,000	—
Total	100	Total	100

[a] Adapted from: Sergio Gutiérrez Olivos and Jorge Riquelme Pérez, *La emigración de recursos humanos de alto nivel y el caso de Chile* (Washington, D.C.: Pan American Union, 1965).
[b] U.S. dollar equivalent.

instances, however, the adjustment has been omitted from analyses of migration that include earnings among the factors analyzed. For example, in their study of high-level migration from Chile, Gutiérrez and Riquelme compare figures for the last salary in Chile and the first salary in the United States at the official exchange rate (see Table 50).

It is unlikely that an adjustment for cost-of-living differences between Chile and the United States could eliminate these extreme differences. On the other hand, it could help explain why more individuals have not migrated in spite of the differentials which appear to favor movement to the United States.

Employment Expectations

Another complication arose when students insisted that, if they were to stay in the United States and be professionally successful, they would need to continue their education, and either finish a degree course which they would not complete if returning to Peru, or go on to a higher degree. The additional costs which might be incurred where more post-graduate schooling is involved will include earnings foregone while continuing the education as well as direct costs. When dealing with individual decisions to remain or return, these cost adjustments are relatively easy to make; earnings do not begin until later, and the cost of education can be included. For social decisions, the anticipated additional education can be disregarded; it presumably occurs only if an individual has already decided to remain abroad permanently, in which case the relevant value of human capital lost is the value upon completing the initial period of education abroad, not the value upon completing additional education after migration.

Starting Salaries versus Earnings Profiles

Do individuals make their valuations of economic alternatives primarily on the basis of an anticipated starting salary, of an expected peak in earnings, or of the entire stream of earnings anticipated? Maximum salary was hard for students to estimate, and, because it typically comes at a later age, it is not weighted as much in economic calculations as a starting salary or a salary ten years after study. The most visible and certain evidence of an economic differential between two alternatives is the starting salary which might be expected in the two settings. In fact, while this is a factor influencing individuals in the choice of a particular job, it is doubtful that they choose their permanent residence on this basis. Moreover, starting salaries are often misleading indices of economic advantage because they reflect a temporary phase in a sequential process: a period of apprenticeship or a period of capital formation so that a private business can be started. The starting salary tells only a part of the future economic story.

A comparison of entire lifetime earnings profiles using discount rates is probably not made consciously by individuals deciding between locations for life work. On the other hand, the fact that $1,000 today is worth more than $1,000 in ten years is easily grasped. When two career patterns bring the same total life earnings, the alternative that puts a large share of the total earnings earlier in life will generally be preferred. It is assumed that individuals have an intuitive feel for comparing entire earnings streams.[10] Such a comparison avoids an excessive reliance on a point in time and its peculiarities. To facilitate comparison, earnings streams can be presented graphically or represented as present values by discounting future earnings for each year back to a decision point, using an approximate discount rate.

Application of the Model to a Private Decision

Individuals could not be expected to make estimates of earnings for each successive year. Consequently, several points in time were chosen, as explained above. Each individual made estimates for these points, and from these, income streams for each person, for the population, and for subpopulations were derived. Figure 6 gives an example for a particular individual. The point estimates are plotted; an earnings curve is derived by linear interpolation. Curves are drawn for earnings estimates in Peru and in

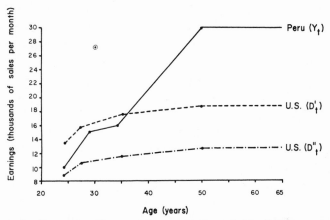

FIGURE 6—Generating Earnings Stream Using Individual Expectation of Earnings: An Example Taken From the Peruvian Student Survey, 1966

Key to Age-Earnings Profiles

	EXPECTED EARNINGS			
	IN THE UNITED STATES			IN PERU
AGE FOR WHICH ESTIMATES WERE MADE	Original estimate, in dollars (D_t)	Adjusted at the exchanged rate, in soles (D_t')	Adjusted to allow for cost of living, in soles (D_t'')	Original estimate, in soles (Y_t)
24	500	13,250	8,878	10,000
27	600	15,900	10,653	. . . . .
29	. . .	. . . . .	. . . . .	15,000
34	. . .	. . . . .	. . . . .	16,000
35	650	17,225	11,541	. . . . .
50	700	18,550	12,429	30,000

the United States, using both unadjusted and adjusted earnings figures.

The two income streams can be fitted into the individual decision models of chapter 6, adjusted for the fact that the student is deciding at point m (the time when studies are completed) rather than at point a (the time study began). The decision to remain or remigrate, viewed from the student perspective at time m, involves the comparison between expected earnings in the U.S. (D_t) and expected earnings in Peru (Y_t) minus transportation costs (Z_t). Symbolically, the comparison is:

$$\sum_{t=m}^{n} \frac{D_t}{(1+r)^{t-m}} \gtreqless \sum_{t=m}^{n} \frac{Y_t}{(1+r)^{t-m}} - \frac{Z_t{}^h}{(1+r)^{t-m-1}}$$

Educational costs have dropped out of the decision model as it is applied here because it is assumed that the costs have already been incurred and are therefore irrelevant. If postgraduate training were associated with the alternative of remaining in the United States, costs of further education would have to be subtracted from the left-hand side of the inequality and Y_t would probably be zero or very low during the years of training. In the example, additional training was not anticipated. If, then, the present value of earnings in the United States are greater than the present value of earnings in Peru (minus travel costs), the student should remain in the United States.

Earnings streams D_t and Y_t for an individual are pictured in Figure 6 and the relevant present values are presented in Table 51, using different discount rates. Transportation is assumed to be $225 or, translated into soles and put on a monthly basis, 550 soles per month. No adjustment has been made for taxes, primarily because there seemed to be no realistic way to estimate an appropriate tax rate for Peru. Tax schedules are available, but it is well-known that compliance with tax laws is less frequent in Peru than in the United States. While dealing with earnings after taxes would probably have reduced United States estimates relatively more than Peruvian estimates, the difference in reductions cannot be calculated.

When calculations are made using the earnings values from Figure 6 and applying a .12 discount rate to United States and Peruvian earnings, present values are virtually the same for the two, with a slight advantage for remaining in the United States. If the discount rate is changed to .08, the advantage shifts to Peru,

TABLE 51—A comparison of present values for estimates of earnings in the United States and Peru, using two discount rates and adjusting for purchasing-power parity[a]

ITEM	$\sum_{t=m}^{n} \dfrac{D_t}{(1+r)^{t-m}}$ (1)	$\sum_{t=m}^{n} \dfrac{Y_t}{(1+r)^{t-m}}$ (2)	Z_t^h (3)	NET (1)−(2)+(3)
U.S. earnings stream, adjusted to soles at the official exchange rate				
r = .12	133,487	131,336	550[b]	+ 2,701
r = .08	199,119	213,010	550	− 13,341
U.S. earnings stream, corrected for cost-of-living differences[c]				
r = .12	89,220	131,336	550	− 41,566
r = .08	133,003	213,010	550	− 79,457
r = .00	494,628	978,000	550	−483,822

[a] Calculated from: Peruvian Student Survey, Interviews and Q-2.
[b] All estimates of earnings are on a per month basis. To obtain the Z_t^h estimate, a travel cost of $225 was converted to soles and divided by 12 to put it on a monthly basis. Z_t^h is not discounted because the decision is at $(t − m − 1) = 0$.
[c] The purchasing-power parity correction was made by multiplying estimates for each year by .67 (the adjustment figure the particular student used in this example, thought appropriate), and then refiguring the present values. In 1966 the exchange was 26.7 Peruvian soles to one United States dollar.

even when transportation costs are subtracted. If United States earnings are adjusted by the individual assessment of cost-of-living differences (this individual estimated that one could live equally well in Peru for two-thirds of the money), the Peruvian stream is clearly preferable.

The particular curve chosen illustrates the difference an adjustment for cost-of-living differences and for differing discount rates can make in the comparative valuing of earnings streams and of human capital. If only starting salaries were compared, the economic alternative would be residence in the United States. If the maximum salaries are compared, Peru is clearly the choice. If the earnings streams are compared without adjusting for the cost-of-living differences, then whether Peru or the United States is the most rational choice depends on the rate of discount chosen as appropriate. If United States earnings estimates are adjusted by the individual's assessment of living differences, the economic alternative is Peru, no matter whether starting salaries, maximum salaries, or earnings streams are compared.

The case presented is not typical; there is no typical case. Estimates for other individuals are not usually as regular as the ones presented in Figure 6. Nor are the alternatives as seemingly indeterminate, depending on assumptions about discount rates or about cost-of-living adjustments. Because there is such variety among the individual cases, no attempt will be made to summarize them. The most important feature of the analysis is well illustrated by the one case presented—that simple earnings differences which seem to favor residence in the United States may not, in fact, reflect an economic advantage for United States residence.

Expected Earnings Streams and Social Decisions

There are few countries outside the United States which provide earnings information, let alone associated individual and demographic characteristics that would allow application of the chapter 6 models to social decisions concerning investment in human resources. To my knowledge, there are no Peruvian age-income profiles (derived from actual earnings figures) from which an appropriate earnings stream could be deduced for a Peruvian student following his study in the United States. As shown in chapter 7, the Peruvian students in the United States are a select group, and within the select group there are readily distinguishable sub-groups. Average income figures from the 1961 Peruvian census do not provide an adequate indicator of the expected earnings for any part of the Peruvian population, let alone for overseas students returning to employment in Peru. In general, census tabulations would grossly underestimate earnings for returning students. Therefore, I decided to generate age-earnings profiles for Peruvian males studying in the United States by combining and averaging individual earnings expectations.

My use of individual expectations to create earnings streams was motivated by more than an absence of other such information. I felt that earnings expectations, in spite of the difficulties involved, provide at least as realistic an operational basis for determining human capital values as the alternative—cross-sectional age-earnings profiles—currently used. Although the earnings expectations are values which individuals assign to themselves rather than values assigned to them by society, there is a strong a priori case for believing they index future earnings streams as accurately as the current method. Individual estimates take disaggregation to the individual level and each individual assigns an appropriate weight to himself in determining the total human capital value for the population being analyzed. When combined, the result is an estimate of the productive value of individuals, *given individual perceptions of the present social economic structure and of how it will change.* Aggregating individual estimates will not help to determine the economically rational ideal any more than using cross-sectional earnings data, but it can indicate the most economic use of resources given the imperfections and constraints of the present and foreseeable future.

It is presumed that when individuals estimate earnings, they take into account their own ability, their connections, their assessment of the economic growth rate, their view of the rigidity (or rate of change) of the social structure, and so forth. It is presumed that an individual who has good connections and little ability, but who expects to earn a high salary, will actually be contributing more to the society (as it is) than an individual with ability but with poor connections who because of this expects to earn a low salary. Individual estimates, then, predict actual rather than potential earnings that can be expected from an individual in a particular context.[11]

The individual estimates contain a clue missed by cross-sectional estimates, as to whether or not individuals anticipate change. If, on the average, individuals expect that their services will be highly valued, even though they are not now so valued, some faith in change is evinced. Anticipated change may be as important as existing inequities in determining whether individuals return home or remain abroad following study.

To explore the utility of individual earnings estimates further, and as a first step toward operationalizing the social decision models of chapter 6, synthetic earnings curves were derived based on the individual estimates. The earnings streams are presented and discussed below.

Creating Synthetic Earnings Streams

Because ages varied, student estimates for starting and subsequent salaries covered all ages from twenty to fifty and even beyond fifty, although any one person made, at most, only four estimates. To create synthetic earnings curves representing the aggregation of all individual estimates, each estimate that could be attached to a specific age was recorded and ages were grouped, first by single years, then in five-year groupings. Initially, the groupings were without reference to who had made them. Means and medians were calculated. The resulting streams are presented in Table 52, for interview respondents, for questionnaire respondents, and for the two combined. All estimates were given equal weight—there was no attempt to adjust for the certainty with which an estimate was made. If an individual made three estimates, all three were included; if only one estimate was made, it was included. Non-respondents were simply ignored.

In general, interview respondents made higher estimates than Q-2 respondents. The two curves are, however, relatively close; close enough, it was felt, that the two could be justifiably grouped. Of the several methods that could be used to smooth the curves, two are presented, in columns 10 and 12 of Table 52: median calculations for five-year groupings and a "moving average" using five-year groupings. Because there were a number of extremely high earnings estimates that pulled mean figures up, medians were chosen as the more accurate general indicator and will be used in further discussion.

TABLE 52—Peruvian student expectation of earnings in Peru following study in the United States (earnings in Peruvian soles per month)[a]

	INTERVIEW			Q-2			TOTAL SAMPLE					
	Earnings			Earnings			YEAR-BY-YEAR			FIVE-YEAR GROUPS		
							Earnings			Earnings		
Age	Mean (1)	Median (2)	N (3)	Mean (4)	Median (5)	N (6)	Mean (7)	Median (8)	N (9)	Median (10)	N (11)	Moving average (12)
20	7,333	5,000	3	3,250	3,250	2	5,700	5,000	5			.....
21	38,966	13,000	3	13,150	10,000	3	24,066	11,300	6			.....
22	10,000	10,000	5	9,786	9,000	7	9,875	11,500	12	10,000	82	11,842
23	11,179	9,750	14	11,639	11,000	18	11,438	12,000	32			11,946
24	12,464	11,250	14	10,708	10,000	13	11,619	12,000	27			11,372
25	11,213	10,000	23	11,364	10,000	11	11,276	10,000	34			11,696
26	11,264	11,500	14	12,164	11,000	14	11,821	14,000	28			13,496
27	12,641	12,000	17	11,958	11,000	12	12,427	15,000	29	12,000	167	14,133
28	15,374	15,500	23	20,018	15,500	22	18,033	15,000	45			15,105
29	17,046	15,000	13	13,944	13,750	18	15,294	15,000	31			16,899
30	16,061	12,500	33	14,969	15,500	16	15,759	15,000	49			17,930
31	24,486	17,550	22	18,042	18,000	12	22,318	18,000	34			19,782
32	19,436	17,000	22	17,862	15,000	13	18,909	15,000	35	16,000	180	20,382
33	29,294	18,750	16	24,876	20,000	25	26,654	20,000	41			23,239
34	16,832	17,500	5	18,281	16,750	16	18,305	17,500	21			23,849

[a] Calculated from: Peruvian Student Survey, Interviews and Q-2.

299

TABLE 52—Continued

Age	INTERVIEW Earnings			Q-2 Earnings			TOTAL SAMPLE YEAR-BY-YEAR Earnings			FIVE-YEAR GROUPS Earnings		
	Mean (1)	Median (2)	N (3)	Mean (4)	Median (5)	N (6)	Mean (7)	Median (8)	N (9)	Median (10)	N (11)	Moving average (12)
35	26,337	20,250	30	27,792	20,000	12	26,755	20,000	42			25,422
36	32,292	26,250	12	14,300	15,000	5	27,000	20,000	17			24,313
37	32,133	25,250	12	19,100	19,000	10	26,209	20,000	22	20,000	112	24,695
38	27,989	20,500	9	16,846	18,000	13	21,414	17,300	22			24,451
39	20,000	20,000	1	14,250	14,500	8	15,044	15,000	9			23,594
40	28,467	21,250	18	23,750	22,500	4	27,609	23,750	22			22,321
41	20,250	20,500	4	21,000	20,000	3	20,600	20,000	7			24,114
42	23,065	20,000	8	16,125	14,250	4	20,750	18,750	12	20,000	52	25,506
43	69,450	69,450	2	21,114	20,000	7	31,856	20,000	9			25,283
44	....	....	0	19,500	19,500	2	19,500	19,500	2			25,914

300

45	29,093	26,000	15	16,250	16,250	2	27,612	26,000	17			28,642
46	15,500	15,500	2	32,500	32,500	2	24,025	24,250	4			29,113
47	33,511	32,500	9	19,400	19,400	2	30,945	22,000	11	24,000	38	29,313
48	52,000	52,000	1	34,500	23,000	4	28,100	25,000	5			32,728
49	17,500	17,500	1			0	17,500	17,500	1			33,067
50	47,621	37,500	14	30,533	26,000	75	33,221	30,000	89			33,312
51			0			0			0			33,035
52			0			0			1			
53	32,000	32,000	1			0	32,000	32,000	1			
54	10,500	10,500	1			0	10,500	10,500	1			
55			0			0			0			
56			0			0			0			
57			0	20,800	20,800	1	20,800	20,800	1	30,000	93	
58			0			0			0			
59			0			0			0			
60			0			0			0			
61			0			0			0			
62			0			0			0			
63			0			0			0			
64			0			0			0			
65	100,000	100,000	1			0	100,000	100,000	1			

TABLE 53—Peruvian student expectation of earnings in Peru following study in the United States, by education and SES (earnings in Peruvian soles per month)[a]

AGE	EDUCATION				SES[b]			
	B.A. OR BELOW		ABOVE B.A.		SES 1, 2 (HIGH)		SES 4, 5 (LOW)	
	Median earnings	Number of estimates	Median earnings	Number of estimates	Median earnings	Number of estimates	Median estimates	Number of estimates
20–24	10,000	29	10,000	14	10,000	44	9,500	18
25–29	12,000	50	11,000	49	14,500	74	10,000	57
30–34	19,000	45	15,000	77	20,000	59	13,000	81
35–39	22,000	22	20,000	55	26,000	30	17,000	63
40–44	22,000	13	18,000	27	25,750	12	20,000	32
45–49	26,000	13	22,000	18	24,250	6	21,500	22
50+	50,000	7	27,000	13	30,000	38	25,000	42
Present value— age 22 r = .12	133,222	..	113,256	..	139,928	..	95,230	..

[a] Calculated from: Peruvian Student Survey, Interviews and Q-2.
[b] For SES levels, see Appendix VI.

Estimates are probably biased downward, not only because medians were used, but because there is a general tendency for individuals to expect and report less than they actually make, because students were not asked specifically to include income from secondary employment (which would have been difficult to anticipate) and because students who had been in the United States for some time tended to make estimates in terms of the Peruvian economic situation at the time they left rather than at present.

Earnings Estimates, Educational Attainment and Socio-economic Status

When earnings estimates are related to educational attainment and to socio-economic status, definite differences appear (see Table 53). It may seem surprising that individuals who only expect to obtain a B.A. or less should have higher earnings expectations.[12] The explanation is partially contained in the SES-earnings cross-tabulation which shows differences between the lower- and higher-SES groupings. We may recall from chapter 7 that higher-SES students tend to be self-sponsored individuals who are returning home to family businesses or large farms and who do not need the certification that an advanced degree provides. The lower-SES individuals are more apt to be sponsored and returning to university positions or to professional employment requiring higher degrees but with lower earnings. Or lower-SES students are those who are planning to remain in the United States. The fact that earnings are more highly correlated with SES than with education raises questions about the value of investing in education without accompanying social changes.

The failure of earnings to reflect educational differences does not necessarily mean that education beyond a B.A. is a poor investment, from either a private or social perspective. When earnings are separated out by amount of education within particular SES strata (see Table 54), we see that higher earnings are directly tied to amount of education for the low-SES group; with higher-SES people the opposite was true, and the BA-or-below people expect a bigger income.

TABLE 54—Peruvian student expectations of earnings in Peru following study in the United States, level of education *within* categories of SES (earnings in Peruvian Soles per month)[a]

AGE	SOCIO-ECONOMIC STATUS[b]							
	HIGH				LOW			
	EDUCATIONAL LEVEL				EDUCATIONAL LEVEL			
	Above B.A.		B.A. or below		Above B.A.		B.A. or below	
	Median	No.	Median	No.	Median	No.	Median	No.
20–24	12,000	19	9,000	25	10,000	9	7,000	9
25–29	15,000	35	15,000	37	10,000	35	9,500	22
30–34	19,000	28	22,000	29	14,000	64	10,000	17
35–39	23,200	18	30,000	11	18,000	54	15,500	10
40–44	17,500	5	35,000	7	20,000	27	20,000	5
45–49	26,000	2	24,200	4	22,000	14	20,000	7
50+	30,000	20	30,000	17	23,300	34	25,000	8
Present value— age 22 r = .12	138,412		148,559		107,193		91,067	

[a] Calculated from: Peruvian Student Survey, Interviews and Q-2.
[b] High = categories 1 and 2 on a 5-point socio-economic scale
 Low = categories 4 and 5 the same scale

For students from upper class families education appears to be primarily a consumption item. Many individuals from the upper strata (Groups I and II in the profiles of chapter 7) contemplated return home to family businesses or farms where they would begin their real training. From a personal point of view, education beyond a B.A. made little or no difference in anticipated earnings. However, it occasionally did serve to provide some technical expertise and often resulted in a respectable "titulo" that might not have been available through the Peruvian university system. These attainments could increase the economic value of an upper-class returnee to Peru even though the increase is not reflected in increased earnings. In effect the training could bring productive potential more in line with earnings—the price an upper class student's services would bring in any case because of his favored position.[13]

For lower-SES students, however, additional educational attainment is reflected in higher earnings profiles. In the university and governmental jobs preferred by (available to?) lower-SES students, salary scales are frequently geared to educational attainment and increased education is specifically rewarded, stimulating investment by individuals in themselves that should prove a social as well as an individual benefit.

Before concluding—on the basis of the relationship between increases in expected earnings and increases in education—that study beyond a B.A. in the United States is a wise investment for lower-class students, an ability factor should be incorporated. The noted increases in expected earnings may simply reflect individual ability, not education. Unfortunately the attempt to obtain grade point averages as a proxy for ability proved unsuccessful, and no measure of student ability is available.

EARNINGS ESTIMATES, NON-RETURN, AND OCCUPATIONAL GROUPINGS

A comparison of the estimated earnings streams for combined categories of the non-return continuum shows little by way of patterned differences, either for Peru or for the United States (see Table 55). When the differences between Peruvian and United States estimates made by non-returning individuals are compared with differences between Peruvian and United States estimates made by undecided, or returning, individuals, there is no clear trend. The fact that *non-returning students'* expectations for earnings *in Peru* are generally *higher* than returning students' expectations tends to support the previously examined student emphasis on considerations other than direct salary considerations in choosing where to work and live. On the surface, it does not support the hypothesis that earnings are a primary factor in decisions because some individuals move and some do not even though expected Peru-U.S. earnings differentials are much the same for those expecting to stay in the United States as for those expecting to return to Peru. The small numbers involved and the reluctance of students committed to staying in the United States to attempt estimates for Peru make firm conclusions impossible.

TABLE 55—Peruvian student expectations of earnings in Peru and in the United States following study in the United States, by non-return (earnings in Peruvian soles per month)[a]

Age	THE NON-RETURN CONTINUUM					
	Non-return (NR1 + NR2)		Undecided (NR3 + NR4)		Return (NR5 + NR6)	
	Median earnings	Number of estimates	Median earnings	Number of estimates	Median earnings	Number of estimates
	PERU					
20–24	12,000	2	10,000	20	10,000	59
25–29	14,000	9	12,000	31	12,000	126
30–34	17,000	13	15,500	34	16,000	132
35–39	35,000	7	15,000	17	20,000	87
40–44	20,000	1	20,000	8	21,250	42
45–49	29,750	2	26,000	9	22,000	27
50+	30,000	5	30,000	14	27,000	73
Present value—age 22 $r = .12$	140,285	..	115,666	..	118,877	...
	THE UNITED STATES					
20–24	17,200	6	18,600	29	17,200	80
25–29	22,100	18	19,900	42	19,900	133
30–34	21,200	17	22,100	29	23,900	99
35–39	26,500	9	37,100	12	31,800	37
40–44	41,900	4	61,400	6	37,500	21
45–49	(74,300)	3	42,100	4	39,800	16
50+	44,000	6	31,800	17	33,100	58
Present value—age 22 $r = .12$	192,904	..	224,917	..	192,049	...

[a] Calculated from: Peruvian Student Survey, Interviews and Q-2.

TABLE 55—*Continued*

AGE	NON-RETURN (NR1 + NR2)		UNDECIDED (NR3 + NR4)		RETURN (NR5 + NR6)	
	Median earnings	Number of estimates	Median earnings	Number of estimates	Median earnings	Number of estimates
DIFFERENCE (THE UNITED STATES − PERU)						
20–24	5,200		8,600		7,200	
25–29	8,100		7,900		7,900	
30–34	3,200		6,600		7,900	
35–39	9,500		22,100		11,800	
40–44	21,900		41,400		16,250	
45–49	(44,550)		16,100		17,800	
50+	14,000		11,800		6,100	
Present value—age 22						
$r = .12$	52,019		109,251		77,172	

An important intervening variable is employment uncertainty. The discriminating effect of job assurance with respect to non-return was shown in chapter 7, but in their earnings estimates, interviewees often made assumptions that they would be able to find employment when they were not at all sure. Presumably Q-2 respondents did the same thing. This leads to an upward bias in the estimates of expected earnings in Peru. If an adjustment could have been made for the probability of employment, the comparison between those more and less inclined to return might be different.

It is not unusual to hear outrage expressed when an engineer or doctor emigrates from a developing nation but to find no parallel if a lawyer leaves. It is frequently asserted that the loss of an engineer is greater than the loss of a lawyer because X country needs engineers for development. Most such arguments, whether right or wrong, are based on a vision of the society as it should be not as it is; need is confused with demand. We can use the earnings estimates to compare occupational groups as seen through the eyes of the Peruvian students.

If engineers are in fact needed more than lawyers, we would expect to find engineers earnings are, on the average, higher than lawyers earnings. If we do not, the assumption of need does not ring true—Peru should be able to show that it is willing to pay for the services of those it claims it needs, particularly if failure to do so results in emigration.

If we find non-return in needed occupations where salaries are high relative to other occupations, there is cause for concern because the incentive system seems to be operating properly. A next step would be to see whether those who are migrating are earning below the average and, if so, whether their earnings are tied to some form of market discrimination that could be eliminated. And local incentives should be compared with those drawing talent away—it may be that even though salaries are high the home country simply cannot pay well enough to meet competing

TABLE 56—Peruvian student expectations of earnings in Peru following study in the United States, selected occupational groups (earnings in Peruvian soles per month)[a]

	OCCUPATIONAL GROUPS					
	MEDICINE		ENGINEERING		SCIENCE	
AGE	Median earnings	Estimates	Median earnings	Estimates	Median earnings	Estimates
20–24	(13,000)	1	10,000	33	10,000	5
25–29	10,000	10	13,000	76	10,000	18
30–34	13,000	15	18,000	74	15,000	25
35–39	16,000	10	21,000	37	18,000	26
40–44	25,000	5	21,000	19	17,000	11
45–49	(17,000)	1	26,000	14	20,000	7
50+	30,000	14	30,000	23	21,000	14
Present value—age 22						
r = .12	120,842	..	141,470	..	115,413	..

[a] Calculated from: Peruvian Student Survey, Interviews and Q-2.

TABLE 56—*Continued*

	OCCUPATIONAL GROUPS					
	AGRICULTURE		EDUCATION		BUSINESS	
AGE	Median earnings	Estimates	Median earnings	Estimates	Median earnings	Estimates
20–24	9,000	6	10,000	5	9,000	24
25–29	10,000	9	10,000	22	12,000	42
30–34	15,000	11	13,000	29	18,000	40
35–39	14,000	8	16,000	29	18,000	21
40–44	15,000	4	20,000	13	12,000	6
45–49	20,000	3	20,000	6	18,000	5
50+	18,000	8	25,000	31	26,000	3
Present value—age 22						
r = .12	99,503	..	104,173	..	114,901	..

	SOCIAL SCIENCE		HUMANITIES		TOTAL[b]	
AGE	Median earnings	Estimates	Median earnings	Estimates	Median earnings	Estimates
20–24	(10,000)	1	.....	0	10,000	76
25–29	11,000	11	(3,000)	2	12,000	192
30–34	17,000	9	7,000	3	15,000	210
35–39	20,000	8	8,000	3	18,000	145
40–44	(25,000)	1	(17,000)	2	20,000	63
45–49	(25,000)	1	.....	0	18,000	38
50+	30,000	3	8,000	3	25,000	137
Present value—age 22						
r = .12	(.....)	..	(.....)	..	113,454	...

[b] The total is for all those who indicated occupations rather than for all those who made estimates.

salaries abroad. In that case, the brain drain complaint has somewhat more force than if it stems from inappropriate incentives or market discrimination at home.

In Table 56, earnings streams are broken down by occupational groups. Using the median values to create lifetime earnings streams (by linear interpolation), present values were calculated.[15]

Perhaps the most interesting feature of Table 56 is the contrast between the high earnings estimates and present values for engineers and the lower ones for scientists. Taking into consideration the fact that scientists were generally working toward a higher degree than engineers, the contrast is even greater. From the finding, we would expect non-return to be higher among scientists than among engineers which it is (Table 32, chapter 7). Furthermore, those scientists who expect to return to lower salaries are, in the main, subsidized while non-returnees are unsponsored. It is not surprising that many students who study engineering are self-sponsored, whereas students in science are more often subsidized. It would appear that if Peru desires to build up its science, it may have to raise rewards as well as subsidize study; if individuals are subsidized for study abroad but anticipated earnings on return are low, then the subsidy might lead to a flight of talent by pricing individuals out of the home market. Interestingly, however, this does not seem to happen in Peru. Possibly earnings differences between Peru and the United States are not as great as imagined. It may be that because living costs are low, subsidized students can afford to return to lower salaries, still obtaining a good rate of return on their educational investment. It is possible that U.S.-trained Peruvians seeking jobs in the United States will be discriminated against in the American job market. It is possible that, even though salaries are not high for returning students, they are much better than what they would have been without study abroad and that this improvement is sufficient to attract individuals home. It is possible that the requirement to return, often written into scholarship agreements of subsidized students, accounts for return. Because most sponsored students have a job guaranteed on return, job certainty and job security also loom large in decisions to return. And finally, it is possible that scientists and engineers are differentially motivated by monetary considerations; the chance to utilize scientific skills may be sufficient to motivate scientists to return. The importance of these components in job opportunity needs to be examined more closely.

Another contrast emerging from Table 56 is that between engineers and doctors. The lower rewards anticipated by medical students is in accord with the present migratory propensities of Peruvian doctors and may help to explain the large percentage of medical students who were undecided about where to settle (see chapter 7, page 252). Peruvian medical students, unlike science students, are usually not sponsored but pay their own way. To obtain an adequate return on their educational investment, doctors must be able to enter private practice in Peru. The number of private practices is limited. When the desire to live in metropolitan areas is added, the expectation of earnings in Peru for doctors trained abroad is not likely to be high unless the trainee has excellent connections and enough money to finance his own clinic. Even then success is not assured. Under such circumstances, one might predict that average expected earnings of doctors would be relatively lower than engineers, as indeed they are.

The relative loss to Peru from emigration of a doctor, engineer, or scientist will depend on the particular individual emigrating, but earnings estimates may be adopted as a gauge for assigning to average individuals in each occupational category, a relative order of economic importance. Peru seems to value engineers more than either doctors or scientists at this time. From this viewpoint, the emigration of doctors does not appear to be as upsetting, economically, as it might otherwise seem. On the other hand, if the more frequent practice of valuing emigrants at their destination (that is, by what they might earn in the United States) is adopted, the loss of doctors relative to engineers would be emphasized rather because doctors in the United States generally earn more than engineers in the United States. As I have suggested throughout the book, valuing losses at home in terms of earnings abroad distorts our picture of losses associated with migration.

One frequently hears complaints that developing nations over-produce university graduates in traditional fields such as law and medicine but that they underproduce engineers. If we accept the observation, we would expect to find lower average salaries in law and medicine than in engineering, which is indeed shown in this study. The market for talented individuals seems to be structured to discourage entry into more traditional fields or, to put it another way, seems to reflect the conditions of supply and demand. This fact suggests that criticism of marginal productivity assumptions on the grounds that the market does not operate properly in developing countries are not as firmly grounded as they may seem at first glance.

SUMMARY

In chapter 8, an attempt was made to operationalize one of the economic decision models developed in chapter 6; the one dealing with the decision to return home or remain abroad following study abroad. Peruvian students were asked to project expected earnings for employment in both the United States and Peru. When expected earnings streams for returning and non-returning students were compared, no firm answers were found concerning the dominance of earnings in decisions to re-migrate or remain. Generally, however, the results did not support the hypothesis that monetary considerations are dominant considerations when deciding to return home. The indeterminacy of the comparison when considered in conjunction with students' ordering of "important considerations" in deciding where to work and live, and with the discriminating power of job assurance in predicting non-return (chapter 7), suggests the importance of non-monetary (but nontheless "economic") elements such as job security or job certainty in the decision calculus.

Theoretical and methodological questions involved in the use of expected earnings streams as an alternative to the more common cross-sectional earnings streams were discussed. Attention was given to the thorny problem of comparing "real" earnings between two countries and a particular measure of purchasing power parity was established.

In private decision models, individual expectations are clearly appropriate. A more difficult question is that of the applicability of average earnings expectations to social valuation of human capital and of their use in social decision models. If the desire is to measure actual (rather than potential) productive contribution, aggregated and averaged individual earnings estimates appear to be useful, providing a weighted measure of productivity for individuals of varying abilities and backgrounds, operating in a specific context.

Earnings streams and present values were established for graduate versus undergraduate students within socio-economic strata. Additional education was associated with increased earnings expectations among lower-status, but not higher-status Peruvian students. No attempt was made to go behind the finding; however, it does point to the faith in, if not power of, education as a means of advancement by those of lower social origins in Peru.

When classified by occupational groupings, earnings estimates provided perspective on the relative loss associated with emigration of an average individual within the respective occupations. It appears that the economic loss to Peru of an average engineer was greater in 1966 than that of an average doctor. Because the earnings of doctors appear relatively low, the observed migration of doctors and the low likelihood of return among medical students (see chapter 7) is not surprising. The same situation pertains to science versus engineering. In short, Peru's economic reward structure appears to be in line with the oft-cited preference for engineers as agents of economic development over scientists and doctors and lawyers. As yet, it seems, science must be highly subsidized to survive and grow.

NOTES

[1] In fact, an intuitive grasp of the economic factors involved allows a more complex economic calculation than models can represent. Individuals may vary the discount rate applied, and allow for uncertainties and discontinuities, but not be aware of the process involved.

[2] The exploration of economic rationality does not conflict with the assumption of economic rationality necessary in establishing the decision models. If individuals are found to diverge from the economically rational, there are two possibilities for explaining the differences: 1, people are not inherently rational, or 2, people are prevented from behaving rationally by imperfect knowledge or market conditions.

[3] Appendix V details the methodology employed in obtaining interviews and in choosing individuals to whom the parallel questionnaire should be mailed. In the appendix, a brief comparison of the marginals for the larger population of 476 with the interview population and with the questionnaire population is made. The questionnaire responses are slightly biased toward graduate students of a lower SES.

[4] I have benefited from comments of Mary Jean Bowman on the following pages of chapter 8.

[5] If property incomes are dependent on residence, a comparison between Peruvian and U.S. incomes would be biased against Peru, particularly for those with higher status in Peru.

[6] "Exclusive dedication" professors are presumably forbidden to work at any job other than their university job. "Full-time" professors must put a certain number of hours into their university jobs but may also work outside the university.

[7] One or two exceptions to this general rule occurred where individuals indicated that one of the two estimates was highly probable. In one case, the estimates given were flip and, in the opinion of the interviewer, were not even semi-serious attempts to arrive at an earnings estimate representing a legitimate expectation; this case was discarded from the estimates. There were undoubtedly some severe errors of judgment, but interviewers did not attempt to judge responses as long as the attempt to answer was judged sincere. If an individual insisted that it was impossible to make an estimate, no estimate was recorded, but not until the question had been asked a second time.

[8] Stanley N. Braithwaite, "Real Income Levels in Latin America," *The Review of Income and Wealth*, XIV, No. 2 (June 1968), pp. 113–82.

[9] *Ibid.*, p. 113. Braithwaite used "a common marketbasket of goods and services whose composition at the item level was considered identical in all situations—thus assuming implicitly that aggregate satisfaction would also be identical, even though variations in tastes, customs, preferences, needs, availabilities, price patterns, and income levels obviously existed throughout Latin America."

[10] Aba Schwartz found that "differentials in life-span earnings pertain somewhat better in explaining the pattern of migration than do differentials in current earnings." *Migration and Life Span Earnings in the U.S.*, p. 4.

[11] Implicit is the assumption that predicted "actual" earnings are at the same time predicted marginal products for individuals, even though there are discriminating markets. This assumption would have to be qualified if individuals were at the same time buyers and sellers of their own services at public expense, or, if employers were obtaining monopsonistic profits at the employees expense. In the first instance, predicted earnings would probably overstate productivity; in the second, they would underestimate productivity.

[12] However, if one looks at the median annual salaries of full-time employed economists in the United States, the same effect is present. *Summary of American Science Manpower, 1966.* NSF 68–9 (Washington, D.C.: National Science Foundation, March, 1968), p. 3.

[13] It is also possible to interpret differences in expected earnings between two social class groupings as reflecting differences in experiential learning outside the formal school system. While the disadvantaged can hope to compensate in some degree by substituting additional formal education they may never be able to close the gap in experience that came with birth and was nurtured by societal distinctions.

[14] When the medians were calculated for occupations, some individuals were classified in each of two occupational groupings. For instance, an industrial engineer, if indicating he would probably become involved in management, was classed both as an engineer and as a businessman. A university professor at the National Engineering University was classed both as an engineer and as a professor.

[15] A 12 per cent discount rate was used to determine present values; it is commonly accepted as a reasonable rate that can be expected from an investment in Peru. Individuals were asked in the survey to estimate what rate they might expect. Generally, estimates were higher than 12 per cent, so the figure probably represents a minimum.

PART V

Implications for Policy

9

SOME IMPLICATIONS FOR POLICY

Academics are frequently caught in the most tempting of traps when discussing migration by assuming that any restriction placed on freedom to move is an infringement on an individual's rights or that migration is a natural corrective process with which, in our best interests, we should not interfere. Policy makers are similarly vulnerable. Pressured by specific problems, their tendency is to assume that immediate and sometimes drastic action must be taken to regulate apparent inequities associated with migration. In so doing, they frequently confuse the effects of migration with the effects of disadvantages which the migration in fact reduces but does not eliminate.[1]

While I prefer the former, more academic position, I think we must accept the fact that there are at present man-made barriers and incentives interfering with the proper functioning of migration as a corrective force, and we must accept that freedom of an individual to move, as other rights, is appropriate only to the extent that it does not result in infringement on the rights of others. The problems associated with migration policy then become matters of degree—when and how much should we intervene in the migration process? A standard of evaluation is implied.

If pressed, most academics would agree that something akin to a Pareto optimum is needed, whereby movement should not only be tolerated but encouraged *if* welfare is thereby increased *and if* no uncompensated losses occur as a result. For purposes of discussion, I will assume that although the first condition is met when high-level persons migrate (i.e. their movement improves their own position and the position of individuals in the destination area by more than it erodes the position of those left behind); the second condition—uncompensated losses may result—may or may not be met.

The problem of uncompensated losses can be attacked in several ways: by denying that uncompensated losses occur, by establishing an equitable means of compensation, or by promoting policies that would eliminate the losses before they occur. I will argue below that because we do not yet have a viable means of estimating the absolute value of human capital losses and gains and because the relationship between human capital losses and other economic gains and losses associated with migration is not well established, *formal* compensation schemes would be, at best, premature. Policy-makers should focus, then, on corrective policies aimed at eliminating losses before they occur or, more realistically, on minimizing losses. In so doing, we must be careful not to eliminate potential gains as well.

Several methods for minimizing losses will be discussed—restricting immigration, making study abroad more relevant to home country needs, and reducing the differentials between areas of origin and destination that act as incentives to migrate.[2] Policies are discussed in relation to foreign study in the United States.

UNCOMPENSATED LOSSES AND COMPENSATING PAYMENTS

I might argue that there are few, if any, cases in which the welfare of those who remain behind is actually eroded as a result of emigration. Forceful arguments supporting this position have been made though they have been met by equally forceful counter-arguments. Although I think the position is frequently overstated, I prefer to carry on the discussion, at least, from the standpoint of those who feel that some losses do occur as a result of migration.

But having accepted the notion that losses (yet to be defined) occur, we might contend that such losses as there are, are in fact compensated through existing channels by counterflows of human and physical capital such as the sending of remittances, the return of individuals trained abroad to the country of origin, the transfer of skills and knowledge and the supplying of highly trained manpower through overseas investments, programs of technical assistance, systems of international loans, and other such programs.

Compensation occupies a critical position in the arguments of those who, in taking a cosmopolitan view of the world, argue for free migration. If a mechanism for compensating losses exists, and migration is, on balance, beneficial, there is no rationale for restricting migration—to hinder the flow would, in fact, be detrimental. Under such conditions, a country might profitably become an exporter of human capital. On the other hand, if compensation does *not* occur and if the welfare of those who remain is eroded, the resulting losses and the magnified imbalances among nations point to a need for corrective policy.

Compensation to losing nations through existing counterflows of talent, knowledge, and funds has not been properly discussed in the literature on brain drains. There is much to be said for the position that counterflows presently provide adequate compensation, but empirical evidence is lacking.[3] And, although there may be offsetting compensation in some cases, it may be lacking in others. For the sake of discussion, then, let us assume, as most nationalists do, that there are uncompensated losses through migration and let us examine one suggestion—that compensating payments be made from nations which gain to nations which lose talent. We are now speaking of compensatory payments linked to estimated gains and losses of human capital. The presumption is that such payments would offset negative effects of the brain drain without doing away with potential benefits. But are such payments appropriate and feasible?

The difficulties involved in attaching a fair and/or appropriate human capital value to a migrating student have been discussed in chapters 5 and 6. However, a hypothetical case may bring the difficulties closer to the surface as we consider policies. Suppose a Taiwanese student graduates from a Taiwanese university. He has difficulty getting a job; the supply of highly-educated individuals in Taiwan exceeds the apparent demand. He decides to migrate to the United States for advanced study and convinces his parents to support him, at least for the first year or two, with the understanding that he will return home when he has finished his degree. He obtains a Ph.D after *six* years, during which he was partially sponsored by a university fellowship and worked as a research assistant. Upon receiving his Ph.D., he discovers that jobs for which he is now qualified are still scarce at home and that he has a good job offer in the United States, so he decides to remain somewhat longer, gaining experience and accumulating some savings before returning home. In order to remain without running into visa problems, he requests a visa adjustment from student to permanent resident shortly after receiving his Ph.D. Following normal procedure, the Immigration Service places his name on a waiting list and he is allowed to remain in the United States until his number comes up (even though the legal grace period of eighteen months normally allowed for practical training elapses in the meantime.) In approximately two years, his request for a visa change is granted.

Viewing this case in isolation and assuming, for the moment, that non-return is permanent, does the United States owe Taiwan money at the time the visa adjustment is made? If so, how much? Do we estimate the human capital value of the student at the time of his arrival or at present? From whose perspective is the estimation to be made—that of the United States or of Taiwan. The question is important because there may be large differences between the U.S. gain and the Taiwanese loss. Assuming the estimate is of the loss to Taiwan, do we estimate loss by using the cost of the student's education in Taiwan before he left for United States study? Do we add in a "maintenance" cost? Or, do we look at what the student might have contributed (as indicated by expected earnings discounted to the present) if he had never come to the United States for study? Or, still considering the loss to Taiwan, do we look at what he might have earned in Taiwan if he had returned home *following* United States study, netting out the costs of his education that were borne by the United States? If the last procedure is followed, what monetary conversion rate do we use?

Would we try to incorporate in our estimates a measure of lost externalities (benefits that would have accrued, for instance, through exercising leadership) the non-returnee might have produced had he returned home? It is sometimes argued that the most important real losses occurring as a result of emigration are associated with externalities. Yet how can we know what these might have been for a particular individual? And if the externalities are attached to an individual (rather than to his occupation), how can we expect a mere transfer of funds to provide compensation? Closely related to the above is the question of quality. How would we adjust our estimate as to the quality of a particular student and of his education?

Now, let us think of the student in our example as compared with others. How would the value of the student in question be balanced against that of a similar student who, instead of remaining in the United States, decided to return to Taiwan at the end of his six years? Should Taiwan reimburse the United States for training provided? Would the base for estimating the increment in human capital value associated with education in the United

States then switch to that of the U.S. dollar cost of his education or to what he might have earned if he had migrated to enter the labor market in the United States rather than to pursue his studies? How would the compensation be calculated if our student remained to work for four years following his degree and then returned home with experience and savings? Should Taiwan then reimburse the United States for training, experience, and savings remitted as set against what would have been earned in the interim in Taiwan?

If we could overcome these conceptual and practical difficulties involved in calculating values (and they probably could be overcome through a series of more or less arbitrary, but agreed upon, decisions), questions would remain. Not the least of these would be the problem of relating human capital flows to other capital flows. Should the monetary values given to human and physical capital be added and subtracted directly? Should we also try to value information flows that are augmented through migration? What weight should a dollar of remittances have in the total reckoning? Here is an area for inventive research and theorizing. In short, we need a firmer basis for accepting or rejecting the present impressionistic statements about the extent to which various counterflows do or do not offset human capital migration losses. Until there is a common denominator, it will be difficult to assess adequately the overall gains and losses through migration. Accordingly, compensation designed to alleviate losses of human capital may actually prove to be an unanticipated subsidy when considering the larger picture. If so, compensation would not be ruled out, but the argument upon which compensatory payments has been built would shift drastically.

But there is another difficulty. On an international plane, suppose Nation A is a developed nation where education is relatively expensive and where anticipated earnings, assuming employment, would be relatively high; Nation B is a less developed nation where neither the cost of education nor the expected earnings are high. How could we justify paying different rates of compensation to A and B when these rates would be determined by their present advantaged or disadvantaged position in world markets? In so doing, we would seem to be accepting the current distribution of wealth and economic status among nations as just.[4] And yet compensatory schemes are suggested with the hope of decreasing gaps between rich and poor nations. Even though elaborate procedures might be built in for constant reevaluations, the assessments would seem to work to the disadvantage of those nations in the worst economic straits.

Finally, consider the possibility that intergovernmental compensatory schemes could reinforce existing labor market imperfections or societal rigidities that are at the heart of much of the migration of talent. Governments could continue their questionable practices leading to export of their discontented, their surplus doctors, their educated lower class, or whatever, thus strengthening their own status quo position while receiving compensation. Under such circumstances, there would be little incentive for the Philippine government, for instance, to reorient its educational system away from the present overproduction of inadequately trained doctors.

In sum, I feel we should postpone (probably discard) formal compensation schemes. Furthermore, we should be open to the possibility that compensating losing countries for their emigrating talent is at least as apt to distort as to improve balances of talent traded among nations.

Having accepted the notion that uncompensated losses exist and having rejected *formal* compensatory schemes, let us look at several policies that have been suggested for correcting losses associated with migration through study in the United States, policies directed at eliminating the losses before they occur. The first set of suggestions involves placing legal restrictions on student migration.

IMMIGRATION RESTRICTIONS AND
RELATED PRACTICES

1. Requiring students to leave the country.

United States proposals to regulate student migratory flows by statute usually involve changes in visa requirements. The proposals have not always been thoroughly thought through. Policy suggestions have often been linked to the recurrent findings that: non-return is much more frequent among student (F) visa-holders than among exchangee (J) visa-holders; and, the rate of non-return among J-visa holders is extremely low. These findings have been paraded periodically and have prompted suggestions that a solution to the problem of foreign student non-return lies in extending the J-visa requirements and requiring all (or select groups of) [5] foreign students to leave the U.S. after completing study (plus eighteen months' leeway for practical training) and prohibiting their remigration to the U.S. for two years after their departure.

Because the nature of the J-visa has been changed somewhat by the recent (April, 1970) legislation,[6] the proposal has less force now than it did before 1970. Even prior to the amendment, however, the proposal was built on tenuous assumptions. Advocates of a blanket J-visa for students as well as exchangees looked at the written regulations and at the correlation between non-return and visa held and incorrectly concluded that holding a J-visa was causally linked to return. They missed the fact that although almost all J-visa holders have returned home following their sojourn in the United States, many or most J-visa returnees have also been older, sponsored students, with jobs waiting for them at home. Controlling for these characteristics, we find relatively little difference between non-return among J- and F-visa holders. (See chapter 7.)

It is not at all clear, then, that extending coverage of the J-visa, as advocated prior to legislative changes in 1970, would have had more than a marginal impact on non-return. Extending the visa to more students would have significantly changed the profile of the J-visa holders and incorporated many more individuals with a high propensity to emigrate—younger, self-sponsored students without assurance of a job at home. Taking into account the legal labyrinth within which visa regulations are embedded, adding U.S. reluctance of strictly enforcing a policy of making people leave the country against their will, considering potential gains the U.S. would stand to make by aiding talented individuals seeking to remain, realizing the pressure that would build for waivers (legal exceptions), and noting the skill with which foreign students (aided by future employers) have been able to maneuver in the past, it is reasonable to assume that students with a strong desire to remain in the United States would have been (and will be) able to do so, J-visa notwithstanding. And the hidden or unrecorded brain drain would certainly have increased (as people waited for decisions, prolonged their period of study, or just shifted about, one step ahead of immigration authorities). This is probably true for the new regulations as well.

To be effective, a broader policy requiring students to leave following their study unless granted a waiver would necessitate governmental pressure on U.S. employers, forcing them to change their hiring practices and to withdraw their insistent support for waiver requests. In the past, even with the limited use of J-visas, pressures for waivers and for special congressional bills to admit a foreigner have been heavy. The tight job market today is relieving the pressure in some fields, but in medicine for instance, the pressure continues. With the increased demands for waivers that would accompany extending the J-visa would come increased costs of adjudication and enforcement.

It is possible that requiring more students to leave would hasten the return home of some students intending to return anyway, but as I will indicate below, an earlier departure from the United States is not necessarily in the best interests of the home country.

With the 1970 changes, departure is required only of J-visa holders who are (1) U.S.- or home-government financed or who are (2) from selected countries and in selected skill categories deemed critical for development.[7] (The latter will be discussed below see p. 334.) Grounds for obtaining a waiver allowing adjustment to immigrant status have been retained and broadened slightly for those who cannot adjust immediately because they fall under (1) or (2) above.[8]

I do not wish to get bogged down in a technical discussion of the new (or old) immigration legislation. However, I do think it is within our purview to speculate about the probable results of a policy which seems to loosen immigration restrictions. Will foreign student non-return increase? I think so. We will probably see an initial jump in the rate of adjustments by J-visa holders, followed by a leveling out of adjustments and waivers at a rate somewhat (perhaps even substantially) above pre-1970 rates. Among undergraduate and graduate university students I doubt that the change will be great. It will probably show up, however, among medical residents and interns or assistant professors and research associates who have also used the J-visa to enter the U.S. Whether such individuals are "students" is a matter of definition. If they are not included as students, I expect to see a relatively small rise in the non-return rate among foreign students following the 1970 legislation.

Related to the probable rise in adjustments from foreign student to immigrant status will be a continuing shift upward in the percentage of high-level migrants who enter the United States initially as students or exchangees.[9] Why? Because a person applying *from abroad* for an immigrant visa (who would be classified as a trained immigrant) must now wait two or three years to come to the United States, whereas he can migrate almost immediately if he applies for a student or exchange visa (which places him in the untrained category), then applies for an adjustment *from within the United States*. While his name is rising to the top of waiting list, he can remain in the United

States.[10] In brief, I am suggesting that more people will use the exchangee visa (and the student visa) as a means of immigration, even though it means stretching the truth.

But caution must be exercised in interpreting increased student non-return and higher percentages of non-returnees among all high-level immigrants if indeed there are to be increases. Specifically, we must recognize that the increases will not necessarily indicate an increased propensity for non-return among those who come to the United States *for study*. It will not mean that the United States will have suddenly become more attractive to students as a place of permanent residence (in fact the movement seems to be in the other direction at the moment).[11] It will not mean that U.S. programs of study will have been more successful in "seducing" students into remaining. It will not mean that increasing percentages of students *in fact* have changed their minds even though more may have perjured themselves. Nor does it mean that U.S. study is necessarily a worse investment for developing nations than it was in the past, nor that all students who adjust their visa will remain permanently. (If students adjust and remain temporarily, the result might even be a net gain to countries of origin, assuming experience and/or capital has been acquired in the meantime that can be used at home.)

One reaction to a higher rate of visa adjustment among "students" could be a move to reduce funds available for foreign student programs under the misguided assumption that by sponsoring study abroad we are adding significantly to non-return. Such an interpretation would only occur if policy makers fail to distinguish between sponsored and unsponsored students and naively assume that the increasing non-return percentages apply equally to each group. Non-return will probably remain low among sponsored students, suggesting that non-return might be more effectively moderated by increasing, not reducing, available funds; that is, by sponsoring more students who could then be selected carefully for specific jobs at home and with the explicit understanding that they would return. As it is, the United States provides a substantial subsidy to other nations at a minor cost through programs of study abroad. Similarly, in those cases where home governments sponsor study abroad, evidence suggests a relatively high return on the investment.

2. Limiting the period of temporary residence following study.

For many professions, a brief period of apprenticeship is necessary before the fruits of a more formal education can be realized. It is difficult, therefore, to know where study ends and work begins in many cases.

In the past, foreign students have been given a period of up to eighteen months following their study during which they can participate in practical training before returning home. The provision is retained under the 1970 law. The eighteen months is, in itself, a period of non-return but has been justified (and I think correctly), in terms of the addition to knowledge and consequent increase in value that can result from practical experience. This will be so even though salary scales in the home country may not take account of the additional experience gained.

There is another positive reason why some students should be given an opportunity to remain temporarily—they wish to accumulate savings that can be remitted to pay off debts accumulated during their education, to provide a nest egg while they seek employment at home, or to build capital with which a business can be started at home. To the extent that such desires are frustrated, the home country may lose by insisting on early departure, even a departure of eighteen months versus three years, for instance.

But the eighteen months, while building professional competence and allowing savings to accumulate, may also induce some non-return that would not otherwise occur by involving foreign students in specific work and by prolonging their time away from families. We do not know how important the period of employment is in actually inducing non-return. We do know that the eighteen months is also viewed as a grace period during which many students who have already made up their minds to remain permanently have a chance to impress an employer with their ability, in hopes that he will support them in their efforts to adjust their visa. It is also used to delay a request for adjustment —until age 26 and the danger of being drafted is behind. A proper balance sheet of the costs and benefits associated with practical training following study has not been drawn. The eighteen-month period following study has not been carefully studied in spite of its important place in the evaluation of migration through study abroad.

Assuming for the moment that a significant amount of non-return is caused by, or made possible by, the existing eighteen-month leeway given students, let us ask what the effect of eliminating the period might be. First, some students would return home without the benefits of the apprenticeship period and without accumulated savings. Second, some potential non-returnees would return home and become involved immediately in work at home that would keep them there, thus making a productive contribution. However, other returnees would not be able to find employment and would spend a good portion of their two years in a discontented search for jobs and in preparing to return to the United States. Third, some students would leave the United States but would not return home, choosing to gain experience and accumulate savings elsewhere. Fourth, some students would simply prolong the period of study until they had accomplished what they would previously have done in the eighteen months. Because their task might be more difficult, however, the net result could be to postpone departure for home beyond that which would have occurred under the 18-month restriction. Furthermore, the search for permanent employment could still occur. It is well-known that students are able to postpone finishing their degree requirements for long periods of time while they work as teaching assistants, instructors, or engineers.

Unless enforcement were extremely rigid, a student who desired to remain would have little difficulty in finding a loophole and eventually adjusting his visa.

Fortunately, there has been relatively little movement toward eliminating the practical training period whether for the above reasons, or simply because it is easier to leave "Pandora's Box" closed. There has been some pressure to extend the period for two years.

One writer, Niland, has suggested that, instead of unrealistically requiring students to indicate, as they must do with F- and J-visas, that they well remain only for their period of study and the limited extension for practical training, we allow application for study and work. Then, he suggests, each student should be held as strictly as possible to a self-imposed deadline for departure—not necessarily eighteen months.[12] His suggestion is based on a careful analysis of what students intend to do during their temporary stay in the United States. Those who intend to stay temporarily, but for a period longer than eighteen months, seem to be primarily interested in accumulating savings which would be remitted. Thus the prolonged stay turns to the advantage of the home country.[13] To take advantage of the delayed return while improving the chances of return, Niland suggests a more rigid set of conditions surrounding conversion to immigrant visa, procedures that would encourage repatriating savings on a regular basis. He also suggests that, after a certain period, taxes be levied by the home country against the U.S. earnings of their nationals (adjusted for remittances). Such policies might be difficult to codify and operationalize but merit serious consideration. Facilitating the repatriation of savings is particularly attractive, for not only is money flowing home, but also a stronger pull home is exerted, at least in theory.

3. *Restricting remigration to the United States.*

Another visa regulation designed to promote home country return has been the requirement that exchangees not only had to leave following study, but had to remain abroad for at least two years before becoming eligible for remigration. Because the regulation did not specify return to the home country for the two-year period, some J-visa holders opted for two years in a third country, usually Canada, and then remigrated to the United States. Although the number of such individuals has apparently been relatively small (statistics have been gathered for only one year), a provision was included in the 1970 amendment that cuts out the third-country option. Now a J-visa holder must reside "in the country of his nationality or last residence for an aggregate of at least two years following departure from the United States." [14] Such a modification may make sense as token evidence (to countries worried about their brain drains) that the U.S. is sincerely interested in getting people *home*, but I doubt it, particularly when juxtaposed as it is in Public Law 91-225 with the liberalizing modifications that open the doors wider. Furthermore, the modification will probably have little or no impact on the magnitude of the brain drain or on the numbers who return home. It may result in some individuals staying in Canada who originally went there with an intention to remigrate to the U.S. after two years. It may result in increased pressure for waivers from those who previously would have gone to Canada or another "third country" before returning to the United States.

4. Restrictions imposed abroad.

Thus far, the discussion of migration restrictions has been limited to the country of destination, the United States. There are, of course, a plethora of emigration restrictions that can be, and have been, imposed by sending nations. In combination, practices such as bonding (i.e., requiring a financial guarantee to be forefeited if non-return occurs) and foreign exchange control probably would have only a marginal influence on flows for study abroad and on return. Students who are going to return anyway submit to the controls. Many self-sponsored students who think they may remain abroad find ways for getting around the regulations. Passport control (there are many variations linked to time abroad, grades, particular fields, sponsorship conditions, etc.) can prove more difficult to circumvent. Nevertheless, if an individual feels strongly that emigration is his best course, it is doubtful that passport control will stop him from migrating. In some cases, the net result of such controls is to block return at a later date of temporary emigrants by making them, in effect, law-breakers who cannot return without paying a penalty. Furthermore, the restrictions probably work selectively—those with connections can more easily circumvent the law.

In my discussion, I have stressed how I think restrictive measures would or would not work rather than stressing how they are supposed to work. The realities of the situation can easily be overlooked. I have tried to alert the reader to look behind "correlates" and behind confusing statistical shifts to processes. I have tried to point out that costs of legislating mass return or even early return may outweigh the presumed but elusive benefits.

MAKING FOREIGN STUDY MORE RELEVANT

Relating Selection, Admission, and Return to Country Needs

It has been suggested that a general basis for selecting students to study in the United States (and for awarding visas) might be a commitment to study in a needed field; students whose specialties would help alleviate national shortages would be favored. Such suggestions often confuse "need," a political concept indicating a desire, with "need" meaning demand as determined by economic interplay of supply and demand factors. In developing nations, the supply of educated manpower often outdistances the demand, an imbalance that is likely to get worse before it gets better. The imbalance is heightened by professionals' preferences for city life and by social rigidities.

There is a fuzziness about the concept of manpower needs that undercuts its usefulness as a basis for policy. As has been shown repeatedly, manpower projections, whether geared to politically chosen goals or whether based on attempts to anticipate future demand, have not provided successful guidelines for educational planning at home. It is not likely that projections of vague manpower needs will be any more helpful as a general basis for issuing visas and judging whether students will or will not return home. If the main point is to reduce non-return, attention should be given to specific jobs, not general needs.

Even if national needs, determined by manpower projections, could be made to correspond with real economic demands, students who wished to go abroad and remain abroad could easily persuade universities to admit them by declaring their intent to study in a needed field. They could transfer to another field on arrival. And students in needed fields, although originally sincere about returning home, would still be subject to the comparative pull of U.S. markets where a demand as well as a need may exist.

The 1970 immigration legislation linking required return among J-visa holders to country-skill listing (see footnote 7) will be subject to the difficulties mentioned above. However, because the provision applies only to J-visa holders, many of whom are sponsored students with specific jobs at home, it will bring about little change in the number who return. In addition, researchers and other non-students who previously came with a J-visa can now migrate with an H-visa if they think they will stay and if the country-skill listing pertains. F-visa holders, from whom the bulk of the adjustments come, are not affected.

Making Courses and Research Work More Relevant

The United States university community has been faulted for failing to provide relevant courses of study and/or research projects for foreign students, both because the skills acquired are not useful upon return home and because "irrelevant" course work heightens the propensity to remain abroad permanently. To deal with the problem, a variety of solutions have been proposed, some of which have already been tried.

Let us turn first to the contention that foreign students do not receive proper guidance in setting up their course of study. There is little doubt that this is true for many foreign students, but the same could be said for United States students. I doubt that a restructuring of foreign student guidance would make course choices more relevant. First, we make an assumption that we know what is relevant. We not only tend to assume that certain areas of study are more relevant than others, but also that specific knowledge gained in specific courses is more important than attitudes adopted or methods acquired. Courses with the most appropriate subject content may or may not produce relevant attitudes and teach relevant methods. Second, there is some question in my mind as to whether any United States person can determine what is most relevant for a particular foreign student, let alone give proper advice to many foreign students from many countries with interests in many fields. Students, including United States students, can easily be misled as well as aided by well-meaning instructors, administrators, or guidance personnel. The student grapevine is a good substitute when choosing courses. In addition, many foreign students who are taking irrelevant courses are doing so by choice, sometimes because they wish to obtain a theoretical grounding that will be useful later, sometimes because they anticipate remaining in the United States. Finally we should leave open the possibility that causality runs from non-return to course choice rather than vice versa.

But let us assume that a large portion of foreign students is not involved in study related to home-country employment and that non-return therefore increases. What alternatives are recommended? One means suggested for circumventing the above difficulties is to provide special schools and institutes for foreign students, keyed either to subject matter or to geographical origin, or to both. In a special school or institute, one can presumably do away with "unnecessary" university requirements that the United States university feels it must impose, such as English literature or United States history. Furthermore, courses can be designed with a particular country or group of countries in mind, something that is extremely difficult to do on a broad scale in any one university because U.S. universities not only *are* oriented, but *must be* oriented toward training U.S. students. I have no quarrel with establishing special schools. However, there are severe limits on the extent to which such programs can be established outside the universities. First, there is the matter of cost. When one thinks of the wide variety of fields and countries we are discussing, the costs appear over-whelming. Second, there is a matter of staffing the institutes. This might be done by borrowing area and subject specialists for short periods of a year or two, but even then talent, if required on a large scale would be scarce. Third, we again make an assumption about what is most relevant. Fourth, the institutes would in all probability draw to them only that part of the foreign student population that is going home. There would be little impact on non-return, for few self-sponsored students would be touched. Finally, in many cases students would have had at least as relevant an education in an alternative existing institution.

Closely related to the complaint about irrelevant courses is the one that foreign students are channeled into research projects totally unrelated, at least in substance, to what they will eventually do at home. There is little doubt that such channeling does occur for many foreign students, particularly for those from developing countries, because the machinery and methodology used here will not be available at home; because the money that underpins much of the research is tied to the exploration of specific United States problems; and because faculty members guide students, consciously or unconsciously, into areas that correspond most closely to their (the faculty's) interests.

To channel students into more relevant fields of research (or more accurately, to prevent their involvement in irrelevant research) it has been suggested that they should not be permitted to work on research projects created by, or dependent upon, government funding. Behind the suggestion is the assumption that government projects frequently involve either applied research applicable only to the United States, or pure research. To assume that U.S. government research will not be relevant to the problems of developing nations is to assume that there is no transfer value in the tasks undertaken and is certainly an exaggeration. But for the sake of argument let us accept the idea that significant numbers of foreign students are diverted from more relevant studies by the availability of government research funds and that some are even induced to remain in the United States. The question remains: Would prohibiting involvement in projects using United States government monies (or even requiring students to pledge to return home) remedy the situation?

First, we should be aware that a blanket law would also cut out participation in relevant research projects funded by the United States government. Second, the problem presumably arises because universities are employing students in accordance with university interest rather than in accordance with home country interest. If this is true and if the student sees his best interest as closer to the university than to the home country, it can be predicted that changing requirements will effect little change in actual practice. There are a variety of ways avoiding outright dishonesty that can be used to involve a talented foreign student in a project.

A third consideration must be to look at the alternatives open to foreign students. If they are not allowed to work on U.S. government projects, there is no guarantee that the alternative will be better. Most of the foreign students who take research assistantships are self-sponsored students who must work to put themselves through school. They will seek other work which may lead to similar sidetracks or may so prolong study that it would tend to increase the rate of non-return.

In a more positive vein, suggestions have been made that universities devise means whereby foreign students can carry out research, particularly at the Ph.D. level, in their home country.

Involvement would thus be in the home country and presumably the risk of non-return would be lowered. In theory, the approach has much to recommend it; in practice, the following problems are encountered. First, even though the topic may be relevant the facilities for doing the research in the home country may be sub-standard. One could argue that if facilities are sub-standard, then the student should choose another research topic because the one he has chosen is not going to permit development of advanced scientific techniques. On the other hand, it may be more relevant to what he will be able to do on return than high-powered research with standard equiment. Second, the student sometimes lacks needed supervision. Third, even though adequate facilities and guidance are available, there is an inevitable tendency for individuals to become side-tracked often in routine administrative duties. The interfering activities may even be constructive activities, but presumably so is the research. If not, it should not have been undertaken in the first place. The problem is one of balancing the present and the future. If we tie research to facilities at hand or to problems of the moment or if we argue that constructive side-tracks should take precedence over less pressing research projects, we are speaking to the present but neglecting the future.

Related to the general question of relevance is the question of overtraining, particularly as seen in the desire by many foreign students to continue on to their Ph.D. It is at the Ph.D. level that many of the complaints of irrelevance arise. It is also at the Ph.D. level that the student becomes eligible for many positions not previously open to him in the United States labor market. I would argue that it is the latter—an enlarged market—that leads to greater non-return among Ph.D.'s and not their involvement in projects that are irrelevant to their home country needs. If this is true, making courses more relevant would not be particularly effective in reducing non-return, whereas holding students to the M.A. level would be. (As the better U.S. universities move toward the elimination of terminal M.A. degrees, the foreign student who wishes to obtain a degree from a well-known institution may be pressured to continue when he probably should have stopped.)

Before moving to the next group of proposals for moderating non-return, let me recapitulate briefly. I have assumed that there are significant national losses occuring through the migration of talent and that these losses are not adequately compensated through the existing counterflows of human and physical capital. The existence of uncompensated losses requires improvement in systems of compensation or some other corrective action. I do not think that formal compensation schemes are either feasible or prudent. For a variety of reasons I have argued that neither the impact of restrictive legislation nor the linking of study abroad to relevant manpower needs promises constructive or effective moderation of migratory flows. What then is left? I come to those policy suggestions that I think are generally most viable: those positive policies designed to induce (not force) students who study abroad to choose employment at home rather than employment abroad following their study.

REDUCING DIFFERENTIAL INCENTIVES TO MIGRATE

My discussion will be divided into two parts, the first dealing with salary differences between potential employment at origin (home) and destination (abroad), and the second dealing with differences in available opportunities at home and abroad, including differences in information about what is available.

As shown in previous chapters, there are many kinds of job satisfaction that individuals seek to maximize when seeking employment. For some, money is of major importance; it not only provides material goods but can also lead to greater social recognition and power. For others, the chance to put professional skills to work in some creative endeavor is more important than money. And there are other sources of satisfaction. Here, I will be concerned primarily with monetary rewards and the manipulation of monetary incentives as a means of inducing return. Others will be picked up below when discussing methods of improving job opportunities.

Monetary Incentives

Two sorts of questions must be asked: Which students will respond to the incentives? and Does the cost of a particular policy outweigh the anticipated benefits that flow from it? In answering these questions, I think human capital estimates can be of some use. (See chapter 6.) Rather than calculating human capital estimates for propagandistic purposes or for inclusion in intergovernmental compensatory schemes, they are most appropriately incorporated into decision models, both private and social. At the private or individual level, such models speak to the first of the above questions by allowing insights into the decision process, particular into the salience of manipulating monetary incentives. At the social level, human capital models can serve as a technique for making project evaluations as human capital values are estimated for different learning situations and locations, then compared to determine the best alternative(s) among many. The models may be applied, for instance, to evaluating the alternate strategies of importing temporary talent from overseas versus sending students abroad. Or they may be applied to assess whether or not repatriation efforts (carrying a cost) are economically sound.

My own application of the models to migration decisions of Peruvian students (see chapter 8) led to the guarded conclusion that non-returning students did not act to *maximize* their earnings. How to interpret the finding is not entirely clear, but it seems that as long a student is able to anticipate (with high probability) employment in his home country in a job that is reasonably interesting and that allows him a reasonable return on his educational investment, he will have a high propensity to return home. Family ties, commitment to development, cultural security, etc., provide enough pulling power that home country salaries can be set considerably below United States salaries yet serve to attract foreign students back home.

At least part of the reason for high return among sponsored students may be attributed to the fact that their out-of-pocket costs are slight and easily recouped at home even though salaries are lower than in the United States. If sponsored students wished to maximize their position, they would probably not return home. Instead they would accept the sponsorship, minimizing costs, and then migrate, maximizing benefits. To discourage such behavior, sponsors are certainly within their rights to require students to return home after completing their studies. But applying the same leverage to self-sponsored students is questionable; it is only with greater difficulty that self-sponsored students are able to recoup their education expenses if they return home. Those students without connections have the most difficult time recouping their investment if they return.

Use of Loan Funds

If the above suppositions are correct and if they bear a relationship to non-return, a case might be made for more extensive use of loan funds tied to graduated "forgiveness." A system similar to that of the United States National Defense Education Act loans might be established whereby partial or total forgiveness would be allowed over possibly four or five years. If it is felt that return in the first two years is crucial, forgiveness might be set at a higher rate for the initial years and taper off in later years. If it is felt that getting students home is easy but retaining them after they have had one or two years to become disillusioned is difficult, the forgiveness provisions might be balanced toward greater forgiveness in the later years. Under the loan system, a student would be obligated to repay the entire loan if he migrated immediately following study and part of the loan if he returned home but remigrated before the period of forgiveness was completed.

Collecting money from emigrant students would pose a practical problem and would require intergovernmental cooperation. It would require establishing a responsible agency in the home country for processing and keeping track of overseas students with loans—several such agencies are operating successfully and might serve as models. Repayment of loans would not cover the entire human capital loss through emigration, but provides a means for recovering some of that loss as well as providing an incentive for students to return home. It is conceivable that the scheme could promote rather than reduce non-return by allowing individuals to go abroad who would not have been able to go abroad on their own. And it is possible that the costs of a loan and forgiveness scheme might outweigh the benefits. Finally, what will be effective for one nation will not work for another. Nevertheless, I think the idea merits a trial run. I will elaborate below in my discussion of an Office of Foreign Study.

Loans tied to forgiveness might also be made available by American universities in cooperation with home-country agencies or independently. Loans would turn, in effect, into scholarships (or partial scholarships) if individuals returned and remained at home. This option differs from the above because it would not involve any flow of funds back to the country of origin, nor any initial expense in the country of origin. It should provide an incentive to return home. A pilot project has been established to test this idea at the University of Minnesota using tuition scholarships.

Non-return and Job Opportunities

Probably the most persistent theme emerging from studies of non-return concerns the relationship between non-return and job opportunity. (See chapters 2 and 7.) High salaries at home in a particular field are of little value if the probability of obtaining employment in that field is slight. Similarly, a high probability of employment in the United States may tip student decisions toward remaining here. Policies aimed at narrowing opportunity gaps may be grouped into: those directed at reducing opportunities in the United States that are open to foreign students; those designed to see that foreign students are aware of employment opportunities at home and, conversely, that employers at home are aware of the availability of foreign-trained students; and those designed to increase the opportunities at home.

Reducing Opportunities in the U.S.

Suggestions to reduce opportunities open to foreign students in the United States take two main forms, legal restrictions on employment of non-U.S. citizens or additional production of U.S. manpower to fill available positions. Interestingly, legal restrictions probably push some foreign students who would not otherwise do so to seek immigration visas. Furthermore, as pointed out above, there are numerous ways of getting around restrictions which would have to be strictly enforced. Although I see a clear relationship between the shortage of U.S. talent and non-return in certain fields, particularly medicine, I think protracted discussion of how the United States should solve its shortages would lead us afield. It is ironic that concern for the losses *other* countries are supposedly suffering should spark us to increase our own opportunities, but there seems to be at least one field, medicine, in which the dependence on foreign talent has been great enough so that discussions of non-return and the larger brain drain lament have had some effect. Indeed, the United States does have a responsibility to "our own" and to foreign governments to alleviate shortages in ways other than importing talent; employment opportunity in the United States is one area over which other nations can exercise little control.

Recruiting Practices and Selection Procedures

Turning now to informing students about available jobs and employers in the home country about available students, the assumption must first be made that there are opportunities; that employers are not only looking for individuals with good training abroad but that students are looking for openings at home. Both non-return research and recruiting efforts of foreign governments point to the importance of providing employment assurance, not just communication channels.

The experience of Canadian, British, Argentine, Ugandan and other recruiting teams suggests that recruiters must have the authority to actually negotiate contracts on the scene. Vague promises of employment are seldom adequate inducement to return. The Indian Manpower Pool, hailed as an inventive scheme for getting individuals home even though employment was uncertain, appears to be only moderately successful because those who have joined often remain in the Pool for extended periods; the desired jobs are not available and the word has been passed to Indian students abroad that what was good in principle is not good in practice.

Recruiting costs money. We do not know whether the recruiting efforts turn up primarily those individuals who would have gone home in any event or whether they induce potential non-returnees to return. More careful attention needs to be given to the costing of recruitment policies before unqualified endorsement can be given. It may very well be that the money spent on recruiting might more profitably be invested in strengthening home institutions, thus providing jobs to which individuals would return of their own volition. Where there is a buyer's market there is little incentive for the firm to recruit actively.

An alternative to recruiting students after or during their period of study abroad is to recruit them before they leave. As an approximation, the subsequent employment expectations of students could be incorporated into procedures for selecting students to study abroad. To the extent that individuals chosen for foreign study do have jobs assured when they leave, the problem of non-return should be considerably reduced because, as indicated above, job assurance not only overrides visa and sponsorship as an important factor in return but seems to operate even though the assured job carries a salary lower than what might reasonably be expected in the United States.

The importance of selecting, for study abroad, individuals who have commitments to specific jobs in specific home institutions has been recognized by most sponsors. International organizations, home and host governments, and foundations usually select with specific positions in mind. But American universities, when judging the many applications from self-sponsored foreign students, do not apply the same principle in their selection procedures. If a procedure could be established for incorporating anticipated employment following study into admission, non-return among foreign students could in my opinion be reduced significantly. There are several possible channels for effecting a method of selection that would incorporate job guarantees into admissions procedures. At present, a cooperative effort is being made by several universities through LASPAU (Latin American Scholarship Program of American Universities) to screen Latin American candidates for financial awards, considering home country employment possibilities as well as individual abilities in making awards.[15] The LASPAU screening could be made more general. Employment assurance could also be incorporated into instructions to overseas alumni or overseas members of professional societies who are commissioned to aid universities in screening potiential candidates. The Institute of International Education has several overseas offices which are available to service U.S. universities in their admissions screening. And finally, as suggested below, agencies monitoring the selection process could be established and run by each country sending a sizable proportion of its educated population abroad for training.

Whether or not employment expectations following study *should* be used in selecting students, particularly self-sponsored ones, is another question. Probably employment assurance should be decisive only in that hypothetical case where two students are equal in other respects, but one has a job assured and is highly likely to return home whereas the second does not have a job promised. One of the dangers of linking admission to job assurance would be that it could strengthen traditional structures of sending nations while depriving marginal students with high ability but low opportunity of using their talents, either through migration or by upgrading themselves in hopes of making good in spite of lack of connections at home. In general, research findings point to a higher rate of non-return among students who are marginal to the society from which they come. "Marginality" is used broadly, incorporating those who differ from the dominant society because of race, ethnic origin, religious beliefs, or social class. Such students may be discriminated against in home employment markets and, lacking connections, be unable to produce an institutional affiliation that would allow them to study abroad. Yet it is just such marginal individuals that theorists have marked as frequent purveyors of change. To deny them the possibility of studying abroad simply on the basis of their failure to secure a position before leaving would be unfortunate. On the other hand, marginal individuals who do have institutional affiliations, that is, individuals who have in a sense already arrived, should probably receive the most favorable attention in selection procedures. Employment assurance, then, should not be a precondition for admission to study abroad, but should probably be incorporated into the decision processes of universities and other organizations faced with the task of choosing from a wide range of foreign students desiring United States study.

Perhaps as important as selecting students with assured jobs is the problem of identifying the expectations of students at the time they leave. Research results do *not* clarify the extent to which non-returning foreign students leave for study abroad with the strong expectation that they may not return home. If the expectation of employment at home is low and the expectation of establishing permanent residence abroad is high on arrival (as I think it is in many cases), it will be extremely difficult, if not impossible, to overcome negative expectations about home country opportunities, particularly from a distance. I therefore think efforts to deal with non-return must be focused less on reducing opportunities open to foreign students abroad or on *ex post facto* attempts to persuade individuals to come home, and more on building positive expectations at the time they leave toward obtaining employment at home. Policies that emphasize the area of origin promise to be most productive in the long run. The problem of non-return begins there.

INCREASING OPPORTUNITIES AT HOME

Student expectations at the time they leave are, of course, a product of their view of the total society in which they live as well as of the particular employment expectations they hold. Therefore, a "quickie" propaganda job before students depart will not have much impact on expectations. In the long run, talent flows will not change in magnitude or direction, and job opportunities and expectations will not increase significantly unless major social, political, and economic changes occur in the sending or donor nations. To discuss such major changes is to enter the ongoing debate about development or modernization or social change and would lead us far afield. Therefore I do not propose to pursue the broader topics at length nor to treat recommendations for increasing opportunities in areas of emigration that are phrased in such general terms as to be virtually meaningless as guides for policy (for example, "eliminate discrimination and bigotry").[16] There is little doubt that emigration and foreign student non-return are indeed closely linked to national and regional imbalances between the number of educated individuals and the number of jobs available, to concentration of jobs in cities, leaving shortages in rural areas when there are at the same time surpluses in cities, to antiquated tax structures, to traditional social structures and value systems, to fundamental corruption leading to squandered funds, and the like. The association, though, is one in which non-return and the brain drain are as much a result as a cause of social and economic stagnation. One must treat the ailment, not the symptom, unless (as many would argue with respect to the brain drain), the ailment is psychosomatic. By now, it should be clear that decreasing emigration will not necessarily spark development; conversely, development can occur while there is an exodus of talent.[17] Among the developing nations, the Taiwanese example is an interesting case in point. While constantly mentioned as one of the major problem nations in discussing of non-return, Taiwan is also cited as a showcase by U.S. technical assistance people. Iran and Korea have also had high growth rates while countenancing high rates of non-return. It is clear that non-return cannot be viewed as a direct offset to technical assistance efforts and that while there may be many reasons why technical assistance programs fail, non-return of foreign students is, almost without exception, a very minor one. x

Emphasizing developing nations, and on a more concrete level, suggestions for improving and increasing home country opportunities are often linked to institution building, i.e., the creation (or strengthening) of a particular organization such as a university, hospital, or research institute. Institution building is expensive and risky.

Not infrequently, efforts to create modern institutions have been swallowed by national systems not yet receptive to the fundamental changes necessary for successful operation of such institutions. Modern structures often hide organizations still functioning in a traditional manner.

We have very little evidence indicating to what extent successful institution building ventures have served as catalytic agents, indirectly creating additional employment opportunities in the larger society or serving as models for upgrading opportunities in existing institutions. Unless institutions have an impact beyond their immediate organization, they will not exert much influence on the magnitude of non-return. They may, nevertheless, significantly influence the *quality* of returning individuals.

From my perusal of the literature on brain drain and non-return, I have concluded that, by and large, the *most* talented individuals in a nation stay at home or return home following study. However, there seems to be a layer of talent remaining abroad after the very top has been skimmed off. It is the A minus or B plus individual, still well above average at home (or in the U.S.) whose loss causes concern. While there are a variety of positions that such individuals could fill at home, the positions are frequently dead-end, routine, and carefully encased in inhibiting social and economic structures.

The major problem of institution building programs has been not to retrieve students sent abroad but to maximize utilization of skills acquired abroad. (Utilization, not non-return, should in fact provide the focus for evaluating such programs.) to this end, most study-abroad plans are related to programs for improving facilities: human capital investments are related to physical capital investments—some more successfully than others. On occasion, students have also been provided with funds enabling them to begin a research project upon return. The "return scholarship" is at once an incentive to come back and an attempt to increase the level of productive utilization of skills. To be successful, however, the subsidy must be attached to pre-existing employment opportunities. The same procedure is therefore not an appropriate means for inducing students without job opportunities to return home.

If our concern is focused on utilization, not non-return, then increasing the *number* of opportunities available at home may be less important than improving *existing* opportunities. My distinction is only a semantic one in the sense that upgrading the quality of existing positions does increase the number of positions, *at a given level.* My previous discussion of monetary incentives suggests that something more than simply upgrading positions by raising salaries is needed. In fact, merely increasing salaries would probably be inefficient. Consideration must also be given to provision of funds and equipment for research, to assuring collegial support, to revamping outmoded structures such as the "chair," or to changing the procedures for validating degrees earned abroad. Funds squandered on unnecessarily high salaries cannot be made available for other reforms.

It is in these matters that *programs* of study abroad have, I think, been effective, and can continue to play a positive role in moderating non-return. Return is extremely high for sponsored students with institutional affiliations. Systematic identification of talented individuals can and does occur as promising persons are selected for study abroad, pursue fields of study with subsequent employment in mind (assured before beginning study), and return home to active participation in an institutional setting.

I have been arguing that tying sponsorship to guaranteed employment in specific institutions as part of an integrated program of institution building provides quality control over return and non-return. There is little that is new in the argument. However, I think there is room for variation on the theme. In particular, I think more individuals with employment experience and institutional affiliations could be encouraged to study abroad *and* return home by use of loans tied to partial forgiveness. If so, funds that would have been used for study abroad could be applied to supporting returnees. Support might mean freeing them from becoming engulfed by the routine tasks that must be performed in any institution, or it might mean subsidizing specific research or publishing projects that would otherwise be put aside.

It is doubtful whether the above suggestions will have much impact on non-return among self-sponsored students. The mere existence of modern institutions does not assure access to them and it is doubtful whether, lacking that assurance, self-sponsored students choosing to study abroad will raise their employment expectations.

More on the Use of Loan Funds

A more likely means of raising expectations and acquiring some control over the migration decisions of self-sponsored students might be the system of loans tied to partial forgiveness that I touched upon earlier. Students wishing to use the loan funds would be required first to show need and secondly to obtain backing of a sponsoring institution willing to give some assurance of employment on return (and willing to back repayment of the loan in case the student decides not to return home).

Requiring students to show evidence of need is not only aimed at avoiding unnecessary subsidies to those students whose parents can afford to pay. It is also included because sons and daughters of wealthy parents are likely to return home even though they study abroad at their own expense. They are apt to be students whose parents have positions waiting for them in the family business on return or who have the necessary connections to assure them jobs. Less wealthy individuals are more apt to remain abroad because they have had to invest relatively large sums without any assurance of employment at home.

Requiring students to seek a sponsor is not only a means of covering repayment of the loans, but is also an attempt to obtain a commitment from both students and home country institutions before students depart. (The "institution" might be the family if the family owns a small business which the student might take over on return.)

The proposal to increase loan funds available to students for overseas study has many potential difficulties. First, the money for the loans would have to be found, and this could be a stumbling block in some cases. The costs of setting up and administering such a program might be prohibitive. And it might be uneconomical in relation to the benefits of the program. It is also possible that recruiting overseas would bring a better pay off than an equivalent investment in loans tied to forgiveness. There would undoubtedly be difficulties in collecting the loans from the returnees as well as from those who remain abroad. Nevertheless, I think the loan program merits serious consideration.

Offices of Foreign Education

To coordinate self-sponsored programs and to administer loan programs, there must be a national agency that deals primarily, if not exclusively, with foreign study. An Office of Foreign Education does not make sense for every country. However, for those countries that train at least 10 per cent of their high-level manpower abroad, such an office would seem logical.

Models for such an agency exist; one of the best is ICETEX in Colombia. By establishing an Office of Foreign Education, the nation would be giving official recognition to the important role international education plays in the formation of human resources and it would be possible to bring that segment of the educational system into the planning process in a systematic manner. Foreign education can be looked upon as an extension of national educational systems and as an official alternative to building new educational institutions at home.

The duties of an Office of Foreign Education could be extremely broad and would probably be limited by available funds. The agency would best be a quasi-governmental or independent one and would not be located in a Ministry, presumably giving it some isolation from at least minor political pressures. It could then receive direct support from the private as well as the public sector. I should think that a variety of overseas corporations would be willing to contribute to the office, and some funding could come from international agencies and foundations.

Among the tasks of the office would be the coordination of programs for study abroad. The office would also be responsible for administering loan funds tied to forgiveness, assessing needs of students, helping them seek institutional affiliations, and collecting loans as they come due. Beyond these basic tasks, it could act as a recruiting agency; serve as a source of information about opportunities for study abroad; aid foreign institutions in their selection of national scholars; provide communication with students while they were studying abroad; and serve as a point of contact on return. I am sure many other functions could be delegated, depending on the needs of the particular country, on the capabilities of the individuals running the office and on the available funding.

As I have described the Office of Foreign Education, it is a home country agency, as distinguished from the United States offices established by the Institute of International Education in several nations, and supposedly carrying out several of the functions described above (only with respect to students desiring to study in the United States).[18] Similarly, United States embassies include a cultural affairs officer (and sometimes an education officer) who is responsible for overseeing programs of study in the United States when the U.S. government participates as a sponsor. Cooperation between the Office of Foreign Education and the various embassies handling their respective programs would be essential.

There is no point in elaborating the structure and functions of such an office in more detail; it would vary considerably from country to country. However, one additional task which the Office of Foreign Education could undertake deserves mention—the task of collecting and publishing statistics on study abroad and non-return. No discussion of non-return or the brain drain would be complete without the almost ritualistic call for improving statistical information. Abiding by custom, I will make one or two specific suggestions.

IMPROVING STATISTICS

In addition to the generally acknowledged need for international and national agencies to standardize definitions and improve data collection procedures, attention should be given to establishing an international matrix of student migration and to incorporating figures on return and non-return among the regularly published data. Data obtained must also be classified in more complete and meaningful ways, allowing researchers to disaggregate information and to relate student migration more directly to general migration, of which it is a part.

As a means of distinguishing high-level migrants from others, consideration should be given to determining the locus and level of previous education—where migrants, students or otherwise, completed secondary school (or their last grade, if secondary education was not completed) and discovering where migrants obtained what highest degree (if educated beyond secondary education). This would allow international patterns of education and work to be abstracted from the data.[19] Thus information would be available for each immigrant on place of birth, place of secondary education, place of highest degree, and place of last residence; this in addition to information about citizenship. The foregoing would also provide an alternative to (or provide a check on) the currently unsatisfactory sorting of migrants into the less talented and more talented in terms of their stated occupation. It would also help pick up U.S.-trained foreigners who were remigrating to the United States after temporary return home. If serious thought is to be given to schemes for compensating nations for their human capital losses associated with migration, educational as well as occupational distributions of migrants must be determined.

I realize I am calling for a degree of sophistication that would severely tax the Immigration and Naturalization Service, given its present technology and organization. In order to allow the more complete information to be collected, processed, and made available in a useful form, agencies responsible for migration statistics will have to think in terms of computerization. In the United States, it is essential that the antiquated, decentralized system now used by the Immigration and Naturalization Service be centralized and computerized. Such a recommendation cannot be made, however, without emphasizing the need for safeguards against unwarranted use of such records; from the standpoint of protecting personal liberties, the present system has much to recommend.

Information is at hand (at UNESCO) that would allow the suggested international matrix showing student migration to be established, but for most nations the data remain at the aggregate level and will probably remain that way for some time to come. And to expect reliable statistics for similar patterns of migration following study (patterns of return and non-return) is not realistic at present, even at the aggregate level. Longitudinal data would be needed that are not easily obtained. The crude aggregate statistics with which we will have to live for some time to come do provide a needed overview, but until international sources have been improved, caveats and qualifications should outweigh contentions and generalizations emerging solely from statistical analyses of official statistics on student migrants and on general migration. This caution must be applied to my own use of UNESCO and IIE data (chapters 2, 3, 4). My search for patterns of study abroad and the use of cross-national comparisons were speculative. The analyses illustrated at once the problems and the potential of the two sources used. Unfortunately, available statistics continue to be used without much thought as to what lies behind them. The demand for better statistics should be accompanied by a demand for more careful handling of available statistics.

A prime example of the indiscriminate use of official figures is the linking of non-return to a count of visa adjustments (from student or trainee visas to immigrant visas) or visa waivers (from exchange visitor visas to permanent resident status). This technique is seldom appropriate. Because United States immigration was conditioned for approximately forty years prior to 1965 by a quota system, and because it now includes a preference system, the ease with which individuals from various nations can enter the United States as immigrants or change their visa status to that of a permanent resident varies widely from nation to nation. On the one hand, the result is an underestimate of the number of immigrants to the United States because individuals arrive and manage to remain for long periods of time—even permanently—without having officially become immigrants. On the other hand there are significant distortions in the amount of brain drain that seems to be associated with study in the United States. Student visas have been used as a means of immigration in the past and will undoubtedly continue to provide a loophole for many individuals who wish to migrate to the United States in the future but who will not be able to do so legally as immigrants.

Given the statistical and definitional problems raised above and in the body of the book, it is even difficult to provide a reasonable estimate of non-return among foreign students in the United States. In chapter 2, I compared a variety of estimates, noting differences in the foreign student populations to which they pertained and differences in the definitions of non-return. Against that background, I presented yet another estimate, using Institute of International Education (IIE) 1964–65 data from their Annual Census of Foreign Students. For all non-U.S. citizens enrolled in institutions of higher education in the United States (including those who held immigrant visas and without regard to level of study, field of study, sponsorship differences, etc.), the rate of *intended* non-return was estimated to be between 15 and 25 per cent (probably closer to the latter figure). This estimate is substantially higher than the 8 to 10 per cent rate frequently quoted, a figure tied either to visa adjustment figures prepared by INS or to analysis of the IIE data, but without giving any attention to students in the IIE survey who were undecided or who did not indicate their intentions to remain or return home.

I cite the higher non-return rate with some misgivings not only because it is tied to a specific definition of non-return (intent), but also because the estimate is subject to being quoted out of context and used as proof that there is a large brain drain associated with foreign student non-return. Such a conclusion does not follow automatically. One first needs to disaggregate the student population in order to see among which groups non-return is occurring. Next, the non-return figures must be placed in a larger context, that of the total migration of talent. Third, rates of non-return are not good indicators of the value of non-return—there is a need to go beyond counting and beyond simple ratios to a system of valuing migrants and their contributions. And finally, it is necessary to consider the timing and motives of the student non-returnees; in particular, attention must be given to whether or not they migrated for study and then decided to stay or whether they migrated at the same time they began study or whether they first migrated and then decided to study but still appear in student statistics as "foreign." When these facets of non-return have been considered, present preoccupation with the problem of non-return, in my opinion, does not seem to be justified. Indeed, it would be unfortunate to allow a summary statistic such as the non-return rate among foreign students in the United States to prod us into general policy decisions regarding all foreign students that we would later regret.

While steps are being taken to improve official statistics, contributions to our knowledge of migration for study and emigration through non-return must continue to come from in-depth studies of carefully chosen student populations. Policy-makers would be well advised to consider the detailed studies as well as the general statistics in formulating their policy. But even with better statistics, the frustrating, fascinating business of describing and analyzing international student migration promises to remain more art than science. Better statistics will take us only a short distance.

A CONCLUDING NOTE

When one goes behind the simple statistics describing the magnitude and correlates of foreign student non-return and when one views non-return in the larger contexts of international migration and of educational investment, it seems to me that one cannot help but be impressed by the positive role of migration for study and by the minor place of emigration through non-return in the total picture. After puzzling through a bewildering array of policy suggestions (many of which I have not touched upon in this concluding chapter), I find that I am impressed by the constructive efforts now being made to assure that study abroad contributes to economic and social development at home and to see that the negative effects of non-return are kept at a moderate level. Without meaning to, I find myself—after several years of working with the topic—in the position of defending, in many respects, the United States programs of sponsored study. While there is room for improvement, I am not ready to indict as irresponsible either the United States as a host nation or the many countries that send students to study here. In official programs the United States government has been relatively attentive to questions of utilization and of return or non-return. When talent losses are real and felt, the losing nations have reacted, not without results. While the United States can more fully support the sending nations in efforts to improve the effects of study abroad, support through additional restrictive immigration measures by the United States is not particularly appropriate or useful. Positive actions initiated in the areas of origin should receive our greatest attention and backing. Investments in people and institutions should be preferred to legal sanctions. In this time of growing isolationist sentiment, it would be unfortunate to succumb to the temptation of cutting back sponsored programs of training and exchange, spurred by the unsupported assumption that such programs are causing a debilitating brain drain.

While I hope the methodological techniques and substantive findings presented here will help us toward a fuller understanding of study abroad in the context of international migration of human resources, I also hope the book has raised many questions. If it has stimulated interest in further research into positive and negative efforts of migration for education or if it has sparked questions about the relationship between migration for education and emigration of the educated, it will have been successful—there is need for work on a broad front. Indeed, the efforts of many persons will be required to produce the blend of practical policy possibilities and theoretical perspective necessary to lead from the present disquiet rooted in relative ignorance to a more positive approach to education and emigration.

NOTES

[1] John B. Lansing and James N. Morgan have made this point in "The Effect of Geographic Mobility on Income," *Journal of Human Resources*, II, No. 4 (Fall, 1967), p. 460.

[2] For policy discussions related to the brain drain and foreign student non-return, see: Adams, chapter 9; George B. Baldwin, "Brain Drain or Overflow?" *Foreign Affairs*, XLVIII, No. 2 (January 1970), pp. 358–72; Herbert G. Grubel, "The Reduction of the Brain Drain: Problems and Policies," *Minerva*, VI, No. 4 (Summer 1968), pp. 541–48; Gregory Henderson, "Brain Drain: An International Overview," New York, UNITAR, 1969 (mimeographed); Niland, chapter VI; C. H. G. Oldham (Rapporteur), *International Migration of Talent From and To the Less Developed Countries*, Report of a Conference at Ditchley Park, 16–19 February 1968 (Ditchley Park, England: The Ditchley Foundation, 1968), pp. 17–26; U.S., *Congressional Record*, 89th Cong. 2nd Sess., 1966, CXII, No. 176 (a speech by Senator Walter Mondale); S. Watanabe, "The Brain Drain from Developing Countries," *International Labor Review*, XCIX, No. 4 (1969), pp. 401–33. By sampling from the above, the reader should be able to cover the range of policy suggestions and viewpoints of writers dealing with brain drain.

[3] One area of compensation that has been cited is that of increased communication from developed to less-developed nations. Migrants presumably feed knowledge back to their area of origin. Although this information flow may occur for some nations and in selected instances, the work of Larry

Litten indicates that a group of scientists in Peruvian universities had almost no professional contact with ex-patriate Peruvians in the United States. Larry H. Litten, "Scientific Communication in Developing Nations: A Study of Media Usage by Professions in Four Peruvian Universities," University of Chicago, Department of Education (Ph.D. dissertation in progress).

[4] I owe this point to Mary Jean Bowman.

[5] In House Report 1215 of March 1968 (p. 11), a recommendation was made that the J-visa be required for all foreign graduate students in the natural sciences and engineering in order to qualify for employment on federally-financed research. Interestingly, however, the recommendation carried an escape clause, "except where extreme hardship would thereby be imposed."

[6] U.S. Congress, *An Act To Amend the Immigration and Nationality Act To Facilitate the Entry of Certain Non-immigrants into the United States and For Other Purposes,* Public Law 91–225, 91st Congress, 1st Sess., April 7, 1970.

[7] The law reads, "financed in whole or in part, directly or indirectly, by an agency of the Government of the United States or by the government of the country of his nationality or his last residence and who at the time of admission or acquisition of status was a national or resident of a country which the Secretary of State, pursuant to regulations prescribed by him, had designated as clearly requiring the services of persons engaged in the field of specialized knowledge or skill in which the alien was engaged."

[8] The grounds for waiver are: 1) hardship to spouse or child, 2) possessing skills essential to a program of official U.S. government interest, 3) return would mean persecution on account of race, religion, or political opinion, and 4) a written statement from the country in question indicating there is no objection to a waiver.

[9] In this discussion, I have purposely avoided bringing in the H-visa, a non-immigrant visa used to bring trainees, individuals of distinguished merit, and other individuals who perform temporary services or labor (if unemployed persons capable of performing such service or labor cannot be found in this country). The H-visa is another potential loophole visa, allowing qualified individuals to get to the United States, then adjust. Universities, for instance, can bring visiting professors for a two-year period (or more) after which the visitor can adjust his status.

[10] The first-come-first-served immigration policy established in 1965 "discriminated against" individuals from the United Kingdom and other Northern European nations who had been able to obtain visas almost at will in the past. In 1969, Filipinos alone, for instance, accounted for approximately two-thirds of the 17,000 third-preference (high-level skills) places available. It should not be surprising that the 1965 law has been amended to give Anglo-Saxon types greater opportunity to migrate, albeit through the side door.

[11] See John Noble Wilford, "Brain Drain to U.S. Reversing," *New York Times* (November 9, 1970), p. 1.

[12] Niland, pp. 98–99.

[13] Niland notes differences by country and urges, as I have, that policy be tailored country-by-country. Simply to talk about less-developed nations is not enough.

[14] Public Law 91–225.

[15] Even LASPAU, however, is concerned about getting people home. In some cases, home country conditions change between the time students are selected and the time they are due to return. Promised jobs can evaporate easily.

[16] Adams, p. 259.

[17] See Education and World Affairs, Committee on the International Migration of Talent, *The International Migration of High-Level Manpower: Its Impact on the Development Process* (New York: Frederick Praeger, 1970).

[18] The IIE offices are only partially successful. For an evaluation of an alternative, see Education and World Affairs (EWA) "The Overseas Selection of Foreign Students, A Report From EWA" (New York: April, 1966).

[19] For example, see Grubel, *Characteristics of Foreign Born and Educated Scientists in the United States, 1966.*

Appendixes

I

AN ANALYSIS OF THE NO ANSWER CATEGORY OF INTENT TO REMAIN PERMANENTLY IN THE UNITED STATES

The large percentage not answering the IIE question of intended permanent residence results partly from census procedures. Where institutions rather than individuals completed the forms, there was no way an individual's intent could be tapped. In great part, however, the non-response rate also reflects uncertainty or reflects a desire not to reveal intentions. This is suggested by the fact that the No Answer category of the variable INTENT is considerably larger than for any other variable (see Table 57). Even allowing for the fact that INTENT was the only truly subjective item on the census form, it is reasonable to assume that non-response is related to individual as well as institutional factors.

If non-response on INTENT is randomly distributed among institutions and individuals, then the distribution of other characteristics within the category No Answer should follow closely the distribution of characteristics for the total population. If the non-respondents are largely weighted with potential non-returnees, the distributions of other variables within the No Answer category of INTENT should closely resemble the distributions within Non-return.

To check the relationship between No Answer and other categories of INTENT, then, cross-tabulations were done with each

TABLE 57—A comparison of the percentage No Answer for various items in the IIE Annual Census of Foreign Students in the United States, 1964–65[a]

VARIABLE	No Answer[b]	
	#	%
COUNTRY	0.0	10
FIELD	1.2	1,047
STATUS	2.5	2,200
AGE	11.6	10,302
SPONSOR	15.2	13,448
TIME	20.3	17,948
VISA	21.1	18,665
INTENT	31.0	28,250

[a] Calculated from: IIE Census forms, Fall 1964.
[b] Base N = 88,556

of the other main variables in the Institute of International Education Annual Census of Foreign Students and percentages were calculated within each category of INTENT. These distributions were done for all individuals and were repeated for males and females taken separately. Because the data were nominal rather than ordinal or cardinal, the most appropriate statistic for testing association seemed to be the Lambda statistic.[1] Table 58 provides an example of the cross-tabulations done. Lambda statistics were calculated for several different dichotomizations in which the non-respondents (the No Answer category) were compared with other categories of INTENT. Table 59 presents Lambda statistics computed for cross-tabulations of INTENT by each of the other major variables. With the exception of VISA, there was virtually no improvement in the predictive power when the Non-return and No Answer categories were separated out, suggesting that the two are quite similar. On the other hand, an increase in the predictive power when No Answer and Return were separated occurred for STATUS, AGE, TIME, SPONSOR, and VISA distri-

TABLE 58—Distribution of academic STATUS within categories of INTENT for the total population of foreign students in the United States, 1964–65[a]

STATUS	INTENT[b,c]									
	NO ANSWER		NON-RETURN		RETURN		UNDECIDED		TOTAL	
	%	#	%	#	%	#	%	#	%	#
Special	10.4	2,731	4.7	446	7.6	3,709	3.7	48	8.0	6,934
Undergraduate	40.3	10,644	67.2	6,435	50.7	24,905	56.9	739	49.5	42,743
Graduate—unspec.	21.7	5,730	1.2	114	1.3	631	1.2	16	7.5	6,491
Graduate—masters	16.5	4,353	15.0	1,438	25.3	12,419	16.8	218	21.4	18,428
Graduate—doctorate	11.1	2,926	11.9	1,136	15.1	7,420	21.4	278	13.6	11,760
Total	100.0	26,404	100.0	9,569	100.0	49,084	100.0	1,299	100.0	86,356

[a] Calculated from: IIE Census forms, Fall 1964.
[b] Excluded from the calculations are:
    NA STATUS 2,200
[c] Lambda statistics:

	Asymmetrical	Symmetrical
No Answer vs. Non-return	0.000	0.000
No Answer vs. Return	0.235	0.094
No Answer vs. Undecided	0.000	0.000
No Answer vs. Non-return, Return	0.230	0.088
No Answer vs. Non-return, Undecided	0.000	0.000
No Answer vs. Non-return, Return, and Undecided ...	0.229	0.087

TABLE 59—Lambda coefficients for cross-tabulations of selected categories of INTENT by STATUS, by COUNTRY, by AGE, by FIELD, by TIME, by SPONSOR, and by VISA, within SEX[a]

ITEM		No ANSWER AND RETURN	No ANSWER AND NON-RETURN
STATUS	Male	.244	.000
	Female	.201	.000
	Total	.235	.000
COUNTRY	M	.079	.012
	F	.097	.080
	T	.079	.023
AGE	M	.201	.002
	F	.240	.085
	T	.209	.008
FIELD	M	.082	.001
	F	.052	.027
	T	.061	.004
TIME	M	.393	.016
	F	.395	.104
	T	.394	.018
SPONSOR	M	.377	.028
	F	.391	.050
	T	.380	.029
VISA	M	.437	.387
	F	.406	.512
	T	.431	.418

[a] Calculated from: IIE Census forms, Fall 1964.

butions. To a certain extent this was a function of the sizes of the categories. However, the evidence is strong enough to leave little doubt that a downward bias was introduced into rates of non-return even when non-respondents were excluded from the base. That is to say, the proportion of non-returnees was probably higher among those who did not answer than it was for the population as a whole.

Although there was apparently little association between the COUNTRY variable in general and No Answer on INTENT, there was considerable variation from country to country in the percentage of individuals who chose not to answer the question on intended residence. The average rate of non-response was 31.9 per cent. Several countries were much higher in their non-response rate. Those above 40 per cent are listed in Table 60.

TABLE 60—Countries with greater than 40 per cent non-response on INTENT, among males[a]

COUNTRY	PER CENT	BASE NUMBER
British West Indies	84.0	25
Rumania	81.5	27
China—unspecified	66.0	1,716
U.S.S.R.	60.7	28
Hungary	56.4	101
Yugoslavia	53.1	162
Poland	50.0	126
Israel	46.7	1,271
Argentina	45.7	521
United Arab Republic	45.0	1,122
Haiti	42.0	169
Iceland	41.9	106
Cuba	41.8	1,874
Belgium	41.8	194
Italy	41.3	550
Austria	40.9	132
West Germany	40.5	1,375
France	40.4	607
Switzerland	40.3	231

[a] Calculated from: IIE Census forms, Fall 1964.

If non-respondents resemble non-returnees more closely than returnees, as suggested above, then these countries should be the ones for whom the calculated rate of non-return has the largest downward bias. To try and draw too much from this listing is unwarranted, but it is apparent that there are two major clusters of countries in the list. The first is a cluster of countries from which return may have been shut off and from which there are fairly large numbers of political refugees (Eastern Europe, China, Cuba, and perhaps Haiti and the United Arab Republic). Argentina is a borderline case in this group, but in 1966 had provided considerable political incentive for emigration. The second cluster is a group of European nations. Where political factors enter, it is logical that individuals would be reluctant to indicate their intentions, and it is logical that there is a greater chance that such individuals remain permanently. No general reason can be given for the higher non-response percentages among European nations. It may be that these individuals are less apt to be committed to either return or non-return, hence are more apt not to answer the question. Assuming that non-respondents are more apt to be non-returnees, the higher rates do support the generalization that non-return is greater among Western European students than among those from less developed regions. The ordering of non-response tends to parallel roughly the country index of non-return developed in chapter 4. Israel stands out as among the top countries on non-response but not among the top countries on non-return.

Table 61 presents the percentage of non-response on INTENT within each category of the main variables considered here. By looking at the variation of this percentage, it is possible to hypothesize which categories may contain a greater bias. For instance, students in both the humanities and engineering are less apt to answer the question of INTENT than are students in other fields. Presumably, this indicates greater indecision or a greater reluctance to report intended residence. If, as has been suggested, those who do not answer have a higher-than-average probability of remaining permanently in the United States, then the estimates for non-return among students in engineering and the humanities will be low.

Bias is not so clear among categories of STATUS because of the

TABLE 61—The percentage of non-response on IN-TENT within each category of FIELD (M1), STATUS, VISA (M1), AGE (M1), TIME (M1), and SPONSOR (M2, M3, M4, M5, M6), males only[a]

Item	Per cent	Base number
FIELD (M1)		
Medicine	29.5	3,384
Social science	30.0	10,080
Science	31.7	12,211
Engineering	34.1	19,042
Agriculture	31.1	3,104
Business	31.9	6,586
Humanities	36.1	10,491
Education	24.9	2,406
Other	27.9	219
All fields	32.4	67,523[b]
STATUS		
Special	41.1	4,690
Undergraduate	26.1	31,801
Graduate—unspecified	90.1	5,367
Graduate—masters	24.7	14,415
Graduate—doctorate	25.0	10,401
All statuses	31.9	66,674[b]
VISA (M1)		
F (student)	20.7	38,267
Immigrant	13.7	5,348
J (exchangee)	16.7	7,351
Other	25.4	2,754
All visas	19.7	53,720[b]
AGE (M1)		
15–17	27.8	593
18–19	23.1	4,408
20–21	23.4	8,059

[a] Calculated from: IIE Census forms, Fall 1964.
[b] Excluded from the total are those who did not respond on FIELD (M1), STATUS, VISA (M1), AGE (M1), TIME (M1), and SPONSOR (M2, M3, M4, M5, M6), respectively. The grand total in each case is 68,238.

371

TABLE 61—*Continued*

ITEM	PER CENT	BASE NUMBER
22–24	25.6	14,726
25–29	29.9	19,698
30–34	30.3	8,284
35–39	29.9	2,895
40+	28.8	1,585
All ages	27.5	60,248[b]
TIME (M1)		
1	20.4	20,131
2	21.1	12,496
3–4	21.3	13,875
5–6	21.4	5,165
7+	21.4	2,626
All times	20.9	54,293[b]
SPONSOR (M2)		
Non-U.S. government	24.0	50,643
U.S. government	15.9	7,206
All sponsors	23.0	57,849[b]
SPONSOR (M3)		
Non-foreign government	23.0	52,283
Foreign government	22.3	5,566
All sponsors	23.0	57,849[b]
SPONSOR (M4)		
Non-U.S. university	22.9	42,780
U.S. university	23.1	15,069
All sponsors	23.0	57,849[b]
SPONSOR (M5)		
Non-private	23.7	49,603
Private	18.6	8,246
All sponsors	23.0	57,849[b]
SPONSOR (M6)		
Non-self	23.9	21,313
Self	22.4	36,536
All sponsors	23.0	57,849[b]

large group of unclassified graduate students. The most logical method of handling this seems to be to group the unspecified graduate students with Masters and doctoral aspirants, to form one category labeled graduate students. The combined percentage of non-response is still large enough (36.4) to suggest that estimates for non-return among students at the graduate level are underestimates. To indicate a downward bias among graduate students is much safer than to support what would appear to be an upward bias in non-return rates for undergraduates. While the downward bias for graduates is in the same direction as the bias introduced by non-response in general, the undergraduate bias runs in the opposite direction. The magnitudes of these biases are not known; hence it is impossible to judge whether the net bias is upward or downward.

None of the categories of SPONSORship is disproportionately high in the number of non-respondents. The low percentages of non-response for both United States government and privately sponsored individuals are most interesting. At least three explanations are possible: 1. These sponsored individuals are in programs which require them to return. There is little or no indecision; hence the percentage who can answer definitely is high. 2. These individuals are afraid to indicate in any way (even by leaving a question blank) that they may fail to live up to expectations that they will return home. This might somehow jeopardize their scholarship. 3. Because these students are sponsored, there is greater accounting. These individuals are not inconspicuous. They are more easily located by foreign student advisors to fill out the census forms.

Among categories of VISA, the lower percentage of non-respondents in the immigrant-visa category supports the validity of looking at relative percentages of non-response in relation to uncertainty and unwillingness to provide information. Logically, there should be a greater degree of certainty concerning residence among immigrant-visa holders. If an immigrant visa has been obtained there should be little need to withhold information. As expected, the percentage of non-response among immigrant visa-holders is lowest of all percentages presented in Table 61.

As AGE increases, there is a slight tendency for the non-response percentage to increase. This might reflect a greater reluctance by older, more sophisticated students to give information. The tendency parallels the previously noted undergraduate-graduate differences.

NOTE

[1] L. A. Goodman and W. H. Kruskal, "Measures of Association for Cross Classifications," *Journal of the American Statistical Association*, XLIX (December, 1954), 732–64. Lambda asymmetric assumes that the columns define the independent variable and the rows, the dependent variable. It can be interpreted as the relative decrease in the probability of error in guessing a unit's row category if there is no information about what column it is in, compared to the probability of error in guessing its row category if its column category is given. In the symmetric case, neither variable is assumed to be independent or dependent. Otherwise the interpretation is the same.

II

A KEY TO CORRELATIONS
IN CHAPTER 4

TABLE 62—A key to indexes and variables used in chapter 4

NAME OF COUNTRY	NON-RETURN INDEX (M & F)[a]	NON-RETURN INDEX (MALE ONLY)[a]	MANPOWER INDEX[b]	INCOME PER CAPITA ($US)[c]	POLITICAL ELITISM INDEX[d]	COMPOSITE EDUCATION INDEX[e]	IMMIGRATION TO THE U.S., 1955–64 (000)[f]
Rumania	83.3	80.0	...	360	251	...	13
Hungary	78.9	79.6	...	490	139	54	57
Cuba	74.8	75.3	...	431	290	36	123
Poland	56.0	60.3	...	475	211	67	83
Ireland	46.3	35.4	87	550	190	...	72
Czechoslovakia	46.2	50.0	...	680	144	69	23
Bulgaria	42.9	50.0	...	365	157	...	...
Germany, F.R.	41.4	38.3	22	927	205	86	315
Netherlands	41.0	43.5	16	836	152	134	50
Yugoslavia	38.6	35.5	...	265	242	60	40
Austria	37.3	29.5	17	670	192	...	24
Italy	33.9	33.8	9	516	181	57	218
Denmark	32.6	26.9	16	1,057	171	77	14
Haiti	31.8	30.6	298	105	444	5	10
United Kingdom	30.8	27.1	34	1,189	185	122	239
El Salvador	26.6	24.5	174	219	285	...	10
Norway	25.9	22.6	55	1,130	142	74	24
Luxembourg	25.0	25.0	11	...	149	...	...

376

Switzerland	24.8	23.9	34	1,428	163	...	18
Spain	24.4	21.7	10	293	173	40	16
Sweden	24.4	18.6	13	1,380	115	79	20
Bolivia	24.3	25.7	69	99	443	15	...
Netherlands Ant.	23.1	17.3	...	160	...	...	...
France	22.8	19.9	5	943	300	108	40
Dominican Rep.	22.6	20.6	...	239	278	15	31
Argentina	22.4	21.6	7	490	157	82	30
Belgium	21.1	18.6	7	1,196	224	124	12
Portugal	20.8	24.6	9	224	43	41	28
Finland	20.1	25.8	10	794	186	89	7
Mexico	20.1	18.8	...	262	359	33	433
Honduras	18.4	17.9	139	194	290	...	10
Iran	17.9	17.8	189	108	383	17	5
Guatemala	17.1	18.0	56	189	203	11	8
U.S.S.R.	16.7	9.1	...	600	219	93	26

[a] Calculated from: IIE Census forms, Fall 1964. Non-respondents were excluded from the calculation.

[b] See Table 63, column 8.

[c] Source: Bruce M. Russett et al., *World Handbook of Political and Social Indicators* (New Haven: Yale University Press, 1964), pp. 149–54.

[d] The political elitism index was developed by Arthur S. Banks and Philip M. Gregg and presented in their article, "Grouping Political Systems: Q-Factor Analyses of *A Cross-Political Survey*," *The American Behavioral Scientist*, IX, No. 3 November 1965), 3–6.

[e] The composite education index was developed by Frederick Harbison and Charles A. Myers in *Education, Manpower, and Economic Growth* (New York: McGraw-Hill, 1964), pp. 45–48.

[f] U.S. Immigration and Naturalization Service, *Annual Report*, 1964 (Washington, D.C.: U.S. Government Printing Office, 1964), p. 48. Figures are in thousands.

TABLE 62—Continued

Name of Country	Non-Return Index (M & F)[a]	Non-Return Index (Male Only)[a]	Manpower Index[b]	Income per Capita ($US)[c]	Political Elitism Index[d]	Composite Education Index[e]	Immigration to the U.S., 1955–64 (000)[f]
Nicaragua	16.1	14.4	117	160	247	::	12
Colombia	15.8	15.2	52	263	291	23	37
Greece	15.6	15.5	40	340	251	49	50
Syria	15.4	14.3	21	173	456	::	2
Ecuador	15.1	15.0	50	189	246	24	19
Panama	15.1	15.9	::	329	254	::	17
Peru	15.1	15.7	::	179	228	30	15
Costa Rica	14.9	14.1	61	357	272	47	10
Jordan	14.9	14.0	55	129	346	::	7
Chile	14.8	13.3	19	379	153	51	9
Barbados	14.3	17.0	::	200	::	::	::
Canada	14.1	15.8	50	1,947	261	102	306
Hong Kong	13,6	15.4	314	272	::	::	5
Uruguay	13.6	13.6	::	478	169	70	::
South Africa	12.5	11.2	10	395	335	40	3
Israel	12.3	13.0	62	726	344	85	13
Lebanon	11.8	10.8	67	362	386	24	4

378

Ceylon	11.6	14.0	8	129	401	..	..
Korea	11.5	11.0	20	144	453	55	15
Iraq	11.1	11.4	38	156	483	31	3
Taiwan	11.1	11.7	56	161	..	48	..
Cyprus	10.8	12.7	..	467	344	..	..
Australia	10.1	7.5	6	1,316	211	138	6
Burma	9.9	11.3	6	57	590	14	..
Venezuela	9.9	8.8	..	648	319	48	8
Brazil	9.6	8.2	..	293	241	21	14
Trinidad	9.6	10.2	..	..	363	..	..
British Guiana	9.3	10.7	4	235	..	..	..
New Zealand	9.3	8.7	..	1,310	233	147	2
Paraguay	9.3	9.4	10	114	213	23	..
Turkey	8.9	9.1	34	220	234	46	9
Iceland	8.6	8.0	7	572	182	..	..
Morocco	8.5	3.9	2	142	506	..	..
Japan	8.3	7.6	6	306	279	111	3
United Arab Rep.	7.9	7.5	..	142	473	40	50
Philippines	7.5	8.8	311	220	421	..	5
Jamaica	7.2	7.1	24	316	421	27	26
Malaysia	7.0	6.8	3	..	530	..	..
India	6.9	7.2	138	73	522	35	5
Mozambique	6.7	6.7	106	70	..	..	..
Saudi Arabia	5.5	5.6	8	170	404	2	..
Vietnam	5.5	5.4	..	76	569	..	..
Kuwait	4.8	4.8	..	2,900	..	..	..

TABLE 62—Concluded

Name of Country	Non-Return Index (M & F)[a]	Non-Return Index (Male Only)[a]	Manpower Index[b]	Income per Capita ($US)[c]	Political Elitism Index[d]	Composite Education Index[e]	Immigration to the U.S., 1955–64 (000)[f]
Rhodesia, S.	4.3	4.3	109	..	..	..	..
Angola	4.2	4.4	..	60	..	..	..
Thailand	3.9	3.6	11	96	354	35	..
Ghana	3.7	3.7	18	172	702	23	..
Indonesia	3.6	2.8	..	131	748	11	18
Tunisia	3.5	4.4	3	173	577	15	1
Laos	3.2	3.7	..	50	485	..	..
Ethiopia	3.0	2.3	27	55	429	1	..
Liberia	3.0	2.9	100	100	382	4	..
Pakistan	3.0	2.9	1	70	553	25	..
Somalia	2.4	2.5	58	57	608	2	..
Sudan	2.4	1.7	4	60	554	8	..
Cambodia	2.1	2.2	6	99	679	..	..
Libya	2.0	2.1	8	60	409	11	..
Afghanistan	1.7	1.9	6	50	302	2	..
Sierra Leone	1.7	1.3	31	..	615	..	..

Country							
Guinea	1.5	1.8	17	..	708	..	..
Nigeria	1.5	1.6	18	78	508	5	1
Congo-Leopoldville	1.4	1.4	..	92	682	4	..
Tanzania	1.1	1.0	19	61	808	2	..
Ryukyu Islands	.8	.9	..	..	..	..	3
Kenya	.6	.4	10	87	..	5	..
Algeria	0	0	0	178	483	..	1
Burundi	0	0	0	..	799	..	..
Cameroon	0	0	0	..	813	..	..
Chad	0	0	0	..	860	..	..
Congo-Brazzaville	0	0	0	..	866	..	..
Dahomey	0	0	0	..	882	..	..
Gabon	0	0	0	..	882	..	..
Ivory Coast	0	0	0	..	867	..	..
Malagasy Republic	0	0	0	45	634	..	..
Malawi	0	0	0	..	428	..	..
Mali	0	0	0	..	862	..	..
Niger	0	0	0	..	901	..	..
Rwanda	0	0	0	..	774	..	..
Togo	0	0	0	50	820	..	..
Uganda	0	0	0	64	556	..	..
Upper Volta	0	0	0	..	874	..	..
Yemen	0	0	0	..	562	..	..

III

VARIABLES AND COUNTRIES USED IN REGRESSION ANALYSES

The following variables and countries were used in the 64-country regression analyses presented in chapter 4.

VARIABLE NAME	DESCRIPTION OF VARIABLES
	CARDINAL VARIABLES
STATUS	The ratio of undergraduate male students to total male students for each country.
SPONSOR	The ratio of self-sponsored male students to total male students for each country.
VISA	The ratio of male F (student)-visa holders to total male students for each country.
AGE	The ratio of male students age 30 or older to total male students for each country.
NON-RETURN	The ratio of male students who indicated their intent to remain permanently in the United States to total male students for each country.
EDUCATION	Index numbers taken from the Harbison and Myers Composite Education Index.
INCOME PER CAPITA	Income per capita in dollars, taken from Russett. The figures are circa 1957, but are used with the assumption that relative position of countries in the listing will not have changed.

VARIABLE NAME	DESCRIPTION OF VARIABLES
POLITICAL ELITISM	Factor loadings from Banks and Gregg's factor analysis of political indicators in *A Cross-Polity Survey.*

DUMMY VARIABLES

E_1, E_2, E_3, and E_4	Derived by cutting EDUCATION into four categories: E_1 ranging from 0–19, E_2 ranging from 20–39, E_3 ranging from 40–79, and E_4 ranging from 80 upward.
I_1, I_2, I_3, and I_4	Derived by cutting INCOME PER CAPITA into four categories: I_1 ranging from 0–99, I_2 ranging from 100–299, I_3 ranging from 300–699, and I_4 ranging from 700 upward.
E_1I_1, E_1I_2 . . . E_4I_4	Derived by cross-tabulating EDUCATION and INCOME PER CAPITA, using the categories outlined above. Each interaction became a separate dummy variable. Empty cells were dropped from the analysis.
P_1, P_2, and P_3	Derived by cutting POLITICAL ELITISM into three categories: P_1 ranging from 0–299, P_2 ranging from 300–499, and P_3 ranging from 500 upward.

RANK ON NON-RETURN INDEX	NAME OF COUNTRY	RANK ON NON-RETURN INDEX	NAME OF COUNTRY
5	Hungary	68	Israel
7	Cuba	72	Iraq
9	Poland	73	Burma
11	Czechoslovakia	74	South Africa
13	Netherlands	75	Korea
14	Germany	76	Lebanon
16	Yugoslavia	80	Paraguay
18	Italy	81	Turkey
19	Haiti	82	U.S.S.R.
22	United Kingdom	84	Venezuela

Rank on non-return index	Name of country	Rank on non-return index	Name of country
23	Denmark	85	New Zealand
24	Finland	86	Brazil
25	Bolivia	88	Japan
28	Portugal	89	Australia
32	Norway	90	United Arab Republic
35	Spain	91	India
36	Argentina	92	Jamaica
37	Dominican Republic	95	Saudi Arabia
41	France	99	Tunisia
42	Mexico	102	Ghana
43	Belgium	104	Thailand
44	Sweden	105	Liberia
45	Guatemala	106	Pakistan
47	Iran	107	Indonesia
53	Canada	109	Somalia
54	Peru	110	Ethiopia
55	Greece	112	Libya
58	Colombia	113	Afghanistan
59	Ecuador	115	Sudan
63	Costa Rica	116	Nigeria
66	Uruguay	118	Congo-Leopoldville
67	Chile	123	Uganda

IV

**ENROLLMENTS AT HOME AND
ABROAD, EDUCATION AT THE
THIRD LEVEL, SELECTED COUNTRIES,
CIRCA 1965**

TABLE 63—Enrollments at home and abroad, education at the third level, selected countries, circa 1965[a]

COUNTRY	TOTAL-STUDENTS (FOREIGN AND NATIONAL) (1)	FOREIGN STUDENTS (2)	NATIONALS STUDYING ABROAD (3)	TOTAL—NATIONALS ONLY (1)−(2)+(3) (4)	TOTAL NON-RETURN-EES[b] (5)	PER CENT FOREIGN (2)÷(1) (6)	PER CENT NATION-ALS ABROAD (3)÷(4) (7)	MAN-POWER LOSS INDEX[c] (8)	PER CENT NON-RETURN[d] (9)
U.S.A.	5,526,325	82,709	13,865	5,457,481	—	1.5	.3	—	—
Canada	283,907[4]	11,284[4]	11,311	283,934	1,440	4.0	4.0	50	14.1
Europe									
Albania	11,937[4]	93	98	11,942	—	.8	.8	—	—
Austria	49,382	9,368[4]	1,171	41,725	75	19.0	4.1	17	37.3
Belgium	75,489[4]	5,000[4]	1,146	71,635	56	6.6	1.6	7	21.1
Bulgaria	100,102	1,048[4]	1,028	100,082	—	1.0	1.0	—	—
Czechoslovakia	141,687[4]	3,303	218	138,602	—	2.3	.2	—	—
Denmark	43,731[4]	643[4]	514	43,602	71	1.5	1.2	16	32.6
Finland	38,775	133[4]	1,069	39,731	42	.3	2.7	10	20.1
France	455,111[4]	35,584[4]	7,370	426,897	215	7.8	1.7	5	22.8
Germany, FR[e]	373,099	26,225	10,491	357,365	816	7.0	2.9	22	41.4
Greece	55,334	1,681	9,053	62,706	253	3.0	14.4	40	15.6
Hungary	51,002	691	1,555	51,866	—	1.4	3.0	—	—
Iceland	1,038[4]	31	423	1,430	5	3.0	29.6	34	8.6
Ireland	20,634[4]	3,364	563	17,833	156	16.3	3.2	87	46.3
Italy	261,358[4]	3,800	3,356	260,914	257	1.5	1.3	9	33.9
Luxembourg	580[4]	48	1,180	1,172	2	11.8	68.9	11	25.0
Netherlands	148,590	1,242[4]	2,134	149,482	248	.8	1.4	16	41.0
Norway	19,528	274[4]	3,623	22,877	128	1.4	15.8	55	25.9
Poland	251,864[4]	1,364	799	251,299	—	.5	.3	—	—
Portugal	32,115[4]	155[4]	811	32,771	31	.5	2.5	9	20.8

Romania	130,416[4]	508[4]	193	130,101	—	.4	.1	—	24.4
Spain	111,133[4]	7,489[4]	2,225	105,869	115	6.7	2.1	10	24.4
Sweden[f]	61,222[4]	—	1,159	61,222	81	—	1.9	13	24.8
Switzerland	30,488[4]	8,649	1,690	22,877	79	28.4	7.4	34	30.8
United Kingdom[g]	225,960[4]	16,396	7,801	217,365	740	7.3	3.6	34	—
Yugoslavia	184,923[4]	1,816	966	184,073	—	1.0	.5	—	—
U.S.S.R.	3,608,000[4]	21,000[4]	—	—	—	.6	—	—	—
Oceania									
Australia	122,620[4]	6,960	1,390	117,050	72	5.7	1.2	6	10.1
New Zealand	47,425[4]	1,056[4]	734	47,103	22	2.2	1.6	4	9.3
Caribbean									
Haiti[h]	1,705[4]	—	672	2,377	71	—	28.3	298	31.8
Jamaica	1,902	675	1,605	2,832	88	35.5	56.7	311	7.2
Trinidad	910	186	1,580	2,304	—	20.4	67.5	—	—

[a] Source: UNESCO, *Statistical Yearbook, 1966* (Paris: UNESCO, 1967). Column 1 figures were taken from pp. 155–169 (Table 2.10, Education at the third level: teachers, students and numbers of students per 100,000 inhabitants) or from pp. 170–202 (Table 2.11, Education at the third level: distribution of students by field of study). Columns 2 and 3: figures were taken from pp. 251–254 (Table 2.15, Education at the third level: number of foreign students enrolled and number of national (students enrolled abroad). Superscripts indicate the year, if other than 1965 (e.g., 4 = 1964).

[b] Calculated from: IIE Census forms, Fall 1964. The rate of non-return among respondents was imputed to non-respondents as well in estimating the total number of non-returnees. See chapter 2 and Appendix I for a discussion of biases.

[c] The manpower index = (5) ÷ (4) × 10,000

[d] Calculated from: IIE Census forms, Fall 1964. Non-respondents were excluded from the calculation.

[e] Includes W. Berlin.

[f] The most recent figure presented by UNESCO for foreign students in Sweden was a 1960 figure of 1,195. It was assumed, for purposes of calculating a manpower loss number, that the number of foreign students enrolled approximately equaled the number of Swedish students abroad; the enrollment in column 1 is repeated in column 4.

[g] Includes Ireland and Scotland.

[h] Figures for Haiti were taken from: *UNESCO Statistical Yearbook, 1965* (Paris: UNESCO, 1966), p. 253 and pp. 308, 309. The column 3 total is for Haitian students in 15 countries: Australia, Austria, Belgium, Canada, Czechoslovakia, France, Germany (F.R. and W. Berlin), Italy, Japan, Spain, Switzerland, Syria, U.AR, U.K., U.S.A.

TABLE 63—Continued

COUNTRY	TOTAL-STUDENTS (FOREIGN AND NATIONAL) (1)	FOREIGN STUDENTS (2)	NATIONALS STUDYING ABROAD (3)	TOTAL— NATIONALS ONLY (1)−(2)+(3) (4)	TOTAL NON- RETURN- EES[b] (5)	PER CENT FOREIGN (2)÷(1) (6)	PER CENT NATION- ALS ABROAD (3)÷(4) (7)	MAN- POWER LOSS INDEX[c] (8)	PER CENT NON- RETURN[d] (9)
Central America									
Costa Rica	6,600[4]	254	616	6,962	43	3.8	8.8	61	14.9
El Salvador	3,624	64	517	4,077	71	1.8	12.7	174	26.6
Guatemala	7,673	243	406	7,836	44	3.2	5.2	56	17.1
Honduras	2,578	180[4]	399	2,797	39	7.0	14.3	139	18.4
Nicaragua	3,343	70[4]	657	3,930	46	2.1	16.7	117	16.1
South America									
Argentina	225,653[4]	13,060	1,310	213,903	168	5.8	.6	7	22.4
Bolivia	11,090	82	899	11,907	83	.7	7.6	69	24.3
Chile	36,503[4]	257	977	37,223	74	.7	2.6	19	14.8
Colombia	37,462[4]	686[4]	2,381	39,157	207	1.8	6.1	52	15.8
Ecuador	12,486	480	761	12,767	64	3.8	6.0	50	15.1
Indian Subcontinent									
India	1,310,000[3]	4,540[4]	10,863	1,316,323	475	.3	.8	3	6.9
Pakistan	229,003	366	2,897	231,534	33	.2	1.3	1	3.0
Ceylon	12,485	16	970	13,439	12	.1	7.2	8	11.6
Middle East									
Afghanistan	3,451[4]	12[4]	501	3,940	3	.3	12.7	6	1.7
Iran	26,000	92	9,834	35,742	679	.4	27.5	189	17.9
Iraq	24,662[4]	1,020	3,724	27,366	104	4.1	13.6	38	11.1

388

Israel	30,273	898	2,626	32,001	199	3.0	8.2	62	12.3
Jordan	2,755	17	15,901	18,639	103	.6	85.3	55	14.9
Lebanon	20,345	10,798	3,249	12,796	86	53.1	25.4	67	11.8
Saudi Arabia	1,568[4]	242[4]	1,683	3,009	32	15.4	55.9	106	5.5
Syria	31,993	7,488	7,150	31,655	69	23.4	22.6	21	15.4
Turkey	91,198[4]	3,325	3,727	91,600	98	3.6	4.1	10	8.9
Asia									
Burma	22,399	16	358	22,741	13	.1	1.6	6	9.9
Cambodia	5,851	104	410	6,157	4	1.7	6.7	6	2.1
China (Taiwan)	85,346	478	8,660	93,528	525	.6	9.3	56	11.1
Hong Kong	10,189[4]	390[4]	4,836	14,635	460	3.8	33.0	314	13.6
Japan	1,085,119	8,266	4,087	1,080,940	289	.8	.4	2	8.3
Korea	141,635	107	6,988	148,516	308	.1	4.7	20	11.5
Malaysia	8,960	106	6,875	15,729	38	1.2	43.7	24	7.0
Thailand	52,037[4]	50	2,973	54,960	64	.1	5.4	11	3.9
Vietnam	23,457[4]	34	3,851	27,274	22	.1	14.1	8	5.5
S. Africa	53,849	2,913[4]	1,475	52,411	52	5.4	2.8	10	12.5
N. Africa									
Algeria	8,177	1,873	1,681	7,985	0	22.9	21.1	0	0
Libya	1,936	110	753	2,579	2	5.7	29.2	8	2.0
Morocco	8,996	998	2,773	10,771	8	11.1	25.7	7	8.5
Sudan	7,701	271[4]	2,179	9,609	4	3.5	22.7	4	2.4
Tunisia	6,230	519	3,592	9,303	3	8.3	38.6	3	3.5
U.A.R.	175,245	16,789	3,572	162,028	105	9.6	2.2	6	12.5

TABLE 63—*Concluded*

COUNTRY	TOTAL-STUDENTS (FOREIGN AND NATIONAL) (1)	FOREIGN STUDENTS (2)	NATIONALS STUDYING ABROAD (3)	TOTAL— NATIONALS ONLY (1)−(2)+(3) (4)	TOTAL NON-RETURN-EES[b] (5)	PER CENT FOREIGN (2)÷(1) (6)	PER CENT NATION-ALS ABROAD (3)÷(4) (7)	MAN-POWER LOSS INDEX[c] (8)	PER CENT NON-RETURN[d] (9)
Sub-Saharan Africa									
Burundi	188	79	111	220	0	42.0	50.5	0	0
Cameroon	1,164	25	1,111	2,250	0	2.1	49.4	0	0
Dahomey	39	8	782	813	0	20.5	96.2	0	0
Ethiopia	2,256	115	811	2,952	8	5.1	27.5	27	3.0
Ghana	4,788	158	1,401	6,031	11	3.3	23.2	18	3.7
Guinea	585[4]	22[4]	558	1,121	2	3.8	49.8	17	1.5
Ivory Coast	1,566[4]	828[4]	505	1,243	0	52.9	40.6	0	0
Kenya	2,758[4]	398	2,433	4,793	5	14.4	50.8	10	.6
Liberia	685	60[4]	371	996	10	8.8	37.2	100	3.0
Madagascar	2,418	112	734	3,040	0	4.6	24.1	0	0
Mozambique	555	2	13	566	1	.4	2.3	138	6.7
Nigeria	8,933	204	3,844	12,573	21	2.3	30.6	18	1.5
Senegal	2,755	1,437	348	1,666	0	52.2	20.9	0	0
Sierra Leone	930	182	473	1,221	3	19.6	38.7	31	1.7
Somalia	61[4]	9[4]	372	424	3	14.8	87.7	58	2.4
S. Rhodesia	639[4]	129[4]	310	820	9	20.2	37.8	109	4.3
Tanzania	115[4]	61[4]	1,477	1,531	3	53.0	96.5	19	1.1
Uganda	1,127[4]	650[4]	1,168	1,645	0	57.7	71.0	0	0

V

METHODS USED TO GATHER INFORMATION FOR "A SURVEY OF PERUVIAN STUDENT ATTITUDES AND EXPECTATIONS"

OBTAINING THE NAMES

The first step in developing a list of Peruvian students was to obtain names of those included in the Institute of International Education censuses of 1964–65 and 1965–66. Although the census is taken in the fall of each year, the process of checking forms, of following up those who did not return forms or who completed them improperly, of coding, and of transferring information to punch cards, delays tabulation and publication until the middle of the following year. By January, however, responses are in, and, with few exceptions, names are available. At this point, in January 1966, the IIE allowed the author to copy names and census information about Peruvian students from the original census forms. Six hundred and sixty-six names were obtained for the 1965–66 school year and were combined with names from the 1964–65 listing. (Institutions and individuals from the 1964–65 census were included to hedge against the possibility that some schools had not yet replied to the 1965–66 request and against the possibility that 1965–66 reporting missed people still enrolled.)

To verify and update names, letters and forms were sent to

Foreign Student Advisors (FSA) at each of the institutions of higher education in which a male Peruvian student had been enrolled according to either IIE census. The FSA at each institution was asked to verify whether the student was male and whether he was still enrolled as of March 1, 1966. If enrolled, the student's address was requested; if not enrolled, his most recent forwarding address was requested. In addition, FSA were asked to add names of male Peruvians currently enrolled at their institution but not

TABLE 64—Adjustments made in delineating the population of male Peruvian students to be included in the mailing list for "A Survey of Peruvian Student Attitudes and Expectations"

ITEM	NAMES ADDED	NAMES SUBTRACTED	TOTAL
Names taken from the IIE 1965–66 Census[a]			666
Excluded as not "higher education"[b]		57	609
Indicated desire not to be contacted[c]		16	593
FSA indicated no longer enrolled		96	497
New students supplied by FSA[d]	164		661
New students found by interviewers[d]	55		716
Independent contact of those who indicated desire not to be contacted[c]	9		725
FSA indicated incorrectly that no longer enrolled	4		729

[a] Original census forms, the Institute of International Education Annual Census of Foreign Students in the United States.

[b] All 57 students were at the New York University Language Institute. See text for explanation of exclusion from the survey.

[c] The original IIE census forms include an option which enables individuals to express their desire not to be contacted. Occasionally, "no contact" was checked by an educational institution for several individuals. In both cases, this option was honored. It was decided, however, that if, in the course of the study, independent contact was made with the student either through a friend or through a foreign student advisor, the "no-contact" names could be reincorporated into the study.

[d] The number of "new" students was adjusted for cases of transfer among United States schools. The 219 students were either missed by the IIE census or were not enrolled at the time the census was taken.

included in the list that had been sent for verification. Responses were received from 95 per cent of the FSA (282 of 297 institutions).[1] Where no answer was received, it was assumed that those Peruvians listed were still enrolled; their names were included in the original mailing list. After adjusting the 1965–66 survey listing of 666 names for those who did not wish to be contacted, for FSA replies, and for new names obtained by interviewers in the field, 729 names had been identified. These names represented a first estimate of the population of male Peruvians studying at institutions of higher education in the United States as of March 1, 1966. Table 64 summarizes the process of obtaining names and of forming the mailing list.

Doubtless some Peruvian students were never identified. Seven "no-contact" students (see Table 64, footnote *c*) were not contacted independently. Also known to be omitted were nine Peruvian males enrolled at Elbert Covell College of the University of the Pacific in Stockton, California. For some reason, they were overlooked in the IIE survey, even though the University of the Pacific is included.[2] In spite of such omissions, it is the author's speculation that at least 95 per cent of the male Peruvian student population, as defined for this study, were included on the mailing list.

OBTAINING THE DATA AND FURTHER DELINEATING THE POPULATION

Three forms were used to collect the information desired: two questionnaires and an interview schedule. The first questionnaire (hereafter referred to as Q-1), was mailed to all 729 individuals. Interviews were conducted with a group selected from among the 729 in a manner to be discussed below. The second questionnaire (hereafter referred to as Q-2) was sent to those individuals who were not interviewed but from whom basic data had been obtained through a returned Q-1.

Questionnaire 1 (Q-1)

Collecting basic information from *all* male Peruvian students was necessary to provide a large enough case base for statistical analysis. The population shifted during the study, complicating the possibility of random sampling at the outset and making it risky. This is discussed below in connection with selecting interviewees.

In its final form,[3] Q-1 was designed to gather basic data for relating individual characteristics, attitudes, conditions of study, and vocational expectations to reasons for study abroad and to the decision to migrate permanently or return to Peru. A preliminary form was pre-tested, first by administering it to several Peruvian students and allowing them to comment on it as they answered questions, and secondly, by mailing out a revised form to Latin American students on the University of Chicago campus. Included in the mail-out was a sheet for listing criticisms. Pre-testing resulted in some revised wording and in considerable cutting of the number of questions asked. All questions concerning income expectations were dropped from Q-1 and were reserved for the interview or for Q-2.

English, rather than Spanish, was used for both questionnaires and the interviews. In large part this was occasioned by time pressures and by the language abilities of the interviewers. If it were possible to rerun the study, Spanish would be used for the questionnaires. For example, a Spanish form would presumably have avoided an occasional misinterpretation of the word primarily in the questions, "Where would you prefer your work to be primarily located?" and "Where do you expect your work to be primarily located?" Although the context seemed clear because the questions followed directly a question concerning expected long-term employer, some individuals translated "primarily" to mean "first" rather than "mainly." Since there is no way of sorting out exactly those cases which involved misinterpretation, the question, which was to have served as a secondary indicator of intent, had to be discarded as ambiguous.

Response to Questionnaire 1

Of the 729 Q-1's mailed, 59 were returned as "Addressee Unknown," were responded to by a friend who indicated that the individual had returned to Peru, or were received and discarded by friends who later told interviewers that the individual was no longer in the United States. (All 59 will be referred to as the "Addressee Unknown" group.) Of the 670 persons receiving the questionnaire, 522 responded—a rate of 78 per cent. To these, individuals were added for whom Q-1 information had been obtained by interview, and individuals not meeting the definition of male Peruvian student were subtracted. Table 65 summarizes these adjustments. The final total 476 represents the working population of full-time male Peruvian students. Frequency distributions and cross-tabulations will refer to this population unless otherwise specified.

For this study, the population of *male* Peruvian students at the particular point in time chosen for the study can be estimated as between 476 (the base number positively identified and contacted) and 710 (the total if all addressee-unknown and non-response individuals are assumed to be still in the United States and studying full time and if an allowance is made for the possibility that an additional 10 per cent of the resultant total were never identified).

In the process of verifying names as of March 1, 1966, using names of Peruvians enrolled as of September 1965, the author hoped to develop a turnover ratio for the Peruvian students within one school year. Again the picture is blurred. However, allowing for the inaccuracies in reporting at both points in time and for the unknown element in the addressee-unknown and non-respondent groups, it seems reasonable to estimate a turnover of 5 to 10 per cent each academic year. The estimate derives from

TABLE 65—Adjustments made in delineating the population of male Peruvian students to be included in the analysis of "A Survey of Peruvian Student Attitudes and Expectations," Q-1

ITEM	NAMES ADDED	NAMES SUBTRACTED	TOTAL
Total students to whom Q-1 was mailed[a]			729
Total students who did not receive Q-1[b]		59	670
Q-1 non-respondents		148	522
Q-1 respondents who did not meet the definition of male Peruvian student:			
Excluded as female		2	520
Excluded as not Peruvian[c]		18	502
Excluded as part time		35	467
Excluded as intensive English[d]		11	456
Excluded as no longer student[e]		11	445
Q-1 information obtained by interview[f]	31		476

[a] See Table 64 for determination of the mailing list.
[b] Questionnaires returned as "Addressee Unknown."
[c] Six were United States citizens; two, Canadian; two, Venezuelan; one, Colombian; two, Bolivian; one, Spanish; two, Italian; one, Philippine; and two, non-Peruvian but of unknown national origin.
[d] A student was omitted if no other courses were being taken concurrently with the English and it was clear that the English was a basic language course rather than a literature course.
[e] Responding were: one high school student, one university instructor, four resident doctors, and five former students who were now working on a full-time basis and no longer attending school.
[f] Q-1 forms were filled out by the author based on the information gathered by interviewers. All information supplied and recorded in this way was factual information which should not have been subject to distortion from the differing manners in which the information was obtained. In all, information was obtained for thirty-six individuals who had not responded on Q-1. Five of these were later discarded as not meeting the definition of student adopted for the study (one was no longer studying, two were part-time students, and two were intensive English students).

the fact that of the 538 students for whom Q-1 information was obtained, 52 (9.6 per cent) indicated they had begun United States study after January 1, 1966. In the group of 476 full-time Peruvian students, 41 (8.5 per cent) had enrolled since January 1, 1966.

Response Bias for Questionnaire 1

To determine how representative the respondents were of the population of male Peruvians, respondents and non-respondents

TABLE 66—A comparison of Q-1 respondents and non-respondents with respect to type,[a] control,[a] size,[a] and quality[b] of institution attended

ITEM	RESPONDENTS[c]		NON-RESPONDENTS[d]	
	%	#	%	#
Type[e]				
University	63.2	334	56.9	62
Four-year college	13.6	72	17.5	19
Junior college	14.2	75	16.5	18
Technical institute	6.3	33	6.4	7
Professional school	2.1	11	0.9	1
Other (commercial, language)	0.6	3	1.8	2
Total	100.0	528	100.0	109

[a] Institutions were categorized by type, control, and size according to information from Christian E. Burckel, *The College Bluebooks,* Book I, Vol. I: *American Institutions of Higher Education* (11th ed.; Yonkers, N.Y.: The College Bluebook, 1965).

[b] Institutions were roughly categorized by quality using the index prepared by Alexander W. Astin, *Who Goes Where to College?* (Chicago: Science Research Associates, Inc., 1965), pp. 57–83. Astin's "Intellectual" index was divided so that high quality institutions were rated 65 or above, medium quality institutions were 50–64, and low quality institutions were below 50 on the index. The measure is, at best, a very rough indicator of one kind of institutional quality.

[c] Excluded from the calculations are those institutions which could not be classified (NC):

    NC Type 10
    NC Control ... 15
    NC Size 17
    NC Quality ... 129

[d] Excluded from the calculations are those institutions which could not be classified:

    NC Type 1
    NC Control ... 3
    NC Size 3
    NC Quality ... 24

[e] No χ^2 is significant at the .05 level for the above.

TABLE 66—*Continued*

ITEM	RESPONDENTS[c]		NON-RESPONDENTS[d]	
	%	#	%	#
Control[e]				
Public	60.4	316	57.9	62
Private, non-sectarian	20.3	106	23.4	25
Private, religious	19.3	101	18.7	20
Total	100.0	523	100.0	107
Size[e]				
Under 1000	6.5	34	3.7	4
1,000–4,999	23.6	123	19.6	21
5,000–9,999	21.7	113	17.8	19
10,000 or more	48.2	251	58.9	63
Total	100.0	521	100.0	107
Quality[e]				
High	10.7	43	14.0	12
Medium	73.3	294	63.9	55
Low	16.0	64	22.1	19
Total	100.0	401	100.0	86

were compared with respect to the only solid piece of information available for all names on the mailing list: institutional affiliation. Table 66 presents these comparisons for type, size, control, and quality of institution attended. There was no significant difference between the two groups on these measures.

Another rough check on the degree to which the respondent population was representative of Peruvian males studying in the United States was made by comparing the distribution of academic status, sponsorship, visa, and field for the working population of 476 students and the "total" population of 613 Peruvian males in the 1964–65 IIE Census. This comparison involves the assumption that there was no significant change in the distribution of characteristics and study conditions resulting from the student turnover between fall 1964, and spring 1966. These comparisons, presented in Table 67, show no significant difference between the two populations of Peruvian males for STATUS, SPONSOR, or VISA, but there is a significant difference on FIELD. In relation

TABLE 67—A comparison of respondents to "A Survey of Peruvian Student Attitudes and Expectations," Q-1, with male Peruvians studying in the United States in 1964–65 and with all male foreign students in the United States, 1964–65

	PERUVIAN MALES				ALL MALES,	
ITEM	IIE, 1964–65[a]		Q-1, 1966[b]		IIE, 1964–65[a]	
	%	#	%	#	%	#
			Status[f]			
Undergraduate	70.0	361	69.7	329	51.3	31,801
Graduate	30.0	157	30.3	143	48.7	30,183
Total[c]	100.0	518[d]	100.0	472	100.0	61,984[e]
			Sponsor[f]			
Self	57.1	281	60.7	289	46.8	27,056
Other	42.9	211	39.3	187	53.2	30,793
Total[c]	100.0	492	100.0	476	100.0	57,849
			Visa[f]			
F (student)	60.4	292	62.5	283	71.3	38,267
Immigrant	20.8	101	15.0	68	10.0	5,348
J (exchangee)	16.2	79	18.5	84	13.6	7,351
Other	2.6	13	4.0	18	5.1	2,754
Total[c]	100.0	485	100.0	453	100.0	53,720

[a] Calculated from: IIE Census forms, Fall 1964.
[b] Calculated from: Peruvian Student Survey, Q-1.
[c] Excluded from the calculations are:

	Peruvian males		All males,
	IIE, 1964–65	Q-1, 1966	IIE, 1964–65
NA STATUS	95	4	6,254
NA SPONSOR	121	..	10,389
NA VISA	128	23	14,518
NA FIELD	3	10	715

[d] Excluded are 82 Peruvian males who were "special" students.
[e] Excluded are 4,690 foreign student males who were "special" students.
[f] χ^2 for STATUS, SPONSOR, and VISA are not significant at the .05 level. FIELD does show a significant difference.

TABLE 67—*Continued*

| ITEM | PERUVIAN MALES | | | | ALL MALES, IIE, 1964–65[a] | |
| | IIE, 1964–65[a] | | Q-1, 1966[b] | | | |
	%	#	%	#	%	#
	Field[f]					
Medicine	3.7	22	5.6	26	5.0	3,384
Social science	13.9	85	8.6	40	14.9	10,080
Science	11.1	68	11.4	53	18.1	12,211
Engineering	31.9	194	37.7	176	28.2	19,042
Agriculture	9.3	57	11.4	53	4.6	3,104
Business	13.4	82	19.5	91	9.8	6,586
Humanities	14.9	91	4.7	22	15.5	10,491
Education	1.3	8	1.1	5	3.6	2,406
Other	0.5	3	. . .	. . .	0.3	219
Total[c]	100.0	610	100.0	466	100.0	67,523

to the IIE 1964–65 group, social science and humanities students seem to be under-represented, while engineering, medicine, and business are somewhat over-represented. This difference may be a reflection of the shifting orientation of students toward the more technical subjects and away from the more traditional ones, or it may be a bias in the sample.

The discussion of response to Q-1 emphasized the total number responding. As important are the extent to which respondents completed all items and the quality of their responses. In general, the No Answer percentage was low, and it was possible to eliminate some No Answers by using the interview information to supplement Q-1 answers. Consistency was remarkable. For the critical dependent variable, no cases of contradictory answers occurred in response to the question of permanent residence or of non-return following study in the United States. There were cases where the interview clearly indicated a definite decision had been made when the Q-1 answer showed Undecided.

The Interviews

Fundamentally, the Peruvian case study was an interview study. It was an interview study not only because the number base precluded extensive statistical analysis, but also because the information most pertinent to an economic examination of decisions would be difficult to collect by paper-and-pencil techniques. Income and occupational expectations involve contingencies which, if obtained by interviews, could prove as valuable as the estimates or projections attempted by respondents. Through the interviews, then, it was possible to obtain a feel for the decision-making process as well as to get facts lending themselves to economic analysis.

Content of the Interviews

The primary purpose of the interviews was to provide data concerning occupational and income expectations of male Peruvian students currently studying in the United States. For each individual, expectations were requested under two main situational assumptions: 1, if after completing United States study, long-term employment is taken in the United States, and 2, if after completing study, long-term employment is taken in Peru. Either 1 or 2 presumably represented a real expectation. Students were also asked to indicate what alternative might have been chosen if United States study had not been possible.

Other economic dimensions explored with each person were: the cost of his education, his assessment of employment opportunity for himself, a judgment of relative salaries required for him to maintain the same standard of living in Peru and in the United States, his time preference for income, contingencies upon which future income would depend, his income estimates for professionals in various occupations in Peru, and his investment priorities.

Also included in the interview were questions concerning

reasons for study in the United States, reasons for choosing to live and work permanently in whatever setting had been chosen as most likely, recruitment policies in Peru and in the United States, communication between Peruvian students in the United States and professionals in Peru, and methods for improving programs of study and methods of selection and orientation of Peruvian students. In addition, some factual questions were included in the interview, both as a means of leading into the interview and as a check on Q-1 answers.

SELECTING AND TRAINING THE INTERVIEWERS

In addition to the writer, two associate interviewers were used in the study. The nature of the task required mature, mobile males, preferably with some knowledge of Spanish and with interviewing experience. (Given the general attitude of the Latin American male toward the academic woman and toward women in general, and given the rigorous travel schedule, women were not considered for interviewing.) In a time of draft calls, chances of meeting the specifications seemed dim, but it was possible to locate two males who were in the same age bracket as the writer (28 to 32), who had interviewing experience, and who had some knowledge of Spanish. All three interviewers were North American. All had done graduate work.

It was assumed that the standardized interview schedule would moderate, though not eliminate, differences among interviewers, even though it involved a number of open-ended questions and called for probing. In addition, the three interviewers spent one week coordinating development of the final interview instrument. Lengthy sessions were held discussing the rationale for—and interpretation of—items finally included. Explanations of the economic theoretical framework to which information collection was geared were made by the primary investigator.

Finalizing the interview schedule included preliminary interviewing in the Chicago area and on the University of Illinois

(Urbana) campus. These interviews, nine in number, formed the basis for critically assessing the schedule (which had already been pre-tested in four interviews by the primary investigator).

In order to facilitate establishing rapport, time was also devoted to familiarizing the interviewers with Peru and Peruvian culture.

SELECTING PERUVIAN MALES TO BE INTERVIEWED

At the outset, a random sampling of male Peruvians was attempted from the mailing list of 661 persons identified by FSA as currently enrolled, but it was immediately evident that a random sample could not be attained. Influencing the choice were time and money constraints; when the random sample was plotted on a map of the United States, it was obviously impossible, given the constraints, to set itineraries which would pick up all individuals so chosen. Even if it had been possible to include all, the shifting nature of the sample as names were added and subtracted during the study would have made random sampling virtually impossible.

The procedure, therefore, became to set itineraries which would cover as much of the population as possible and which would preserve the broad geographic and institutional coverage desired. The assumption was that spreading the sample by types of institution and by geography would also spread the sample in terms of individual characteristics. As will be shown, this procedure did produce a diverse interview sample, paralleling in many respects the population defined by responses to Q-1. However, it is not a random sample, and statistical extrapolation from those interviewed to the entire population of male Peruvian students studying in the United States is not fully justified.

THE INTERVIEW SAMPLE AND NON-RETURN

Because the study was directed toward non-return, an attempt was made to include as many non-returnees as possible. In spite of this intention, the percentage of returning and non-returning students did not differ significantly between the Q-1 population and the interview population. Table 68 compares answers to the question, "Where do you plan to settle permanently?"

CONTACTING THE STUDENTS

One interviewer was routed to California by way of Colorado and Utah; the second was sent through the Central States from Iowa to Texas; and the third was assigned territory along the East Coast from Vermont to Georgia. The only area omitted from the study which had a concentration of Peruvians was Florida. Although the Midwest between Illinois and Eastern Pennsylvania was omitted, this is not an area which attracts large numbers of Peruvians, in spite of its great number of institutions of higher learning.

TABLE 68—A comparison of full-time male Peruvian students who responded to Q-1 with the subpopulation of those interviewed, on intended long-term residence[a]

LONG-TERM RESIDENCE[b]	Q-1 RESPONDENTS[c]		INTERVIEWED STUDENTS[c]	
	%	#	%	#
Peru	73.1	315	74.4	137
U.S. or third country	6.5	28	9.2	17
Undecided	20.4	87	16.4	30
Total	100.0	430	100.0	184

[a] Calculated from: Peruvian Student Survey, Q-1 and interviews.
[b] χ^2 is not significant at the .05 level.
[c] Excluded from the calculations are:
    NA among Q-1 respondents 46
    NA among interviewees 4

The actual process of selecting those to be interviewed was as follows:

1. Interviewers were provided with two lists of individuals,

each with names arranged by institution and with institutions ordered to fit the itineraries already arranged. The first list was derived from names drawn when trial sampling the original mailing list of 661. The primary purpose in using this sampling was to spread interviews in a weighted manner over a variety of institutions rather than to provide a scientifically chosen random sample which, as has been mentioned, could not be attained. The second list of names provided alternatives at each institution and/or location who were to be sought if first choices could not be contacted.

2. Interviewers made contacts as they went. In many cases it was expedient to choose from the list of alternatives rather than trying repeatedly to contact first choices. This led to considerable crossing over between lists. Once contacted, students were, in the main, very cooperative and willing to give of their time. Contacting individuals proved most difficult in the large cities.

RESPONSE TO THE INTERVIEW

Interviews were completed with 208 persons. Of these 208 interviews, 20 were set aside because they did not meet the definition of Peruvian student (13 were part-time students, 3 were non-students, 4 were intensive English students), leaving a total of 188. Interviews ranged from thirty minutes to five hours, averaging slightly under two hours. Interviewers developed rapport in their own manner, and a standard explanation of the project was provided for the interviewer to fall back upon if needed.

Questionnaire 2 (Q-2)

Questionnaire 2 represented an attempt to collect, by correspondence, information similar to that requested in the interviews. As has been mentioned earlier, it was felt that the interview was a much more appropriate method for dealing with questions of income and occupational expectations. Q-2, then, was an experimental supplement.

The questionnaire was mailed only to those individuals who responded to Q-1 and who had *not* already been interviewed; 330 Q-2's were mailed out and 135 returned, for a response rate of only 41 per cent. Of the 135 responses, 120 were by individuals who met the definition of male Peruvian student. Table 69 indicates the relationship between Q-2, Q-1, and interview samples.

TABLE 69—Distributions of students in the Peruvian Student Survey, by type of response for selected variables[a]

CATEGORY	INTER-VIEWED STUDENTS	Q-2 RESPOND-ENTS	COMBINED INTERVIEW AND Q-2	Q-1 RESPOND-ENTS
Intent				
NR1	4.2	3.3	3.9	3.4
NR2	5.8	2.5	4.6	4.6
NR3	14.4	10.0	12.7	12.6
NR4	3.2	13.3	7.1	12.8
NR5	29.3	23.4	26.9	27.5
NR6	43.1	47.5	44.8	39.1
Total[b]	100.0	100.0	100.0	100.0
Base N	188	120	308	476
Academic status				
Undergraduate	68.4	57.1	64.1	69.8
Graduate	28.9	37.0	32.0	26.6
Other	2.7	5.9	3.9	3.6
Total[b]	100.0	100.0	100.0	100.0
Base N	187	119	306	473

[a] Calculated from: Peruvian Student Survey.
[b] Excluded from the calculations are:

	Interview	Q-2	Q-1
NA Intent	0	0	0
NA Academic status	1	1	3
NA Sponsor	0	0	0
NA Field	3	1	10
NA SES	0	0	0
NA Visa	4	3	23

TABLE 69—*Continued*

CATEGORY	INTER-VIEWED STUDENTS	Q-2 RESPOND-ENTS	COMBINED INTERVIEW AND Q-2	Q-1 RESPOND-ENTS
		Sponsor		
Sponsored	39.4	48.3	42.9	39.3
Unsponsored (self)	60.6	51.7	57.1	60.7
Total[b]	100.0	100.0	100.0	100.0
Base N	188	120	308	476
		Field		
Medicine	6.5	3.4	5.3	5.6
Social science	8.6	12.6	10.2	8.6
Science	13.0	13.4	13.2	11.4
Engineering	38.3	34.5	36.8	37.7
Agriculture	11.4	12.6	11.8	11.4
Business	18.4	16.8	17.8	19.5
Humanities	2.7	5.9	3.9	4.7
Education	1.1	0.8	1.0	1.1
Other	....	....	....	....
Total[b]	100.0	100.0	100.0	100.0
Base N	185	119	304	466
		SES		
1 (High)	16.5	18.3	17.1	20.0
2	20.7	20.0	20.5	20.0
3	27.2	11.7	21.1	20.0
4	20.7	20.8	20.8	20.0
5 (Low)	14.9	29.2	20.5	20.0
Total[b]	100.0	100.0	100.0	100.0
Base N	188	120	308	476
		Visa		
F (student)	67.4	56.4	63.2	62.5
Immigrant	14.7	12.0	13.6	15.0
J (exchangee)	16.8	27.3	20.9	18.5
Other	1.1	4.3	2.3	4.0
Total[b]	100.0	100.0	100.0	100.0
Base N	184	117	301	453

NOTES

[1] The high response rate from FSA was undoubtedly aided by the endorsement of Mr. Jack Kerridge, FSA at the University of Chicago. Of the fifteen institutions from which no reply was received, five apparently had no Peruvians currently enrolled according to the IIE, five were contacted in the field by interviewers, leaving only five institutions of the original 297 unaccounted for.

[2] These names emerged in an appendix to Hearings on the International Education Act. Of the ten names listed there, one had been added to the mailing list of the survey because he was mentioned by a friend studying at another California school. U.S. Senate, *Hearings on the International Education Act*, pp. 584–85.

[3] For a copy of the questionnaire, see Robert G. Myers, "Study Abroad and the Migration of Human Resources" (unpublished Ph.D. dissertation, University of Chicago, 1967), Appendix 12.

VI

THE SOCIO-ECONOMIC INDEX

The following indicators, taken from responses to Questionnaire 1 (Q-1), were combined into a composite socio-economic index using a principal-components analysis:[1]

Father's education
Mother's education
Father's occupation
Father's income
Number of servants employed full time
Type of high school attended

The composite index was judged to be more appropriate than any individual indicator; although the correlations among individual indicators were not high, they all seemed to contribute to a general factor which could be labeled SES. In addition, the method generated scores for all individuals. Students who did not respond on one or more items were incorporated into the index by assigning a mean score on the missing item and using the mean in combination with other items for which information was known. This procedure undoubtedly pushed some individuals toward the middle of the SES scale. Students were arranged in order of their factor loadings on the SES factor and divided into quintiles, which were then used for cross-tabulations.

NOTE

[1] For a discussion of the principal-components analysis, see William W. Cooley and Paul R. Lohnes, *Multivariate Procedures for the Behavioral Sciences* (New York: John Wiley and Sons, 1962), pp. 151–85.

Index

INDEX